Studies in the Philosophy of S‹

Volume 7

Editor-in-Chief
Raimo Tuomela (Prof. Emer., University of Helsinki, University of Munich)

Managing Editors
Hans Bernhard Schmid (Prof., University of Vienna)
Jennifer Hudin (Lecturer, University of California, USA)

Advisory Board
Robert Audi, Notre Dame University (Philosophy)
Michael Bratman, Stanford University (Philosophy)
Cristiano Castelfranchi, University of Siena (Cognitive Science)
David Copp, University of California at Davis (Philosophy)
Ann Cudd, University of Kentucky (Philosophy)
John Davis, Marquette University and University of Amsterdam (Economics)
Wolfgang Detel, University of Frankfurt (Philosophy)
Andreas Herzig, University of Toulouse (Computer Science)
Ingvar Johansson, Umeå University (Philosophy)
Byron Kaldis, University of Athens (Philosophy)
Martin Kusch, University of Vienna (Philosophy)
Christopher Kutz, University of California at Berkeley (Law)
Eerik Lagerspetz, University of Turku (Philosophy)
Pierre Livet, Universite de Provence
Tony Lawson, University of Cambridge (Economics)
Kirk Ludwig, University of Florida (Philosophy)
Uskali Mäki, Academy of Finland (Philosophy)
Kay Mathiesen, University of Arizona (Information Science and Philosophy)
Larry May, Vanderbilt University (Philosophy and Law)
Georg Meggle, University of Leipzig (Philosophy)
Anthonie Meijers, University of Eindhoven (Philosophy)
Seumas Miller, Australian National University and Charles Sturt University
(Philosophy)
Elisabeth Pacherie, Jean Nicod Institute, Paris (Cognitive Science)
Henry Richardson, Georgetown University (Philosophy)
Michael Quante, University of Münster (Philosophy)
John Searle (Philosophy, University of California at Berkeley)
Michael Tomasello (Developmental Psychology, Max Planck Institute, Leipzig)

More information about this series at http://www.springer.com/series/10961

Héctor Andrés Sánchez Guerrero

Feeling Together and Caring with One Another

A Contribution to the Debate on Collective Affective Intentionality

 Springer

Héctor Andrés Sánchez Guerrero
Department of Child and Adolescent
 Psychiatry and Psychotherapy
University Hospital Münster
Münster, Germany

Studies in the Philosophy of Sociality
ISBN 978-3-319-81587-9   ISBN 978-3-319-33735-7   (eBook)
DOI 10.1007/978-3-319-33735-7

Printed on acid-free paper

This Springer imprint is published by Springer Nature
The registered company is Springer International Publishing AG Switzerland

For Eliana

Acknowledgments

This book is a revised version of my doctoral thesis entitled 'Feeling Together and Caring with One Another: A Contribution to the Debate on Collective Affective Intentionality' which I submitted and defended at the University of Osnabrück in 2013. There are many persons who, in different ways, made it possible for me to complete the research from which this contribution originated and the manuscript of this book.

First of all, my profound gratitude goes to Achim Stephan for continuously supporting me in ways that went beyond the academic guidance provided by a good thesis supervisor during the years I spent as a research assistant and PhD candidate at the University of Osnabrück. In general, I would like to express my gratitude to all the members of the group 'Philosophy of Mind and Cognition' of the Institute of Cognitive Science at the University of Osnabrück for providing an atmosphere characterized at the same time by academic support and intellectual freedom.

A very special thanks goes out to Hans Bernhard Schmid, whose philosophical work has always been a source of inspiration for me, for forcing me to clarify in a number of respects the view of collective affective intentionality I articulated in my doctoral dissertation.

I am deeply grateful to Armin Egger, Asena Paskaleva, Annika Reinersmann, Nicolás Sánchez Guerrero, and Jan Slaby for reading one or the other chapter of my manuscript and making helpful suggestions that allowed me not only to improve in clarity and precision, but also to attenuate the edges of my clumsy English. In this last respect, I particularly want to thank Rudolf Owen Müllan, who read the complete manuscript before submission and made important suggestions concerning a more idiomatic use of a number of expressions.

Some of the ideas I develop in this book have appeared, in a more rudimentary stage, in contributions I made to edited volumes. Some of the thoughts that compose the second chapter of this book (Chap. 2) were initially articulated (in German) in a paper entitled 'Affektive Intentionalität, die fundamentale Begründbarkeit unserer Emotionen und die Unbeschreibbarkeit des depressiven Erlebens' (2012) that appeared in the journal *Psychoanalyse: Texte zur Sozialforschung*, 3/4 (30), 369–380. Considerations that are at the heart of Chaps. 4, 5, and 6 can be found in my contribution (in German) to the book *Affektive Intentionalität: Beiträge zur welter-schließenden Funktion der menschlichen Gefühle* (2011) as well as in a paper I contributed to the book *Institutions, Emotions, and Group Agents: Contributions to Social Ontology* (2014). I am indebted to the reviewers of these papers as well as to the anonymous reviewer of the manuscript of this book for their helpful suggestions.

My deepest gratitude goes to my parents and my wife's parents for the invaluable support they provided us by lovingly taking care of our children, Simón and Antonia, at different moments in the course of the last years.

I dedicate this book to my whole family. However, I am particularly grateful to my wife, Eliana, who amorously supported me throughout the long process of writing my doctoral dissertation and the manuscript of this book, and, for months, took over many of my household responsibilities to enable me to focus on this project. I have no words to express my heartfelt gratitude for her infinite patience and loving support. This book is for her.

I also would like to mention that my work would not have been possible without the financial assistance of Deutsche Forschungsgemeinschaft (DFG) and Arts and Humanities Research Council (AHRC). These two foundations supported the research project *Emotional Experience in Depression* in the frame of which I worked as a research assistant at the University of Osnabrück during the time I was completing my doctoral dissertation.

Contents

Chapter 1
Introduction

Abstract This introductory chapter discusses the challenge of providing a phenomenologically adequate account of collective affective intentionality and states
the main claim of the book. It delineates the subject matter and limits the scope of
the inquiry by explaining why certain expressions which seem to refer to the ability
at issue do not really point to the kind of phenomena the book intends to elucidate.
Drawing on Max Scheler, I point to a human ability that becomes actualized in situations in which, in an interrelated way, two or more individuals come to understand
their emotional feelings as feelings that constitute one and the same experiential act.
The discussion emphasizes that any account of collective affective intentionality
should offer a principle to differentiate between situations in which the individuals
involved are feeling together and situations in which they merely are feeling alongside each other. After addressing the difficulties of reconciling a number of insights
gained in the course of different philosophical debates, I suggest that the study of
our ability to participate in episodes of joint feeling sheds light on the fundamental
issue concerning the kind of beings we humans are. Appealing to a characterization
of transcendental arguments offered by Charles Taylor, I explain my way of proceeding which is based on the idea that we can explicate experiential phenomena by
specifying their conditions of intelligibility. In closing the chapter, I outline the
general structure of the argument to be developed in this book.

Keywords Affective intentional community • Collective affective intentionality •
Conditions of intelligibility • Feeling alongside each other • Feeling together •
Fellow-feeling • Group mind • Sense of togetherness • Shared affectivity • Subject
of emotion

1.1 Feeling Together: What a Discussion on Collective Affective Intentionality Is About

Our everyday discourse suggests that we humans can share at least some of our
affective experiences. We can do so not only in the sense that we can tell each other
about these experiences, but also in the sense that we can come to *feel together*. This
book examines our ability to participate in such episodes of joint feeling. It proposes

© Springer International Publishing Switzerland 2016
H.A. Sánchez Guerrero, *Feeling Together and Caring with One Another*,
Studies in the Philosophy of Sociality 7, DOI 10.1007/978-3-319-33735-7_1

1

an answer to the question as to the *ground* of this ability. The arguments to be developed here aim, thus, at elucidating the *nature* of our faculty to share in what I shall call episodes of collective affective intentionality. The proposal will be that our capacity to participate in such moments of affective community is grounded in an ability that is central to our human condition: our ability to care with one another about certain things. In developing this suggestion, I shall provide a phenomenologically adequate account of collective affective intentionality, i.e. an account that takes seriously the idea that feelings are central to our emotional relation to the world.

In delineating our subject matter and limiting the scope of the present inquiry, in a first move I would like to explain why certain expressions which could seem to refer to the ability just mentioned do not really point to the kind of phenomena this book intends to elucidate. I am referring to utterances that convey that a given person has some grasp of the affective condition of another individual. These are utterances that seek to make explicit that the person at issue knows, understands, or imagines how someone else is feeling; or that she is, furthermore, able to 'put herself in the shoes of this other person' (cf. Goldie 2000, p. 176).

At first, one might consider it worth noting that at least some of these utterances clearly refer to some fundamentally *cerebral*, i.e. to some affectively detached, involvement with the feelings of another person. This is the case when a statement refers to a situation in which someone, probably on the assumption that she understands the particular circumstances that are affecting the relevant other person, asserts that she *knows* or *imagines* how this other person is feeling. The main reason, however, why the expressions we are considering do not point to the kind of phenomena this book aims to explain is not primarily related to the cognitive, rather than affective, nature of the intentional acts at issue. Indeed, some of the linguistic expressions just mentioned point to an affective phenomenon that could be thought relevant in this context. Peter Goldie makes the point by observing that 'in gaining a grasp of another's emotion, we often also respond emotionally ourselves' (2000, p. 176). At least some of the expressions under consideration could, thus, be said to not only reveal some genuinely affective aspect of the intentional relation at issue, but also point to some sharing of feelings. Goldie lists a number of ordinary phrases that clearly refer to an eminently affective interpersonal relatedness. He includes expressions such as 'feel for someone', 'empathize with someone', 'sympathize with someone', 'resonate to their feelings', as well as phrases that are more clearly metaphorical in character such as 'our heart goes out to them' (cf. p. 176). The reason why not even these expressions could be taken to refer to the kind of ability this book aims to elucidate is because they either refer to some intentional act that is *directed towards the feelings of another individual* or suggest that someone is feeling *on behalf of another person*. In other words, the reason for disqualifying these expressions as expressions that concern the ability at issue is not because they fail to reveal the affective nature of the invoked intentional acts; or because they fail to point to some sharing of feelings. Rather, the reason is that the present inquiry deals with those situations in which we come to feel *with* other individuals, as opposed to coming to feel *for* them. Moreover, the arguments to be developed in the course of this philosophical investigation exclusively concern situations in which the participants may be thought to feel with one another in a very specific sense, namely in the sense that they could be thought to *feelingly* understand a particular situation as *pertaining to them in a very special manner*—in a manner I shall, of course, characterize in the course of this analysis.

For the purposes of setting up the discussion, at this point, it should suffice to say that the kind of joint feeling this work seeks to elucidate is not a matter of our capacity to *grasp, engage, or even affectively 'resonate' with the feelings of other persons*. Rather, it is a matter of our capacity to *jointly* (i.e. *together with concrete others*) *respond to certain worldly occurrences in an affective way*. Put another way, our explanandum consists of pluripersonal affective acts that arise in a number of circumstances that may be taken to constitute a single class of situations for the following reason: they all put the participants to *be in touch with an aspect of the world in a manner that may be argued to be both properly affective and genuinely collective*. The human capacity I am pointing to becomes, thus, actualized in those everyday situations in which, in an interrelated way, two or more individuals come to understand their emotional feelings towards some occurrence *as feelings that immediately connect them to one another*.

Now, it could be argued that this first attempt to limit the scope of the inquiry has made out of the tacit assumption that serves as a point of departure something worth questioning. Can we really take for granted that there is some human ability to feel together which may be told apart from the class of capacities actualized in those situations in which a person comes to 'resonate' with the feelings of another person? Can we assume that there is a distinct way of being in touch with the world that deserves to be called collective affective intentionality?

One of the ways in which contemporary philosophers have begun to make a case for the existence of what may be thought to be a sui generis form of intentional world-relatedness—one which could be argued to be fundamentally affective and authentically collective—is by pointing to a normally inconspicuous, but, from a philosophical point of view, peculiar linguistic practice: we sometimes attribute emotions to groups of individuals as well as to ourselves in a plural grammatical form.[1] Take, as an example, statements such as 'The football team felt a slight annoyance with the referee', 'The committee feels shame for having overseen the evident plagiarism', or 'The army felt sorry for the victims'; or expressions such as 'We are happy about the undefeated season' or 'We feel sorrow about India'. These are the kinds of quotidian utterances I referred to at the very beginning of this introductory section. But do these expressions really suggest that we can share our affective experiences in a manner that, in some fundamental respect, differs from the way in which two individuals share an emotion when one of them comes to sympathize with the feelings of the other, or when two people come to simultaneously experience

---

[1] This is the way in which Margaret Gilbert (1997, 2002) has opened up the debate to which this book aims at contributing: the analytic philosophical debate on collective affective intentionality. We shall discuss Gilbert's influential work in later chapters (cf. the discussion in Sects. 3.2, 3.3, and 8.2).

the same kind of emotion as a result of what is usually called emotional contagion? Furthermore, can we take these statements to refer to a distinct mode of world-relatedness? In other words, do utterances of the sort just listed really allow us to speak of such a thing as a collective affective intentional response to some worldly occurrence?

A more sophisticated attempt to make a case for the existence of such a form of intentionality can be found in a proposal that has come to be seen as the locus classicus of the philosophical interest in the kind of phenomena I am pointing to. In a short but enlightening taxonomic study offered at the beginning of his book *The Nature of Sympathy* ([1913] 2008), the German phenomenologist Max Scheler has drawn attention to a distinctive, and rather demanding, mode of shared affectivity. This is a form of shared affectivity that, as Angelika Krebs (2010, p. 10) insinuates, has tended to be overlooked not only before but also after the publication of Scheler's book.[2] Scheler does so by differentiating four forms of *fellow-feeling* [*Mitgefühl*], as he calls the class of phenomena I am denoting by the general term 'shared affectivity'.

In this brief study, Scheler defends the view that there are situations in which it is warranted to speak of an *immediate feeling-together* [*unmittelbares Miteinanderfühlen*].[3] He makes a formidable effort to tell these situations apart from those in which other varieties of pluripersonal affective phenomena could be described. In contrast to what occurs with the phenomenon he calls immediate feeling-together, these other forms of shared affectivity have received some attention from philosophers and scientists alike. In Scheler's view, they have often been confused with each other, though. The three other forms of shared affectivity from which Scheler distinguishes the phenomenon of immediate feeling-together are: *emotional contagion* [*Gefühlsansteckung*], *emotional identification* [*Einsfühlung*], and *fellow-feeling 'about something'* [*Mitgefühl 'an etwas'*].

Scheler illustrates the category he calls emotional contagion by writing: 'We all know how the cheerful atmosphere in a "pub" or at a party may "infect" the newcomers, who may even have been depressed beforehand, so that they are "swept up" into the prevailing gaiety' ([1913] 2008, p. 15). He completes this illustration by mentioning situations in which 'laughter proves "catching", as can happen especially with children' (ibid.), as well as situations in which 'a group is infected by the mournful tone of one of its members, as so often happens among old women, where one recounts her woes, while the others grow more and more tearful' (ibid.). Scheler

---

[2] A number of phenomenologists have—either acknowledging their intellectual debts (such as in the case of Edith Stein) or not doing so (such as in the case of Martin Heidegger)—exploited some of the thoughts articulated by Scheler in this brief study. But until recent times these ideas have tended to elude the Anglo-American tradition of philosophical thought. That Scheler's thoughts have begun to circulate in the context of the analytic philosophical debate on collective intentionality can be seen as an achievement of Anita Konzelmann Ziv, Angelika Krebs, and Hans Bernhard Schmid's.

[3] In the English version I am quoting from, Peter Heath translates Scheler's term 'unmittelbares Miteinanderfühlen' as *immediate community of feeling*. Krebs (2010) prefers to talk of *joint* or *common feeling*.

is eager to emphasize that in a case of 'pure' emotional contagion 'there is neither a *directing* of feeling towards the other's joy or suffering, nor any participation in her experience' (ibid.). He explicates this remark by writing that 'it is characteristic of emotional infection that it occurs only as transference of the *state* of feeling, and does *not* presuppose any sort of *knowledge* of the joy which others feel [...]; only by inference from causal considerations does it become clear where [the feeling at issue] came from' (ibid.).[4] Despite the fact that he is discussing this phenomenon as a form of *Mitgefühl*, Scheler concludes that it is too obvious that emotional contagion 'has nothing whatever to do with *genuine* fellow-feeling' (p. 17; my emphasis).

The same holds true for what he characterizes as '[a] true *sense of emotional unity*' (p. 18). For Scheler, this emotional identification (or *feeling of oneness*, as it has also been translated) 'is only a heightened form, a limiting case as it were, of infection' (ibid.). The point is that '[in a case of emotional identification] it is not only the separate process of feeling in another that is unconsciously taken as one's own, but his self (in all its basic attitudes), that is identified with one's own self' (ibid.). One of the examples Scheler provides in order to illustrate this category concerns 'the phenomenon of mass self-identification with the "Leader"' (p. 19).[5]

So, in Scheler's view, there are only two varieties of shared affectivity that amount to an authentic feeling-with-one-another: fellow-feeling (or sympathy) 'about something' and immediate feeling-together. Scheler differentiates these two kinds of phenomena by discussing a very dramatic situation. He writes:

> Two parents stand beside the dead body of a beloved child. They feel in common the 'same' sorrow, the 'same' anguish. It is not that A feels this sorrow and B feels it also, and moreover that they both know they are feeling it. No, it is a *feeling-in-common*. A's sorrow is in no way an 'external' matter for B here, as it is, e.g. for their friend C, who joins them, and commiserates 'with them' or 'upon their sorrow'. On the contrary, they feel it together, in the sense that they feel and experience in common, not only the self-same value-situation, but also the same keenness of emotion in regard to it. The sorrow, as value-content, and the grief, as characterizing the functional relation thereto, are here *one and identical* (pp. 12–13).

In this short passage, Scheler clearly identifies what permits us to understand these two forms of genuine fellow-feeling as two completely different categories of pluripersonal affective phenomena. The relevant difference lies in the fact that in a case of sympathy 'about something' (in this example expressed in the form of a feeling of commiseration) the person who is sympathizing with another person is, as Scheler writes, feeling 'upon' the feeling of this other person (who is *directly* affected by the

---

[4] Scheler observes, moreover, that one could get 'infected' by merely coming into contact with a given 'affective atmosphere'—he mentions the serenity of a spring landscape, the melancholy of a rainy day, and the wretchedness of a room. Scheler writes: 'For such contagion it is by no means necessary that any *emotional* experiences should have occurred in [another] person' (p. 15). It is worth noting that the sense in which we could speak of a shared emotion here is extremely weak, to say the least.

[5] Scheler offers a number of other examples and discusses them in some detail. Among these examples, he mentions the identification in 'primitive thought' of an individual with a totem animal (or with an ancestor) as well as certain cases of hypnosis (cf. pp. 19ff.).

occurrence at issue). So the kind of affective relatedness that is instantiated in a case of sympathy 'about something' only actualizes our human capacity to feel on behalf of another person, as I have put it above, and not necessarily our ability to feel with this other person that something is a certain way. What is special about the situation described by Scheler is, however, not only that the involved individuals are emotionally directed towards one and the same occurrence. Rather, what is special here is that these individuals are emotionally directed towards this occurrence *in a very particular manner*: in a manner that allows them to understand their emotions as constituting *one and the same experiential act*.

In this short fragment, Scheler does not only differentiate the phenomenon of immediate feeling-together from the phenomenon of sympathy 'about something'. Furthermore, he makes clear that he finds it absolutely relevant to distinguish between immediate feeling-together and what I shall call a mere feeling-alongside-each-other (which has also been called a 'merely parallel feeling' [cf. Krebs 2010], and may be characterized as a convergence of individual emotions [cf. Salmela 2012, pp. 38ff.]). Moreover, Scheler makes it clear that, not even in the case that were their having a similar affective experience in a parallel way to be *common knowledge* among the individuals involved, it would be warranted to assert that these individuals were feeling together (in the sense that is relevant here). This is one of the reasons why the mode of feeling-together we are interested in could be claimed to amount to a very demanding form of shared affectivity. Having seen what differentiates these two forms of fellow-feeling (sympathy 'about something' and immediate feeling-together), let us try to specify what they have in common—let us see what it is that makes these two kinds of affective phenomena *genuine* forms of *Mitgefühl*.

As Krebs (2010) remarks in her clarifying reconstruction of Scheler's classification, the first thing to note is that having an affective experience *in common* is not a matter of understanding or, as Scheler writes, 'visualizing' each other's emotion.[6] Scheler emphasizes that in a case of joint feeling *of whatever sort*—and this is what makes all forms of fellow-feeling genuinely affective phenomena—the involved individuals are 'going through the [affective] experience itself' ([1913] 2008, p. 9). The sense of connectedness at issue here is, thus, not a matter of what Theodor Lipps (1905) calls *projective empathy* [*Nachfühlen* or *Einfühlen*], as Scheler is anxious to observe. What sympathy 'about something' and immediate feeling-together have in common—the reason why these two varieties of shared affectivity deserve being called genuine forms of *Mitgefühl*—is that, as Scheler puts it, they both amount to '[a] sort of "participation" in the other's experience' (p. 9). In the case of immediate feeling-together, this participation in the experience of another is given

---

[6] In the paper I am referring to, Krebs does not only make an effort to illuminate Scheler's classification of different forms of sympathy by discussing Scheler's classification of four distinct forms of social unity, in his book *Formalism in Ethics and Non-Formal Ethics of Values* ([1913–1916] 1973). Furthermore, she explains the way in which Edith Stein ([1922] 1970) elaborates on Scheler's view. I am not going to reconstruct the debate Scheler's proposal opened up in phenomenological circles, but we shall come back to Scheler's analysis (cf. the discussion developed in Chap. 4).

by an actualization of our ability to be affectively directed towards the same value-situation *in a joint manner*.

Scheler argues that between these different forms of fellow-feeling one could describe a number of foundational relations. That is to say, those forms of fellow-feeling that are more demanding may be said to presuppose other (less demanding) forms of shared affectivity.[7] He insists, however, that the phenomenon of immediate feeling-together constitutes a category in its own right, for the reason that it cannot be exhaustively explained in terms of other forms of fellow-feeling; the point being that its *essence* [*Wesen*]—what I have preferred to call its nature above—may be argued to be *a completely different one*.

On the basis of the discussion developed so far, concerning the essence of the phenomenon we are interested in, it may be argued that something that is special about expressions such as 'The committee feels shame for having overseen the evident plagiarism' or 'We are happy about the undefeated season' is that they strongly suggest that there is a mode of affective response to the demands posed by the world *in virtue of which a number of human individuals come to constitute some sort of transient affective community*.[8,9] Is this the key to a satisfactory answer to the

---

[7] Scheler argues that the more demanding forms of 'sympathy' presuppose less demanding forms of shared affectivity in a diachronic sense (i.e. genetically) and also synchronically.

[8] Drawing on Edmund Husserl's remark to the effect that 'the first community' [*die erste Vergemeinschaftung*] is 'in the form of a common world' [*in Form einer gemeinschaftlichen Welt*] (cf. [1929] 1999, p. 121), in this introductory section I shall make use of the term 'transient affective community'. The point in doing so is to avoid having to take too much for granted at this stage of the discussion. What is central to the thought that in the situations we are interested in the participants come to transiently constitute an affective community is the idea that, in reference to something that occurs in a world that is common to them, they come to be transiently united with one another by means of what Antonio Calcagno, following Gerda Walther, calls 'the experience of oneness' (2012, p. 92; cf. Walther 1923, p. 132).

[9] The issue concerning what we normally mean when we attribute an affective state to a group of individuals is profoundly controversial. The problem is that it could be contended that it is unwarranted to conclude from a series of observations that concern our ordinary way of talking that we are inclined to understand (let alone that we are justified in understanding) certain groups as legitimate subjects of affective states. Bryce Huebner makes the point as follows: 'We often speak and write in ways that appear to ascribe emotions to [...] various human and non-human entities, as well as objects. "Susanne *regrets* her decision to live in this neighborhood"; "Germany *regrets* its genocidal past"; "My cat is *unhappy* when she finds her food bowl empty"; and, "My car *was angry* when I finally started it after over a year". But while such sentences occur in ordinary language, this does not establish that Susanne, Germany, my cat, or my car can be in emotional states' (2011, p. 90). Concerning this issue, Gilbert makes the following claim: 'People who make collective emotion ascriptions do not generally see themselves as speaking in a fanciful or humorous fashion. There are no implicit scare quotes as in "We *feared* the worst," or, for that matter "*We* feared the worst"' (2014, p. 19). Gilbert's attempt to explicate everyday collective emotion ascriptions is grounded in the assumption that the default interpretation of a statement such as 'We are very excited!' takes it to be the ascription of an emotion to *us* (the participants), as opposed to being an ascription of an emotion to me, on the one hand, and her, him, or all other involved individuals, on the other (cf. Gilbert 2014). For two insightful discussions that touch on the issue concerning what we might be whishing to say when we ascribe emotions to groups of individuals, see Konzelmann Ziv (2007, 2009).

question concerning the nature of our ability to participate in episodes of collective affective intentionality?

To this suggestion it may be objected that there are situations in which one could be willing to attribute an emotion to a more or less defined group of individuals, but definitively not be inclined to assert that these individuals constitute some community. Imagine a number of car drivers who have been stuck for hours in a massive traffic jam. We would probably have no reservations about speaking, for instance, of the annoyance shared by the involved individuals. But it is questionable that we could meaningfully speak of some sort of community in this context. On the other hand, without having to refer to a determinate set of individuals, we could convey the idea that there is some affective condition that exhibits an eminently collective character. So it might be objected that we do not seem to have to take for granted the existence of some particular community in order to understand a situation as one in which the talk of a collective emotional response is warranted. In her analysis of the semantic properties of expressions that suggest that certain emotions may be shared, Anita Konzelmann Ziv asks us to consider the following statement made by a journalist who is reporting on the funeral of Winston Churchill: 'Not since the war has there been such a shared emotion' (2009, p. 85).[10] One could be tempted to argue that this statement tacitly refers to a determinate set of individuals—to the set composed by those individuals who are factually taking part in the funeral ceremony at issue. But the statement is not clearly a description of the affective state experienced by a definite number of individuals. It may be understood as a portrayal of the 'affective atmosphere' that holds sway at a given moment, as some philosophers may be prepared to say.[11] Despite the fact that in none of these two sorts of cases we could point to a group that may merit being called an affective community, so the objection goes, both kinds of situations could invite us to speak of a collective emotion. Let me try to take advantage of this objection in a number of steps.

To begin with, statements that primarily concern a certain affective atmosphere do not exemplify the sorts of expressions that suggest that, under certain conditions, we can come to feel together. There probably are situations in which it could be extremely difficult to differentiate between what is usually called an affective atmosphere and what I call a collective affective intentional episode. I mean those situations in which part of the relevant affective atmosphere is determined by the emotional responses of a number of individuals, like in the case of the joyful energy radiated by a stadium full of pumped up fans.[12] But in principle, one should be able to pick up those situations in which the *occurrent* emotional responses of a number

---

[10] Konzelmann Ziv declares to have taken this excerpt from *The Weekend Telegraph*, 31.01.1965.

[11] Konzelmann Ziv herself talks of an 'atmospheric reality' of the scene at issue which may be perceived by an external observer (see p. 85).

[12] This book does not deal with the idea of an affective atmosphere. Let me briefly state, however, what is usually meant by the term 'affective atmosphere' in the relevant philosophical discussion. A radical proposal invites us to *generally* understand emotions as atmospheres that can *as such* never be localized in some particular subject (cf. Schmitz et. al 2011). But it is fair to assert that in the pertinent literature the term 'affective atmosphere' is normally employed to refer to varied environmental features (and this could include the occurrent emotions of other individuals) that

of individuals do not merely contribute to some affective ambiance that dynamically sustains the affective states of the participants, but are, furthermore, *the basis for their participation in a joint affective response to certain demands posed by the world*. Let me clarify what is at stake by explicating why we cannot really exclude the utterance of the journalist who is reporting on Churchill's funeral ceremony as a statement that refers to a joint feeling of the sort we are interested in.

Despite the fact that, as just emphasized, the statement of the journalist does not clearly refer to a determinate group of individuals, the example of a communal mourning on the occasion of Churchill's funeral, as we may preliminarily call it, could help us to understand the idea that something like an affective community comes to be constituted by the participants in a case of collective affective intentionality. Let me state the point as follows: whoever came to share in this 'moment of communal mourning' would do so to the extent to which she would become aware that, at this very moment, she is grieving *together with*, and not *merely alongside*, the other individuals involved in the relevant situation.

So the objection we are dealing with allows us to see something that is absolutely fundamental: our analysis has to be able to shed some light on the fundamental difference between situations in which the individuals involved are *feeling together* (as one could take the participants in the communal mourning on the occasion of Churchill's funeral to be doing) and situations in which they are merely *feeling alongside each other* (as is likely to be the case in a situation such as an exasperating traffic jam). Moreover, one could claim that what ultimately has to be explained, in order to offer a philosophical account of collective affective intentionality, is precisely what grounds this fundamental difference. At any rate, the distinction just mentioned allows me to specify what it is that can (and what it is that cannot) be taken for granted at the very beginning of this inquiry. There uncontroversially are situations in which the participants' emotional responses are interrelated in such a way that it would be weird (and ultimately incorrect) to assert that the individuals involved are feeling alongside each other. That is, there are situations in which it intuitively makes perfect sense to speak of a *genuinely joint* emotional response. The task of someone interested in elucidating what collective affective intentionality amounts to consists in specifying the presumed state of affairs a statement such as 'they are feeling together, and not merely alongside each other' is intended to refer to. It does not consist in determining whether or not there is a difference *at all* between these two sorts of situations. This is not to suggest, however, that we can take for granted that certain groups could be understood as supraindividual bearers of emotional states. So, in assuming that episodes of genuinely collective affective intentionality are possible and that we humans normally possess the ability to participate in such episodes, I am not taking for granted that certain groups could have emotions *of their own*—emotions that are over and above the participants' feelings. We shall have time to deal with this issue later, for the moment, let us continue to

---

tend to *evoke* certain affective states (and not others) *in human subjects of affective experience*. For an interesting discussion on the topic, see Anderson (2009).

survey the terrain by further exploring the idea that the expressions we are interested in could point to the momentary constitution of some sort of affective community.

Konzelmann Ziv contrasts the statement made by the journalist reporting on Churchill's funeral with an utterance made by Japan's former Prime Minister Koizumi, who, on a given occasion, is said to have uttered the following words: 'We express our deep remorse and heartfelt apology' (2009, p. 85).[13] This example may also be taken to cast doubt on the suggestion that the individuals involved in a collective affective intentional episode could be taken to constitute a sort of affective community. The reason is as follows. To the extent to which Koizumi is speaking for, or in the name of, a particular group he represents—say, the group constituted by all Japanese nationals—one could understand the statement under consideration as a statement by means of which an emotion (remorse) is attributed to a *determinate* group of individuals. However, it is rather obvious that we cannot take each Japanese citizen to be experiencing such a feeling of remorse. At least two questions arise here. The first question is the question as to who should, in such a case, be taken to constitute the particular kind of group I have, in a provisory way, called a transient affective community. Are all Japanese alluded to, i.e. even those who do not feel remorse? The second question concerns the more general issue as to what would be required for us to *adequately* speak of such a community.

As to the first question, it is important to note that to take all Japanese nationals to constitute the relevant affective community would be at odds with a remark made above: a collective affective intentional episode, as I want this notion to be understood, is a situation in which a number of individuals come to participate by means of their *occurrent* emotional feelings—feelings that bring them to immediately feel connected to one another. As we shall see (in Sect. 3.3), however, at least Margaret Gilbert (2002) would be prepared to claim that, without experiencing any specific feeling, a number of individuals could participate in what she calls a collective feeling.[14]

While trying to answer the second question, we could benefit from a further example offered by Konzelmann Ziv who asks us to consider the following statement uttered by a member of a group of environmentalists: 'We love the concept of car-sharing … Unfortunately, not everyone shares our enthusiasm' (p. 86). Konzelmann Ziv observes that '[t]aken together, the two parts of the utterance seem to suggest that the class of the lovers of car-sharing is open in the sense that everyone from the class of non-lovers of car-sharing can join in' (ibid.). At first sight, this remark renders the idea that, in feeling together, a number of individuals come to constitute some kind of community more puzzling, since it stresses the openness of the class of sharers of an affective attitude. We can begin, however, to solve the general issue concerning the condition a number of individuals have to fulfill, in order to, on a given occasion, come to transiently constitute an affective community

---

[13] In the relevant passage, Konzelmann Ziv is addressing a different problem. She is interested in the difference between the observing point of view, the function of which is descriptive, and the experiencing point of view, the function of which is expressive, as she writes (cf. 2009, pp. 84–85).

[14] Gilbert (2002) discusses the specific case of so-called collective guilt feelings.

by trying to answer the following question: what is required for someone who does not belong to the group of lovers of car-sharing to come to be part of this group?[15]

The crucial point here is to appreciate that it would not be sufficient for a person to become a member of the relevant community to come to love the idea of car-sharing. If this person is to come to really co-constitute the group the environmentalist is tacitly referring to, she has to, furthermore, come to *at least non-thematically understand herself as someone who shares the attitude at issue with the relevant others* (in this case with the other members of the group of lovers of car-sharing). The upshot is that we can assert that, in coming to feel in a genuinely joint manner, a number of individuals *necessarily* come to understand themselves as members of some transient affective community. For we could not make sense of the idea that these individuals have come to feel together (as opposed to merely having come to, in a parallel way, experience an emotion of a particular type), were we not to assume that they have come to understand themselves as individuals who constitute some sort of collective emotionally directed towards some occurrence.[16]

So we are now in a position to make a grounded claim concerning the necessity of presupposing that there are situations in which, in emotionally responding to certain requirements of the world, we come to constitute (with certain others) some transient affective community. This claim has its foundation in the insight that we would otherwise have no possibility to spell out the difference that exists between two clearly distinct sorts of situations: on the one hand, those situations in which, in emotionally responding to a particular occurrence, one comes to feel immediately joined to certain other individuals, and on the other hand, those situations in which, being aware that one's emotional response coincides with those of a number of other individuals, one does not come to feel affectively tied to them.[17]

On the basis of this reflection, we could venture a preliminary answer to the second question posed above. Talk of a transient affective community is warranted just in case the involved individuals non-mistakenly understand their situation as one in which they are *jointly oriented towards something in an emotional way*. Of course, this leaves us with a big task ahead: that of elucidating what the expression 'non-mistakenly' means in this context.

But the train of thought developed so far does not only permit us to offer an initial answer to the question concerning the condition a number of individuals have to

---

[15] This example is not ideal, since the mentioned lovers of car-sharing may be argued to share an emotional attitude, and not an occurrent emotion.

[16] Gilbert points out that '[o]ne who says "We are excited," if asked who "we" are, may well say, for instance, "the football team"' (2014, p. 18). According to Gilbert, even in those cases in which it is not possible to invoke what she calls a 'familiar *collectivity concept*' the following holds true: 'if one can properly ascribe an emotion to us, then we constitute a collectivity' (p. 26). We shall come to better understand this claim in the course of our discussion.

[17] I take it to be uncontroversial that in certain contexts we experience a momentary affective condition as a state we share with concrete others in a manner that is—at least at a pre-theoretical level—worthy of being characterized as a genuinely joint feeling, while in others we merely come to have a sense that we are feeling alongside other individuals who seem to evaluate the situation at issue in a similar way.

fulfill in order to transiently constitute a group of individuals who are feeling together. Rather, they open up a series of questions that concern the grounds of the sense of feeling together (with certain others) which we have in certain situations.

One could argue that it is possible to look at the situations at issue in two completely different ways. One could be inclined to conceive of the relevant group as something that is brought to life by, and exhausts itself in, the affective responses of the involved individuals. The intuition here is that the invoked group is just as ephemeral as the relevant emotional response. Moreover, one could think that the constitution of such a group is something that is profoundly contingent and regulated by conditions that are, so to say, external to the participants. A certain constellation of factors has brought the individuals at issue to momentarily synchronize their emotions, as it were, and in this context experience some affective closeness to one another. Alternatively, one could think that the possibility of coming to constitute an affective community in a situationally specific manner is grounded in what may be seen as a more basic psychological fact: as soon as a number of individuals come to see themselves as members of a particular group, they become prepared to respond to certain requirements of the world in ways that are *completely different* to those in which they would have responded to these same occurrences had they not considered themselves as a part of this group.

The proposal to be developed in this book exploits the latter sort of understanding of the relationship at issue. I believe that the only way to stop the regress of questions concerning what makes possible the constitution of what I have called a transient affective community is to assume that the individuals involved *always already* understand themselves as members of some group when they come to be affected by a given occurrence in such a way as to feel affectively connected to one another in the immediate manner that is at issue. This conviction is based on the following thought: even if we were able to list all 'external' conditions that amount to the specific constellation in which such a community can emerge (as a result of some 'synchronization' of emotions), we would be urged to explicate *what makes possible the experience* the involved individuals have to the effect that they (at least transiently) constitute an affective community. (As we have seen, it is this sort of experience that we have to take for granted if we are to speak in a meaningful way of some genuinely joint feeling.) In due course, we shall come to understand the claim that what makes possible the experience that we (the participants) transiently constitute some affective community is the fact that we, in a sense, already take ourselves to, together with the relevant others, constitute some group when we emotionally respond to a particular occurrence. At the risk of getting ahead of myself, let me claim without argument that what is central here is the capacity to understand one's emotional response as a constitutive part of *our* response.

There is a further issue opened up by the insight that, in coming to feel together, one comes to see oneself as constituting a certain community. Invoking the popular saying, according to which a sorrow shared is a sorrow halved and a joy shared is a joy doubled, Konzelmann Ziv points out that we do not only seem to think that some of our emotions are shareable. Furthermore, we seem to believe that their being shared could modify their intensity and probably also their quality. In this context, she observes that we seem to think that 'an emotional experience reveals through some feature of its quality or intensity whether it is shared or not' (2009, p. 83). If this is so, a central task here consists in spelling out what this feature could be that allows us to understand some of our emotional experiences—and only some of them—as experiences that are shared in the demanding manner that is at issue. Moreover, we have to account for the specific relationship that holds between the alleged 'modification' in the phenomenology of our emotional experiences and our understanding of ourselves as individuals who (together with the relevant others) constitute a certain group. Having said that, let me summarize this first train of thought, thereby stating what this book is about.

The present inquiry seeks to elucidate the nature of the phenomenon Scheler has pointed to.[18] Although it addresses our capacity to share emotional feelings, it does not deal with all forms of shared affectivity. It is restricted to the phenomenon of collective affective intentionality. So the sort of feeling-together I shall try to shed some light on exclusively concerns situations of a very particular sort. In these situations a number of individuals come to emotionally respond to some occurrence in such a way as to experience their emotional engagement with the world as one which affectively, and in an immediate manner, connects them to one another. The aim of this book is to explain what it is that brings the participants in such a situation to understand the affective condition they are experiencing as a response that connects them to one another in such an immediate way. This is what a debate on collective affective intentionality could be taken to ultimately be about.

1.2   A Motivation for Exploring Our Ability to Participate in Episodes of Joint Feeling

The idea of a joint emotional feeling has tended to elude the contemporary philosophical discussion. As Angelika Krebs (2010, p. 10) observes, current philosophical reflection has just begun to re-discover this phenomenon.[19] In an attempt to

---

[18] I shall make an effort to *make sense of the suggestion* that there is a form of world-directedness that merits being called collective affective intentionality. In the remainder of this book I shall, however, not really try to *support the existential claim* that there are situations in which a number of individuals can be said to be feeling together. I believe that this is something that has already been done. (And it has been done in a way that is much more compelling than I could do myself.) Scheler's case study, it may be argued, falls short of an argument that conclusively establishes the existence of the phenomenon at issue. But I think that the illustration is as vivid as it can be. Moreover, I believe that, although this phenomenon has just begun to attract the attention of philosophers again, the legitimacy of the phenomenon is something everyone should be able to see— at least everyone who has had this rather common, but unique, sort of experiences. In other words, someone who after having read Scheler's example remains skeptical about the legitimacy of the phenomenon itself is probably not going to be persuaded of the existence of this class of phenomena by the cases discussed in this book.

[19] The situation is not radically different in other theoretical contexts. In the introductory chapter of their compilation entitled *Collective Emotions*, which testifies the growing interest in our human

reanimate this line of inquiry by locating the discussion in the context of two very prolific ongoing debates, namely the debate on collective intentionality and the one on affective intentionality, Hans Bernhard Schmid has coined the term 'collective affective intentionality' to which I have been appealing.[20,21] Schmid characterizes the situation from which he departs in his effort to develop this notion as a 'research lacuna' that is profoundly surprising, given the attention the intentional character of human emotions has attracted in contemporary philosophical debate on our affective life (cf. 2009, p. 59).[22]

One could certainly suspect that it is the foreseeable difficulty of the endeavor aimed at defending the view that certain groups could be regarded as subjects of affective experience which has brought contemporary philosophers to shy away from the idea of a collective affective intentional response to the requirements of the world. But could the avoidant attitude towards this idea be based on some prejudice, i.e. in some (unarticulated) pre-theoretical assumption that may be dismantled with some effort?

To neutralize the strong intuition that groups cannot be understood as legitimate subjects of affective *experience* is definitively not an easy task.[23] Even relatively open-minded contemporary approaches to the idea of a group mind seem to warn against trying to defend the view that certain collectivities may be understood as subjects of emotional experience. Let us take a brief look at some of these approaches.

In order to avoid a question-begging starting point, Georg Theiner and Timothy O'Connor propose to answer the question as to whether groups can be seen as subjects of cognitive states in general—as to whether there is some sense in which we can speak of a 'group mind'—by appealing to what they call an 'ecumenical, "big tent" approach to cognition' (2010, p. 82). The main idea here is that the cognitive character of a system could be understood as something that permits of degrees.

---

capacity to share affective states, Christian von Scheve and Mikko Salmela (cf. 2014, pp. xivff.) point out that the heterogeneous class of phenomena they call collective emotions has for a long time been a topic of interest for researchers and theorist in the social and behavioral sciences, though definitively not a central one.

[20] As far as I can see, the technical term 'collective affective intentionality' can be traced back to Hans Bernhard Schmid's contribution to the fifth International Conference on Collective Intentionality (held from August 31st through September 2nd, 2006, in Helsinki, Finland).

[21] One could also mention the debate on extended cognition as well as the one on distributed cognition as debates for which the idea of a collective affective intentional state could be relevant. The reason why I have not mentioned these debates is because the present work aims at bridging the two discussions I have referred to in the main text.

[22] Schmid addresses particularly the neglect of shared affective phenomena in the debate on collective intentionality. It would be warranted to speak of a reciprocal neglect of the collective dimension in the context of the ongoing debate on affective intentionality.

[23] Bryce Huebner (2011) and Hans Bernhard Schmid (2014b) both refer to an experiment conducted by Joshua Knobe and Jesse Prinz (2008) which could be taken to show that we are disinclined to understand groups as legitimate subjects of feeling, even though we are not entirely reluctant to attribute emotions to groups. Schmid makes the point as follows: 'People are inclined to ascribe *intentionality* to corporations, but not *consciousness*' (2014b, p. 5).

Depending on whether or not (and to which extent) they meet certain requirements, we can ascribe to particular systems more or less 'mindfulness' (cf. p. 83).[24] It is certainly important to note that Theiner and O'Connor address the issue in terms of cognitive states, and not in terms of psychological states, let alone in terms of experiential states.[25] But this basic theoretical decision can hardly be argued to affect the discussion, as far as the problem I am pointing to is concerned. For the authors make room for the possibility of conceiving of an experiential state as a cognitive state that meets *all* the listed criteria for mindfulness. So Theiner and O'Connor do not neglect the experiential dimension, which is the dimension one may argue to be critical here. On the contrary, they explicitly address this aspect of what we, following their suggestion, may call a highly cognitive state. They do so in terms of a criterion they label 'consciousness' (or 'criterion C').[26] In other words, in their account, the capacity a system possesses to be in cognitive states that exhibit some experiential character is relevant to the question concerning the degree of mindfulness attributable to this system. One immediately sees, however, that not even the relatively permissive frame of what Theiner and O'Connor call a big tent approach makes it an easy task to argue for the idea that certain groups can be regarded as subjects of *full-fledged* mental (i.e. experiential) states; unless one has already made plausible the critical idea that, at least in certain cases, phenomenal consciousness can be ascribed to the relevant group as such. Indeed, quite at the beginning of their inquiry Theiner and O'Connor write: 'We currently see no compelling evidence that there are any groups which satisfy condition C' (p. 84). Having concluded that there is a sense in which we can speak of emergent group cognition, at the end of their paper they make the following remark:

> [G]roup cognition is here taken to occur without any dubious sort of collective consciousness. Group cognitive states and processes of the sort suggested by contemporary empirical theories do not entail that there is a conscious, self-aware subject of them. [...] How we should think about phenomenal consciousness in particular is quite unsettled. But it seems clear that none of the group cognition–friendly theories give reason to posit collective consciousness on any of the most promising philosophical accounts of the nature and function of consciousness (whether physicalist or dualist).
>
> [...] In our reconstruction, we have already granted that the repertoire of cognitive capacities displayed by groups need not—and typically does not—live up to the full-fledged mentality of individual human beings (pp. 106–107).

It seems, hence, that, as soon as we agree that occurrent emotions are eminently experiential states, the big tent approach proposed by Theiner and O'Connor ceases

---

[24] For a list of the relevant criteria, see Theiner and O'Connor (2010, pp. 82–83).

[25] As Theiner and O'Connor observe, '[i]n cognitive science and related fields, the relevant meaning of *cognition* is partly inspired by but nevertheless to be distinguished from what we would ordinarily consider as instances of mental states or activities' (p. 82).

[26] Theiner and O'Connor specify what condition C is about as follows: 'Condition C is meant [...] to cover the phenomenal aspects of consciousness. [...] Our implicit assumption here is that A-consciousness [access consciousness] can be reduced to a composite of other conditions' (pp. 83–84).

to be helpful for a theorization of emotional states the bearer of which is some group.

In the context of the debate on collective intentionality, Philip Pettit (2002) has argued that there are some collectivities that, besides being understandable as legitimate subjects of intentional states, can be understood as persons proper. The point is that these collectivities normally exhibit a sufficiently coherent group perspective which could be differentiated from the perspective of the involved individuals. Pettit takes it to be a defining characteristic of persons that they can be held accountable for failures to unify their intentional states (and their actions) in accordance with rational constraints. Holding them accountable for these failures, Pettit suggests, presupposes understanding the collectivities at issue as agents that are able to recognize their intentional states (and actions) as their own. So, in Pettit's view, certain groups—namely those groups he wants to understand as institutional persons—fulfill a criterion that only highly cognitive systems fulfill: these groups possess the capacity to become aware of themselves as cognitive agents.[27] However, defending a view that may certainly also be taken to be liberal, Pettit explicitly rejects the idea that we can ascribe phenomenal consciousness to the groups he alludes to.

In a similar vein, and drawing on David Velleman's defense of Margaret Gilbert's notion of a *plural subject* (cf. Velleman 1997, p. 38), Bennett Helm argues for the idea that certain collectives—Helm speaks of *plural robust agents*—can be said to have emotions (cf. 2008, pp. 33ff.). Helm's point is that these collectives exhibit a coherent evaluative perspective that becomes expressed in some of the emotions of the individuals who constitute them. One easily recognizes, however, that Helm does not conceive of the collective itself as a subject of emotional *feeling*. Helm writes: 'there is a genuine, non-metaphorical sense in which plural agents have their own emotions, desires, etc., albeit a sense that is not exactly the same as that in which individual agents do' (2008, p. 34).

The lack of prospects for the endeavor aimed at making plausible the picture of a group *experiencing* an emotion seems to be so clear that, developing a sort of modus tollens argument, Margaret Gilbert (2002, 2014) prefers to question a basic assumption that seems to be operative here. This is an assumption that could be taken to make problematic the suggestion concerning the idea that there are emotions the bearer of which is some group. As we shall see in a later chapter, Gilbert rejects the idea that, in order to support the view that certain groups can be understood as legitimate subjects of emotion, we have to be able to make sense of the idea of an emotional experience that somehow emerges at the level of the group.

Approaching the issue from a completely different perspective, Schmid (2008, 2009), as we shall discuss in detail, arrives at a similar conclusion: although feelings are absolutely central to genuinely emotional responses, the plausible intuition that we can find no phenomenal consciousness at the group level does, in certain situations at least, not preclude the meaningful talk of some feeling of *ours* which is not merely a feeling of yours, on the one hand, and a feeling of mine, on the other.

---

[27] Theiner and O'Connor call it 'criterion R'.

So it seems fair to conclude that the tendency to disregard the idea of a collective affective intentional state is not based on an unreflected and questionable assumption to the effect that groups cannot be understood as legitimate subjects of what we may call full-fledged emotions.[28] Moreover, there is at least one recent attempt to tackle this issue which, contrary to what it intends to establish, makes it painfully clear that, if the intuition that groups cannot be seen as subjects of emotional states properly so called is a prejudice, it is one we are far from being able to dismantle.

Building on the theoretical framework known as distributed cognition (cf. Hutchins 1995a), Bryce Huebner has recently tried to challenge what he characterizes as a 'received wisdom in philosophy and the cognitive sciences' (2011, p. 89). He refers to the view that only individuals, and not groups, can be in genuinely emotional states. Huebner makes it his business to show 'that there is substantial philosophical and empirical support for the existence of collective emotions' (p. 90). By 'collective emotions' he means emotions had by the relevant group *itself*. Huebner is eager to contrast this idea of a state being collective from a use of the term 'collective' that is common among social psychologist, sociologist, and philosophers alike. He refers to this, in his view, rather weak notion of a collective mental state by observing, with Robert Wilson (2001), that 'ascriptions of mental states [to groups] often function as claims about certain psychological states *of individuals* that tend to be manifested only within the context of particular group relations' (Huebner 2011, p. 91; my emphasis). So what Huebner is interested in showing is that there are *genuinely* collective emotions, as he calls the states alleged to emerge at the group level, which could not be exhaustively characterized in terms of the emotional states of a number of individuals in group contexts.

Huebner's argument for the existence of such collective emotions is based on the idea that 'some groups exhibit the computational complexity and informational integration required for being in genuinely emotional states' (p. 89).[29] He takes this proposal to elaborate on the work of a number of cognitive scientists and philosophers who, as he puts it, 'have moved away from an exclusive focus on the

---

[28]There probably are theories of consciousness that do not rule out the possibility of collective consciousness. Bryce Huebner mentions the theories of Dennett (1991) and Lycan (1987). But most contemporary philosophers would frown at the idea of some sort of collective *phenomenal* consciousness. Deborah Tollefsen (2004) and Hans Bernhard Schmid (2009) talk of 'the specter of the group mind' in this context.

[29]Huebner's argument operates on the basis of a functionalist view of what emotions are. He writes: 'I assume that emotional states are *at least* representational states with intentional contents; regardless of what other constraints must be placed on emotion, I assume that such states must *at least* have the function of carrying some information about the world' (p. 95). In this order of ideas, Huebner makes the following claim: 'I hold that fear has the function of carrying information about dangerous things in our environment and I argue that collective fear must also be a representational state that has the function of carrying information about danger' (ibid.). Useful as it may be for an initial conceptualization of emotions at the group-level, this functionalist view does not allow us to understand what is special about the states we normally call emotions. The problem, as we shall see, is that as soon as we take seriously some of those other 'constraints [that] must be placed on emotion' the idea of an emotion the bearer of which is the relevant group itself becomes profoundly mysterious.

implementation of mental states in aggregations of neurons to focus instead on the ways in which mental states can be implemented by collections of people' (p. 94).[30] Huebner's claim is that the emotional representations that are at the heart of genuinely collective emotions should be taken to be states the bearer of which is the relevant collective itself; the point being that these representational states can be said to be *situated in the group* (cf. p. 102).[31]

Huebner is perfectly aware that it may be objected that collectivities are not the sort of entities that are likely to have emotional *experiences*, 'no matter how rich the representational capacities of [the] collectivity [at issue] are' (p. 104). He counteracts this sensible objection by arguing that some emotional states are completely non-conscious in the sense that, even if there is 'something it is like to be' a person who is in this state, there is no unitary phenomenal quality consciously accessible to the person at issue that can be identified by her as an emotion of this or that sort.[32] He claims that this idea of a 'completely non-conscious emotion' is compatible with a wide range of empirical data that suggest that the neuronal processes that instantiate an emotion do not always yield a conscious recognition that one is in an emotional state (cf. p. 106).[33] The point of Huebner's argument is as follows: as soon as one were to recognize that 'phenomenal consciousness could be so radically dissociated from awareness as to be inaccessible to introspective monitoring and completely unreportable' (p. 107), one would have no reason to rule out the possibility of a non-accessible collective representation that is properly emotional in nature; or, more generally, and as Huebner prefers to put it, 'the possibility of collective phenomenal consciousness' (ibid.).[34]

Appealing to the collective fear that, as he claims, may be argued to have been exhibited by the McCain-Palin campaign during the closing days of the United States presidential campaigns in the fall of 2008, Huebner submits that there are

---

[30] Huebner refers to the work of Baber et al. (2006), Brooks (1986), Giere (2002), Hutchins (1995a, b), Knorr Cetina (1999), and Sutton (2006).

[31] The idea is not merely that these representational states are not localizable at the level of the involved individuals. Furthermore, the idea is that they are the result of some computationally complex processes that occur at the level of the group and allow for the informational integration required by a genuinely emotional state.

[32] Huebner writes: 'the disjointed experience of [certain bodily] changes in isolation cannot merely be "summed up" to generate an aggregate phenomenology of fear. That is, while there is something that it is like to feel your heart race, to feel tension in your muscles, and to feel short of breath, the experience of these physiological changes alone is not sufficient to yield an experience *of fear*' (p. 105). In so arguing, Huebner is elaborating on an argument developed by Laura Sizer (2006), who claims that moods are dissociable from the experiences of moods.

[33] Huebner refers to the work of Damasio (1999, 2001), de Gelder et al. (2005), LeDoux (1996), Prinz (2004a, b), and Tsuchiya and Adolphs (2007).

[34] In a last move, Huebner responds to the objection that, given that they must be implemented by radically different sorts of mechanisms, collective representations and individual representations could not be understood as belonging to the same psychological kind. He does so by appealing to the well-known idea that mental states are multiply realizable. He writes: 'Emotions [...] require only the right sort of functional organization and there are numerous ways in which the relevant sorts of functional roles can be implemented' (p. 113).

situations in which '[the] distribution of computational resources across [a given] collectivity suggests a computational architecture that is likely to have been sufficient for producing [an emotional] representation' (p. 115). He observes that in such a situation '[t]he redeployment of attention, the reorientation of cognitive processes, and the production of action tendencies all [could be argued to play] an important role in generating the behavior of the [group] itself' (ibid.). The claim is that, although we could in such a situation attribute certain emotions to the involved individuals, the response of the collectivity would best be predicted and explained by appealing to the computational systems governing the behavior of the group.[35] The last point, however, does definitively not establish what the argument as a whole is supposed to show. For, even if we were to agree that the coordinated activity of the members of such a group could best be explained in terms of a sort of collective representation, one could wonder why we should understand such a collective representation as an *emotional* representation. Is the point here that the invoked processes, and the response of the group, could be said to be 'quick and dirty', as Joseph LeDoux (1996) famously claims an emotional response is?

Although he is arguing from a functionalist point of view, Huebner seems to not be drawing exclusively on the idea that any computationally complex response of a system that is fast enough and refrains from making use of refined conceptual representations deserves being called an emotional response.[36] If he makes an effort to make plausible the idea that there are emotions that, in his terminology, are completely non-conscious, i.e. emotions which the relevant subject is (despite having some bodily sensations) not aware of, it is because his ultimate claim is a bolder one. Huebner puts it bluntly as follows: 'if an individual can be in a phenomenally unconscious emotional state, then a collectivity can as well' (p. 107).

It is not entirely clear whether in so claiming Huebner is simply arguing for the idea that we can speak of a genuinely collective representation that is properly emotional as soon as the integrated computational processes at the level of the group are complex enough *and* 'the individual members of this [group are] clearly in a state of agitation' (p. 115). Alternatively, one could take him to be arguing for the following idea: we can assume, on the basis of the computational complexity and informational integration a particular group exhibits at a given moment, that this group is (as such) undergoing certain processes that are associated with genuinely collective phenomenal consciousness; the point being that this phenomenal consciousness could, however, be entirely dissociated from any kind of awareness of it.[37]

---

[35] Huebner argues that there are some patterns in the behavior of the group which an observer that focused on the behavior of the individuals who compose this collectivity would overlook (see p. 116).

[36] He does, however, claim that 'emotional representations are generated when quick-and-dirty computations are carried out to reorient the cognitive activity of an organism' (p. 98).

[37] Something that speaks in favor of this interpretation of Huebner's claim is that he suggests the following analogy: in the same way in which the neural structures involved in an emotional process are not aware of the emotions they implement (i.e. they have no awareness whatsoever of the fact that the relevant person is in a phenomenally conscious state), the individuals involved in the

The first interpretation of Huebner's conclusion leaves us with a claim that is much to weak to establish what the whole argument seeks to show: that in certain cases the group *as such* is in a genuinely emotional state. For the 'agitation' that, in Huebner's view, makes a properly emotional representation out of the representational state at the group level is the agitation of the individual members of the group, as opposed to being the agitation of the group as such. The second interpretation leaves us, on the other hand, with an argument that, being profoundly scientistic in spirit, is absolutely speculative, as far as its ultimate conclusion is concerned. For one could wonder whether the claim is at all falsifiable that a collective exhibiting a given computational complexity and informational integration is in a phenomenally conscious state which is *in principle unreportable*.[38]

At any rate, besides failing to make us feel comfortable with the image of a group *experiencing* an emotion, this argument has a basic problem: it does not allow us to advance our understanding of situations in which a number of individuals can feel justified in *actually having a sense* that they are feeling together (and not merely alongside each other). These are the situations—the absolutely quotidian situations—we are interested in. Furthermore, there is a fundamental objection one could raise against Huebner's approach to the idea of a collective emotion. One could argue that the whole proposal is set up to solve a problem that does not really exist. For contrary to what Huebner claims at the very beginning of his paper, and as we shall come to better understand in the course of this inquiry, in order to make sense of the idea of a genuinely collective affective response, we are not urged to defend the idea of an emergent, supraindividual emotional state.[39] There just is no clear reason why we should abstain from characterizing a situation in which the participants are not misguided by their sense that they are emotionally responding to some occurrence in a joint manner as a *properly* collective affective intentional episode. Our task certainly consists in explicating what it means for these individuals not to be misguided by such a sense of togetherness. But we definitely cannot take for granted that it necessarily means that the collective they together constitute is *itself* experiencing an emotion. But if it is not obvious that we are required to defend the rather counterintuitive idea that an emotional experience can take place at the level of the group, what is it that has brought contemporary philosophers to shy away from developing the idea of a collective affective intentional relation to the world?

According to Schmid, the neglect of the affective dimension in the theory of collective intentionality has a root that is different to the problem just considered. Schmid argues that this neglect is strongly related to the way in which intentionality,

---

instantiation of a genuinely collective emotion could be completely unaware that the collectivity they constitute is (itself) in a properly emotional (i.e. phenomenally conscious) state (cf. p. 107).

[38] Although he does not discuss it as a problem, Huebner seems to recognize this fundamental difficulty. He writes: 'After all, once we have decided to entertain the possibility of phenomenal consciousness that is *in principle* inaccessible and completely unreportable, all empirical bets are off' (p. 107).

[39] Not even Scheler's claim that the participants in a genuinely joint feeling characteristically experience their emotions as constituting *one and the same feeling* does imply the idea of an experiential state had by some entity at the supraindividual level.

on the one hand, and affectivity, on the other, have been conceived of in modern philosophy. He observes that the idea of an affective form of intentionality has been overlooked not only in the context of recent debates on collective intentionality, but also in the wider history of the philosophical theory of intentionality (cf. 2009, p. 59). Schmid points to a second reason for this neglect which is, in a sense, complementary to the one just considered. As we shall discuss in detail in a later chapter, one of the 'fronts of battle' in the contemporary philosophical debate on emotions is defined by two positions that share the inability to capture the idea of an authentically affective intentional state. On the one hand, we find a number of positions based on what may be interpreted as an intentionality-free conception of emotions: the so-called feeling theories of emotion. On the other hand, we find a view of emotions that tackles the issue of their intentionality by appealing to the traditional belief-desire model: the so-called cognitivist view of emotions for which our emotions are insofar intentional as they are, or fundamentally involve, judgments (cognitive states) and/or action tendencies (conative states). Schmid observes that in such a context the neglect of the affective dimension of collective intentionality loses its prima facie puzzling character. For if our intentional relation to the world can be theorized without any reference to our affectivity and the intentionality of an emotion can, in turn, be reduced to the intentionality of those cognitive and conative elements assumed to constitute our emotions, there is no reason to devote philosophical efforts to a special theory of collective affective intentionality. Indeed, as Schmid points out, the claim that 'the philosophers of collective intentionality have neglected the analysis of collective affective intentionality by focusing on the cognitive and conative dimensions of intentionality [may be taken to] amount to a simple *category mistake*' (p. 61). The point is that it may be claimed that '*shared intentions and shared beliefs are what the intentionality of shared emotions is all about*' (ibid.). In other words, since those situations one could be intuitively inclined to understand as cases of collective affective intentionality may be accounted for in terms that are already familiar to the ongoing discussion, it seems that a separate debate on collective affective intentionality should be seen as a superfluous one. There is, to put it bluntly, nothing else to be accounted for in this context.

So it may be argued that, in appealing to the term 'collective affective intentionality', I am linking the present work to a debate that for at least one of two reasons may be doubted to be worth contributing to: because it is rather obvious that an 'interesting' notion of collective affective intentionality—one which is grounded in the idea that certain groups can be regarded as legitimate subjects of emotional experience—is not viable and/or because the discussion to be developed is likely to be redundant.

I believe that, contrary to the spirit of such a critical remark, we can find in this situation a particular motivation for trying to develop a solid idea of a genuinely collective and, at the same time, properly affective intentional response to the demands posed by the world. The challenge consists in bridging the gap between some apparently incompatible insights gained in the course of the debate on collective intentionality and the one on affective intentionality. In particular, it must be shown that there is a sense in which we can talk of genuinely *affective* collective intentional responses to the demands posed by the world, even though groups cannot be understood as legitimate subjects of (emotional) experience. This becomes a real philosophical problem as soon as we agree that, given that the intentionality of an emotion cannot be reduced to the intentionality of other (non-properly affective) world-directed states accepted to be shareable, it is not trivially true that a group of individuals can emotionally respond to the requirements of the world in a manner that merits being called *collective*.

I believe that the apparently critical point of departure for the intended exploration is absolutely ideal not only because the two ongoing philosophical debates that touch on the subject matter of this inquiry are extremely active, but, furthermore, because, as we shall see, a number of highly interesting ideas articulated in the context of these two discussions could be said to be waiting to be exploited in the context of a theory of collective affective intentionality. I have to confess, however, that the present contribution is not basically motivated by the academic aspiration of linking the debate on collective intentionality and the one on affective intentionality. Primarily, it is motivated by the conviction that, in making sense of the suggestion that there is a distinct mode of world-relatedness that deserves to be called collective affective intentionality, we are shedding some light on the fundamental issue concerning the kind of beings we human individuals are. The intuition is that collective affective intentionality could be regarded as a phenomenon that in an outstanding manner expresses our human nature. To put it another way, one of the main goals of this book is to show that in such situations in which a number of individuals come to jointly actualize their ability to feel together, these individuals come to actualize in a demanding and particularly rich manner a fundamental human ability; an ability that defines our very mode of being. I am alluding to our ability to make of certain concern-based projections something in terms of which we can exist as a person of a particular kind. This is the reason why an inquiry the subject matter of which is our faculty to feel together is going to end up being an explication of what it means for two or more individuals to care about something in a properly joint manner. Having said that, let me turn to a series of metatheoretical (methodological) remarks.

1.3   A Way of Approaching Our Ability to Feel Together

In the opening paragraph of this chapter I declared that the present work aims to reveal the nature of our ability to feel together. This announcement could have raised false expectations in some of my readers. The reason is because the meaning of 'revealing the nature of X' that is operative here does not correspond to the one that is prevalent in theoretical endeavors that aim at *functional*, and ultimately *causal*, explanation.[40] By explicating what I mean by the phrase 'to elucidate the

---

[40] For a cognitive scientist, for instance, to elucidate the nature of a given human (or animal) capacity usually means: to define the operation of an information-processing system that can be said to

nature of our capacity to feel together', I shall clarify the way in which this proposal intends to make plausible the idea that a genuinely joint emotional response expresses our human nature in an outstanding manner.

To begin with, the argument of this book can be understood as an attempt to bring to light the *essence* of the phenomenon of collective affective intentionality. That is to say, it can be understood as an attempt to answer the question as to what this phenomenon *basically amounts to*. One way in which this question could be tackled is by elucidating *what it means for us* to understand a particular occurrence as an instance of the relevant kind of phenomenon. This is what I shall try to do here. In particular, the analysis to be developed aims at explicating what it is to understand a situation as one in which we (the participants) are actualizing our ability to feel together.

Despite the fact that it aims at elucidating what it is that permits us to understand a particular situation as an episode of joint feeling, the inquiry to be developed here cannot be understood as a form of conceptual analysis. The reason is because it does not proceed by conceptually 'breaking-down' our vernacular notion of a joint feeling into its constituent parts.[41] So I shall not primarily try to determine a set of independently necessary and jointly sufficient conditions for the truth of an assertion concerning the occurrence of the phenomenon I call a collective affective intentional episode. My way of proceeding is much more akin to a mode of argumentation that is quite uncommon in contemporary philosophy of mind, and much more so in cognitive science. I have in mind a mode of argumentation that is based on the idea that one could differentiate and explicate experiential phenomena by specifying their particular *conditions of intelligibility*.[42] What I shall offer here is, hence, an

---

correspond to the ability at issue, to decompose this operation into a number of sub-systems that can be argued to implement it, and to explain the operation of these component systems in terms of certain neuronal mechanisms. Indeed, this broadly is the way in which Huebner, following Dennett (1978), describes what, on his favored approach, *has to be done* if one is to offer an explanation of a capacity in terms of individual mental states (cf. 2011, p. 94).

[41] In other words, although this work points to certain relations that could be said to hold between particular *ways of conceiving of* a number of different phenomena, it cannot be understood as a conceptual analysis for the following reason: it constantly shifts from one concept to a *completely different* one; it illuminates the notion that serves as an explicandum in terms of a number of notions which *we do normally not take to be conceptually linked to this explicandum*. To this extent it offers—or at least this is its intention—a philosophically informative *explication of the ability at issue*, as opposed to offering an *analysis of a given concept that is related to this faculty*; it offers something that, at least in certain contexts, could suitably replace the explicandum. (I have been led to this meta-philosophical consideration by the talk held by Raphael van Riel, under the title 'Three Conceptions of Explication – Two In, One Out', at the eighth international conference organized by the German Society of Analytical Philosophy [GAP], which took place at the University of Constance from September 17th through 20th, 2012.)

[42] I could have talked here of conditions of *possibility*—and this would have brought some of my readers to immediately understand how my argument is intended to function. But it seems to me that the term 'conditions of possibility' is a rather unclear one. For it is a term that can be (and is often) used to refer to *factual* (or *empirical*) conditions that causally contribute to the realization of something. This is the reason why I prefer to talk of conditions of intelligibility. In so doing, I am following Bryan Baird (2006), who makes use of this expression in the context of an attempt to

intentional explanation of what a joint feeling is. The goal of this book is, therefore, not to provide a plausible model of some psychological capacities that could be assumed (or shown) to be involved in those cases in which we come to actualize our ability to feel together; a model which would not only explain some relevant data, but which would furthermore permit us to make some empirically testable predictions. Rather, I shall seek to articulate—in the sense of trying to express in words or to make explicit—something we have already understood (usually in a non-thematic way).

I am not sure whether the argument to be developed here deserves being called a transcendental argument, but since it is inspired by this class of arguments, I would like to further explain my procedure by appealing to a characterization of transcendental arguments offered by Charles Taylor. Taylor writes:

> The arguments I want to call 'transcendental' start from some feature of our experience which they claim to be indubitable and beyond cavil. They then move to a stronger conclusion [...] by a regressive argument, to the effect that this stronger conclusion must be so if the indubitable fact about experience is to be possible (and being so, it must be possible) (1978–1979, p. 151).

The indubitable fact at issue here concerns the idea that we humans can have emotional experiences that are structured by what I call a sense of togetherness. Specifically, it concerns the idea that there are emotions we immediately understand as part of some joint feeling, and which can be usually differentiated from emotions we take ourselves to have in a merely parallel manner—alongside certain others. It is true—and this is what the adverb 'usually' is intended to signalize—that in particular situations we could have doubts concerning, not only the factive character of this sense of togetherness, but furthermore the presence of such a character of sharedness in the relevant experience.[43] But this does not render our point of departure instable. For, if it is true that we can have doubts of the sort just described, we can do so only on the condition of having understood that, as far as this sense of togetherness is concerned, we can have (at least) two different kinds of experiences. That is to say, only on the basis of the assumption that feeling-together has an experiential character that is in some respect different from the one feeling-alongside-each-other exhibits, we can meaningfully try to determine whether or not—and meaningfully doubt that—our affective experience is accompanied *in a particular situation* by some sense of sharedness. This is the basis for the regressive argument

---

stress the transcendental nature of the arguments developed in John McDowell's *Mind and World* ([1994] 1996). Baird's point is that McDowell's critics have often failed to take sufficient notice of this character of the proposal.

[43] Imagine two persons who are married to each other, but who are no longer sure that they are still sharing a *common life*, as we often say. Assume that in relation to some of their simultaneous emotional responses to certain occurrences they do not have serious doubts that they are having similar affective experiences. They could have a vague impression that some of their, in some sense, still synchronized emotions exhibit a character that is different from the one most of these sorts of emotions used to exhibit years ago. They could express this impression by asserting that these experiences somehow do no longer clearly feel like *our* emotional responses to the relevant occurrences.

to be developed here.[44] But let me try to further characterize the nature of my claims by pointing to a feature Taylor takes to be characteristic of transcendental arguments.

Taylor begins to make the point as follows: '[transcendental arguments] consist of a string of what one could call indispensability claims. They move from their starting points to their conclusions by showing that the condition stated in the conclusion is indispensable to the feature identified at the start' (p. 159). The point Taylor is making here is one we have already touched on: the basic claim of an argument of this sort is that we could not understand the phenomenon at issue as being the way it has been claimed to be (in the premise of the argument), were we not to take for granted the condition stated in the conclusion of the argument. Taylor continues this discussion by making an observation that pertains to the grounds of plausibility of these sorts of arguments. He writes: 'these indispensability claims are not meant to be empirically grounded, but a priori. [...] I would suggest further that they are supposed to be self-evident' (ibid.). It is this 'self-evident' character I have tried to point to by writing that my argument will attempt to articulate something that we, in a way, already understand.

Now, to be self-evident does not only mean for a claim to be grounded in a particular kind of certainty. A self-evident claim should not require too much argument in its favor, or so one might expect. But as we have just seen, even the claim that is intended to serve as a starting point for this chain of indispensability claims requires some efforts aimed at making it plausible. It seems that one has to paradoxically *bring others to see* what is claimed to be self-evident. Indeed, there is something disturbing concerning the claim that such an argument can *elucidate* the nature of the phenomenon at issue. We expect of that which is intended to illuminate something else to be clearer than what has to be illuminated. But, as we shall see, the conditions my argument seeks to formulate can, in a number of respects, be said to be more obscure than the explicandum itself: in order to formulate these conditions, I will be compelled to introduce a number of technical terms and to develop very strange ways of talking; ways of talking that sometimes border on the metaphorical. The reason for this lies precisely in the fact that the primary goal of the argument is to articulate a number of conditions of intelligibility of the emotional experiences that are at the heart of a collective affective intentionality. This implies trying to put into words aspects of our experiences we do normally not talk about, aspects for which everyday discourse does often not provide a vocabulary. Our ordinary language is relatively good in capturing what our experiences are about, but we do not normally need to formulate what Taylor calls the 'boundary conditions' of these experiences. It is these limiting conditions—conditions beyond which the experiences at issue would not be *comprehensible* as experiences of the particular sort they are—which the present argument seeks to articulate.

---

[44] It might be argued that a feeling is just a feeling. That is to say, that there is no such thing as a feeling structured (or accompanied) by a sense of sharedness or togetherness. But note that someone who argues in this way would not merely find the argument to be developed here dubious. She would find *any* argument concerning the phenomenon of feeling together worth questioning—or not even that. For it is the legitimacy of the phenomenon itself that she would doubt.

Specifically, the present work seeks to make plausible the following thought. If we are to make sense of the claim that we are beings that can participate in a genuinely joint feeling, we have to understand ourselves as beings with a particular ability: under certain conditions at least, we can come to care about certain things in a joint manner. If we are, in turn, to make sense of the suggestion that we are beings that can care with one another about certain things, we have to understand ourselves as beings that share, *in a non-entirely weak sense of 'sharing'*, what Martin Heidegger characterizes as a care-defined mode of being. It is in the context of such a consideration that I shall eventually identify the grounds of our ability to feel together with our ability to, in certain situation, press ahead towards the actualization of certain possibilities we (the involved individuals) share. Appealing to a series of Heideggerian thoughts, I shall argue for the idea that our ability to feel together is existentially grounded in our ability to press ahead towards the actualization of certain abilities we (the participants) *together are*. The claim is going to be that caring with one another may be argued to be a matter of our human ability to, as I shall put it, *be our shared possibilities*. In closing this introductory chapter, I would like to outline the general structure of the argument to be developed in this book.

The first part of the book aims at a specification of the philosophical problem to be solved. In the course of this discussion I shall furthermore determine the terms in which the issue will be treated. In the two chapters that follow this introduction, I shall discuss some basic presuppositions of as well as some theoretical challenges posed by the idea that there is a distinct mode of world-relatedness that merits being called collective affective intentionality. I shall begin to do so by presenting, in Chap. 2, a particular view of our emotional relation to the world. This is a view that, as I shall try to show, captures both the genuinely affective and the authentically intentional nature of human emotions (Sects. 2.2 and 2.3). In this context, I shall introduce the idea of a *felt understanding* (Sect. 2.4). In order to establish a frame for assessing the virtues and defects of the most influential account of what may seem to be an instance of collective affective intentionality—namely Margaret Gilbert's account of so-called collective guilt feelings—, in Chap. 3, I shall discuss some of the central issues that motivate the general debate on collective intentionality (Sect. 3.2). Against this background, and having discussed a criticism that has been repeatedly leveled against Gilbert's proposal, I shall introduce the notion of *feeling-towards together* as a notion apt to capture the affective, the intentional, and the shared character of the acts that actualize the ability we are concerned with (Sect. 3.3). Chapter 4 continues this discussion by examining Schmid's attempt to take to the collective level the idea that the intentionality of an emotion is inextricably intertwined with its phenomenology. The chapter begins with the exposition of a concrete problem which, according to Schmid, has to be solved if we are to provide a phenomenologically adequate account of collective affective intentionality, i.e. an account that takes seriously the idea that feelings are central to emotions (Sect. 4.2). It continues with a discussion of Schmid's solution to the problem exposed (Sect. 4.3) and closes with an attempt to articulate a particular question left open by this illuminating proposal (Sect. 4.4). In the course of this last move, and following a suggestion made by Schmid himself, I shall try to redefine the task to be accomplished in order to make room for the idea that feelings are at the heart of collective affective intentionality.

The second part of the book articulates the proposal that participating in an episode of joint feeling is a matter of emotionally manifesting that we (the participants) care about something in a joint manner. In Chap. 5, I shall discuss some preliminaries required for a proper understanding not only of this proposal, but also of the claim that those emotional acts that actualize our ability to feel together are prime features of our human nature. I shall begin to do so by discussing a theory of affective intentionality that captures particularly well the relationship between our emotions and our capacity to care about certain things, namely Bennett Helm's account of felt evaluations (Sect. 5.2). On this basis, and seeking to ground the analysis of collective affective intentionality in Heidegger's theme of a care-defined mode of being, I shall suggest that human intentionality may be understood in terms of our essentially shareable and affectively enabled belongingness to the world (Sects. 5.3 and 5.4). This discussion is intended to bring to light some relevant continuity between those emotions through which we participate in an episode of collective affective intentionality and 'ordinary' cognitive or conative intentional acts that are neither properly emotional in nature nor formally collective. Against this background, Chap. 6 delineates my view of collective affective intentionality and clarifies what is distinct about this form of world-relatedness (Sects. 6.2, 6.3, and 6.4). In the course of this discussion, I shall introduce two further notions: the notion of *caring-with*, and the notion of *feelings of being-together*. Chapters 7 and 8 basically flesh out the view articulated in the preceding chapter. They do so by explaining the relationship that holds between Heidegger's notion of care and my notion of caring-with. Chapter 7 begins with a discussion of Heidegger's claim that our mode of being is defined by care, and explicates his suggestion that a human person always 'exists' in terms of some of her possibilities (Sects. 7.2 and 7.3). On this basis, I shall argue for the idea that there are situations in which we humans exist as some particular group we co-constitute (Sect. 7.4). In Chap. 8, I shall elaborate on this last thought by discussing the fundamental ability we humans have to *be our group*. After discussing what I call the minimal feeling of being (a member of) a particular group (Sect. 8.2), I shall explicate my notion of caring-with in terms of a distinct mode of caring that is at the basis of those pluripersonal acts by means of which a number of individuals come to jointly press ahead towards the actualization of certain possibilities they share (Sects. 8.3 and 8.4).

By way of this argument I shall not only try to make plausible the idea that the emotions that permit us to participate in a moment of affective intentional community may be understood as acts that beautifully express our human nature. I shall also try to show that one of the reasons why the debate on collective affective intentionality is worth having is because it permits us to better understand the relationship between two apparently conflicting philosophical pictures of ourselves. The first of these pictures, which we inherited from ancient Greek philosophers, can be regarded as a platitude—a strange platitude we seem to not yet fully understand: we human individuals are essentially social beings. The second picture could also be claimed to have a long tradition, but it seems to me that it has found its most concise articulation in Heidegger's claim that we are essentially creatures for whom our own existence is an issue.

Part I
Feeling Together: A Philosophical Problem

Chapter 2
Felt Understanding: A View of Affective Intentionality

Abstract In this chapter I clarify the sense in which we can speak of an essentially affective mode of intentionality. I argue that this mode of openness to a world that, to put it in McDowellian terms, is 'embraceable in thought' cannot be exhaustively characterized in terms of the intentionality of other mental states, such as beliefs, desires, and intentions. Emphasizing the strong relationship between the intentional character of our emotions and their rational intelligibility, I argue that human emotions are best characterized as responses properly so called and examine the complex structure of our human affective responses. The chapter closes with an attempt to spell out the specificum of affective intentionality. I suggest that the best way to capture the genuinely affective nature of our emotional world-relatedness is by conceiving of this mode of openness to the world in terms of our capacity to feelingly understand particular situations as being a certain way and therefore meriting and calling for certain sorts of responses. In this context, I coin the notion of acts of felt understanding. This discussion allows me to provide an overview of the contemporary debate on affective intentionality and determine the terms in which I want the topic of this book to be discussed.

Keywords Affective intentionality • Emotional response • Feeling towards • Felt understanding • Multilayered intentional structure • Openness to the world • Rational intelligibility

2.1 Introduction

If we are to make sense of the idea that there is a distinctive form of human world-relatedness that deserves to be called collective affective intentionality, we have to, in a first step, clarify in which sense we can speak of an *essentially affective mode of intentionality*. Here the task does not merely consist in explicating what it means for an affective state to be about a particular object or occurrence. Furthermore, it has to be shown that this mode of openness to the world cannot be exhaustively characterized in terms of the intentionality of other mental states, such as beliefs, desires, and intentions. Put another way, we have to try to understand in which sense affective intentionality, as it has been recently argued, may be said to amount to a

© Springer International Publishing Switzerland 2016   31
H.A. Sánchez Guerrero, *Feeling Together and Caring with One Another*,
Studies in the Philosophy of Sociality 7, DOI 10.1007/978-3-319-33735-7_2

sui generis form of world-relatedness that is on a par with the intentionality of beliefs, desires, and intentions, but cannot be reduced to the aboutness of these propositional attitudes. This is exactly what I shall try to do in this chapter.

The chapter begins with a general discussion of the view of our emotional relatedness to the world on which I shall elaborate in the remainder of the present work. While exposing this view, I shall emphasize the strong relationship between the intentional character of our emotions and their rational intelligibility (Sect. 2.2). The point I shall try to make in this first move is as follows: something that allows us to claim that our emotional responsiveness amounts to an openness to a world that, to put it in McDowellian terms, is 'embraceable in thought' is the fact that we can rationally justify what someone has done, thought, or said by invoking a particular emotion. In this context, I shall argue that human emotions are best characterized as responses properly so called. I shall continue to recommend this view of emotions by examining the complex structure of our human affective world-relatedness as well as the relationship between this multilayered structure and the rational intelligibility exhibited by our emotions qua responses proper (Sect. 2.3). The chapter closes with an attempt to spell out the specificum of affective intentionality. I shall suggest that the best way to capture the genuinely affective nature of our emotional world-relatedness is by conceiving of this mode of openness to the world in terms of our capacity to *feelingly understand* particular situations as being a certain way and therefore meriting and calling for certain sorts of responses (Sect. 2.4). The discussion developed in this chapter will allow me to, first, determine the general terms in which I want the topic of this philosophical exploration to be discussed, and second, to provide a very general overview of the contemporary debate on affective intentionality.

2.2 Emotional Responses: A View of Our Affective Openness to the World

Emotions have been traditionally understood as *responses* to particular worldly occurrences. These emotional responses, at least typically, involve a number of bodily changes (some of them experienceable by the subject of emotion) and a series of behaviors that may be understood as characteristic expressions of the particular way in which the responding individual has been affected by the relevant occurrence.[1]

Already in Aristotle's various treatments of what he calls *the passions of the soul* [*pathê tês psyches*], we encounter a picture that delineates this understanding of emotions as responses. According to this picture, our human emotions could be

---

[1] As we all know, we sometimes respond in an emotional way to something we have just imagined, remembered, anticipated, or erroneously taken to be the case. I should therefore better have spoken of *assumed* occurrences. Since this would further complicate a statement that is already intricate enough, I decided to omit the 'assumed' in this context.

understood in terms of complex states that normally involve both what we, following Kant, might call a *receptive capacity*—this is what is behind the central image of a subject being affected in a particular way by certain sorts of occurrences—and an *expressive* or *behavioral component*—a tendency to undergo certain changes and/or behave in certain ways.[2]

It is by appealing to Aristotle that, in a short remark, Peter Goldie makes a number of points that allow us to appreciate what is fundamentally right about the suggestion that our human emotions are best conceived of as responses. Goldie writes:

> What Aristotle's discussion of the emotions in his *Rhetoric* brings out is the relationship between beliefs on the one hand, and desires on the other; or, more broadly, between recognition and response [...]. Even if, metaphorically, beliefs and desires have opposing directions of fit, and even if some relevant recognition on an occasion does not logically or conceptually imply the presence of any response, there is, in our emotional experiences, an *intimate relationship between recognition and emotional response* which needs to be understood (2000, p. 28; my emphasis).

In this passage, Goldie does not only make a claim concerning the phenomenology of our emotions, namely that, *in our emotional experiences*, recognition and response, as he calls these two aspects of the world-directed character of a typical human emotion, are intimately entangled.[3] He also touches on a number of fundamental issues that concern the way in which our emotions are related to worldly occurrences. In coming to appreciate what is ultimately at stake here, we shall come to recognize a first particularity of the distinctive mode of world-directedness that has begun to be called *affective intentionality*. Moreover, as I shall try to show, a particular reading of this passage allows us to understand the extent to which our human emotions may be claimed to exhibit an intentional character *in a rather demanding sense of the technical term 'intentionality'*. Let me anticipate the point by stating that an understanding of what is at issue in Goldie's remark permits us to appreciate the sense in which our human emotions may be claimed to amount to responses *strictly so called*.

To begin with, an important thought one could take Goldie to be articulating in the passage just quoted pertains to the inadequacy of any attempt to capture the world-directed character of our emotions in terms of the intentionality of *either* the cognitive states (i.e. beliefs or judgments) *or* the motivational states (i.e. desires, intentions, or action tendencies) which may be argued to constitute human emotions. What Aristotle seems to have recognized—what Goldie seems to understand as a fundamental insight of Aristotle's view of emotions—is that, in order to

---

[2] Aristotle does, of course, never discuss the issue in these terms. Moreover, he offers no definition of what emotions *in general* should be taken to be. Rather, he usually proceeds by discussing specific 'passions of the soul'. He often does so in such a way as to bring to the fore those sorts of situations to which these affective responses may be said to be, not merely typically, but furthermore, *appropriately* related (cf., for instance, Aristotle 1984).

[3] This is a phenomenological claim Robert Roberts also makes while listing a number of facts an adequate account of emotions should be able to accommodate. He articulates the point as follows: 'Emotions are typically experienced as unified states of mind, rather than as sets of components (for example, a belief + a desire + a physiological perturbation + some behavior)' (1988, p. 184).

characterize the world-directed character of a typical human emotion, we ineluctably have to appeal to both cognitive *and* conative states.

But Goldie could be taken to be making a more radical point. This point could be stated as follows: the image that guides much of the contemporary philosophical discussion about our intentional relation to the world—the notion of a direction of fit—seems to fall short when it comes to trying to capture the complex relationship that holds between our emotions and the world. It seems that, if we decided to stick to the prevailing metaphor, we should, at a minimum, abandon the assumption that the intentionality of every single world-directed state could be characterized in terms of one of two opposing directions of fit.[4] In other words, we have to make room for the idea that certain mental states—among them human emotions—typically have a *double direction of fit*.[5]

But we could do more. We could radicalize the view I am ascribing to Goldie in such a way as to underscore what is important in the quoted remark concerning the idea that human emotions are best conceived of as responses. We could do so by showing that the notion of a response already entails what Goldie calls a recognition. Furthermore, by trying to spell out what a response proper is, we could begin to understand the complex structure of our affective intentional relation to the world. I shall begin to do so by making some remarks that pertain to what I take to be a sufficiently demanding notion of a response, apt to make clear that, being basically a kind of reaction to something—a manner of 'working against' or 'upon' a particular change or event—, a genuine response goes beyond a purely physiological reaction to a specific stimulus.

---

[4] John Searle, the contemporary philosopher who has made this notion of a direction of fit popular, acknowledges at the very beginning of his influential book *Intentionality: An Essay in the Philosophy of Mind* that one of the limitations of his account is that it does not address the intentionality of affective states (see 1983, p. vii). In the course of the discussion, however, he comes to make a strange suggestion that concerns the intentionality of an emotion. He asserts that the direction of fit of an emotion may be said to be 'null' (see pp. 8–9). Whatever exactly he means by 'a null direction of fit', Searle's (undeveloped) view of affective intentionality is radically different from the one I am beginning to sketch here.

[5] I am proposing that *we could take* Goldie to be hinting at the fact that this idea of a direction of fit might mislead us in our attempts to capture the nature of our affective relation to the world. But not even in the section that follows the passage just quoted, and in which under the heading of the 'recognition-response tie' he discusses the relation between the receptive-recognitional and the responsive-expressive aspects of an emotion, does Goldie explicitly make any claim concerning what I am construing here as a sort of bidirectional intentionality characteristic of emotions. (Drawing on Richard Wollheim [1999, pp. 45–51], Goldie criticizes the notion of a direction of fit, but he clearly has other reasons for so doing [cf. 2000, pp. 25ff.].) Since this idea of a sort of bidirectional intentionality is one we shall discuss below in detail, while examining Bennett Helm's notion of a felt evaluation (in Sect. 5.2), I shall not insist here on the possibility of reading Goldie this way. At any rate, Goldie's point seems to be that, even though they are *analytically differentiable*, as far as our emotional experiences are concerned, the recognitional and the responsive aspects of our affective relation to the world are inextricably intertwined. As I shall argue in what follows, this feature of our emotional experiences is related to the venerable idea that emotions are best understood as responses.

It is certainly true that in a number of different contexts we use the words 'response' and 'reaction' interchangeably, and it is also true that we quite often talk of a human emotional reaction while trying to characterize a certain comportment or experience. There are, however, contexts in which we would clearly prefer to replace the term 'response' by the term 'answer'. I think that we could begin to elucidate what is central to a 'sufficiently' demanding notion of a response—and to appreciate the extent to which our emotions are best characterized as responses—by exploring what an answer is.[6] Two interrelated points come to mind.

First, an answer is an act guided by some effort at sense-making. As soon as we come to understand a person's behavior as an answer, we come to understand it as *an expression of her having worked out what is at issue,* as opposed to understanding it as *the sheer result of certain processes she has undergone.* That is, we come to understand this behavior as something this person has, in a sense, accomplished *in light of* her having understood a particular situation as one that calls for a certain sort of comportment. This point is surely an extremely delicate one, since the root 'act' is part of the term 'reaction', but not of the term 'response' or of the term 'answer'. So it could seem that I am attempting to determine what is special about the sorts of reactions responses are by appealing to a feature a reaction of whatever sort could be claimed to exhibit. The key to understanding what is at issue in the claim that an answer is an act guided by some effort at sense-making is to appreciate that an answer is a way of conducting oneself that *makes visible a particular understanding* of the pertinent situation.[7] Indeed, were the relevant behavior to be 'mechanically' triggered (say, by stimulating a certain region of the brain) in abstraction from the meaning-giving context of *a pertinent requesting situation* (i.e. in abstraction from all the varied circumstances that could be argued to *call for such a response,* and which are the ones the subject at issue is assumed to have

---

[6] Although we seldom speak of an emotional answer in the sense I am trying to convey, this move is motivated by the fact that the term 'response' (but not the term 'answer') has been employed by a number of philosophers (who, in so doing, are following a usage that is common among biologists) to refer to sheer physiological reactions. As I shall argue, the idea of a response/answer (but not the idea of a reaction) is strongly related to—indeed, can be said to imply—the idea of a point of view. As we shall come to see, this idea of a point of view (or of a particular view of the world, as I shall prefer to call it) may be argued to be central to our intuitive understanding of what an emotion is.

[7] This holds true even in those situations in which a person's answer does not involve any salient behavior, for instance, when someone responds by remaining silent and doing nothing, where we can take this person's 'doing nothing' to express her having understood the relevant situation as being a certain way and calling for this quietness. So, in suggesting that our emotional responses should be understood as answers to certain demands posed by the world—and to this extent as acts, and not as sheer reactions—, I am not meaning to suggest that *all* our emotional responses could be conceived of as *actions* properly so called, i.e. as something we perform. I do not think that we should go so far as Jean-Paul Sartre ([1939] 2002) and Robert Solomon (1976) do in construing our emotional responses as strategies we, more or less consciously, make use of. Rather, I am interested in stressing the idea that an emotional response is a form of comportment apt to make evident the way in which the relevant subject, *in understanding the relevant situation as being a certain way,* is situated with regard to it.

understood), one would be justified in doubting that this behavior deserves to be called an answer.

Second, an answer is not only always an answer *to something* (a question or demand), but also always *someone's* answer to such a demand: an agent's way of comporting *itself* towards the pertinent occurrence. In order to conceive of some activity as an answer, we have to take for granted a responding agent acting against the background of a particular perspective—of a particular view of what is at issue. Consider a situation in which one gets an anonymous response to some request one has posed. Take, for instance, a non-signed letter that does not refer in any way to its remitter. In such a situation, one would attribute this response—provided, of course, that one is taking the anonymous message to amount to an answer—, if not necessarily to a particular individual, at least to what we might call an institutional person; namely to that institutional person to which one has directed one's request or demand. I do not wish to put too much weight on the concept of a person here, although, drawing on Goldie, I shall stress below that in everyday life we approach our emotions from a personal point of view. All I want to emphasize is that we seem to only be able to understand a reaction as a response on the condition of having presupposed an agent that possesses, and comports itself against the background of, *a particular view of the world.*[8]

Let me sum up this first train of thought by stating that a response proper is an agent's way of comporting itself towards some event it has understood as a request or demand of a certain sort.[9]

So it is certainly true, as Goldie points out, that the recognition of something as being a certain way does not logically (or conceptually) imply the presence of a response of a certain sort. And to be sure, I do not mean to suggest that one cannot differentiate in the case of a typical emotion between what Goldie calls the recognition and what he calls the response. Furthermore, as we all know, it is at least to some extent possible to avoid behaviorally expressing one's emotional understanding of a given situation as being a particular way. But the notion of a response—if we do not make use of it in order to merely refer to the reaction that follows a given

---

[8] The positive phototaxis of a sunflower, for instance, can only metaphorically be said to amount to an answer proper. The reason is because it is hard to understand the mechanical behavior of a sunflower, which is certainly related to some worldly occurrences in a sufficiently systematic way, as a response to something the sunflower, in some not purely metaphorical sense, *takes to be a certain way*. It is sunlight that *causes* the sunflower to 'turn its head' in a certain direction, but it is not *in light of its taking* the illumination conditions to be a particular way that the sunflower does so.

[9] There is a further aspect of responses proper which is related to the idea that to offer a response implies having understood something as constituting a certain sort of request. This is an aspect to which Goldie devotes considerable attention in his discussion of the recognition-response tie: one can normally cultivate one's responses in a way one cannot cultivate one's physiological reactions, for instance. This is the reason why one is accountable even for certain responses one could be said to be *in the grip of*—as it is sometimes the case when one comes to be *affectively touched* by something. One is probably not responsible for a given emotion *at the very moment* one experiences it, but one is, to some relevant extent, responsible for the profile of emotional responses one has developed in the course of one's life.

stimulus—implies *having understood something as being a certain way and therefore meriting the sort of answer that is at issue*. To put it briefly, although it is true that a given recognition does not require a given response, a particular sort of response presupposes the understanding of an occurrence as a demand of a particular sort—it does presuppose a specific recognition.

In the last section of this chapter I shall develop this thought that emotions are responses strictly so called by defending the idea that *a human emotion is essentially a form of understanding* (cf. the discussion in Sect. 2.4).[10] But before we come to see in which sense precisely emotions may be conceived of as forms of understanding, and what is the specificum of those forms of understanding we call emotions, I would like to explicate the extent to which this philosophical conception of emotions as answers of a particular sort is related to a quite intuitive way of looking at our human affectivity. This is a view of our emotional responsiveness that may be argued to be at the very root of our everyday use of emotional vocabulary in our attempts to explain some of our human actions. Let me begin to make the point as follows: we seem to understand our emotions as states that, from a rational point of view, are *fundamentally intelligible*. In other words, we normally succeed in locating our emotions in the explanatory dimension John McDowell ([1994] 1996), following Wilfrid Sellars (cf. 1956, pp. 298–299), calls *the logical space of reason* (as opposed to having to locate them in the 'realm of law'). Let us consider.

Besides emotions, there are a number of behavioral reactions that are elicited in a rather systematic way by particular occurrences. Take, for instance, a musculoskeletal reflex or the withdrawal reaction that follows one's touching a hot object. In contrast to what we normally do when we explain some of these other sorts of reactions, in everyday talk we usually do not explain our emotional responses by merely pointing to their *causes* or *elicitors*. At least as far as exemplary emotions such as fear, anger, or joy are concerned, we find it natural to explain the relationship between our affective condition and the worldly occurrence at issue in such a way as to try to bring to light some *reasons* we had to respond the way we did.[11] Although

---

[10] I am well aware that this suggestion could bring some of my readers to worry at this point about the possibility that this discussion might result in a far too intellectualistic view of affective intentionality. But my hope is that, as the discussion proceeds, these worries should dissipate.

[11] There is no view of human emotions apt to accommodate *all* the diverse states, conditions, and dispositions some philosopher or scientist has at some point called an emotion. Moreover, in everyday talk we use the term 'emotion' to refer to a variety of conditions that could be said to, at best, constitute an extremely heterogeneous class. But I think that there are states—and I have in mind what Goldie calls *emotional episodes*, i.e. occurrent, experienced psychological states—that paradigmatically represent the class of emotions. A non-exhaustive list of 'exemplary human emotions' would include: fear, anger, joy, sorrow, shame, envy, jealousy, grief, and remorse. These are not only the sorts of emotions we most frequently invoke in everyday talk, while seeking to explain some of our acts, but also the ones scientists and philosophers usually study. As I shall remark below in a different context (cf. footnote 31), I do not take love to amount to a typical emotion. The reason is because love can be expressed by means of a variety of emotions. Nor do I understand the sudden intense feeling that brings us to, for instance, jump up after having been exposed to an unexpected and loud sound, and which we call fright, to amount to a genuine emotion. Fright—and perhaps we should better talk here of frightful surprise—, as opposed to fear, is much too similar

they often exhibit an automatic character, we are inclined to explain our emotional responses by appealing to intelligible *motives* in light of which they become rationally understandable, and not by invoking certain physiological mechanisms, as in the case in which we want to explain some behavior we understand as a reflex. Moreover, in everyday discourse we normally make use of emotional vocabulary when we are looking for *adequate reasons* for a given action, and not merely for the causes of a certain behavior.[12] This, I think, is in part reflected in the differentiated way in which, in ordinary discourse, we link the occurrence or object at issue with our emotional condition or response. Even though in most cases we could use the conjunction 'because' in order to articulate in words a relation that can, broadly speaking, be understood as one of cause and effect, we usually prefer to say that we are afraid *of...*, angry *with...*, or happy *about...*; where that which is stated after the relevant preposition designates an intentional object, and not simply a material cause. Of course, you could, for instance, bring your walking partner to understand why you all of a sudden got paralyzed by literally pointing (with a finger) to a furious dog that is in front of you (and of which your partner was not aware), and in this situation it would make perfect sense to call the dog you are pointing to 'the cause of your fear'. But as we shall discuss below (in Sect. 2.3), this is only possible because this pointing-to is always already full of meaning, so to speak. It is not a mere pointing to the material elicitor of your emotion. Let me try to briefly illustrate the point.

Imagine that a person who works in the stock market brings one of her colleagues to understand the sudden transformation of her facial expression by pointing (with her finger) to the computer screen that has begun to display some red numbers.[13] If not only this other person but also we (while reading the example) are able to make sense of this person's facial expression as (a part of) a response of fear, it is only because we already understand (at least to some relevant extent) what the displayed numbers *could signify to her*. For there is nothing intrinsically frightening in a screen that displays certain numbers.

The point I am trying to make is that we have good reasons to conceive of human emotions as states that bring us to be in *immediate* touch with a world *that is the*

---

to a reflex. The problem is not the automatic character of the reaction we call fright. The problem is that a frightful surprise does not present a given situation as being a certain way. It is normally only after having been exposed to some frightening stimulus that one, seeking to understand the situation, begins to 'register the world' in order to look for that which has caused one's fright. (Even the psychologist and neuroscientist Jaak Panksepp [1998] takes surprise, in general, to be much too simple to be understood as a genuine emotion.) But the relation between fright and fear is a complicated one. Not only because they probably have a number of common biological roots, but also because we can normally assert of the intentional object of our fear that it is worth being frightened.

[12] This is the insight that, in the late 1950s and early 1960s, gave birth to the philosophical view of emotions that has come to be known as the cognitivist approach. We shall discuss this position and a second one (the so-called feeling theory of emotion) below (in Sect. 2.3). Together they have framed the terms in which the current debate on affective intentionality is carried out.

[13] Here, I am elaborating on an example offered by Goldie; an example to which we shall come back (see footnote 44 below).

object of meaningful thoughts and articulated experiences, and not merely with a physical environment organized by certain natural forces and laws (as may be claimed to be the world to which our reflexes, for instance, immediately relate us).[14] Put another way, our emotions actualize an ability to *understandingly* (and feelingly, as I shall emphasize below) relate to an *intelligible* world. This is something that tends to become blurred in certain accounts of affective intentionality according to which one might construe our emotional responses as reactions on a par with reflex-like organismic reactions.[15] These accounts, I believe, fail to recognize that an adequate account of our emotional world-relatedness should be sensitive to our pre-theoretical inclination to understand human emotions as states that, to appeal to a distinction made by McDowell, can *justify* some of our acts, as opposed to merely *exculpating* them (cf. [1994] 1996, p. 8). What these accounts ultimately overlook is that we normally understand our emotions as constitutive elements of what McDowell calls our *openness to a world that is essentially 'embraceable in thought'* (p. 33). Let me specify what this means.

McDowell's notion of an openness to the world involves much more than the idea that our experiences—and, in consequence, our empirical judgments—are not merely causally related to certain worldly occurrences. What is central to this image of an openness to the world is the idea that, in non-deceptive cases, our experiences, as McDowell, paraphrasing Wittgenstein (cf. [1953] 2001, §95), writes, *do not stop anywhere short of the facts* (see McDowell [1994] 1996, p. 29). If we are to make sense of the idea that a veridical experience is apt to justify a belief (or judgment) to the effect that something is such-and-such, we have to refrain from the temptation of construing experience in terms of unarticulated sense data, and stick to the phenomenological fact that to have an experience is to have an experience *to the effect that such-and-such is the case* (cf. McDowell [1994] 1996, pp. 24ff.). I am arguing that this general claim concerning human experience, mutatis mutandi, holds true for paradigmatic emotional experiences. If we are to make sense of the idea that an emotion can justify (and, in this sense, motivate) certain acts (as opposed to merely causing them), we have to avoid the temptation of construing emotional experience in terms of non-relational feelings that could merely inferentially be linked to certain kinds of occurrences, and stick to the idea that *an emotional feeling is an articulated experience that typically presents a situation as being a certain way*. I shall elaborate on this consideration below.

A second thought that is central to McDowell's image of an openness to the world concerns the idea that the *conceptual capacities* that are *passively* operative in experience—the capacities in virtue of which an experience can present something as being a particular way—open up a world to us which is independent of, but,

---

[14] I do not mean to suggest that we live in two different worlds. Nor am I suggesting that a human behavior is either a physiological reaction or an intelligible response. The point is simply that we are likely to understand some of our human reactions as rationally intelligible responses, while others do, for different reasons, not allow for such an interpretation.

[15] At least certain sorts of emotions (e.g. fear) tend to be conceived of in neuroscientifically inspired theories of emotions as reflex-like reactions (cf., for instance, LeDoux 1996).

in a particular sense, not external to, the mind. McDowell writes: 'The fact that experience is passive, a matter of receptivity in operation, should assure us that we have all the external constraint we can reasonably want. The constraint comes from outside *thinking*, but not from outside what is *thinkable*' ([1994] 1996, p. 28). It is to the extent to which it belongs to the realm of the essentially thinkable that the world we are able to (emotionally) experience—the world presented by our (emotional) experiences as being such-and-such—can be argued to be embraceable in thought. This is the idea I have tried to articulate by suggesting that our emotions typically actualize an ability to understandingly relate to a world that is always already intelligible. We definitively have to conceive of emotional experience as the result of *one's being passively acted upon by the world*, since this is the idea that our emotions actualize some receptive capacity. But, as we shall discuss below, an emotion is understandable as a state that at the same time discloses and constitutes the significance things *really* have (cf. the discussion in Sect. 5.2). This significance, as it should become clear below (in Sect. 2.3), is not understandable if one overlooks a number of links that are conceptual (and rational) in nature. To this extent a typical emotional experience amounts to an ideal example of how our spontaneity is operative in our receptive capacities, to use, yet again, a McDowellian slogan.[16]

We will have time to come back to most of the considerations just articulated.[17] I would like, however, to support the basic thought that our emotions put us in touch with a world that is always already intelligible by observing that even in those situations in which we, in the end, fail to *make sense* of what we have taken to be an emotion, our point of departure is clearly the assumption that it makes sense to try to understand what rationally justifies this behavior we are inclined to understand as an emotional response. To this extent, human emotional responses can be argued to typically be intelligible responses.[18]

Now, the idea that human emotions are typically intelligible, in the sense of being typically apt to rationally justify certain acts, is, of course, not the idea that an emotional evaluation of a certain situation is always in accordance with what a calm and cerebral judgment would tell us to do in this situation. As Goldie is eager to

---

[16] It is important to note that the idea that conceptual capacities are involved in *all* those forms of 'recognition' that are apt to justify an act does not imply the idea that what has been recognized has to be *conceptualized* (i.e. at least mentally brought to words) in order to count as experience. Nor does it imply that the object of an emotional experience (or of an experience more generally) is a proposition. In general terms, the object of an emotional experience is the situation towards which the emotion is directed; a situation the emotion at issue presents as being such-and-such. The fact that the situation towards which some emotion is directed can normally be captured by means of a proposition to the effect that some state of affairs is such-and-such has misled a number of philosophers and brought them to construe human emotions as attitudes towards propositions.

[17] We shall touch on some of these issues in the course of the discussion that composes this chapter (particularly in Sect. 2.3), but we will really discuss these ideas in Sect. 5.2.

[18] Given the sense of 'response' I am interested in, the expression 'intelligible response' may be regarded as a pleonasm. For it is precisely to the extent to which our emotions are normally rationally intelligible that we can conceive of them as responses proper.

emphasize, intelligibility is 'a thinner notion than rationality' (2000, p. 12).[19] In very general terms, emotions are rationally intelligible in that personal, normatively constrained motives for having an emotion can be articulated in the frame of a rationally coherent narrative. Goldie fleshes out this idea that our emotions are rationally intelligible by observing that our emotions can normally be said to be proportionate or disproportionate, appropriate or inappropriate (cf. p. 23). Our human emotions, in short, can be warranted or unwarranted, as Helm (2001) prefers to put it, and this is something a number of other human reactions that are systematically elicited by concrete occurrences cannot be said to be. A musculoskeletal reflex, for instance, might be taken to be exaggerated (or, on the contrary, to be extremely diminished), and this could help the clinician to detect certain pathologies. But these 'abnormal' reactions are usually not understood as unwarranted or inappropriate responses. Moreover, there are a number of situations in which, in invoking an emotion, we are not only explaining a given behavior, but furthermore, putting this behavior under a light that *allows it to appear as a genuine action*; as an 'action out of emotion', as Goldie calls it (cf. 2000, pp. 37ff.).[20] Put another way, at least in some cases, in invoking an emotion, we are not just explaining and justifying a concrete behavioral segment, but furthermore, *rendering sufficiently intelligible a fragment of the relevant person's life* (cf. Goldie, p. 16).[21] In order to complete this train of considerations concerning the adequacy of conceiving of our emotions as responses proper—as personal answers to certain demands posed by the world—, I would like to come back to my claim that our emotions may be argued to be intentional in a rather demanding sense of this technical term.

To be sure, the sense of the adjective 'intentional' that I have in mind is one which corresponds to a widely accepted understanding of the philosophical term of art 'intentionality'. Most contemporary philosophers would agree that a mental state can be said to be intentional—and it is worth noting that most contemporary philosophers reject the idea that *all* mental states are intentional—if we can provide a straightforward answer to the question concerning what this state is about. The reason why I may be taken to construe our emotions as states that are intentional in quite a demanding sense of 'intentionality' is hence not that I am suggesting that the customary notion of aboutness falls short of a notion apt to capture the world-directed character of typical human emotions, i.e. that our emotions are intentional in a sense that is somehow stronger that the common idea of being about something. Rather, the point is that some philosophers are inclined to argue that emotions are intentional in a sense that does not necessarily imply the idea of being about

---

[19] To be sure, Goldie opposes rationality strictly so called to intelligibility (cf. 2000, p. 5).

[20] Goldie argues that actions out of emotion are *fundamentally* different from actions not out of emotion (see p. 12). His point is that actions out of emotion do not seem to be adequately explicable in terms of *feelingless* beliefs and desires (at least not from the personal point of view).

[21] In this context, Goldie distinguishes between objective (impersonal) explanations and third-personal explanations. He argues that third-personal accounts are still *personal* in the sense that, in offering such an account, one is explaining the behavior of other individuals 'without losing sight of the fact that these other people have a point of view, just as [one] do[es]' (p. 2).

something. I believe that a human emotion can typically be said to be about a particular situation and that this is related to the possibility we normally have to understand our emotions as responses proper. Let me develop this point.

It could be contended that, in appealing to the notion of aboutness, I am calling into question our very first conclusion: that an emotional experience typically has a double direction of fit. Concretely, it may be objected that, in appealing to the customary notion of aboutness, I am restricting myself to the cognitive aspect of a typical human emotion (to its mind-to-world direction of fit); the intuition being that a characterization of affective intentionality in terms of the aboutness of our emotions tends to overlook the fact that we also understand emotions as motivational states.

As we shall discuss below, there is an aspect of the world-directed character of our emotions in relation to which there seems to be sufficient consensus: our emotions can easily be conceived of as evaluative states. At a minimum, hence, we should conceive of the intentional character of our emotions as a matter of their *evaluative aboutness*. In so doing, I believe, we would already have overcome the problem to which the objection is trying to point. For to say that the intentionality of a human emotion can be understood in terms of this emotion's particular evaluative aboutness is to say that an emotion typically presents an aspect of the world as being a certain way and *therefore* meriting a certain sort of response. In other words, given the evaluative nature of the intentionality that is characteristic of our emotions, in saying that a human emotion is typically about something, I am not neglecting the motivational aspects of the intentionality of our emotions. On the contrary, I am underscoring the idea that an emotion is typically experienced as a state that exhibits a double direction of fit, as opposed to being experienced as a condition which is somehow composed by attitudes that have diverging directions of fit.[22]

But besides allowing us to underscore the idea of a sort of bidirectional intentionality characteristic of emotions, the claim that our emotional feelings exhibit the feature I am calling evaluative aboutness captures an attribute of the intentional character of human emotions that allows us to conceive of them as *straightforwardly* intentional states. The feature I have in mind concerns what is sometimes called the *perspectival nature*, or the *aspectual character*, of genuinely intentional states. The point is a rather simple one: when something appears in experience as the object of an intentional act it always appears *under a particular aspect*.[23] In the

---

[22] It may be objected that this talk of an emotional response being merited fails to capture the automatic character many of our emotional responses exhibit. It is true, I think, that this way of talking does not make sufficiently clear that the emotional presentation of a situation as being a certain way quite often *urges* (or *immediately moves*) us to respond in certain ways, and not in others. But I believe that we should be careful not to construe our emotional responses as something we cannot resist, so to say. Were it true that our emotional responses are absolutely automatic reactions (much the way reflex-like reactions are), it would make no sense to speak, as psychologists often do, of cognitive strategies of emotional regulation.

[23] This is one of the reasons why I prefer to frame the discussion in terms of presentations [*Vorstellungen*], as Franz Brentano did (cf. [1874] 1995, Book II, Chapter 1), and not in terms of *re*presentations, as it is customarily done in cognitive science. I believe that the idea of presenting something in experience—an idea that involves the image of something being 'given' to the mind

case of our emotions, the aspect at issue is an evaluative one. By bringing the relevant circumstance to be understood as a situation that merits a response of a certain sort, an emotional experience refers back to the *evaluative perspective of the pertinent subject*. We will have time to discuss this issue in detail (particularly in Sect. 5.2). So let us turn our attention to a different point that is also related to the claim that human emotions are intentional in a rather demanding sense of the word.

In his paper 'Intentionality as the Mark of the Mental' (1998), Tim Crane persuasively argues for the idea that we should not spell out Franz Brentano's claim that mental states are characterized by their intentionality in terms of the idea that a mental state is always about some state of affairs that can be captured by means of a proposition. If we are to make sense of Brentano's intuition that intentionality may be understood as the specificum of those states we call mental states, Crane argues, we should, more generally, conceive of intentionality in terms of the directedness of the mind towards certain objects; objects that can, correspondingly, be said to be 'given' to the mind.[24] One of the points Crane stresses in this context is that not all intentional states are understandable as propositional attitudes (to the effect that a given state of affairs is such-and-such). Crane writes: 'I do not question the applicability of the notion of a propositional attitude itself, but rather the tendency in some contemporary philosophers to see the propositional attitudes as the sole home of the concept of intentionality' (1998, p. 246). Following Crane, and conceiving of what he calls bodily feelings as intentional feelings that are directed towards one's own body, Goldie suggests that we should prefer to conceive of the intentionality of our emotions in terms of their directedness towards particular objects, and not in terms of their aboutness or ofness. A central issue here seems to be the idea that 'emotions can be directed onto objects which are not states of affairs' (2000, p. 16).[25]

Let us grant that to exhibit the feature that is usually called aboutness—and I shall say something about what it is to exhibit this feature below—is arguably not necessary for a state to be intentional, as Crane points out. Let us concede,

---

in some particular way—is, in a respect that is relevant here, much more specific than the idea of (internally) representing something that obtains 'outside' (in the world). For there is a sense in which to represent just means to 'stand for' something else. In cognitive science the term 'representation' is often used in this sense, which loses track of the idea that intentional objects are 'given' to the mind under a certain aspect.

[24] Brentano's idea of something being 'given' to the mind should not be confused with the idea Sellars and McDowell are criticizing when they talk of the 'myth of the given'. For Brentano, what can be said to be 'given' to the mind is an intentional object, and not some sense datum.

[25] In claiming that our emotions are intentional in that they are typically directed towards particular objects (as opposed to being about certain states of affairs), however, Goldie conceives of our emotions as states that are intentional in a relatively strong sense of the word. For what he has in mind are *objects of experience*. Goldie's notion of intentionality is by far stronger than, for instance, the one appealed to by someone who, recurring to the idea of an 'ability to detect danger', and given the capacity the neuronal system involving the amygdala has to systematically elicit certain physiological reactions in the presence of certain kinds of stimuli, characterizes a given state of this brain system as an intentional state, without figuring out whether or not there is something the relevant subject is (at least in principle) able to *experientially understand* as frightening or threatening.

furthermore, that there is a sense in which one could affirm that every emotion is ultimately directed towards a particular object (in a broad sense of 'object' which does, however, not include states of affairs or situations).[26] This is hardly a problem for the view of our affective relation to the world I am outlining here, since, as already hinted at, few philosophers would be prepared to argue that to exhibit the feature that is usually called aboutness is not sufficient for a mental state to be considered an intentional state.[27] Indeed, this is ultimately the reason why I may be taken to be endorsing (and defending) a view of affective intentionality that conceives of our emotions as states that are intentional in a rather demanding sense of the word. In my view, a typical human emotion fulfills a condition that is sufficient, but probably not necessary for us to speak of an intentional state.

I believe that, if there is some uneasiness with the suggestion that our emotions are typically about certain situations which they present as being such-and-such, it probably stems from the wrong impression that, in saying that a human emotion normally exhibits the feature of aboutness, one is necessarily suggesting something along the following lines: in experiencing an emotion, we are (at least mentally) engaging with some proposition; a proposition to the effect that the situation at issue is such-and-such.[28] Let me try to dismantle this worry.

The claim that an emotional experience is normally about a certain situation which it presents as being such-and-such certainly involves the idea that our emotional experiences usually have some *articulated* content. That is to say, emotional experiences typically have some content proper; they do not merely point to something. But as William Blattner (1999, pp. 71ff.), drawing on Hubert Dreyfus (1991) and Charles Guignon (1983), observes, it is important to distinguish between two different senses in which the content of an experience may be said to amount to an articulated content.[29] In saying that the content of a particular experience is an articulated content, we may, on the one hand, be saying that this content has already

---

[26] As we shall see below when discussing Bennett Helm's notion of an emotion's focus (in Sects. 2.3 and 5.2), what ultimately permits us to find intelligible a particular behavior as an emotional response is a particular object—and by 'object' I mean a diversity of things such as a material thing, a person, a particular project, or even an idea—that appears to the relevant subject as worth caring about. We shall come to understand why the fact that our emotions are always directed, in an at least indirect way, towards a particular object is not in tension with the phenomenological fact I have been stressing throughout this section: emotional experiences are typically about particular situations which they present as calling for a certain sort of response.

[27] Of course, to exhibit this feature is not sufficient for something to be an intentional *mental* state. Certain linguistic and artistic entities (e.g. an utterance or an oil painting) can be said to be intentional precisely to the extent to which they can be said to be about something, but they are not (themselves) mental states. Searle (1980) begins to solve this problem by talking of *derived* (as opposed to *original*) intentionality in the case of intentional entities that are not (themselves) mental states.

[28] I think that this is what ultimately brings Goldie to suggest that we should capture the intentional character of our emotions in terms of their directedness-towards, and not in terms of their aboutness.

[29] In the relevant passage, Blattner is tackling the issue of the significance of an articulated comportment, and not discussing the issue of the meaningful content of an experience.

been brought to (or put into) words. But we could, on the other hand, merely be saying that this content exhibits an intrinsic structuredness; that it possesses a differentiated organization in virtue of which its elements can be discriminated and logically related to one another in some particular way. I believe that the immediate object of an emotional experience—that which is presented in the relevant experience—can normally be said to be articulated in the sense of possessing some structuredness that allows us to differentiate and, at the same time, interrelate a number of elements. This can be said to be the case precisely to the extent to which an emotional experience can usually be claimed to present a situation *as being such-and-such*. This does, however, not imply the idea that the content of an emotion has always already been brought to (mental) words when one comes to respond in a certain way.

Indeed, one could claim that it is only because an emotional experience normally exhibits this structuredness that we could, *if required*, bring the content of this experience to words by means of a statement to the effect that the situation at issue is such-and-such. Moreover, the distinction just mentioned allows us to accommodate the intuition that creatures that have not (yet) mastered a human language can be in experiential states that are sufficiently similar to those we human adults normally call emotions. Drawing on Guignon (1983, p. 118), we could say that the meaningful comportment of a human infant can make evident that she or he has understood the relevant situation as being a certain way; this comportment can make evident that she or he possesses some mastery of the emotional significance of the situation at issue, despite the fact that she or he lacks mastery of the articulate structure of human language and is not able to bring to words her or his experience (cf. Blattner 1999, p. 75). In closing this section, I would like to come back to a point we have just touched on, namely the widely shared idea that our emotions are evaluative in nature.

As a matter of fact, not every event or circumstance is able to emotionally affect us, i.e. not every occurrence can bring us to respond in the manner we ordinarily call an emotion. This is something philosophers have at all times been aware of. Indeed, as a consequence of the obvious character of this fact, a particular view concerning the characteristic feature of what we may call emotion-eliciting events has become philosophically commonplace. According to this view, emotion-eliciting events are normally occurrences that, for whatever reason, *are an issue for* the subject of emotion. To put it in slightly different terms, emotion-eliciting events amount to (assumed) occurrences that are, in one way or another, *significant to the relevant individual*.

According to Ronald de Sousa (cf. 2010, p. 1), we could mention Plato, Aristotle, Hobbes, Descartes, Spinoza, and Hume as examples of classic philosophical figures that have drawn on this intuition that emotions essentially involve, or could even be characterized as, responses to the significance something has. The list of contemporary philosophers who either explicitly or tacitly endorse this very general view concerning what an emotion could be said to be a response to is interminable and includes theorists that probably disagree in substantial ways concerning other aspects of our emotions.[30]

So it could seem that, as far as the world-directed nature of typical human emotions is concerned, there are at least two broad intuitions that are widely shared (although philosophers with different inclinations tend to understand them in different ways): on the one hand, the idea that our emotions can be understood as responses, and on the other, the idea that emotions are evaluative in nature. Pleased to recognize that these two intuitions do not exclude each other, one could feel encouraged to synthesize them in order to offer what may seem to be a more precise description of the sort of intentionality that is characteristic of our emotions by claiming that human emotions are basically *evaluative responses*.

Although this is an adequate characterization of typical human emotions, it is important to note that it is not accidental that these two basic intuitions concerning the nature of our emotions do not exclude each other. There is a sense, I agree, in which our emotions could be said to exhibit a clearer evaluative character than other psychological states which can also be understood as responses. But we are not confronted here with two entirely independent intuitions. For as soon as we conceive of a given behavior as someone's response to something, we enter a normatively constrained dimension that requires us to understand this behavior as one that exhibits some evaluative character. As we shall see below, in discussing Helm's account of affective intentionality (in Sect. 5.2), we cannot make sense of a fragment of behavior as a personal evaluative response—and this means that we cannot understand it as an emotion—, unless we assume that this behavior *expresses a for the most part coherent evaluative view of the world*; a view of the world that is unified by a number of rationally defined constraints.

To sum up, the notion of affective intentionality on which the present proposal elaborates is not exhausted by the rather unproblematic idea that '[e]motions are typically elicited by external events' (Prinz 2004b, p. 3). Indeed, the point of departure for this exploration is not even the relatively more specific (and relatively more demanding) idea that our emotions are intentional in the sense of being understandable as instances of a general organismic capacity to *detect* and *react to* certain worldly events. Rather, my notion of affective intentionality relies on the thought that our emotions are typically about particular situations which they present as being such-and-such; that our emotions usually have an articulated content.[31] A

---

[30] The idea that emotions are responses to the significance something has to the relevant subject is presumably what brings Robert Roberts (1988) to qualify his claim that emotions are construals by saying that emotions are serious *concern-based* construals. Roberts understands our emotions as states that have (and can serve as) reasons, and not merely (as) causes. On the other side of the spectrum, and as an expression of the naturalistic inclination that characterizes most of the philosophical contributions made in the frame of cognitive science, we find proposals that conceive of these 'significant' events as biologically relevant events and, ultimately, as survival-related events (cf., for instance, Jesse Prinz 2004b).

[31] It has been repeatedly argued that certain emotions are not directed towards states of affairs or situations, but only towards particular objects. Love and hate are typical examples here. As already mentioned, I agree with Roberts (1988, p. 203) who claims that love is not a typical emotion, but

human emotion, I have insisted, typically presents a situation as meriting a response of a particular sort.[32] Accordingly, many of our emotional responses can be easily understood as actions proper; as deeds that have been rationally motivated by our having understood the relevant situation as being this or that way.[33] In the sense of 'intentional' that is relevant here, emotions are intentional in that they bring us to be in touch with a world that is embraceable in thought by disclosing, constituting, and

---

an attitude or disposition that can be expressed by means of innumerable emotions; emotions that are typically about certain situations. The same holds true for hate.

[32] It may be objected that the idea that our emotions always present a situation as being a certain way clashes with an intuition many philosophers (and non-philosophers alike) seem to share with psychoanalysts: not all our emotions are conscious (cf. Lyons 1980, p. 6). The discussion about non-conscious emotions is, however, obscured by at least two ambiguities. On the one hand, the term 'non-conscious emotion' could refer to either of the following: first, to an occurrent emotion that exhibits some phenomenal character of which the relevant subject is not aware (in the sense of not having noticed or identified it), or second, to an emotion that has no experiential character whatsoever. On the other hand, by 'emotion' one could mean an occurrent and felt *emotional episode*, as Goldie calls it, or a longstanding dispositional state that involves a series of thoughts, desires, tendencies to act in certain ways, and *at some point* emotional feelings. It goes without much argument, I think, that there is no such thing as a *completely* non-conscious emotional episode. As Aaron Ben-Ze'ev observes, the idea of an *unfelt feeling* amounts to 'an obvious absurdity' (2000, p. 55). (For an argument against the intuition that the notion of an unfelt feeling constitutes a contradiction in terms, see Leighton 1986.) The feelings one could take to express an emotion of which the relevant subject is not aware—an emotion she does not notice being in—normally amount to mere bodily sensations. These feelings are not of such a nature that we could take them to present a particular situation as being a certain way. Indeed, this is probably the reason why, in these situations, one does not assimilate these feelings with an emotion of this or that sort (or with an emotion at all). However, if by means of a reflective interpretation of one's comportment one can come to the conclusion that, at the relevant point, one was experiencing this or that emotion (although one was not aware of it), it is only because one can understand this comportment as a logical consequence of one's having understood a situation (or a series of situations) as being a certain way. The intuition that emotions typically present a given situation as being a certain way—the idea that in emotionally responding to some occurrence the situation at issue is 'given' to the mind—does not imply that the subject of an emotion is always thematically aware of what is being presented. It only involves the idea that this subject has evidently understood the requirement imposed by the world. Very often this understanding, which may be thematized in a further move, is eminently practical, it is a matter of 'knowing how' to deal with the relevant occurrence.

[33] In conceiving of an emotion as a state that presents something as being a particular way, one is not necessarily endorsing the idea that an emotion is a sort of perception of some objectively (subject-independently) existing value, which Jesse Prinz (2004b), for instance, explicitly claims an emotion to be. For one could conceive of our emotions—and we could take Ronald de Sousa (1987), Robert Roberts (1988), and Amélie Rorty (1980) to be doing so—, as ways of rendering certain features of a concrete state of affairs or object *experientially more salient*, thereby presenting the situation at issue in certain terms (and not in others). To capture this idea, Roberts appeals, as already mentioned, to the notion of a construal. As he tells us, '[c]onstruing seems to involve dwelling on or attending to, or at a minimum holding onto, some aspect' (1988, p. 187). Roberts states: 'A construal, as I use the word, is a mental event or state in which one thing is grasped in terms of something else' (p. 190). Roberts is eager to observe that '[p]henomenologically [...] a construal is not an interpretation laid over a neutrally perceived object, but a *characterization of the object*, a way the object presents itself' (pp. 191–192). This is an important point which I shall discuss below by appealing to Heidegger's idea that experiencing something always means interpreting some situation (in a non-necessarily thematic way).

adjusting an intelligible evaluative view of this world. This broad picture of our affective relation to the world, I think, allows us to better understand the role emotions play in the conduct of our human lives.

In the next section I shall make an effort to further recommend the idea that the demanding sense in which human emotions can be said to be intentional is strongly related to their being conceivable as responses proper. I shall do so by discussing the complex structure of our emotional openness to the world.[34]

2.3   The Complex Structure of Our Emotional Openness to the World

The idea that human emotions are typically about particular situations has a long tradition in Western philosophical thought. However, in the context of the contemporary philosophical discussion, the intentional character of our emotional responses has been the object of an intense debate. The centrality of this topic in the current debate does not only reflect the complexity of the matter. As we shall see, it could be seen as an effect of the merely partial adequacy of both the proposal that (in the Anglo-American tradition) reopened the philosophical interest in our affective life and a particular response to this proposal. I am referring, on the one hand, to the so-called *feeling theories*, and on the other, to the *cognitivist accounts* of emotion. Ultimately seeking to motivate a third view, which we shall come to discuss in the next section (Sect. 2.4), in what follows I shall briefly examine the two positions mentioned. As we shall see, each of them could be argued to capture something important at the cost of neglecting another aspect that is fundamental to our intuitive understanding of our human emotional life. This examination will end up in a discussion of the complex intentional structure of typical human emotions and the relationship between this multilayered structure and the rational intelligibility of our emotional acts. By way of this discussion, I shall try to consolidate the claim that human emotions are best understood as responses proper.

The basic tenet that defines 'classical feeling theories of emotion' concerns the idea that an emotional feeling may be conceived of as a phenomenally marked psychological state that permits a first-person awareness of the physiological state of one's body. This view has been traditionally associated with the work of William James (1884) and Carl Georg Lange ([1885] 1922) who simultaneously, but separately, articulated a proposal that ultimately identifies emotions with certain bodily sensations.[35] James and Lange both suggested that an emotional feeling is understandable as the *characteristic experiential expression* of a determinate ensemble of

---

[34] Here, I am following Helm (2011) who introduces the image of a multilayered intentional structure that characterizes those intentional states we call emotions (cf. also Sánchez Guerrero 2012).

[35] Given a number of fundamental points of agreement, these separately developed theories have come to be regarded as a unique locus classicus of the view I am attempting to characterize. It is, therefore, common to speak of the James-Lange theory.

automatic bodily changes that occur in reaction to an event of a certain type. It is on the basis of the *specific* phenomenal quality of the sensations that accompany the relevant physiological changes, they proposed, that the experiencing subject can classify the reaction at issue as instantiating a particular *type* of emotion.[36]

When developing their view of emotions James and Lange took into consideration the basic observation that motivates talk of affective intentionality: the observation that there is some rather systematic relationship between our emotional reactions and certain sorts of worldly occurrences. They accounted for this relation in broadly mechanical terms: a *non-affective* intentional state (a perceptual state) brings about a certain set of physiological reactions which, in turn, cause the characteristic bodily sensations we, as they argued, call an emotion. This view of our emotional relation to the world has an appeal that is, at least in part, based on its capacity to accommodate the pre-theoretical intuition that *feelings are at the heart of our affective life*. As far as the intentional nature of human emotions is concerned, however, classical feeling theories of emotions have been argued to be unsatisfying in a number of respects. I shall mention only three of them.[37]

First, although feeling theories of emotion accommodate the idea that emotional feelings are usually related to particular worldly occurrences, it fails to make sense of the image of a genuinely emotional experience that is *itself* intentional in character. The controversial idea that the bodily sensations James and Lange assimilate with emotions are intentional does, at any rate, not explicate the discussed capacity human emotional feelings have to present an aspect of the world as being a certain way.[38] Put another way, a basic problem of this view is that it does not permit us to

---

[36] The philosophical and the scientific literature are both full of reviews of the so-called James-Lange theory. For this reason, and given that I am interested in a particular aspect of those views on emotion I shall discuss in this section—namely their capacity to make sense of the idea of a genuinely affective and, at the same, time genuinely intentional relation to the world—, I shall abstain from offering a detailed review of the position developed by James and Lange. In what follows, I am going to emphasize some ideas that are central not only to this view, but to the debate this proposal triggered. For an informative reconstruction of the position developed by James and Lange—one which stresses the differences between James' and Lange's original view and the theory recently developed by Damasio—, see Prinz (2004b, pp. 4ff.). For a review anchored in an attempt to show that the view developed by James and Lange remains a dynamic force in contemporary emotion research, see Friedman (2010).

[37] Put in its extreme form, the main objection raised against classical feeling theories of emotions in the context of the debate on affective intentionality states that these theories leave no room for the idea of a genuinely intentional affective relation to the world. We shall immediately see to which extent this could be argued to be the case. For an introductory overview, not only of this concrete debate between 'feeling theorists' and 'cognitivist and appraisal theorists', but also of a number of different discussions that are part of the current philosophical debate on emotions, see de Sousa (2010).

[38] The idea that the bodily sensations referred to by Lange and James are intentional is insofar controversial as there is room for dispute concerning whether we should conceive of bodily feelings as (intentional) experiences *directed towards* one's own body or as (non-intentional) mental states *localized in* one's body. But independently of how this issue will eventually be decided upon, this idea of a systematic relatedness to certain bodily states is not able to explicate the intuition at issue.

feel comfortable with the idea of a feeling that *puts us in touch with an intelligible world.*[39] As we have seen, the latter seems to be the intuition that is at the root of our everyday use of emotional vocabulary while trying to explain the rational motives of certain human actions.

Second, and related to the preceding point, James and Lange include in their picture both a receptive capacity (a perceptual state) and a reactive component (a bodily reaction). They identify, however, the emotion exclusively with (the aware-ness of) the reactive component. As we have discussed above, our idea of becoming emotionally affected in a particular way by a certain occurrence is the idea of pas-sively actualizing a receptive capacity that is part of our human understanding; it is the idea of coming to *affectively understand a situation* as being a particular way. There is little room for this idea in the theory just exposed.

Third, even if we were to agree that we could take the picture *as a whole* to be the picture of an authentically intentional relation between a subject and its world, one could argue that this view makes us prone to confound the emotion's elicitor with the emotion's intentional object. As we have seen above, while discussing the example of the person who works in the stock market, what physically elicits an emotion does not necessarily correspond to that which this emotion could be taken to be about. At any rate, it does not necessarily correspond to that which we would have to bring to light in order to render intelligible the emotion at issue, were we asked about our reasons for having responded the way we did.

Considerations along these lines have brought a number of philosophers to reject classical feeling theories of emotion.[40] In the meantime, it has become customary to group together a number of different responses to the exposed proposal under the label 'cognitivist theories of emotions'. In a stricter sense the term 'cognitivist' has been used to characterize those theories that take an emotion to *essentially* be a judgment.[41] In what follows I shall refer with the label 'cognitivists' to all those theorists that are explicitly or tacitly committed to two related, but distinct, ideas: first, the idea that in order to classify a token emotion as an instance of a given type of emotion we have to consider its intentional content, and second, the idea that, as far as its intentionality is concerned, the phenomenology of an emotion plays no role whatsoever. By discussing two problems of classical feeling theories to which cognitivists have repeatedly pointed, I shall try to offer a picture of the spirit of this 'early' philosophical response to James' and Lange's proposal.

---

[39] Prinz's embodied appraisal theory can be read as an attempt to solve this concrete problem.

[40] As far as the philosophical discussion is concerned, Errol Bedford (1956–1957) and Anthony Kenny ([1963] 2003) have to be seen as the pioneers of the first wave of criticism of feeling theo-ries. In psychology the criticism of feeling theories had begun earlier. However, the objections raised by psychologists have been less clearly focused on the issue of the intentionality of our emotions. For an informative review (in German) of this psychological debate, see Traue and Kessler (2003).

[41] One might prefer the term 'judgmentalist' to characterize these theories. The accounts developed by Jerome Neu (2000), Martha Nussbaum (1990, 1994, 2001), and 'the early' Robert Solomon (1976) are often mentioned as examples of the judgmentalist view.

The first of these problems does not directly concern the mentioned incapacity of classical feeling theories to capture the intentional character of our emotions. Rather, it targets the central tenet of these theories concerning the issue of the individuation of an emotion (i.e. the issue about how to differentiate individual emotions). I am alluding to the claim that a particular emotion can be classified as an instance of a given type of emotion in reference to the quality of the pertinent bodily sensations; sensations that, as is assumed, are systematically associated with a certain pattern of physiological changes. The problem is that the bodily changes assumed to be characteristic of an emotion of a certain type could in the case of most emotions hardly be said to be *specific* for this type of emotion. This physiological unspecificity makes less plausible the idea that a qualitatively characteristic feeling apt to make a person aware of her own bodily state could individuate some organismic reaction she is undergoing as instantiating a given type of emotion.[42] As I shall explain below, this problem is at least indirectly related to the mentioned incapacity of feeling theories to accommodate the idea that our emotional experiences are genuinely intentional in nature.

A second weakness of feeling theories cognitivists have pointed to—one which is more directly related to the issue of affective intentionality—concerns an insight I have stressed above: our emotions can typically be said to be warranted (or unwarranted), given the circumstances in which they arise. Non-relational phenomenal qualities—whatever exactly they turn out to be—can hardly be characterized as being warranted or unwarranted. The problem is that the picture of emotions provided by feeling theories invites us to conceive of the relationship between an emotion (in their view, a bodily sensation of a certain sort) and the occurrence it is evoked by as an entirely contingent (merely causal) one. As we have begun to see in the previous section, the relationship between an emotion and its intentional object may be argued to be conceptual and normatively constrained. The latter is a thought Anthony Kenny articulated in the beginning of the debate on affective intentionality by means of the following observation: 'One cannot be afraid of just anything, nor happy about anything whatsoever' ([1963] 2003, p. 134). The object of one's emotion has to have certain properties that make it appear dangerous, if one is to make sense of the idea that one's feeling is a feeling of fear or that one's action is an action out of fear. The relevant property characteristically varies from one type of emotion to another, but it holds true for emotions of all types that they *necessarily* present their object as having some attribute of a specific sort. Moreover, and as we shall discuss below (in Sect. 5.2), the relationship between an emotion and its object is such that there is a sense in which one could say that, given certain circumstances, a particular subject *ought to* have certain emotional experiences (and not others).

---

[42] Most authors who raise this issue refer to an experiment conducted by Stanley Schachter and Jerome Singer (1962). Schachter and Singer show that, depending on specific contextual clues (manipulated in their experiment), a person tends to interpret the arousal she is experiencing (as a result of her having been injected with epinephrine without knowing it) in one of two different ways: as a state of euphoria or as a state of anger. This is thought to show that the bodily sensation alone is insufficient to determine an experienced physiological arousal as an emotion of this or that kind.

Although the two points of criticism just exposed are independent of each other, there is a strong relation between them. One could state the ultimate criticism leveled by cognitivists against feeling theories in such a way as to bring to the fore the connection between these two problems as follows: it is because they have failed to see the conceptual (rather that merely causal) nature of the relationship between an emotion and its intentional object that classical feeling theories have failed to recognize that what differentiates one type of emotion from another is not its allegedly typical (non-relational) phenomenal quality, but that which these two different experiences can be said to be about; their typical intentional character.[43]

In their attempts to defend the idea that, in order to target the individuation-relevant differences between emotions of diverse sorts, we have to address their intentional content, philosophers have introduced a series of technical terms that allow us to appreciate the precise sense in which its being about its object could be said to determine the class to which a particular emotion belongs. By appealing to distinctions drawn in this context, it is possible to explicate, first, the extent to which we can talk of a complex intentional structure that is typical of human emotions, and second, the extent to which this idea of a multilayered intentional structure is related to the idea that emotions typically put us in touch with a rationally intelligible world.

At the most basic intentional level, emotions can be argued to typically have a *target* understood as 'an actual particular to which [this token] emotion relates' (de Sousa 1987, p. 108). If I respond with fear when I see the dog of my neighbor, *this particular dog* constitutes the target of my emotion of fear. If I get angry because a car driver has ignored the zebra crossing while I was seeking to cross the street with my six-year-old son, *this particular comportment of the car driver* constitutes the target of my anger.[44] The first thing the cognitivist response to feeling theories of emotion has brought us to see is that the intentional nature of emotions is not exhausted by their typically having a target. It has done so by pointing to the fact that the reference to the target of an emotion fails, not only to explain in which sense this emotion can be said to be about (and not merely causally related to) its object, but furthermore to illuminate in how far the intentional content of a particular emotion may be claimed to individuate this token emotion as belonging to a specific

---

[43] According to Matthew Ratcliffe, cognitivists have offered a distorted picture of James' position (cf. 2008, pp. 219ff.). Even if Ratcliffe is right, it is fair to say that the picture of feeling theories I have sketched above is the one against which cognitivists have reacted.

[44] As Goldie points out, the target of an emotion is in a very broad sense of the term 'object' an object, for it can be a thing, a person, a state of affairs, an action, or an event (see 2000, p. 17). Goldie suggests that even at this apparently basic level the determination of the intentional object of an emotion is not completely straightforward. His point is one we have already touched on: the target of an emotion does not have to coincide with the physical stimulus that elicits this emotion. To illustrate the point, Goldie offers an example on which I have elaborated above. He writes: 'the sight of red numbers on a computer screen in London might bring about your fear, but the object of your fear is falling bond prices in the Japanese markets (in which you are too heavily invested for your own good)' (2002, p. 250, note 11).

type of emotion. The obvious problem here is that we can have an ample variety of emotions directed towards the very same target in different situations.

In the context of the contemporary debate on emotions, Kenny ([1963] 2003) was the first philosopher to observe that, besides having a targeted nature, emotions may be argued to have what he calls a *formal object.*[45] In the meantime, it has become common to use the term 'formal object' to refer to a certain property that may be claimed to be implicitly ascribed by an emotion to its target. My emotion of fear in the presence of my neighbor's dog, for instance, may be said to ascribe the property of dangerousness to this particular (targeted) dog. It does so in that it presents this dog *as being dangerous or worth being frightened.* If I get angry with a car driver who has ignored the zebra crossing, my anger presents the disrespectful comportment of this car driver *as being insulting or worth protesting against.* This specific property an emotion typically ascribes to its target is defined by the formal object that characterizes the *type of emotion* this token affective response instantiates. An affective state that presents its target as worth being frightened *is* an instance of the emotion we call fear and an emotion that presents its target as being offensive *is* an instance of the emotion we call anger. Put another way, any response of fear is directed towards 'the dangerous' and any response of anger towards 'the offensive'.[46] This is the sense in which the idea that an emotion always has a specific formal object can be argued to solve the problem concerning the individuation of emotions.

This basic distinction between an emotion's formal object and its target permits us to understand the claim that emotions should be seen as states that have a rather complex intentional structure. An analysis of this complex structure permits us, in turn, to better understand the idea that an emotion is about a particular situation, and does not merely point to some worldly event that has elicited it. As already mentioned, the idea that emotions are typically about particular situations—the idea that they are intentional states in a rather demanding sense of the technical adjective 'intentional'—is strongly related to the idea that our emotions can normally be said to be warranted (or unwarranted), given certain circumstances. A first point one can make in order to explicate this idea is that the warrant of an emotion is related to the plausibility of the relationship the emotion at issue proposes exists between its target and its formal object. The point touches on the following fact: we are normally

---

[45] In his discussion of the difference between the particular (or material) object—what we have called here the target—and the formal object of an emotion, Kenny attributes to the medieval scholastics this idea of a formal object of an intentional state (cf. [1963] 2003, pp. 132ff.). As Jan Slaby (2007) observes, Martin Heidegger ([1927] 1962, §30) may be taken to have 'anticipated' the distinction at issue, although he addressed the issue in completely different terms.

[46] One of the most common objections raised against the idea of a formal object concerns the circularity of the characterization of certain emotions (e.g. joy or embarrassment) in terms of their alleged formal objects (the joyful, the embarrassing). (For a criticism along these lines, see Gordon 1987, p. 70.) As we shall see below (in Sect. 5.2), this circularity can be said to be of a non-vicious sort. Prinz (2004b, pp. 62ff.) proposes evading this circularity by conceiving of the formal object in terms of what Richard Lazarus (1991) calls the 'core relational theme' of an emotion. (For a summary of Lazarus' main point, see Prinz [2004b, pp. 14ff.].)

not urged to render intelligible an emotional response the target of which can straightforwardly be said to possess the properties tacitly ascribed. My being afraid of my neighbor's dog would be *immediately* comprehensible, if this dog had some features that permitted us to regard it as a dangerous animal. But, if my neighbor's dog were a small and old poodle that has lost most of its teeth, I may see myself compelled to make my fear intelligible (i.e. I may feel urged to show its being warranted, appropriate, and/or proportionate) by embedding my response in a more detailed narrative framework.

So we can initially understand the intentionality of a typical human emotion as a matter of the capacity this affective state has to disclose something (a concrete feature) *in* something (the target of this token emotion), thereby presenting this target *as* something that has a particular property defined by the formal object that characterizes the type of emotion it instantiates. To differentiate between the target's *particular* features that permit an intelligible ascription of the relevant property and the *typical* quality defined by the formal object—the quality towards which the pertinent type of emotion is characteristically directed—, Goldie distinguishes between *determinable* and *determinate* features of an object. He writes:

> If Peter is afraid of the bull, then there will be some feature of the bull which Peter thinks it has. If this feature is a determinable one (its being dangerous), then he will think it is dangerous in virtue of its having certain determinately dangerous features (having long horns which could harm him, perhaps), even if he is not able to say what they are. And if the feature which he thinks it has is a determinate one, then it ought to be possible for Peter to explain why this determinate feature falls under the determinable one. Thus, according to this idea, if Peter did not believe that there was something potentially harmful about the bull's long horns, then it would be puzzling, to say the least, why he should feel fear of the bull in virtue of its having this feature (2000, pp. 21–22).

This last distinction certainly complicates the issue sufficiently to warrant the talk of a multilayered intentional structure. But the frame of tacit references that constitute the complex intentional structure of an emotion is even more intricate. My neighbor's dog may have some features that make it 'objectively' dangerous (say, for instance, the tendency to behave in an unpredictable way, in addition to an evidently very strong jaw, and a remarkable agility). But even if this were the case, the capacity this *manifestly* dangerous dog has to *appear to me* as worthy of fright (as opposed to merely appearing as an animal that has some objectively hazardous features) would depend on the extent to which I take myself to be able to cope with this encounter with the animal. Were the dog to clearly be kept under tight control by my neighbor, my running away in terror would be unwarranted, inappropriate, and/or disproportionate. My comportment would also appear so, were it clear that, as part of my training as a police officer, I had developed a number of skills and abilities that allowed me to bring under control this dangerous animal, if required. What this remark is intended to bring to the fore is that we can evaluate an emotion as warranted or unwarranted only in reference to the intelligible evaluative view of the world of the subject of emotion. Specifically, we can find an emotional response warranted only on the assumption that the occurrence in question is related to something that is an issue for the relevant subject. An encounter with my neighbor's dog can be said to be worthy of fright, given not only certain features this animal possesses, but also my limited capacity to cope with such an encounter, only on the assumption that it is an issue for me not to become hurt, damaged, or negatively affected in one way or another. So the ultimate ground of intelligibility of a human emotion has to be spelt out in terms of a sort of double condition. We can understand a segment of human behavior as a warranted emotion only on the condition that, first, there is some background intentional object to which this behavior is related (which is not necessarily the target of this emotion) that can be claimed to be positively or negatively affected by the occurrence at issue, and second, this background intentional object is understandable as something the relevant subject cares about.[47] Bennett Helm, the philosopher who has, in my view, more clearly articulated this thought in the contemporary debate, illustrates the point as follows:

> [M]y fear of earthquakes and my anger at you for throwing the baseball in the house are both made intelligible in light of the import my prize Ming vase has for me, for it is this vase that the earthquake threatens and it is in virtue of your callous disregard for the vase that you offend me (2001, p. 69).

In order to refer to this background object that makes intelligible the evaluation implicit in an emotion, Helm coins the notion of an emotion's *focus* (cf. p. 69). Helm insists that only the significance this focus has to the relevant subject can serve as an ultimate 'standard of warrant' for the evaluation implicit in the emotion at issue.[48] If what ultimately warrants my anger at the car driver who has ignored the zebra crossing while I was seeking to cross the street with my son is the import my son's wellbeing has to me, my son constitutes the focus of my emotional response.

One could sum up this train of thought—in such a way as to characterize the complex intentional structure of a typical human emotion—by making two claims that jointly underscore the idea that human emotions are best conceived of as responses strictly so called. First, the genuinely intentional character of a human emotion can be understood in terms of the capacity this emotion has to disclose something (a determinate feature) in something (the target of this token emotion), thereby presenting this target as something that possesses a given evaluative property; a determinable property defined by the formal object of the type of emotion this token emotion instantiates. Second, the property defined by the formal object of this emotion is a property which *qua evaluative property* makes reference to and is only comprehensible in light of the significance something (the focus of the token emotion at issue) has for someone (a subject of concern who *as such* has a fundamentally intelligible evaluative view of the world). There is no reason to identify the intentional object of an emotion with the worldly occurrence that seems to have

---

[47] Of course, one could point to a further ground of intelligibility of every emotional response. In order to understand a fragment of behavior as an emotional response, we have to already have understood the individual at issue as a subject of concern; as a being that *can* care about certain things and occurrences. We will have time to address this point below (in Chap. 7).

[48] This is a fundamental insight to which we shall come back below (in Sect. 5.2). As it will become clear in the course of this discussion, Helm is not an exponent of the cognitivist view—at any rate, not an exemplary one.

elicited it. For each of the elements just listed may be said to be part of the intentional content of an emotion; each of these elements co-constitutes what this emotion is about and could, correspondingly, be appealed to in our attempts to render the behavior at issue intelligible by invoking the pertinent emotion.

Now, it is definitively a merit of the cognitivist response to classical feeling theories that it has provided us with some fundamental conceptual tools that allow us to understand in which sense an emotion can be said to be a form of understanding. In recent times, however, a number of philosophers have raised a series of objections concerning what they take to be the fundamental ground of inadequacy of this view of emotions: its incapacity to explain what differentiates an emotion from a non-affective intentional state; its incapacity to capture the *emotionality* of emotions, as Helm puts it (cf. 2001, pp. 38ff.). This failure of the cognitivist view, these philosophers have argued, is a consequence of its having tended to neglect the central role feelings play in our intuitive understanding of what an emotion is.

The awareness of this shortcoming of the cognitivist view of emotions has led to two different developments. The first one is a sophistication of the James-Lange theory that has become popular thanks to the work of the neurologist Antonio Damasio (1994, 1999, 2003) and the philosopher Jesse Prinz (2004b). It has become common to use the label 'neo-Jamesian theories of emotions' to refer to these sorts of accounts. In particular Prinz's perceptual theory of emotion might be taken to accommodate the thought that is central here: the thought that responding emotionally in a particular situation implies having understood it as being a particular way and meriting a response of certain sorts. However, Prinz's account includes this central aspect of an understanding of the relevant situation by arguing—as James basically also did, though in a theoretically enriched way—that certain bodily sensations are triggered by the perception, i.e. by a non-affective recognition, of certain classes of situations. In so arguing, Prinz fails to accommodate the idea that an emotional feeling *is itself* (and is not merely systematically related to) a world-directed experiential state. To this extent, he fails to solve the basic problem of feeling theories, as far as the criticism leveled by the second response to the cognitivist view is concerned.[49]

In the following section, I shall characterize the mentioned alternative view developed in response to the judgmentalist picture. This is a view which attempts to respect both the intuition that feelings are central to our affective life and the intuition that emotional feelings are genuinely intentional experiential states apt to rationally motivate some of our actions, without 'falling back' into some sort of (sophisticated) feeling theory of emotions. As we shall see, the advocates of this third view, which I shall recommend as the right point of departure for a theory that construes emotions as responses proper that are genuinely affective, achieve this by

---

[49] For this reason I am not going to deal with this sort of development of James' and Lange's view. Bennett Helm (2009) offers a critical assessment of neo-Jamesian theories in which he acknowledges that these theories can be seen as an improvement not only over classical feeling theories, but also over the cognitivist view.

arguing that—as it is not unusual in philosophical discussions—the two positions that have framed the contemporary debate share a false premise.

2.4 World-Directed Feelings and Felt Understanding

As we have seen, a human emotion can normally be said to present its target as being a certain way; as having a certain property defined by the formal object that characterizes the type of emotion this token affective state instantiates. Typically, the property in question is such that its recognition could be said to merit, or call for, a certain sort of response. That is to say, the property defined by the formal object is characteristically an evaluative property.[50] There is thus a clear sense in which we can speak—as a number of philosophers have done—of an evaluation implicit in every human emotion; an evaluation that, as just discussed, is rationally intelligible in light of the significance the focus of this emotion can be said to have for the subject of emotion.

Elaborating on this common idea concerning the evaluative nature of our emotions, some philosophers—judgmentalists—have proposed to conceive of our emotions as judgments or beliefs about the value of certain things or occurrences. Robert Solomon, for instance, writes: 'My shame *is* my judgment to the effect that I am responsible for an untoward situation or incident' (1993, p. 187; as quoted by Goldie 2000, p. 24).[51] Something that motivates judgmentalists to explore the idea that emotions *just are* judgments is the intuition that we could analyze the intentionality of an emotion in terms we are already familiar with, namely in terms of the about-ness of non-emotional, cognitive world-directed states (or of combinations of cognitive and motivational states) that may be claimed to constitute our emotional responses. Put another way, the leading intuition is that we could get rid of any residual discomfort with the claim that a typical human emotion can normally be said to be about its object by showing that our emotions (and, specifically, their world-directed character) can be analyzed in terms of 'ordinary' propositional attitudes. That is to say, by showing that the intentionality of our emotions is not sui generis, as Joel Marks (1982, p. 227) puts it.

Although this line of thought has been extremely influential in the current analytic philosophical debate on emotions (particularly during the 1970s and 1980s) the source of its contestability is a rather obvious one. As it has been repeatedly observed, one certainly can have those beliefs judgmentalists identify with a given

---

[50] It is McDowell (1979, 1985), as Goldie (2000, p. 30) acknowledges, who proposes that what it is for something to exhibit an evaluative property is, in part, for it to merit a certain sort of response.

[51] It has to be mentioned that, as far as the tenet that an emotion *essentially* is a judgment is concerned—a tenet that, as Solomon himself recognizes, '[relegates] all [bodily feelings] to the causal margins of emotion, as merely accompaniments or secondary effects' (2004, p. 85)—, Solomon has moderated his position. He writes: 'I am now coming to appreciate that accounting for the bodily feelings (not just sensations) in emotion is not a secondary concern and not independent of appreciating the essential role of the body in emotional experience' (ibid.).

type of emotion without having the relevant emotional experience. Thus, to be in a genuinely emotional state seems to be something more (or perhaps something entirely different) than just having a series of beliefs and corresponding desires. Moreover, this 'something more' (or 'something different') seems to be precisely what amounts to the distinctively affective character of those intentional states we call emotions.

One could regard the argumentative move that leads from the widely shared intuition that emotions characteristically have an evaluative character to the conclusion that they are evaluative judgments as an unnecessary one; as a move by means of which the philosophical response to feeling theories—a response the fundamental merit of which consists in having allowed us to understand the complex intentional structure of our emotions—, unfortunately, went awry.[52] But a number of philosophers seem to be inclined to think, rather, that this argumentative step only makes evident that the whole approach is misconceived.[53] Independently of their willingness (or unwillingness) to appreciate the achievements of cognitivist theories, most critics of the cognitivist approach agree that the basic problem of this view of emotions resides in its tendency to provide over-intellectualized (or 'cerebral') accounts of affective intentionality that lose sight of the genuinely affective nature of our emotional relation to the world.

In recent times, this dissatisfaction with the orthodox cognitivist view has taken the form of a criticism along the following lines: having stressed the aboutness of our emotions at the cost of neglecting their phenomenology, cognitivist theories of emotions have become blind to the sui generis character of affective intentionality. In this context, some philosophers (Goldie 2000, 2002; Ratcliffe 2008; Slaby and Stephan 2008; Stocker 1983) have begun to explore the idea that the intentional and the phenomenal aspects of our emotions could be claimed to be intertwined in such an inextricable way as to make the intentionality of an emotion be a matter of its specific phenomenology.[54]

In a diagnostic spirit, these philosophers have observed that both feeling theorists and cognitivists have reduced the phenomenology of our emotional experiences to the bodily sensations that accompany some of our emotional responses, thereby overlooking a theoretical possibility suggested by our everyday discourse: we could conceive of at least some of our feelings as states that are directed towards worldly objects and occurrences.[55] Endorsing the central insight of the cognitivist view—the

---

[52] It seems to me that Goldie offers a moderate criticism of cognitive theories along these lines (cf. 2000, pp. 22ff.).

[53] This is the line of (more radical) criticism I take Bennett Helm, Matthew Ratcliffe, and Jan Slaby to be advancing.

[54] According to Íngrid Vendrell Ferran (2008), this is a view the so-called realist phenomenologists have defended at the beginning of the twentieth century.

[55] As Roberts observes, those philosophers who made strong the idea that emotions are not feelings failed to pose the question as to *which kinds of feelings* emotions are not (cf. 1988, p. 185). Roberts notes that even Gilbert Ryle (1971), who offered a very differentiated taxonomy of feelings, neglected the idea that emotional feelings could be taken to constitute a class of feelings that is distinct from all the other classes he identified. It is not only for reasons of simplicity that I have

idea that we cannot individuate an emotion by referring exclusively to its *non-relational* phenomenal quality—, these philosophers have focused on the content of our emotions, but tried to reject the idea that this content is exhausted by the that-clause of those judgments (evaluative propositions) by means of which we could, if required, make explicit what the emotion in question is about.

In one of the most elaborated attempts to elucidate the extent to which the intentionality of an emotion may be claimed to be intertwined with its phenomenology, Peter Goldie (cf. 2000, Chapter 3; 2002) differentiates two distinct kinds of feelings involved in a typical emotional episode: *bodily feelings* and *feelings towards*.[56] He argues that, as an effect of their normally being held together in a unitary emotional experience, we tend to run these two sorts of feelings together in our ordinary way of speaking of affective experiences (cf. 2002, pp. 247ff.). By pointing to an ambiguity of the expression 'to feel something', Goldie brings us to an awareness that in talking of emotional feelings we are not necessarily referring to certain bodily sensations, as cognitivists and feeling theorists alike could be accused of having assumed. For the expression 'to feel something' may be employed in the sense of feeling something (in the world beyond one's own body) *to be a particular way*.

Goldie begins by observing that in a typical emotional episode we can often recognize 'the feeling from the inside of the condition of one's body as being a certain way or as undergoing certain changes' (2002, p. 235; cf. 2000, pp. 51ff.). This is what he calls a bodily feeling. When I am in fear, for instance, 'I feel the hairs go up on the back of my neck' (2002, p. 235). Goldie is eager to point out that certain bodily feelings could probably be said to characteristically accompany some physiological processes that instantiate specific types of emotion, but they do not permit one to classify a token emotion as an instance of a certain type of emotion, *unless one has already (and by other means) identified these sensations with the relevant type of emotion*. Goldie makes the point by writing that '[a bodily feeling]

---

reconstructed the contemporary philosophical debate on emotions in terms of the dichotomy between feeling theories of emotions on the one side and cognitivist theories on the other. However, early enough in the course of this debate we find developments that cannot be easily classified in one of these two positions. As far as the idea that emotional feelings are feelings of a particular sort—feelings that have an intentional content proper which is evaluative—is concerned, one has to mention here Patricia Greenspan's (1988) claim that occurrent emotions are best understood as 'propositional feelings'. In a later paper, Greenspan articulates the idea as follows: 'Emotional affect or feeling is *itself* evaluative—and the result can be summed up in a proposition' (2004, p. 132; my emphasis). In this paper, Greenspan points to the amphibious nature of her proposal. She writes: 'My own view emerged from modification of judgmentalism, but I have concluded that it amounts to a version of the feeling view with enough structure to allow for rational assessment of emotions' (ibid.).

[56] Goldie differentiates between emotion and episode of emotional experience. He writes: 'An emotion [...] is a complex state, relatively more enduring than an emotional episode, which itself includes various past episodes of emotional experience, as well as various sorts of disposition to think, feel, and act, all of which can dynamically interweave and interact' (2000, p. 11). This distinction allows Goldie to avoid a very strong claim: the claim that emotions *essentially* involve feelings. The idea is that an emotion could be said to typically involve feelings *at some point during its existence*.

is not of such a nature that it can provide a prima facie reason, in and of itself, for believing that one is experiencing the emotion' (2002, p. 238). He explicates this claim by observing that 'there is nothing *intrinsic* to the experience of, for example, the hairs going up on the back of your neck to suggest that it is characteristic of a feeling of fear' (p. 240). In accordance with the cognitivist view, Goldie asserts that the reason why bodily feelings cannot individuate a token emotion is because they 'alone cannot reveal to you what your emotion is about' (p. 241).[57] So it is only once an emotion has been individuated by reference to its intentional content that one is able to associate a bodily feeling with a type of emotion. He writes: 'the bodily feeling becomes recognisably one of irritation, or of excitement, once one is already aware that it is that emotion that one is feeling' (p. 238).

Goldie stresses the inferential and contingent nature of the relationship between a bodily feeling and the corresponding emotion by pointing out that the existence of such a relationship 'is something that the child comes to *learn*' (p. 250, note 10; cf. 2000, pp. 29ff.). His ultimate point here is that to have bodily feelings of a certain sort is neither necessary nor sufficient for us to have an emotion of a particular kind. Goldie writes:

> Intuitively, it might seem rather obvious that bodily feelings which are characteristic of an emotional experience are not necessary for it. (They also seem not to be sufficient, for they can be caused in some way which has nothing to do with an emotional experience; furthermore, first-personal authority about this cannot be relied upon—subjects can, and do, 'confabulate'; see Nisbett and Wilson 1977 and Griffiths 1997.) They seem not to be necessary for at least two reasons […]: it is possible to have an emotion which involves bodily changes, but without having bodily feelings—without being conscious of the bodily changes which are part of the emotion; and it surely seems correct to say that there are certain sorts of emotion which might have associated feelings, but which do not have associated *bodily* feelings (pride, perhaps) (2000, p. 52).

In order to refer to the second kind of feelings involved in a typical emotional episode, Goldie coins the mentioned notion of a feeling towards. This is a term that aims at capturing the idea that in an emotional episode there always is some feeling that may be said to be directed towards the intentional object of one's emotion. Such a feeling can be claimed to be intentional to the extent to which it can be claimed to present its target object 'as being a particular way or as having certain properties or features' (2000, p. 58). In fear, for instance, we *feel* the object in question *to be* dangerous; we feelingly understand its dangerousness. Feeling towards, Goldie writes, can be understood as 'thinking of with feeling' (ibid.).

Central to this proposal is the claim that a certain kind of feeling that constitutes a typical emotional experience does not *merely point* to something in the world. It does not simply bring the subject to infer that a given object or situation is likely to be this or that way, as certain bodily sensations (as mere experiences of the body) could perhaps do. Rather, this kind of feeling (as an experience of the world) can be said to *present* this object or situation in certain terms or under a particular aspect.

---

[57] As already mentioned, Goldie submits that bodily feelings are intentional in the sense that they are directed towards something, namely (a part of) one's own body.

It can be said to bring the relevant object or situation to appear in experience as having a particular evaluative property that calls for a certain sort of response. According to Goldie, a feeling towards may be said to have a 'content [...] individuated in [such] a sufficiently fine-grained way [as] to capture *a subject's way of thinking*' (2002, p. 241; my emphasis); as opposed to having 'a content [...] individuated purely in terms of reference' (ibid.). Goldie illustrates this difference as follows:

> Oedipus wanted to marry Jocasta; he did not want to marry his mother: 'that he marry Jocasta' and 'that he marry his mother' are different contents, even though in every possible world where Jocasta exists, he would marry his mother by satisfying his desire to marry Jocasta, for 'Jocasta' and 'Oedipus' mother' refer to the very same person. It is thus perfectly intelligible that Oedipus should feel horror when he realised that Jocasta was his mother, and thus that he had—unintentionally—married his mother (ibid.).

Feelings towards are, hence, not merely systematically related to certain worldly occurrences. Furthermore, they have some content proper that—to put it in the terms I have employed above—constitutes and expresses a particular view of the world.

Matthew Ratcliffe objects that, in categorically contrasting bodily feelings and feelings towards (or psychic feelings), Goldie and Stocker are double-counting the pertinent feelings (cf. 2008, p. 35). He argues, furthermore, that we would not be able to offer a clear idea of what gives our acts of feeling towards their *felt* character, were we not to acknowledge that feelings towards also *are* bodily sensations (ibid.). I believe that Ratcliffe is right. But I also think that the *analytic* distinction between affective experiences the object of which is the body and affective experiences the object of which is the world is essential—although it might probably be better to talk of different *aspects* of a yet unified emotional experience that is bodily rooted through and through. For, as discussed above, it is the character of the relevant affective experience of the world—which is captured by its formal object—, and not the one of the bodily sensations involved, that defines the type of emotion the feeling at issue instantiates; and there is no logical or empirical rule whatsoever that permits us to infallibly infer from the character of the relevant bodily sensations which character the world exhibits in a particular emotional experience. Understanding this permits us to conciliate the (empirical) claim concerning the unspecific and unnecessary character of bodily sensations *of a particular sort* as a part of a given emotional experience with the conceptual claim that *some* bodily sensation is necessary for us to understand an evaluative state as an (occurrent) emotion proper. A fear response, for instance, could, but does definitively not have to, involve an experience of muscular tension. The same person might rather experience a diffuse abdominal discomfort in a different situation she also takes to be dangerous. Such a discomfort, as we all know, is not necessary, either, for us to speak of a response of fear. Moreover, these sensations (and other bodily sensations that may be described) are not exclusive of our responses of fear. In a given situation the experienced muscular tension could be the somatosensory aspect of this person's taking the relevant situation to be rather insulting. So, in some cases it is *through* her muscular tension and in others *through* her abdominal discomfort that a person *feels* the situation at issue to be dangerous (and the list of bodily sensations that may be described in a situation in which one is frightened by something is quite long). In some other situations *through* a similar experience of muscular tension the same person could come to rather understand the pertinent situation as meriting a response of anger. But in each situation in which it is appropriate to speak of an occurrent emotion there is some bodily sensation that confers to the person's understanding of the situation as being a particular way and meriting a response of certain sorts its felt character. Goldie makes the point by claiming that 'the feeling towards is infused with a bodily characterization' (2000, p. 57). To this extent we can, indeed, take the relevant feelings towards to just be the pertinent bodily sensations: there is no additional affective entity involved. But we completely lose the possibility of *definitively* settling the question concerning the kind of emotion a feeling instantiates, if we focus on the body-directed aspect of the experience (which cannot be systematically 'translated' into the description of a particular kind of world-directed experience). And we completely lose sight of the specificum of affective intentionality, if we disentangle the world-directed character exhibited by a typical emotional experience from the feeling aspect (as add-on theories of emotions do). This, I think, warrants Goldie's emphasis on the distinction between the (non-relational) bodily sensations that instantiate an emotional experience and the world-directed affective experiences these sensations make possible.[58]

---

[58] At this point, an objection raised by an anonymous reviewer of the manuscript of this book could be answered. The objection targets the claim that the specificum of affective intentionality concerns the inextricable intertwinement of phenomenology and intentionality in paradigmatic instances of emotion. It does so by pointing to cases in which the bodily sensations a subject is inclined to associate with the relevant emotion and the intentional object of this emotion are *not* brought together in a world-directed emotional experience; the point being that in these cases, the phenomenology of the relevant emotion is exhausted by the relevant (non-relational) bodily feelings. The reviewer appeals to the idea that these bodily sensations may, in a second move, acquire a 'borrowed intentionality' (cf. Goldie 2000, p. 57) by being (retrospectively) associated with this person's understanding of the object as being a certain way. He argues, that such a 'non-conscious emotion', as we may call it (cf. the discussion above [in footnote 32] concerning the idea of non-conscious emotions), has an intentional structure even before the person has become aware of this world-directedness. He takes this to suggest that the intertwinement of intentionality and phenomenology is not a necessary feature of human emotions, but something that is contingent on the subject's awareness and attention during an emotional episode. The reviewer concludes that a sharp differentiation between emotional feelings with borrowed intentionality and emotional feelings with intrinsic intentionality (as being different *in kind*) is not warranted if the difference in experience depends on whether or not the subject is aware of the particular object of emotion when the emotional reaction takes place. This interesting objection, I think, fails to note that we could never settle the question concerning whether these bodily sensations constitute a genuine emotional experience, were we not able to understand them as feelings apt to present an aspect of the world as being a certain way and meriting a certain sort of response. In other words, the act of reflection that brings to light the fact that these feelings constitute an emotional response does not *retrospectively confer* intentionality on a feeling that was not originally part of a world-directed evaluative state. Rather, this act of reflection discovers the fact that the relevant sensations were, in a sense, always already intentional (although the subject was, at the relevant moment, not able to recognize this world-directedness). Indeed, not every bodily sensation can acquire borrowed intentionality by means of an association of ideas. If I reflectively recognize the causal and systematic link between my toothache and the presence of the dentist, my toothache does not become an

Presumably seeking to elude the charge of over-intellectualization that accounts of affective intentionality which stress the conceptual relation between an emotion and its object are likely to face, Goldie points to a further ambiguity of the expression 'to feel something'. He writes:

> I think that there is quite a deep ambiguity in the meaning of '*A* feels emotion *E*': in one sense we mean that *A* has those feelings which are part of his being unreflectively emotionally engaged with the world; in another sense we mean that *A* is reflectively aware of having certain feelings which he recognizes as being *E*-related feelings—either bodily feelings or feelings towards something, or both (2000, p. 64).

In this context, Goldie appeals to the distinction between reflective and non-reflective forms of consciousness (cf. 2000, pp. 62ff.) and construes the phenomenon of feeling towards in terms of an 'unreflective [conscious] emotional engagement with the world beyond the body' (2002, p. 241).[59] His point is not merely that feeling towards should be seen as a basic form of consciousness in the sense of being something that cannot be reduced to other conscious mental acts. Furthermore, he wants to underscore that having an emotional experience is a matter of actualizing an ability that does not presuppose some thematic self-awareness. Goldie writes: 'Feeling towards is [...] something that a creature which is incapable of self-reflective thought—a dog or a toddler, for example—could achieve' (ibid.).

Now, since such a view of affective intentionality has some evident advantages over both classical feeling theories and cognitivist theories of emotions, all seems to come down to the plausibility of the claim that our emotional experiences can be said to have some content that, in a way, goes beyond the that-clause of the proposition by means of which we could capture what a particular emotion is about. One of the ways in which one could attempt to make room for the possibility of such

---

intentional experience that presents the dentist as being a certain way. To this extent it is true that an emotional feeling that 'acquires' borrowed intentionality and an emotional feeling that from the very beginning exhibits an intrinsic world-relatedness are not different in kind. But this is because the act that leads to a borrowed intentionality does not create intentionality. What is borrowed, to put it in a different way, is only the experiential access to the particular character exhibited by the relevant object or situation. (So it is not true, as the reviewer suggests, that theories of affective intentionality have to presuppose that our emotions are always entirely transparent to us.) Indeed, although he articulates the point in a way that makes the view liable to the mentioned objection leveled by Ratcliffe, Goldie explicates this idea of a borrowed intentionality by contrasting his theory to the one offered by James in such a way as to suggest that the bodily feelings can 'become' intentional not as a matter of an association of ideas, but because they are a constitutive part of an experience that is always already intentional. He writes: 'For James, the object of the frustration [...] does not become transformed into an 'object-emotionally-felt' until there is the bodily feeling to combine in consciousness with the 'object-simply-apprehended'. I say, rather, that the [object of the frustration] is an object-emotionally-felt from the moment you begin to feel frustrated by it, arising (in this case) prior in time to the bodily feeling in your chest of being hemmed in; then, I say, the two feelings come together in consciousness so that the bodily feeling becomes, through borrowed intentionality, directed towards the [object of the frustration]' (2000, p. 57).

[59] To be sure, one can have world-directed feelings towards one's own body. These feelings, Goldie (2002, p. 251, note 14) writes, are not bodily feelings. For in this case the object of the emotion is the *body image*, and not the *body schema*. (For the distinction between body image and body schema, see Gallagher 1995.)

content is by appealing to the image of a sort of *non-propositional content*, understood as a content that is not capturable by a proposition to the effect that some worldly state of affairs is such and such. Although he explicitly allows for the possibility of such non-propositional emotional content, I believe that Goldie's way of tackling the issue is a somewhat different one.[60] One could read the argument I am to reconstruct in what follows as an argument that does not try to establish the existence of some non-propositional emotional content, but rather seeks to show that being directed towards something in an emotional way is a matter of having *a completely different pre-thematic understanding* of the pertinent situation.

Goldie elaborates on an example Michael Stocker offers in an attempt to capture the difference between merely knowing something to be a certain way and having an emotional experience—a feeling—to the effect that it is this way. Stocker writes:

> [H]aving fallen on the ice, the very same knowledge of (and wishes to avoid) the dangers of walking on the ice are 'emotionally present' to me. They concern me to the point of my being afraid. Before the fall, I had only an intellectual appreciation of the very same dangers (and a rather pro-forma desire to avoid them). Then I only saw the dangers, now I also feel them (1983, pp. 20–21; as quoted by Goldie 2002, p. 242).

Goldie emphasizes that the fundamental difference between the (previous) knowledge that the ice is dangerous and the emotional experience of this dangerousness does not simply lie in the richer (non-relational) phenomenal quality exhibited by the emotional experience. Rather, the before-after difference is a matter of the transformation of our very understanding of this dangerousness, and insofar, Goldie argues, a matter of some fundamental differences in the content of these two intentional states. Although both intentional acts refer to the very same dangers, 'for no new dangers have come into view' (p. 243), 'the dangerousness of the object, and the determinate features towards which the thought is directed, is grasped in a different way [after having slipped on the ice]' (ibid.). This difference, Goldie suggests, allows us to talk of different contents, *despite the fact that by means of the very same proposition we could state what both intentional states are about.*

Goldie insists that the transformation in the manner in which one understands this dangerousness (after having slipped on the ice) cannot be conceived of in terms of the addition, as it were, of a further element (the bodily sensation) to the purely cognitive way of thinking of these dangers. Rather, Goldie submits, 'one's way of seeing [these dangers] is *completely* new' (ibid.; my emphasis). He supports this suggestion by pointing to a series of effects this novel understanding could be argued to have on the rest of our mental economy. These effects, he argues, are not exhausted by the fact that we gain 'new powers and potentialities of thought and

---

[60] Psychologists (appraisal theorists) have normally no problem whatsoever with the idea of a non-propositional content. This seems also to be the route Richard Wollheim (1999) takes in order to make plausible the idea that the content of an emotion is not exhausted by the content of a proposition able to specify what this emotion is about. Goldie draws on Wollheim in a number of respects and, as far as this point is concerned, one certainly could take him to be doing so. He writes: 'I do not want this notion of content to be taken to imply that content must be capturable in terms of a proposition' (2002, p. 241). As I shall immediately explain, one could, however, take Goldie to be following a completely different strategy; one I find more plausible.

imagination' (p. 244). There are also functional differences that parallel the transformation of our understanding: 'what was before "a rather pro-forma desire to
avoid the dangers" is now an emotional desire to avoid them' (p. 245). So one could
maintain that Goldie is not arguing for the idea of a non-propositional affective
content that 'supplements' the propositional content of the evaluative judgment
attributable (on the basis of his emotional comportment) to the subject of emotion.
Rather, he is offering an argument to the effect that a belief (or judgment) and an
emotion have to be understood as two *completely different forms of understanding*,
even in those cases in which there is some proposition that is apt to capture what
both this emotion and a particular belief (or judgment) attributable to the relevant
subject are about.

Now, one could find plausible the suggestion that our capacity to relate to worldly
occurrences in an emotional way brings us to see certain states of affairs in completely different ways, but consider this suggestion to be unsupportive of the claim
that feeling towards should be seen as a basic and non-reducible intentional phenomenon. In other words, even finding Goldie's argument persuasive, one could
remain skeptical about the claim that there is a sui generis form of intentionality that
deserves to be called affective intentionality. For there is a clear alternative: we
could conceive of this new way of thinking-about in terms of an 'affective color-
ation' of our *perceptual-cognitive* relation to the world. Moreover, the easiest way
to account for the fact that by means of the very same proposition one could articulate the content of both the judgment that motivates the rather pro-forma desire to
avoid the dangers of walking on the ice and the emotional evaluation that underlies
someone's resistance to walk on the ice (after having slipped on it) is by construing
the affective understanding that in the second case motivates the avoidant behavior
in terms of a sort of *emotional interpretation* of the situation at issue.

I am sympathetic to the idea of an emotional interpretation. I believe, however,
that it is wrong to assume that we have to conceive of such an interpretation in terms
of a second-order mental act directed towards the thematic content of some first-
order (non-affective) perceptual act. The objection we are considering could be
argued to rest on a view of what it is to interpret a situation that is inadequately
informed by the notion of interpretation that guides the endeavor classically called
hermeneutics. According to this view, an interpretation is an (intellectual) act by
means of which someone comes to disclose the 'deeper' meaning of some structure
that already in its 'surface' offers an explicit content (typically a text). In the context
of an attempt to develop a phenomenological approach to human existence, which
he calls the hermeneutics of facticity, Martin Heidegger offers a view of experiential
understanding that may help us to develop an alternative picture of what the emotional interpretation could be of. He does so by developing the idea of a *primary
(non-explicit) understanding* of Dasein (cf. [1927] 1962, §§31–33). In the section of
Being and Time in which he begins to develop this idea, Heidegger emphasizes that
one's immediate understanding of the situation one is in could be taken to be a matter of one's 'being able to manage something' [*einer Sache vorstehen können*],
'being a match for it' [*ihr gewachsen sein*], or 'being competent to do something'
[*etwas können*] (cf. [1927] 1962, p. 183; [1927] 2006, p. 143). What in this context

motivates Heidegger to talk of a form of understanding that is prior to any thematic articulation is the simple fact that we normally do not make any statement about the world when we engage practically with it (cf. [1925/26] 1976, p. 144).[61] The thought could be stated in such a way as to begin a reply to the objection we are considering by pointing out that a *thematic* understanding of a certain situation *merely brings to words* something we have already understood in a pre-predicative way;[62] the point being that there is room for conceiving of our emotional interpretation of worldly occurrences in terms of a *pre-thematic* experiential understanding that actualizes a fundamental intentional ability.

Seeking to finally address what is special about those actualizations of our openness to the world which we call emotions, I propose to conceive of an occurrent emotion as a *felt understanding* of some situation. I believe that this image of a felt understanding lies at the heart of Goldie's notion of feeling towards. It is basically the image of an emotionally expressed personal view of the world that, if required, may be captured by means of a proposition, but which is usually expressed in a rather practical manner, i.e. in the way in which the subject in question engages with a world she takes to be a certain way—a world she takes to merit certain sorts of responses. The term 'felt understanding' allows us, hence, to refer to the way in which the world *immediately* strikes the subject in emotional experience. Moreover, this basic idea of a felt understanding can be exploited in such a way as to make an even bolder claim to the effect that the intentional and the phenomenal aspects of an emotion are inextricably intertwined. Helm, whose theory of emotions as felt evaluations I shall examine below (cf. the discussion in Sect. 5.2), has repeatedly argued that understanding the peculiar nature of affective intentionality requires of us to be able to spell out the sense in which (occurrent) emotions may be said to *be* feelings. The point being that it is insufficient to claim that emotional episodes typically *involve* some pleasant or painful sensation, as some cognitivists have claimed. For there is a sense, Helm maintains, in which occurrent emotions can be said to *be* pleasures and pains. Moreover, emotions of different types may be characterized in terms of pleasures and pains of different sorts. As Helm suggests, 'to be afraid is to be pained by danger, to feel hope is to be pleased by the prospects for success, to feel frustration is to be pained by repeated failure to attain some good, etc.' (2001, p. 59). Drawing on this basic thought, Helm provides a detailed elucidation of, first, the sense in which feelings towards are evaluative in nature, and second, the sense

---

[61] This notion of a primary understanding is one Heidegger begins to prepare in the frame of his winter-term lecture 1921/22 by discussing what he calls 'the hermeneutic situation' (cf. [1921/22] 1985). (For a reconstruction of this idea of a primary understanding that connects it to motives Heidegger believes to find in Aristotle, see Kisiel [1993, pp. 227–275] and Gutiérrez Alemán [2002, pp. 95–114].) Heidegger relates this notion of a primary understanding to the particular mode of being of Dasein, which, as he argues, is defined by a sense of potentiality-for-being (or a sense of ability-to-be, as I shall, following William Blattner [1999], call it). We will have time to spell out what this claim amounts to (in Chap. 7).

[62] Heidegger famously writes: 'In [interpretation] the understanding appropriates understandingly that which is understood by it. In interpretation, understanding does not become something different. It becomes itself' ([1927] 1962, p. 188).

in which they can be said to exhibit a double direction of fit. We will have time to discuss these thoughts. For the moment, this remark should suffice to close a first discussion aimed at making sense of the idea that there is a distinct mode of world-relatedness that deserves to be called affective intentionality.[63]

On the basis of some of the insights gained so far, in the next chapter I shall begin to address the issue of collective affective intentionality. My overall goal in this chapter will be to motivate the idea that an adequate account of collective affective intentionality has to conceive of this phenomenon as a matter of what we, extending Goldie's central notion, could call our capacity to *feel-towards together*.

---

[63] As my reader shall see (particularly in Sect. 5.2), my view of affective intentionality is strongly inspired in Helm's idea that emotions are best conceived of as felt evaluations. One could, hence, wonder why I want to populate the (terminologically overpopulated) philosophical debate on emotions with yet another term, namely with the term 'felt understanding'. Why do I not just recommend Helm's account at this point and make use in the rest of the work of his definition of emotions as felt evaluations? The reason is because I want to stress Goldie's and Stocker's idea that an emotional experience of some situation as being a certain way basically amounts to a completely different (pre-thematic) way of *understanding* this situation. The term 'felt evaluation' may instead suggest (although this is not Helm's view of the matter) that something is given to 'our faculty of understanding' and *then* evaluated. As already stated (in the main text above), I believe that the term 'felt understanding' allows us to refer to the way in which the world immediately strikes the subject in emotional experience as meriting a particular sort of response.

Chapter 3
Our Ability to Feel-Towards Together: Collective Affective Intentionality Preliminarily Conceived

Abstract In this chapter I begin to address the issue of collective affective intentionality by discussing some of the considerations that animate the general debate on collective intentionality—a debate that turns on the question of what it is to share an intentional attitude in a sufficiently demanding sense of the verb 'to share'. I eventually express my preference for a membership account that stresses the relational nature of collective intentionality as well as the normative character of the tie between the participants. In accordance with an objection repeatedly leveled against Margaret Gilbert's account of so-called collective guilt feelings—which constitutes one of the most prominent exceptions to the tendency to neglect the realm of the affective in the early debate on collective intentionality in analytic philosophy—, I argue that a theory of collective affective intentionality able to capture the affective, the intentional, and the collective nature of the phenomenon at issue has to take as its point of departure the idea that collective affective intentionality is a matter of joint actualizations of our human faculty to feel-towards together. My main goal here is to provide a first glimpse of what has to be done in order to offer a philosophical account of collective affective intentionality which could be considered adequate in light of important insights gained in the course of both the debate on affective intentionality and the general debate on collective intentionality.

Keywords Collective affective intentionality • Collective guilt feelings • Collective intentionality • Feeling-towards together • Joint action • Plural self • Shared intention

3.1 Introduction

In the preceding chapter I focused on the topic of affective intentionality. I discussed some of the main issues that motivate the contemporary philosophical debate on our affective relation to the world in a way that sought to support the following claim: affective intentionality is a matter of our ability to feelingly evaluate concrete situations as being a certain way and therefore meriting and urging certain sorts of responses.

© Springer International Publishing Switzerland 2016   69
H.A. Sánchez Guerrero, *Feeling Together and Caring with One Another*,
Studies in the Philosophy of Sociality 7, DOI 10.1007/978-3-319-33735-7_3

I began this discussion by examining an insight that stands at the beginning of the current debate on affective intentionality: we tend to understand human emotions as intelligible answers to some pressing questions posed by the world, as opposed to understanding them as sheer organismic-physiological reactions elicited in a purely mechanical way by certain worldly occurrences (Sect. 2.2). In this order of ideas, by drawing on Bennett Helm, I pointed out that we are inclined to understand a human emotional comportment as a behavioral segment that expresses and co-constitutes a particular evaluative view of the world. I explicated this claim by elaborating on Helm's suggestion that there is a complex arrangement of tacit references that may be argued to form a multilayered intentional structure typical of human emotions. I suggested that the possibility we have to make sense of a human comportment as a reaction that involves all the intentional references discussed is at the core of the possibility we have to understand this comportment as a personal answer to the demands posed by a world that, as McDowell puts it, is embraceable in thought (Sect. 2.3). By means of this discussion I tried to support the claim that human emotions are best conceived of as responses strictly so called.

Against the background of this view of our emotional life, I addressed the idea that the experiential content of an emotion is not exhausted by the that-clause of the judgment by means of which one could articulate what this affective evaluation is about. Seeking to specify what is special about our capacity to emotionally evaluate a situation as being a certain way and therefore urging certain sorts of responses, I eventually recommended conceiving of our affective openness to the world as constituted by what I proposed to call acts of felt understanding (Sect. 2.4). This last move was motivated by a thought that has become central to the current debate on affective intentionality: in order to make sense of the claim that there is a properly intentional and, at the same time, genuinely affective form of world-relatedness, we are compelled to make room for the idea that the aboutness of a typical human emotion and its distinctive phenomenology are inextricably intertwined; the idea being that, for this reason, affective intentionality may be argued to amount to a sui generis expression of our human openness to the world.

In this chapter, I shall begin to address the issue of collective affective intentionality. I shall do so by exposing some of the considerations that animate the general debate on collective intentionality; a debate that turns on the question of what it is to share an intentional attitude in a sufficiently demanding sense of the verb 'to share' (Sect. 3.2). In the course of this exposition I shall discuss a simple classification of the positions that dominate this philosophical discussion. By these means I shall contextualize Margaret Gilbert's account of so-called collective guilt feelings. This is an account which should be seen as one of the most prominent exceptions to the tendency to neglect the realm of the affective in the early debate on collective intentionality in analytic philosophy. I shall close this chapter by critically examining Gilbert's proposal (in Sect. 3.3). In accordance with an objection leveled against this account as well as with some of the results of the discussion developed in Chap.

2, I shall propose to preliminarily conceive of a collective affective intentional episode in terms of a joint actualization of our human ability to feel-towards together.
My main goal here is to provide a first glimpse of what has to be done in order to
offer a philosophical account of collective affective intentionality which could be
considered adequate in light of certain important insights gained in the course of
both the debate on affective intentionality and the general debate on collective
intentionality.

3.2   Collective Intentionality: Some Issues That Animate the Debate

There are situations in which we coordinate our actions with those of other individuals in order to achieve some common goals. At least some of the experiences
we have in these situations are characteristically marked by a sense that we (the
participants) are *doing something together*. This is a form of experience which may
be argued to differ in some fundamental respect from the experience that one merely
is engaged in this activity *alongside the relevant others* (cf. our discussion in Sect.
1.1). What exactly this difference consists in is something we have to elucidate.[1] At
this point it might be suggested, though, that two individuals who are involved in a
genuinely joint action understand themselves as forming some sort of plural agentic
identity, i.e. that they understand themselves as performing the relevant act *as one*.[2]

There also are situations in which we do not hesitate to ascribe actions to social
groups such as corporations, orchestras, committees, families, parliaments, sport's
teams, or nations, to list but a few. We are inclined to do so, even though we are
perfectly aware that it is through (or in virtue of) the deeds of the individuals
involved that these groups act. In these cases, the assumption that the participants
share the mentioned sense of plural agentic identity may be argued to play a fundamental role in our inclination to understand the relevant deeds as constituting some
collective acts.

In the course of the last 25 years, this intuition concerning a sense of plural agentic identity has motivated a number of philosophers to explore the notion of a

---

[1] It is a central part of my task in this book to specify the respect in which the experience that we
(the participants) are emotionally responding to some occurrence in a joint manner differs from the
experience that we are doing so in a purely parallel way. Since this difference can be argued to be
a special case of the general difference between doing something together and doing it alongside
each other, to understand what a joint action amounts to is of great relevance to our discussion.

[2] For an empirically oriented philosophical exploration of the phenomenology of joint action, see
Pacherie (2012). For a psychological study that supports the intuition that two individuals who are
involved in a joint action automatically form a pre-reflective plural agentic identity (what the
authors call a 'we' identity), see Obhi and Hall (2011).

genuinely joint agency and to speak of *genuinely collective intentions*.[3,4] On the basis of the idea that intentional acts performed in social contexts ultimately have to be seen as acts of individual subjects, the idea of a genuinely collective intentional act has given rise to a conceptual tension which Schweikard and Schmid (2013) call *The Central Problem of Collective Intentionality*. Let us try to understand what this philosophical problem consists in.[5]

In the paper in which the very term of art 'collective intentionality' has been coined, John Searle ([1990] 2002) claims that we could never explain genuinely joint action in terms of *formally* individual intentions, i.e. in terms of intentions expressed in the form 'I intend to do such-and-such' (I-intentions). In order to explain joint actions, we necessarily have to invoke intentions expressed in the form 'we intend to do such-and-such'; the point being that these we-intentions, as he calls them, cannot be reduced to I-intentions. Searle illustrates the point by comparing two sets of persons performing the very same sort of movements in different contexts.

Individuals enjoying a sunny day in a park compose the first set. Having been suddenly bothered by a rainfall, they, *independently of each other*, begin to run

---

[3] Given the primary interest in the notion of a joint agency, the term 'collective intentionality' has not always been directly associated with the notion of intentionality Brentano re-introduced into the contemporary philosophical discussion about mental phenomena. At the beginning, it was mainly the idea of having a common aim, purpose, or goal that attracted the interest of philosophers.

[4] Cognitive psychologists have also been interested in the topic of joint action. (For a concise review of some recent findings from developmental psychology, cognitive psychology, and cognitive neuroscience that have contributed to our understanding of the mechanisms underlying pluripersonal, coordinated action, see Sebanz et al. 2006.) However, their notion of a joint action is often more permissive than the one defended by certain philosophers whose work we are going to discuss in this chapter (e.g. Searle, Tuomela, and Gilbert). Sebanz et al., for instance, offer the following working definition: 'joint action can be regarded as any form of social interaction whereby two or more individuals coordinate their actions in space and time to bring about a change in the environment' (2006, p. 70). As we shall see, it could be objected that such a definition fails to stress that, independently of the degree of coordination exhibited by the participants' behaviors, we can speak of a *properly joint* action just in case we can also speak of a joint intention (as opposed to having to speak of a sheer convergence of individual intentions).

[5] There are philosophers who have offered what we, following Margaret Gilbert (1989), could call *summative accounts* of collective intentionality (other authors have preferred to call them *aggregative accounts*). The intuition defended (or the assumption made) by these philosophers is that the ascription of an intentional state to a collective just suggests that this intentional state may be ascribed to all (or, at least, to most of) the individuals involved. For reasons we shall discuss in this section, the defenders of this view amount to a minority. According to Gilbert, even Anthony Quinton (1975–1976), who is often mentioned as an exemplary defender of this sort of view, '[just] assumes the simple summative account *en passant*' (2004, p. 105, note 12). As we shall immediately see, not all the authors who find these summative accounts of collective intentionality inadequate share the intuition that a collective intention cannot be exhaustively explicated in terms of formally individual intentions plus a number of principles of interaction (cf. Bratman [1993, 1999], Kutz [2000a], and Miller [1992]). For two very informative and, at the same time, introductory overviews of the general debate on collective intentionality, see Tollefsen (2004) and Schweikard and Schmid (2013).

looking for a centrally located shelter. In this situation, Searle observes, one could take each individual's action to rely on an intention expressed in the form 'I am running to the shelter'. Searle concludes: 'In this case there is no collective behavior; there is just a sequence of individual acts that *happen to converge on a common goal*' ([1990] 2002, p. 92; my emphasis). This could be argued to be the case even if the individuals involved were to have mutual knowledge of each other's intentions. The second set is composed by a number of persons who begin to run to the very same shelter as part of an outdoor ballet they are jointly performing. Searle argues that, even if the movements of the individuals who constitute these two sets were indistinguishable, the actions of the individuals taking part in the joint performance and the actions of the individuals, independently of each other, running for shelter may be said to be 'clearly different internally' (ibid.). The 'internal' difference at issue is given by the fact that in the case of the individuals involved in the ballet performance their actions may be said to rely on an intention expressed in the form 'we are running to the shelter'. By means of this example Searle attempts to show that '[t]here really is such a thing as collective intentional behavior that is not the same as the summation of individual intentional behavior' (p. 91). Regardless of whether this conclusion is warranted or not, Searle's example allows us to appreciate the unspecificity of the phrase 'to share an intention'. For there is a clear sense in which the individuals of the first set may be said to be sharing an intention, namely their formally individual intention to go for shelter. To the extent, however, to which it is compatible with the idea that the intentions of the involved individuals *just happen to* have the same content, this sense of 'sharing' should be taken to be too weak to serve as the basis for the concept of a genuinely joint action. In the second situation, in saying that the individuals involved are sharing an intention, we are, at any rate, making use of a clearly stronger notion of a shared intention. Moreover, in this case some of the formally individual intentions of the participants may be easily understood as intentions that are derived from *their* shared intention.

Philosophers interested in the idea of a collective intentional behavior are normally interested in attitudes shared by a number of individuals in a relatively strong sense of the verb 'to share'. As we shall see, this does not necessarily commit them to the idea that we can speak of a genuinely collective intentional behavior only in case the group *itself* can be understood as the subject of the intention at issue. There is, thus, no agreement concerning the claim that we-intentions are necessarily intentions the bearer of which is the collective *as such*. Put another way, a collective intention is not always assumed to be a collective's intention.

Although the initial interest, as mentioned above, was to explore the idea of a joint action, a series of considerations have gradually extended the scope of this line of inquiry.[6] These considerations quite often turn on the idea of a collective responsibility that accompanies the notion of a joint action. Given that in ascribing actions

---

[6] The concept of a joint action still amounts to one of the central issues in the debate on collective intentionality. There certainly are good reasons for this. As Margaret Gilbert puts it: 'If one does not understand what it is for one person to do something with another, one cannot have much of a grasp of the social domain' (2007, p. 32).

and responsibilities to collectives we are ultimately attributing beliefs and desires to them—or so one could argue—, we are pressed to make an effort to understand the meaning of our (tacit or explicit) ascription of these and other propositional attitudes to groups.

The majority of the philosophers contributing to this debate seem to reject a prima facie plausible answer to the question concerning the meaning of these attributions. This answer is based on the idea that these ascriptions are always metaphorical in nature. There probably is enough room for dispute concerning whether the rejection of this view involves the rejection of the idea that attributions of intentions and intentional behavior to groups are purely instrumental in character, i.e. the idea that such an ascription is basically a heuristic tool. Most philosophers involved in the debate seem, however, to assume that these attributions are not grounded in purely pragmatic considerations concerning our capacity to predict and explain the performances of certain groups by appealing to collective intentional states; the point being that these ascriptions could be argued to refer to 'something real'.

To account for the intuition that there is some literal sense in which we could speak of a collective intentional state has, however, not been an easy task. This is basically due to the discomfort that the idea of a group mind (and particularly the idea of a collective form of consciousness) causes in the contemporary philosophical discussion.[7] Here we find the ground of the Central Problem of Collective Intentionality: the clash between the intuition that a collective intentional state cannot be reduced to individual intentional states and the intuition that mindfulness properly so called is always an attribute of certain organismic individuals, and never a property of groups as such.

In this context, a number of philosophers seem to have imposed on themselves a seemingly concrete task: to show that it is possible to conceive of collective intentionality in such a way as to respect, first, the assumption that only individuals can be said to be in genuine (conscious) psychological states, and second, the intuition (or set of intuitions) that underlie the sort of methodological individualism that is customary in a number of contemporary social sciences. Searle explicitly argues that any valid account of collective intentionality has to meet two conditions of adequacy. First, it must be compatible with the idea that society is nothing over and above the individuals who comprise it; the ultimate point being that any intentional state is in the brain of some individual. Second, it must be compatible with the idea that any (formally) collective intentional state may be *mistakenly* had by an isolated individual. Searle writes: 'I could have all the intentionality I do have even if I am radically mistaken, even if the apparent presence and cooperation of other people is

---

[7] According to Georg Theiner and Timothy O'Connor (2010, p. 78), the group mind thesis fell out of grace with the rise of behaviorism and operationalism. Referring to Wegner et al. (1985), Theiner and O'Connor observe that 'the main problem was that the group mind seemed to lack its own body. Hence it remained unclear where to look for its properties, and how to measure them' (ibid.). In the context of cognitive science, some philosophers of mind have been defending for over 20 years the idea of distributed cognition. But not even in this frame we find a clear sense in which we could speak of a phenomenal consciousness the bearer of which is the collective itself (cf. the discussion in Sect. 1.2).

an illusion, even if I am suffering a total hallucination, even if I am a brain in a vat' ([1990] 2002, p. 97). These are conditions Searle characterizes as 'commonsensical, pretheoretical requirements' (p. 96, footnote 1).

The mere formulation of this task may be thought to already contain a possible solution to the problem. Indeed, Searle catalyzed the debate I am trying to reconstruct by suggesting that the collective character of those intentions we seem to have to invoke in order to explain genuinely joint action is a matter of a formal peculiarity they exhibit: these intentions make reference to a group. On this view, collective intentions are mental states each of the participating individuals has in a 'we-mode'. These we-intentions are primitive in the sense that they cannot be reduced to I-intentions. They can normally be understood as the result of the identification of the participating individuals with a group they jointly constitute and their corresponding willingness to cooperate with the other members of this group.[8] The idea, as Margaret Gilbert—in the context of a critique of Searle's position—formulates it, is as follows: 'In order that there be collective behavior [...] each individual member of the supposed collective must have an appropriate we-intention "in his head"' (2007, p. 38).

Although Searle sets his account of collective intentions off against the one offered by Tuomela and Miller (1988)—an account Searle takes to be 'typical in that it attempts to reduce collective intentions to individual intentions plus beliefs' ([1990] 2002, p. 93)—the idea of a we-mode intention is traditionally attributed to Raimo Tuomela (1984).[9] According to Tuomela, however, it was Wilfrid Sellars (1963, 1968, 1980) who first 'argued for the necessity of employing other-regarding intentions, which he calls *we-intentions*' (Tuomela 1995, p. 425). Hans Bernhard Schmid and David Schweikard (2009, p. 32) maintain that Sellars may have picked up the term from Robin George Collingwood ([1942] 1947).

The suggestion that some of our mental states are immediately understood by us (the bearers of these states) as psychological states that are common to us (the participants) is one we also seem to find—framed, of course, in a completely different way—in the continental phenomenological tradition to which the debate on collective intentionality has been rather impermeable until quite recently.

---

[8] Searle argues that 'the notion of a we-intention [...] implies the notion of *cooperation*' ([1990] 2002, p. 95). This leads him to reject the proposals of philosophers who, as he thinks, have tried to analyze a we-intention in terms of I-intentions plus common knowledge (Searle, in particular, targets Tuomela and Miller [1988]). Searle writes: 'One can have a goal in the knowledge that others also have the same goal, and one can have beliefs and even mutual beliefs about the goal that is shared by the members of the group, without there being necessarily any cooperation among the members or any intention to cooperate among the members' (ibid.). Searle's point is that even the most promising attempts to reduce we-intentions to I-intentions fail to provide sufficient conditions for cooperation.

[9] Tuomela has rejoined that Searle's criticism misfires, the reason being because Searle has failed to see that the analysis offered by Tuomela and Miller (1988) 'is not meant to be reductive but is rather meant to elucidate the irreducible notion of we-intention in a functionally informative way' (Tuomela 2005, p. 358).

Probably influenced by Heidegger, in §55 of his *Cartesian Meditations* Husserl speaks, as mentioned above (cf. Chap. 1, footnote 8), of 'the first community' which, as he writes, is 'in the form of a common world' ([1929] 1999, p. 121).[10] Drawing on David Carr (1973), Eric Chelstrom proposes that Husserl is arguing here for the idea of a *cogitamus*, which may be said to *open up* the intersubjective world (cf. 2011, pp. 89ff.). Chelstrom stresses the grounding character of the experiences at issue here by writing that 'intersubjective moments of experience, instances where there is a non-reducible *we,* can be understood as foundational for higher order intersubjective meanings' (p. 89). In support of this interpretation of the notion of a first community Chelstrom refers to a claim Husserl makes in §48 of the Meditations. Husserl writes: '*not all my own modes of consciousness are modes of my self-consciousness*' ([1929] 1999, p. 105; as quoted by Chelstrom, p. 94; italics in original).[11] Chelstrom maintains that it is elaborating on this line of thought that Aron Gurwitsch comes to speak of '"mental processes [that are] appertinent to the We" [*Wir-Erlebnisse*]' (1979, p. 28; as quoted by Chelstrom, p. 96). This is an idea Gurwitsch unpacks by writing:

> Included in the sense of every mental process [...] there is also the co-presence of those others which is co-apprehended through the 'we' (and, more particularly, co-apprehended as effecting these mental processes together with me). On the basis of the immanental co-presence of others pertaining to the sense of these mental processes—others together with whom I effect the mental processes in question—these mental processes are determined specifically as *ours* and are distinguished from those that are specifically mine (1979, p. 28; as quoted by Chelstrom, p. 96).

So the idea is that we could provide an initial characterization of a particular sort of experiences we humans can have—among them those experiences that are accompanied by a sense of joint agency—by referring to what might be called a sense of *ourness*.[12] The intuition that such a sense may be claimed to structure the experiences at issue has been defended in the frame of different intellectual traditions.

There is a peculiarity of these sorts of accounts that allows them to meet the first condition of adequacy stated by Searle: accounts of collective intentionality along

---

[10] This idea of a common world that is at the root of our human capacity to (actively or passively) constitute communities of different sorts and degrees of complexity is one we shall intensively deal with below (in Sect. 5.3).

[11] A view has begun to circulate, according to which the phenomenological tradition of thought would have 'anticipated' some insights that guide the current analytic philosophical debates on collective intentionality and social ontology (cf. Calcagno 2012; Schmid 2005, 2009; Schmid and Schweikard 2009). A reference to Husserl's work is, however, not the best way to anchor the idea of a genuinely collective world-relatedness in the tradition of phenomenology. As Caminada writes, 'since his "transcendental turn" [Husserl] has often been accused of being a representationalist and therefore of falling victim to a monological, solipsistic account of intentionality' (2014, p. 197). Most defenders of the view just mentioned refer rather to the work of Adolf Reinach (1922), Edith Stein ([1922] 1970), Gerda Walther (1923), and Dietrich von Hildebrand ([1930] 1955). For a compelling attempt to bring to light the phenomenological 'prehistory' of the analysis of collective intentionality, see Schmid (2005). Here I am only concerned with the idea of a *formally* plural intentionality that may be argued to be at the root of any collective intentional state.

[12] We shall come back to this idea of a sense of ourness below (in Sect. 4.3).

these lines are at the same time individualist and collectivist. They are individualist concerning the subject (bearer) *of* the intentional sate at issue—for it is a particular individual who has the relevant intentional state—, and they are collectivist concerning the subject's mode of the intentional state in question—for, according to this view, the self-understanding implicit *in* the intentional acts at issue characteristically exhibits a collective character.[13] Seeking to capture this difference, Schmid distinguishes between *subjective* individualism and *formal* individualism (cf. 2003, p. 205). Chelstrom makes the point by writing that '[t]he *intending* subject, the conscious subject, is not equivalent to the *subject of intention* or subject matter of acts of consciousness, i.e. it is not the syntactical subject referenced in and through an intentional act' (2011, p. 91).

Regardless of the preferred terminology, the recognition of this particularity of the accounts just presented allows us to provide a basic taxonomy of theories of collective intentionality. Following Anita Konzelmann Ziv (2007), I shall use the term 'membership accounts' to refer to those accounts that rely on the intuition that we should conceive of collective intentional episodes in terms of interrelated mental states that, in virtue of a formal feature capturable by Tuomela's notion of a 'we-mode', tacitly refer to some group, but are had by a number of individuals who regard themselves as members of this group. Membership accounts are to be contrasted with a second type of accounts, for which we shall reserve the term 'collectivist accounts'.[14] A few lines below, we are going to discuss the main feature of this second kind of theories.

If we can talk of two general classes of accounts of collective intentionality it is because solutions along the lines just sketched failed to satisfy everyone.[15] Particularly Searle's account, which can be characterized further as an *internalist* membership account of collective intentionality, has been repeatedly criticized for allowing for the possibility of something like a solipsistic collective intention, i.e. for proposing that we could speak of a collective intention in cases in which a single individual had an intention of the form 'we intend to do such-and-such'. The problem is not merely that, as Anthonie Meijers puts it, '[i]n case these participants do not exist in the real world, there is simply no collective intentionality' (2003, p. 179).

---

[13] Let me make a remark aimed at preventing a possible misunderstanding related to this talk of a subject's mode. The term 'mode' has been used in the context of analytic philosophy of mind to designate the *psychological* mode (belief, desire, hope, etc.)—or, if you prefer, the attitude—the content of which is captured, for the sake of analysis, by a given proposition. In this order of ideas, Tim Crane (2001, p. 32), for instance, argues that the general structure of intentionality may be captured as follows: Subject—Intentional Mode—Content. What we, following Tuomela, are calling here a 'we-mode' corresponds to a mode of what Crane calls the subject.

[14] Konzelmann Ziv takes up the expression 'membership account' from Margaret Gilbert's (1997) membership account of shared guilt. As we shall see, Gilbert changed her mind and ended up providing a collectivist account of so-called shared guilt feelings (cf. Gilbert 2002). Appealing to Schmid's distinction, one could preliminarily characterize what we are calling here a collectivist account of collective intentionality as an account that is both subjectively *and* formally collectivist.

[15] It would be fair to count the summative (or aggregative) view as a third class of accounts of collective intentionality, although, as already mentioned, few philosophers defend it.

The problem is furthermore that this counterintuitive implication of the account may be taken to point to a more general inadequacy of the approach: Searle's internalist approach fails to stress the *relational nature* of genuinely joint agency (and of genuinely collective intentionality). It fails to respect the intuition that the individuals' actions that constitute a collective action—or a collective intentional behavior, as Searle prefers to call it—should be interrelated in a way that is much more substantial than the mere overlap of their plural self-reference.[16] As a consequence of this failure, it has been objected, Searle's account conceives of a collective intention as a sheer 'correlated series of we-intentions' (Gilbert 2007, p. 41); that is to say, as 'a series whose elements [merely] fit together in the right way' (ibid.).[17] As should become clear in the second part of this book, I find this line of objection not only warranted, but also absolutely crucial.

Drawing on the intuition that the idea of a joint action is the idea of a plural act that arises from the coordination of the participants' actions, Michael Bratman (1993, 1999) offers a radically different account of 'shared intentions', as he prefers to call the phenomenon. Referring to Alan Donagan (cf. 1987, p. 95), Bratman suggests that the thought according to which '"the study of intention" is in part the "study of planning"' (1993, pp. 97–98) could 'serve as a basis for reflection on the phenomenon of shared intention' (p. 98). Bratman's initial premise is the idea that one of the fundamental roles intentions *in general* play is to plan and coordinate the behavioral components that constitute a given action.

In this context, Bratman contends that the term 'shared intention' does not allude to 'an attitude in the mind of some superagent consisting literally of some fusion of [...] two [or more] agents' (ibid.). Nor does this term refer to some overlap of individuals' psychological states that exhibit a congruent we-mode. Rather, it refers to a particular sort of situations in which a specific kind of interpersonal relationship can be described. Such a relationship presupposes a series of interrelated (ordinary, i.e. formally individual) intentional states had by the participating individuals.[18]

---

[16] Gilbert (2007) critically discusses Searle's approach to what he calls collective intentions. She tends to deny Searle's account the status of an account of collective intentionality. Gilbert writes: 'As [Searle's] discussion develops, indeed, it seems that his main interest is not so much in developing a complete account of **we-intentions**, but rather in emphasizing that the primary constituents of **we-intentions** are we-intentions, not I-intentions' (p. 39). By '**we-intention**' (boldly written) Gilbert means 'the intention of a group [as such]—whatever that may amount to' (p. 35, footnote 19).

[17] Gilbert illustrates the problem by means of the following example. 'Suppose Ben is currently thinking, with respect to himself and Elaine, "We intend to get married". Indeed, he expresses himself thus to his parents. Elaine is in a similar position. And each assumes the other would sincerely say the same thing if prompted to do so. If a **we-intention** was a series of correlated we-intentions, and so on, then it would be the case that there was a **we-intention** to get married, the members of the "we" being Ben and Elaine. But surely the description of the situation so far is not enough to show that they do. If Ben's parents learn that Ben and Elaine have never discussed getting married with one another, they would surely judge Ben's announcement to be inaccurate' (2007, pp. 42–43).

[18] Being an account that brings to the fore the relational nature of the phenomenon at issue, Bratman's proposal should be understood as a subjectively individualist account of collective

Bratman's idea is that the individuals' intentions that are part of a shared intention basically coordinate the individuals' actions that constitute the relevant joint action. They do so by making sure that the plans (and subplans) of the participants mesh together. In so arguing, Bratman ultimately construes a shared intention as 'a [complex] *state of affairs* consisting primarily of appropriate attitudes of each individual participant and their interrelation' (p. 99; my emphasis), as opposed to construing it as a particular kind of mental state.

This proposal is set up to avoid the counterintuitive implication of the internalist (individualist) view mentioned above, and it certainly succeeds in doing this. A basic problem of Bratman's account is, however, that it may be argued to transform (or even deform) our ordinary notion of an intention (cf. Tollefsen 2004). For we normally use the term 'intention' to refer to a mental state the content of which specifies an aim, purpose, or goal, and not to refer to a complex state of affairs, as Bratman does here.

One could defend Bratman, however, by maintaining that, although his (technical) notion of a shared intention does not naturally extend our vernacular notion of an intention, his account succeeds in specifying *what has to be the case* for an ascription of a shared intention to be correct.[19] In other words, Bratman makes an effort to spell out in which situations we could feel comfortable in speaking of a genuinely shared intention. This is something Searle, for instance, may be argued to not even have attempted to do in the contribution discussed. Gilbert articulates the criticism as follows: 'It seems […] that in order fully to understand what a we-intention is one needs to understand what a **we-intention** is' (2007, p. 41); the point being that 'one needs to know what we-intentions assume or presuppose' (ibid.).[20] So one could definitively argue that one of the strengths of Bratman's approach is precisely that it makes clear that collective intentions, as Gilbert puts it, 'are not a purely mental phenomenon' (p. 44).[21] This idea that collective intentionality cannot be conceived of as something that is 'purely mental' is particularly important. At a minimum, it should lead us to differentiate the *intentional acts* that are at the root of

---

intentionality, i.e. as an account that seeks to respect the idea that only individuals are legitimate subjects of intentional (psychological) states. In fact, Bratman's account is, furthermore, formally individualist, since it seeks to explain shared intentions in terms of formally individual intentions (I-intentions).

[19] Bratman writes: 'We intend to *J* if and only if[:] 1. (*a*) I intend that we *J* and (*b*) you intend that we *J*[.] 2. I intend that we *J* in accordance with and because of 1*a*, 1*b*, and meshing subplans of 1*a* and 1*b*; you intend that we *J* in accordance with and because of 1*a*, 1*b*, and meshing subplans of 1*a* and 1*b*. 3. 1 and 2 are common knowledge between us' (1993, p. 106).

[20] In the passage from which I am quoting, Gilbert is not defending Bratman, but criticizing Searle.

[21] As far as this point is concerned, Schmid's view of collective intentions is similar to the one just exposed. Schmid writes: 'Collective intentions are not intentions of the kind anybody "*has*" not single individuals, and not some super-agent. For collective intentionality is not subjective. It is relational' (2003, p. 214).

the phenomena we are interested in from the *moments of intentional community* I call episodes of collective intentionality.[22]

But there is a second line of objection to Bratman's account of shared intentions. To be sure, objections along these lines may also be raised against Searle's account of collective intentions. These objections concern the idea that intending something presupposes being, at least in principle, able to bring about what one intends to do, in the sense that the intended action must be, to a relevant extent, under one's control. The problem is that it seems that, having ruled out frank coercion, one cannot control the actions of the other individuals involved in what Bratman calls a shared intention; at least not in the way alleged to be presupposed by our vernacular notion of an intention.[23]

Bratman (1999) responds to these series of objections by coining the technical expression 'intending that'. This maneuver seems effective, but it has been protested that it changes the subject matter of discussion (cf. Tollefsen 2004). I believe that this latter objection becomes innocuous as soon as one takes Bratman to be after an articulation of that which has to be the case for an ascription of a shared intention to be correct.

At any rate, even an account along these lines, which excludes the counterintuitive idea of a solipsistic collective intention by emphasizing the relational nature of a genuinely shared intention, has failed to satisfy everyone. The problem is that Bratman's account may be contended to also fail to show that an intention shared in a strong sense of the verb 'to share' is something completely different from a non-accidental overlap of individuals' intentions. In other words, it may be objected that Bratman merely provides an account of highly coordinated aggregate action, as opposed to offering an account of genuinely joint action. To provide an account of collective intention and action, it has been objected further, is to explain in which situations—under which conditions—the relevant group, as Gilbert puts it, 'can plausibly be regarded as having an intention *of its own*' (2002, p. 123).

Following this line of objection, I find it crucial to differentiate between a highly coordinated (aggregate) pluripersonal behavior and a genuinely joint action. For one can certainly perform a number of actions alongside certain others, i.e. in a purely parallel manner, in a way that is, nevertheless, highly coordinated with certain actions and goals of the relevant others. Take the case of someone who, seeking to arrive at some particular goal without delays and accidents, coordinates his actions as a driver with those of a number of individuals who have taken the same road (on the assumption that these others have a similar goal and also coordinate their actions as drivers with his deeds). In this way he contributes to the, in a sense,

---

[22] I agree with Sellars, Tuomela, and Searle, among others, that, in order to account for a collective intentional act, we are compelled to invoke non-reducible we-intentions. As my reader shall see, the idea that there are formally plural mental states (that cannot be reduced to their formally singular counterparts) is also central to my account of collective affective intentionality, and particularly to my notion of an act of feeling-towards together.

[23] For criticisms along these lines, see Baier (1997) and Stoutland (1997).

shared goal of non-congested vehicular traffic.[24] I doubt, however, that, in order to make sense of the idea of a genuinely joint action, we have to show that there is a sense in which the pertinent group of individuals can be conceived as a sort of supraindividual centre of intentional attitudes, as the *real* bearer of the shared intention at issue. In particular, I believe that one does not need the idea of a supraindividual centre of intentional attitudes in order to differentiate the two sorts of cases that have to be distinguished: cases in which one does something together with certain others and cases in which one does it merely alongside these others. But let us continue to characterize the positions that determine the 'classic' analytic philosophical debate on collective intentionality.

---

[24]There is a relatively recent development in the debate on joint action that may be argued to challenge the distinction between highly coordinated pluripersonal behavior and genuinely joint action. The advocates of the challenging view (cf., for instance, Pacherie 2011; Tollefsen 2005; Vesper et al. 2010) accuse 'classical' theorists of joint action of having offered a picture of collective behavior that 'imposes more normativity on shared intentions than is strictly needed and […] requires too much cognitive sophistication on the part of agents' (Pacherie 2011, p. 173). Contrary to what the central figures of the established debate have done, these authors do not try to characterize that which makes joint actions *intentionally* collective. Aiming at a minimalist model of collective behavior, they rather emphasize the online coordination exhibited by some of the movements and perceptual processes of the individuals involved. In this way, they seek to evade the idea of a structure of interconnected (formally collective) intentions. One can hardly accuse these authors of claiming that highly coordinated (in the sense of sufficiently synchronized) pluripersonal behavior *just is* joint action. Matti Heinnonen distinguishes two kinds of contribution these minimalist accounts make to the debate on joint action. He writes: 'The "complementarists" seek to analyze a *functionally different kind* of joint action from the kind of joint action that is analyzed by established philosophical accounts of shared intentional action. The "constitutionalists" seek to expose *mechanisms that make performing joint actions possible*, without taking a definite stance on which functional characterization of joint action is the appropriate one' (2016, p. 168; my emphasis). But precisely for this reason one can also hardly understand these accounts as alternative accounts of the sort of collective (intentional) behavior that has interested the 'classical' theorists of joint action. As discussed above (cf. the discussion in Sect. 1.1), the point of departure of the present study is the thought that, at a minimum, a theory of collective affective intentionality has to be able to *in a principled way* differentiate those situations in which the involved individuals are feeling together from those other situations in which they merely are doing this alongside each other. A phenomenologically adequate account of collective affective intentionality has to articulate the principle at issue with regard to the participants' emotional responses *as experienced by them*. Without further qualification, the idea of a sufficiently high degree of online coordination (or synchrony) does not serve as a basis for the formulation of such a principle. The reason is because it does not exclude cases of highly synchronic emotional responses that are experienced by the participants as responses they are exhibiting in a merely parallel way. This is the reason for not discussing these minimalist accounts of collective behavior in the main text. In line with the minimalist approach, John Michael offers an account of 'how shared emotions can facilitate coordination without presupposing common knowledge of complex, interconnected structures of intention' (2011, p. 355). Unfortunately (for our purposes), he operates with an extremely undemanding notion of shared emotions—one which rather captures cases of emotion that is perceived (from a second- or third-person point of view), and which, at any rate, does not offer a basis for a robust concept of collective affective intentionality. Michael writes: 'Shared emotions are defined for the purposes of this paper as affective states that fulfill two minimal criteria: (a) they are expressed (verbally or otherwise) by one person; and (b) the expression is perceived (consciously or unconsciously) by another person' (ibid.).

On the basis of the idea that a genuinely collective intention should be construed as a collective's intention (i.e. as an intention the bearer of which is the collective understood as a single centre of intentional attitudes), Gilbert has repeatedly argued that accounts of the two kinds considered so far fail to recognize that certain normative relations are at the core of a properly collective intention (and of a genuinely joint action).[25] These are normative relations that arise from the fact that the individuals involved in a truly joint action have come to constitute what Gilbert calls a *plural subject* of intention (and action).

Gilbert develops this thought by pointing out that to form a genuinely collective intention, for the individuals involved, means to generate a series of obligations and expectations that entitle them to rebuke each other when they fail to perform their part in the intended joint action (cf. 1990, p. 3).[26] Gilbert claims that a collective intention is always grounded in some *joint commitment* of certain members of a population 'to intend as a body to do that thing' or 'to do (as a body) a certain thing' (cf. 1989, Chapter 4; 1990). A joint commitment, Gilbert claims, comes into existence when *each* of the participants expresses (though not necessarily in a verbal way) his or her willingness to take part in the commitment at issue (cf. 1990, pp. 6ff.). As she puts it: 'each must openly express his or her readiness to be jointly committed with the relevant others, in conditions of common knowledge' (2002, p. 126).

Gilbert stresses that in a joint action not only the fact that all other relevant individuals have committed themselves to the success of the action at issue, but also the obligations and entitlements brought about by these commitments are common knowledge among the individuals involved (cf. 1990, p. 7). She is particularly eager to emphasize that a joint commitment does not amount to a set of matching personal commitments. A truly joint commitment is a commitment on which two or more persons agree *together*, i.e. simultaneously and interdependently (ibid.). Moreover, having generated a series of obligations and entitlements, without some additional agreement, a joint commitment cannot be rescinded *unilaterally* (cf. Gilbert 1990, p. 8). Only when each of the participants has agreed to rescind the joint commitment at issue the obligations and entitlements it generated cease to exist. Such a commitment could, of course, be unilaterally *broken*, but in so doing, the individual who is breaking the commitment would not cancel out the obligations it brought about.

On this basis, Gilbert submits that a social group should be seen as a special sort of entity that is constituted by a plurality of individuals who are strongly tied to one another by joint commitments to do such-and-such—where 'doing such-and-such' is broadly construed so as to include intentional states of different sorts. She goes so far as to argue that our vernacular notion of a social group is the notion of a plural subject of some intentional act (cf. Gilbert 1989, Chapter 4). The point is that, being understandable as a sort of plural subject, a social group can be regarded as the legitimate subject of certain intentional attitudes.

---

[25] Anthony Meijers (2003) raises a similar objection against Searle's account.
[26] We shall discuss this claim in detail below (in Sect. 8.2).

This idea that in cases of genuinely collective intentionality the relevant group should be understood as the proper subject of the intentional attitude at issue amounts to the basic claim of the position we are calling the collectivist view of collective intentionality.[27] During the last 20 years, Gilbert has defended it by extending her analysis of what it is to do something together, in a first step, to the analysis of collective beliefs, and, finally, to the analysis of what one may, at first sight, be inclined to call a collective affective intentional attitude.[28] In what follows, we shall take a look at the first of these developments of Gilbert's theory. (In the next section we shall discuss Gilbert's attempt to extend her plural subject account to the realm of the affective.)

Gilbert's point of departure is the thought that it is neither necessary nor sufficient for a number of individuals to collectively believe that such-and-such that they all believe this to be the case. Concerning the non-necessity of this condition she writes: 'Often what is taken to determine the collective belief in such cases is a formal voting procedure where the opinion that receives the most votes is deemed, for that reason, to be the opinion of the court, the union, or whatever' (2004, p. 97). As to the non-sufficiency of this prima facie plausible requirement, Gilbert provides the following example:

> Consider a court. A certain matter may not yet have come before it. It would then seem right to say that, as yet, the court has no opinion on the matter. The individual justices may, at the same time, have definite personal opinions about it. What they now think, however, is not relevant to the question of what the court now thinks (p. 98).

So, in order to participate in a collective belief, the involved individuals do not have to also *personally* believe the proposition at issue to be true. Nor do they have to behave as if they *personally* believed it to be true. On the other hand, it does not suffice for a number of individuals to participate in a collective belief to *personally* take the corresponding proposition to be true and behave in a way that corresponds to their *personal* assent to the truth of this proposition. For they would not *jointly* believe what is at issue, were they to understand their respective belief as a belief *they individually have alongside each other.*

On this view, in order to participate in a collective belief the individuals involved have to respect their obligation to do their part to make the case that pertinent endeavors be conducted on the assumption that the belief in question is the belief of their group. According to Gilbert, we can talk here of an obligation for the following reason: 'Once a group belief is established, the parties understand that any members who bluntly express the opposite belief lay themselves open to rebuke by other

---

[27] Besides Gilbert, one could mention Russell Hardin (1988), Philip Pettit (2002), and probably Bennett Helm (2008) as philosophers who, in specific contexts, defend (or assume) a collectivist view of collective intentionality.

[28] Already in her paper 'Modeling Collective Belief' Gilbert (1987) offered an account of collective beliefs along these lines. This account, however, can be understood as an extension of her plural subject account of joint action (cf. 1989). Gilbert herself explains why: 'Due to the vagaries of publishing, the 1987 article was written after the 1989 book was sent to the press' (2004, p. 104, note 6).

members' (p. 99). In other words, in the case of a collective belief, too, each of the individuals involved has a standing that allows her or him to rebuke the other members of the group for expressing a view that conflicts with the collective belief at issue.

In this context, Gilbert establishes three conditions of adequacy for an account of collective belief. She writes:

> It should explain how the existence of a collective belief that p could give the parties the standing to rebuke each other for bluntly expressing a view contrary to p. It should not suppose that all or most of the parties must personally believe that p. Nor should it suppose that if all or most of them believe something then they collectively believe it (p. 100).

On this basis, Gilbert claims that 'it is both necessary and sufficient for members of a population, P, collectively to believe something that the members of P have openly expressed their readiness to let the belief in question be established as the belief of P' (p. 100). So we can speak of a collective belief whenever the involved individuals have expressed their willingness to do their part to bring it about that they believe *as a group*. She brings it to the following formula we are already familiar with: '*A population, P, believes that p* if and only if the members of P are jointly committed to believe as a body that p' (ibid.). The idea is that '[it is b]y virtue of their participation in a *joint* commitment [that] the parties gain a special standing in relation to one another's [belief-expressing] actions' (ibid.).

A number of philosophers (cf. Meijers 1999, 2002 and Wray 2001) have objected to this proposal by pointing to the difference between accepting a proposition and having a belief. The point is that a group might probably be said to accept a proposition, but not to have a belief properly so called. To these sorts of objections Gilbert rejoins by claiming that we should refrain from deciding whether collectives can really have beliefs based on our intuitive understanding of what it is to be in the psychological state we call a belief. One way of approaching the issue of collective cognitive states, Gilbert suggests, is by examining the contexts in which everyday ascriptions of such states are generally considered true or false 'with the aim of arriving at a perspicuous description of the phenomena people mean to refer to when ascribing collective cognitive states' (2004, p. 97). The idea is that, although 'it is likely enough that collective beliefs differ in important ways from the beliefs of individual human beings' (p. 103), 'many of the features traditionally claimed to characterize belief in general can be argued to characterize collective beliefs' (ibid.). This last remark suggests that Gilbert does not really expect from a theory of collective belief that it be able to show that certain groups can be understood as bearers of a psychological state of the sort we normally call a belief. She seems not to expect this, even though she, in general, requires of a theory of collective intentionality that it be able to show that the group at issue can plausibly be regarded as having some intentional attitude of its own.

The best way to make sense of this apparent contradiction, I think, is by taking Gilbert to also be articulating what has to be the case (in the world, and not merely in the head of the participants) for the ascription, in this case, of a collective belief to be correct. The key to dissolving this apparent inconsistency is, hence, to differentiate the *psychological states* that are at the root of a collective intentional attitude (of the relevant sort) from the *state of affairs* that merits being called a collective intentional episode (of the relevant sort). Such a state of affairs always involves a number of individuals who have the appropriate psychological attitudes, which, on this account, include some joint commitment to, in this case, believe as a group that something is such-and-such and act in accordance with this belief.

Before we tackle the specific issue of collective *affective* intentionality in the next section, I would like to briefly articulate what I take collective intentionality (in general) to be. There is nothing original in my *general* view of collective intentionality, since it merely integrates into a single picture diverse insights mentioned throughout this discussion.[29] The formulation of this view only seeks to articulate some conditions of adequacy the theory of collective affective intentionality that I shall develop in the second part of this book—qua theory of a special case of collective intentionality—has to fulfill.

To begin with, I believe that the term 'collective intentionality' can refer to two related but different things. First, it can refer to a *capacity* or *set of capabilities* certain minded creatures (human beings, paradigmatically) exhibit. Here I mean the capacity to be intentionally directed towards particular objects, states of affairs, values, projects, etc. in what can be taken to be a properly joint manner, as opposed to being directed towards these intentional objects in a private or purely parallel manner.[30] Second, it can refer to certain sorts of *situations* that centrally involve a number of individuals who are jointly directed towards some intentional object. These *episode*s of collective intentionality are not themselves mental states, but, as pointed out, they essentially involve individuals comporting themselves towards something on the basis of mental states of a peculiar sort, namely of (non-misleading) we-intentional states.[31]

---

[29] Among the theories mentioned above, the one defended by Schmid (2005 and elsewhere) most closely corresponds to my view of collective intentionality. The theory of collective *affective* intentionality I am to develop in the second part of this book also elaborates on some motives of Schmid's (2008, 2009) view of what it is to share a feeling (in a strong sense of the verb 'to share'). My proposal also builds significantly on Bennett Helm's (2008, 2010) work on shared evaluative perspectives and plural agents. This work does not figure centrally in debates on collective intentionality, but it definitively has to be seen as an important contribution to this area of scholarship. The only reason for ignoring this contribution here is that I extensively discuss Helm's work elsewhere in the book (cf. the discussion in Sects. 5.2 and 6.2).

[30] Michael Tomasello (2008) suggests that this ability (or set of abilities) is at the ground of other faculties that are commonly taken to differentiate us from other primates.

[31] This book treats both the acts that actualize our capacity to feel together and the moments of affective community I call episodes of collective affective intentionality. As mentioned above, my main goal is to explicate the claim that there is a distinct form of human world-relatedness that deserves to be called collective affective intentionality. This goal may seem to exclusively concern the pertinent ability. A complete understanding of our ability to feel together, however, involves an understanding of the type of state of affairs the individuals who take themselves to be participating in a moment of affective intentional community assume to be the case. In the course of this discussion, we shall, therefore, also get a clear idea of what an episode of collective affective intentionality amounts to.

As a condition of the possibility of their being jointly directed towards an intentional object two or more individuals have to (a) be similarly open to this object's being, i.e. they have to share a basic understanding of its mode of being, and (b) be open to one another as subjects who share a common world and are, to this extent, candidates for some joint intentional act. In order to *actually* be intentionally directed towards something in a joint manner two or more individuals additionally have to (c) be in a particular intentional state that is directed towards the relevant object, where it is fundamental that (d) this intentional state be such that it can be argued to tacitly refer back to some particular 'we' they, in the relevant situation, jointly constitute. The latter is an oblique reference that points to what, drawing on Schmid (2014a), may be called the plural self of the intentional acts at issue.[32] Finally, (e) the fact that the participants' intentional states refer back to one and the same group cannot be a matter of sheer coincidence. That is to say, the individuals involved must stand in a certain objective relationship to one another. This is a relationship that warrants the claim that their understanding themselves as members of the relevant 'we' is not misleading.[33]

So I take the criticism raised against Searle's internalist account to be absolutely warranted. Talk of collective intentionality just makes no sense in cases in which there is only one individual involved. However, I agree with Searle (and, to this extent, with Tuomela, among others) that what makes out of an intentional state an act by means of which someone participates in an episode of collective intentionality is not exclusively the fact that it has some *content* that can be said to be shared. The collective character of those intentional acts through which people come to participate in a moment of intentional community is also a matter of their *mode*. To this extent, I do not favor accounts along the lines of the one offered by Bratman, i.e. accounts that reduce collective intentional attitudes to formally individual intentional states. I believe, however, that Bratman is pointing to something fundamental when he stresses that the intentional states of the participants in a collective intentional act have to be interrelated in a substantial way.

---

[32] Schmid makes the point by writing that '[p]otential joint intenders have to see each other in a different light than simply as agents who act on their own private agenda and who have social cognition of whatever order' (2014a, p. 8). The idea has also been articulated in terms of a sense of community (or sense of 'us') that is central to a genuinely collective intentional act (cf., for instance, John Searle [1990] 2002). It is important to note that the participants must be able to understand themselves as constituting some particular 'we' on the basis of the intentional states through which they participate in the relevant episode of collective intentionality.

[33] Were we not to include such a factual relationship in our picture, we would not be able to differentiate between situations in which the individuals involved are in a we-intentional state in a merely parallel way and situations in which they are in a we-intentional state in a properly joint manner. Schmid makes the point as follows: 'the mere fact that you happen to have the belief that we are a team, and that I, by some coincidence and perhaps in a dream, happen to have the same thought, does not make us a team. It is not enough for you to have the appropriate belief, and for me to have that belief; at least, it has to be true that we have the belief *together*' (2014a, p. 10). In the course of the discussion developed in the second part of this book, I shall explicate what this relationship amounts to.

Agreeing with Bratman in this last respect, I believe that the eminently *relational nature* of collective intentionality is not exhausted by (and not grounded in) the practical coordination of the participants' acts. A genuinely joint act is not merely a highly coordinated pluripersonal act. So I believe that Gilbert is right in claiming that, in virtue of their conceiving of themselves as constituting a group directed in a particular way towards something, the participants in a collective intentional act come to occupy a space that is *normatively structured* by expectations (rights and obligations) of a particular sort.[34]

Finally, I believe that there is a sense in which the group constituted by the participants in a collective intentional episode may be understood as the subject of the relevant intentional state. It is important, however, to note that this does not imply that in a case of genuinely collective intentionality there is some additional supraindividual bearer of intentional attitudes. A collective intentional attitude is an intentional attitude had by the participating individuals *as a group*. Moreover, as it has been pointed out (Schmid 2014a; Tollefsen 2002; Tuomela 1992), an account of collective intentionality based on Gilbert's idea of a plural subject can be claimed to take for granted what it aims at explaining.[35] In this context, Schmid (2014a) persuasively argues that there is only one way to elude this circularity, without falling into an infinite regress: one has to locate the collective quality of the intentional act at issue in the plural character of the (non-thetic) self-awareness it involves qua intentional act.[36] This is the sense in which the collective character of those intentional attitudes that are at the root of a moment of intentional community could be said to also be a matter of the *subject*.[37] In particular, and as we shall see (in Sect. 4.3), it may be said to be a matter of what Schmid calls the *phenomenal subject*.

To sum up, I believe that the most plausible account of collective intentionality construes it as a relational phenomenon at the heart of which we find intentional states of individuals that refer back to some group (they take themselves to constitute) and generate a particular sort of normatively constrained relatedness among the participants. Insofar as it is grounded in the idea of formally collective intentional states had by individuals who are not mistaken in understanding themselves

---

[34] I furthermore believe that there is an implication of this particular kind of relationality that characterizes a collective intentional act. This implication concerns the issue that one's membership in a particular 'we' in the context of a collective intentional episode is not factually but normatively determined. If one, on a given occasion, *fails to participate* (as expected) in some collective intentional act, one is not necessarily immediately excluded from the relevant intentional community. In many cases one is only urged to justify one's failure. In principle, only in those cases in which this failure becomes the rule, the membership in the relevant group becomes questionable.

[35] Schmid articulates the criticism as follows: 'Forming a plural subject, it might seem, is something that has to be *done*, and we can only do it *together*. If, however, plural subjects are the result of joint actions or even just joint attitudes, we are in an infinite regress, since ex hypothesi, joint actions and attitudes presuppose a joint subject' (2014a, p. 11).

[36] We are going to deal with this idea below (in Sect. 4.3).

[37] Here, I am trying to characterize my view of collective intentionality in terms of Schmid's (2009; cf. also Schweikard and Schmid 2013) differentiation of theories that locate the collective character of genuinely collective intentionality in either the content, the mode, or the subject of the relevant intentional states.

as members of a particular group, the most plausible account of collective intentionality is, in my view, a membership account.

In the next section, and ultimately seeking to determine the general terms in which an adequate account of collective affective intentionality should be formulated, I shall critically examine Gilbert's attempt to provide an account along the lines of her plural subject theory of what she takes to be a collective feeling.

3.3   Collective Affective Intentionality and Our Ability to Feel-Towards Together

Gilbert (2002) makes an effort to show that an extension of some of the ideas formulated in her previous works may allow us to understand the sense in which certain groups of individuals could be said to feel an emotion of a particular kind in a genuinely collective manner. Unsurprisingly, Gilbert extends her plural subject account to the sphere of the affective by discussing the issue of so-called collective guilt feelings.[38] Her main proposal is that collective guilt feelings could also be understood in terms of a certain joint commitment on which the involved individuals have agreed. Gilbert writes: 'For us *collectively to feel guilt over our action* A is for us to be jointly committed to feeling guilt as a body over our action A' (2002, p. 139). In accordance with the view exposed in the preceding section, Gilbert completes this thought by claiming that '[f]or us *collectively to feel guilt over our action* A is for us to constitute the plural subject of a feeling of guilt over our action A' (ibid.).

Gilbert motivates this approach in a number of different ways. She begins by suggesting that, if people are prepared to talk of a collective guilt feeling, it is because they probably think that there is 'something real' to which these attributions refer (see p. 118). She continues by trying to show that the guilt of a group can, and must, be sharply distinguished from the guilt of any of its individual members (cf. pp. 129ff.). At some point she suggests — or so one could take her to be suggesting — that only an account of collective guilt feelings based on the idea of a joint commitment can explain the moral force we usually attribute to such feelings (cf. pp. 139–140).

I shall not comment on these suggestions.[39] Rather, in what follows I shall focus on Gilbert's attempt to show that a collectivist view of collective guilt feelings is

---

[38] The reason why this should not come as a surprise is not only because, as already mentioned, the idea of a collective responsibility surrounds the idea of a joint action, but also because the issue of collective guilt (broadly construed as collective bad conscience) constitutes a rather common philosophical topic. Indeed, when reading the first part of the mentioned paper in which Gilbert motivates her account, one gets the impression that she has not been driven to extend her plural subject account to the realm of the affective by a general interest in emotional phenomena, but by an interest in collective moral responsibility.

[39] For a criticism concerning the first of these points, see Konzelmann Ziv (2007). (Cf. footnote 42 below.)

necessary if one is to account for what she takes to be the ordinary notion of a collective guilt feeling. Gilbert proceeds by showing that two alternative accounts of collective guilt feelings are inadequate as general accounts of collective guilt feelings; the point being that they only capture some of the phenomena we are inclined to associate with the term 'collective guilt feelings'. These accounts are instances of the other two classes of accounts of collective intentionality we have distinguished above: aggregative accounts and membership accounts (which Gilbert characterizes as a second sort of aggregative accounts [cf. pp. 133ff.]).

The first proposal as to the nature of collective guilt feelings Gilbert explores concerns the idea that a collective guilt feeling may be understood as a summation of feelings of personal guilt. By 'feelings of personal guilt' she means feelings of guilt had by a particular person *over an action of hers*, i.e. feelings of guilt the intentional object of which is an action performed by the same person who is experiencing guilt. Gilbert argues that there are two main problems with such an account. She observes, firstly, that the intentional object of a collective guilt feeling, as we often understand this idea of a collective guilt feeling, is *the collective act of a certain group*, i.e. something we (the participants) have, in some relevant sense, *done together*. As she points out, '[i]t is hard to see how an account in terms of personal guilt can accommodate this [basic] consideration' (p. 131).

For Gilbert, a second problem of these sorts of accounts is that they require that all members of the relevant population feel guilt in relation to some contributory action of their own (cf. p. 131). She takes this requirement to be implausible. Gilbert writes: 'There surely are cases of collective action where we cannot expect all of the members to feel this way, or in which they simply do not feel this way, cases in which — at the same time — it is not obvious that a collective feeling of guilt is ruled out' (pp. 131–132). I shall comment on this claim below.

The second proposal Gilbert examines concerns the idea that a collective guilt feeling is constituted by what she calls 'membership guilt feelings'. This basically is the idea of a number of individuals who understand themselves as members of a given group and *personally* feel guilt *over something their group has done*.

A clear virtue of such an account is that it accommodates the fact that the term 'collective guilt feelings' is commonly used to refer to emotions the intentional object of which is a particular action that may be attributed to the relevant collective (as opposed to being attributed to certain members of this group). Gilbert argues that, contrary to what Karl Jaspers ([1947] 2001, pp. 80–81) seems to have thought, these sorts of feelings would be completely intelligible in case the individuals at issue were to be parties to the joint commitment that lies at the heart of the relevant collective action. However, she contends that an account of collective guilt in terms of membership guilt feelings fails to capture all the situations to which we refer by means of the term 'collective guilt feelings'. The reason is as follows: 'It is true that, here, a group's action is the object of a feeling of guilt. But the feeling does not have a collective subject' (p. 137). The problem is that '[t]he group *itself* does not seem to be the subject of a feeling of guilt' (p. 138; my emphasis).[40]

Against this background, Gilbert articulates the plural subject account of collective guilt feelings sketched above. Being aware of the puzzling character of the idea of a number of individuals who are jointly committed to feeling something, Gilbert provides a concise answer to the question concerning what exactly the parties involved in a joint commitment to feel guilt as a body are committed to. She writes: 'They are to act as would be appropriate were they to constitute a single subject of guilt feelings. Or, perhaps better, they are to act so as to constitute, as far as is possible, a single subject of guilt feelings' (p. 139).

The phrase 'as would be appropriate *were they to constitute a single subject of guilt feelings*' is very telling. It betrays that Gilbert does not require the individuals involved to be committed to *collectively experiencing* certain sorts of feelings—whatever exactly this could mean. Gilbert makes the point slightly more explicit by writing:

> This does not mean that they are to act so as to constitute, as far as possible, a single *individual human* subject of guilt feelings (ibid.).

In the abstract of the paper I am quoting from, we find a formulation that completes this idea. Gilbert writes:

> The parties to a joint commitment of the kind in question may as a result find themselves experiencing 'pangs' of the kind associated with personal and membership guilt feelings. Since these pangs, by hypothesis, arise as a result of the joint commitment to feel guilt as a body, they might be thought of as providing a kind of phenomenology for collective guilt (p. 115).

Since this account is meant as a response to Christopher Kutz's (2000b, p. 196) prima facie plausible claim that a collective cannot respond affectively to expressions of recrimination—the point being that only its members can—, we have to try to understand the extent to which, according to Gilbert, we can affirm in certain situations that the collective *itself* is responding in an affective manner. In the course of this discussion, we shall come to understand why Gilbert stresses the expression 'individual human' in the remark just quoted.

Gilbert begins to argue for the idea that in certain situations the response of the relevant group may be said to amount to a genuinely emotional response by observing that there is no particular sensation that *necessarily* has to accompany an experience of guilt *in general*. She generalizes the claim by asserting that '[p]articular emotions may not require a specific phenomenology' (p. 119). Gilbert concedes that a phenomenally rich state of consciousness—she calls such a state a 'feeling-sensation'—normally accompanies our experiences of guilt. Endorsing the judgmentalist view of emotions discussed above (in Sect. 2.3),[41] she argues, however,

---

[40] This is an intuition concerning what it means to feel something in a genuinely collective manner that Gilbert shares with other philosophers. As we have seen (cf. the discussion in Sect. 1.2), this is the intuition that motivates Huebner's (2011) talk of genuinely collective emotions.

[41] Gilbert draws on Martha Nussbaum (2001) and Jerome Shaffer (1983).

that all that is needed for us to feel guilt (both individually and collectively) is a judgment concerning the morally reprehensible character of the acts we feel guilty about. She writes:

> I can imagine saying that I felt guilty about something without meaning to imply that any particular phenomenological condition was satisfied. The central if not the sole thing at issue would be my judgment that I was wrong to do whatever it is I say I feel guilty about. The very nature of any associated pangs or twinges as pangs or twinges of guilt could only be assumed if this judgment were present (p. 120).

Gilbert suggests that we should not presume that it is already clear what feeling guilt amounts to. In this context, she warns us against the temptation to construe the phenomenon of collective guilt feelings on the basis of our intuitions concerning what it is *for an individual human* to feel guilt. Rather, we should embrace what she calls the *broad* method, which, first, takes into consideration guilt feelings attributed to both individuals and groups, and in a second move, extrapolates from both of these in order to decide what it is to feel guilt more generally. Her point is that after having done so '[o]ne might [...] want to say that groups did not feel guilt in quite the same way that individuals did. [But i]t would not be necessary to say that they did not feel guilt at all' (ibid.).

One easily gets the impression that, when speaking of 'collective guilt feelings', Gilbert is using the term 'feeling' in a way that differs from what she has in mind when she talks of feeling-sensations. Applying the principle of charity, one could argue that Gilbert is referring to what Goldie calls feelings towards. The problem is that Gilbert could too easily be accused of assuming that bodily sensations exhaust the 'specific phenomenology' of emotions, to use her words. This impression that there is something strange in Gilbert's use of the word 'feeling' (when she talks of guilt feelings) is in line with the fact that the most common objection raised against her account of collective guilt feelings concerns the phenomenological inadequacy of this proposal as an account of a collective *affective* intentional state (cf. Konzelmann Ziv 2007; Salmela 2012; Schmid 2008, 2009; and Wilkins 2002).[42] In

---

[42] There are other objections that are worthy of mention. Taking for granted that emotions are routinely ascribed to groups, Gilbert claims that these ascriptions are not based on some 'sense of fantasy or metaphor' (2002, p. 121). As already mentioned in the main text, she asserts that '[the fact t]hat people are prepared to speak in this way, and frequently do, at least suggests that they think that there is something, *something real*, to which [these ascriptions] refer: the feelings of a group' (p. 118; my emphasis). Konzelmann Ziv (2007) casts doubt on both the assumption that ascriptions of guilt feelings to groups are common and the claim that people making these sorts of ascriptions are normally referring to a feeling they think to be had by the group *itself*. A further objection Konzelmann Ziv raises concerns an assumption of what she takes to be Gilbert's second line of argument. The assumption is that self-ascriptions that display the form 'We feel p' *necessarily* refer to feelings of collectives. Konzelmann Ziv observes that plural sentences *in general* are open to both distributive and collective analyses: 'A collective analysis of the proposition "These books are expensive", for example, states that the proposition is true if the collection of books referred to is expensive, while a distributive analysis takes it to be true if each of the books is expensive' (p. 478). Konzelmann Ziv points out that '[t]he logical grammar of [such a] proposition does not determine which analysis is the right one; this depends largely on contextual parameters' (ibid.).

other words, what most philosophers involved in this discussion have tended to criticize in Gilbert's account is not her notion of a plural subject of guilt. Rather, the problem is Gilbert's suggestion that the possibility to invoke some collective judgment (or belief) to the effect that a particular action of the relevant group was morally wrong warrants talk of a collective guilt *feeling*. Burleigh Wilkins makes the point by writing that '[at least] the total absence of any phenomenological accompaniments would be extremely puzzling' (2002, p. 152).

As we have seen, Gilbert does not simply neglect the phenomenal aspect of the state she calls a collective guilt feeling. Gilbert does make a claim concerning this aspect. She writes: 'it seems most likely that there are phenomenological accompaniments of collective guilt feelings. These will include feeling-sensations experienced by individual human beings and occurring, in that sense, in the minds of these individuals' (p. 141). To the question concerning whether these feeling-sensations should be understood as 'pangs of personal guilt' or 'pangs of membership guilt', she offers the following answer: 'Clearly, from a phenomenological point of view there may be no way of deciding this issue: a pang is a pang is a pang. One needs to look at the context in which the pangs occur' (ibid.).

I believe that Gilbert is correct in claiming that, first, without contextual clues a bodily sensation is just a bodily sensation, and second, it is our understanding of the pertinent situation that can bring certain sensations to be intelligible as 'pangs' of collective guilt. But despite Gilbert's attempt to include in her picture the phenomenal dimension by referring to certain feeling-sensations, the account just exposed has two problems that pertain to its phenomenological inadequacy. These are problems on which we have already touched. Let me make them more explicit.

The first problem is that it is hard to see to which extent the invoked joint commitment to 'feel guilt as a body' is not merely a joint commitment to judge a certain action of the relevant group to be wrong. The issue is that such a joint commitment, which in itself only amounts to a sort of evaluative norm that *may* be expressed emotionally, has *not necessarily* to give rise to a genuinely affective state.[43] Wilkins makes the point as follows:

> It does not suffice for you to say that individual members of your plural subject may experience 'pangs' of guilt, because that is consistent with saying they may not.... From the point of view of philosophers trying to understand collective feelings of guilt, this is just the kind of scenario you might expect to encounter unless you provide a full blown account of such feelings as necessarily having some phenomenological component (2002, p. 153).

Appealing to a distinction made by Stocker on which we have already touched above (in Sect. 2.4), one could radicalize Wilkins' objection by arguing that, having reduced a guilt feeling to the evaluation this emotion may be said to express, Gilbert has made it impossible to distinguish between *mere pro forma* and *genuine* (i.e. actually felt) collective guilt. To put it bluntly, Gilbert's account may, in the best case, be argued to be a persuasive account of a group belief to the effect that a

---

[43] Following Arlie Russell Hochschild (1983), Salmela observes that 'a joint commitment to collectively feel an emotion amounts to the creation of a group-social *feeling rule* for a group of individuals, but not necessarily to an actual emotion' (2012, p. 36).

certain action of the pertinent group was wrong. But it falls short of an account of a collective affective state. This is the consequence, one could further argue, of her having endorsed a view of affective intentionality that is unable to account for the properly affective nature of our emotional relation to the world.

The second problem, which is related to the previous one, concerns Gilbert's unthematized assumption that the 'specific phenomenology' of a particular emotion is determined exclusively by the accompanying bodily sensations; in this case by the, as she observes, rather unspecific 'pangs' that are part of some instances of guilt. As we have discussed in detail above (particularly in Sect. 2.4), the intentional character of our emotions may be said to fundamentally be a matter of certain intentional feelings that can be differentiated from these bodily sensations: of feelings towards. These feelings are not only at the heart of an emotion's intentional character. Qua genuine feelings they co-determine the 'specific phenomenology' of this emotion. Indeed, one may claim that some feeling towards is always *the most salient constituent* of the specific phenomenal character that is proper to an emotion of a certain kind. For such a feeling corresponds to that which one is required to describe when characterizing the relevant experience as an experience of a particular emotional sort. As mentioned above, to feel fear is not basically to feel the hairs on one's neck rising, but to feel a particular situation to be dangerous.

To sum up, having endorsed the judgmentalist view of emotions—and with it the assumption that the phenomenology of an emotion is exhausted by certain non-relational bodily sensations—, Gilbert has failed to see that to experience a guilt feeling over an action of one's group means to *feelingly understand* this action as a wrong one (as opposed to merely judging it to be wrong). So one could argue that, contrary to what Gilbert asserts, there is a necessary phenomenological condition of feeling guilt. Moreover, one could maintain that the necessary phenomenological condition of feeling guilt over a personal action is clearly different from the necessary phenomenological condition of feeling guilt over an action of one's group.

Of course, one could see oneself and certain others as blameworthy for an action of a group one together with these others constitutes and, furthermore, act in a way that corresponds to this self-understanding without having to experience full-fledged episodes of guilt. But if one is to claim that this comportment amounts to an action out of guilt—and by 'guilt' I mean, of course, the feeling of having done wrong, and not the fact of having committed a specified or implied offense—, at some point one has to have *feelingly* understood the group action at issue to be wrong. To put it briefly, the inadequacy of Gilbert's account as an account of a collective affective intentional state is based on her failure to appreciate that there is a phenomenological condition of collective guilt which fully corresponds to the intentional condition of collective guilt she adequately characterizes.

Can this problem of Gilbert's elaborated and, in a number of respects, illuminating account be amended? I do not want to discard this possibility. But it is important to emphasize that, if an amendment were possible, it would definitely not be a matter of stressing the salience of certain feeling-sensations that accompany actual (full-blown) experiences of guilt. If we are to take seriously the idea that affective intentionality amounts to a sui generis form of openness to the world—one in which certain sorts of feelings, namely feelings towards, play an absolutely central role—our attempt to make sense of the idea of a collective affective intentional episode has to rely on a completely different approach.

Concretely, and as Hans Bernhard Schmid (2008, 2009) has argued, we have to try to extend to the collective level the idea that affective intentionality is a matter of world-directed feelings. Put another way, we have to try to construe the phenomenon of collective affective intentionality in terms of *people together feeling towards something*, in terms of particular actualizations of what I shall call *our human ability to feel-towards together*. In closing, let me point to some 'initial unclarities' that might guide our inquiry—and our attempt to construe the phenomenon of collective affective intentionality in terms of interrelated actualizations of our capacity to feel-towards together.

To begin with, I think that it is plausible to assume that, as Konzelmann Ziv puts it, '[t]he enabling condition for sharing one feeling episode is the feeling's immediate responsiveness to one and the same object' (2009, p. 100). But already at this point we find ambiguities. It will be necessary to clarify what exactly is meant here by 'object'. Do the participants' emotional feelings have to share the target, the formal object, and/or the focus?[44]

Konzelmann Ziv claims that there is a second condition fulfilled in those situations in which it is warranted to speak of a participation in one and the same feeling-episode; a condition she takes to be 'seemingly trivial'. We have to be able to understand the participants' emotional responses as affective states that have the same phenomenal quality (cf. p. 100). But what does this exactly mean? And is it really trivially true that the participants' feelings have to exhibit the same quality—whatever this turns out to mean—in order for these individuals to (correctly) understand their emotional response as a joint feeling?

At any rate, Konzelmann Ziv is absolutely right in arguing that these two conditions are 'by far not sufficient to delineate immediate co-feeling from type-identical feeling that is responding to one and the same object' (2009, p. 101).[45] So the crucial question will be the question as to the ultimate ground of the difference between genuine co-feeling and sheer affective parallelism.

We already have an intuition that may lead us to an answer to the latter question. Part of the difference at issue can be attributed to the sense of togetherness that structures the former, but not the latter, affective experiences. That is to say, we should look for the ground of this difference in the particular relationship that holds between the individuals involved, *according to these individuals themselves*. Put another way, we should begin our inquiry concerning the nature of our ability to feel-towards together by exploring the basic fact that in a collective affective

---

[44] As we shall see below (in Sect. 4.4), Schmid (2009) argues that, in order to constitute a shared emotion, the participants' emotional feelings do not have to have the same target. Nor do they have to have the same focus.

[45] The example Konzelmann Ziv gives is very illustrative: 'People feeling desperate towards the state of values of crashing stock markets fulfill both characteristics without immediately co-feeling their despair' (p. 101). This is a point we have already touched on.

intentional episode the participants *take themselves* to be responding to the requirements of the world in a joint manner; the fact that, in actualizing their ability to feel-towards together, the participating individuals come to see themselves *as standing in a particular relation to one another*.

So a basic task will consist in providing an account that explains the relationship between our understanding ourselves as members of a particular social group (at a given point in time) and having affective experiences marked by the mentioned sense of togetherness (in the presence of other individuals who co-constitute this group).[46] As observed above (in Sect. 1.1), this ultimately means to articulate the central condition fulfilled in those cases in which the individuals involved are feeling towards something in a genuinely joint manner and not in those other cases in which they merely are doing so alongside each other.

Seeking to articulate a more specific question that could guide our inquiry concerning what it is to interrelatedly actualize our ability to feel-towards together, in the next chapter I shall examine Schmid's phenomenologically inspired account of shared feelings. This is an account that, at least in the context of the current debate on collective intentionality, has to be regarded as the unique attempt so far to develop the idea that collective affective intentionality is a matter of world-directed feelings. After discussing Schmid's view of shared feelings, I shall distance myself from his claim that, in order to provide a phenomenologically adequate account of collective affective intentionality, we have to show that feelings, despite their eminently subjective nature, are shareable in the same sense in which we, to use an example offered by Schmid, can share a bottle of wine. In my view, in so arguing Schmid is unnecessarily limiting the theoretical possibilities we have for elaborating on the intuition I have presented in this chapter as the right point of departure for a phenomenologically adequate theory of collective affective intentionality: the idea that we have to conceive of collective affective intentional episodes in terms of interrelated actualizations of our human ability to feel-towards together. The view of

---

[46] I am aware that, in framing the issue in terms of a subjective sense of togetherness, I am making my proposal susceptible to an objection we are already familiar with: the objection concerning the possibility of a solipsistic (formally) collective intentional state. I believe that there is no real threat posed by the recognition that someone could experience a *misguiding* intentional feeling that is marked by what I am calling here a sense of togetherness, since this does not invalidate the whole approach. For it is possible to argue that the existence of such a feeling is, in a sense, *parasitic* on the very possibility we have to participate in real collective affective intentional episodes (whatever exactly this turns out to mean). One way in which one could begin to dismantle the worries at issue here, I think, is by addressing not only the concrete situation in which someone is experiencing such a feeling, but also what we could call *the historical preconditions* of such a feeling, thereby making clear that a genuine collective affective intentional state is grounded in some already existing relationship between the participants. At any rate, what this (anticipated) objection reminds us of is that collective affective intentionality (and collective intentionality more generally) cannot merely be a matter of feeling togetherness—although, as I have been arguing, it is absolutely fundamental to have some sense that the relevant experience is *our* experience. This, however, is not really a problem, since collective affective intentionality may be preliminarily argued to be a matter of feeling affective togetherness *in a genuinely joint manner* (whatever exactly this turns out to mean).

collective affective intentionality I am going to develop and recommend in the second part of this book should be seen as an attempt to spell out what it is to share in a moment of affective intentional community that does not take too seriously certain metaphysical worries mentioned in the introductory chapter (cf. our discussion in Sect. 1.2).

Chapter 4
Shared Feelings and Joint Feeling: The Problem of Collective Affective Intentionality Specified

Abstracts In this chapter I discuss Hans Bernhard Schmid's account of shared feelings which elaborates on the idea that affective intentionality is a matter of world-directed feelings. I reconstruct the philosophical problem Schmid is seeking to solve, which I call The Problem of Shared Feelings. This problem concerns the conflict between two deep-seated intuitions: the intuition that we humans can come to feel together and the intuition that only individuals, and not groups, can be understood as legitimate subjects of feeling. I expose Schmid's solution to this riddle which attempts to show that feelings can be shared in a non-metaphorical sense of the verb 'to share'; the point being that collective affective intentionality can be claimed to be a matter of shared feelings. Seeking to motivate a suggestion concerning the terms in which we should conceive of collective affective intentionality, I articulate a question Schmid's proposal may be argued to leave unanswered: what does it mean for two (or more) qualitatively different feelings to 'match' one another? I argue that, in order to offer a qualified answer to this question, we could appeal to a suggestion Schmid may be taken to make in a later version of his analysis of shared feelings: at the heart of a collective affective intentional episode we always find a shared concern. This thought, I propose, indicates a direction we could take in order to spell out a phenomenologically adequate account of collective affective intentionality along the lines of the view proposed at the end of Chap. 3.

Keywords Collective affective intentionality • Feeling together • Ontic subject • Phenomenal subject • Plural self-awareness • Sense of ourness • Shared concern • Shared feelings • World-directed feelings

4.1 Introduction

In the first chapters of this book I commenced to argue for the idea that there is a distinctive form of human world-relatedness that deserves to be called collective affective intentionality. I did so by providing a critical overview of the two ongoing philosophical debates that are most directly pertinent to the present inquiry. In Chap. 2, I critically reconstructed the debate on affective intentionality and recommended conceiving of an occurrent emotion as an evaluative state that typically

© Springer International Publishing Switzerland 2016
H.A. Sánchez Guerrero, *Feeling Together and Caring with One Another*,
Studies in the Philosophy of Sociality 7, DOI 10.1007/978-3-319-33735-7_4

presents a given situation as being a certain way and therefore meriting (and urging) a response of a certain sort (Sects. 2.2 and 2.3). Seeking to underscore the genuinely affective nature of such an evaluative state, I eventually proposed to conceive of our affective world-relatedness in terms of acts of felt understanding (Sect. 2.4). In Chap. 3, I turned to the specific topic of collective affective intentionality. I began to approach the issue by discussing a number of crucial insights and fundamental disagreements that frame the general debate on collective intentionality (Sect. 3.2). In the course of this theoretical contextualization, I discussed a very simple taxonomy of the positions that determine this debate. This taxonomy is based on the distinction between aggregative accounts, membership accounts, and collectivist accounts of collective intentionality. Drawing on diverse objections leveled against these different accounts, I eventually expressed my preference for a membership account that stresses the relational nature of collective intentionality as well as the normative character of the tie between the individuals involved. In the last part of the chapter I examined a proposal that, in the context of the current debate on collective intentionality, may be seen as the most influential attempt to account for a collective affective intentional attitude, namely Margaret Gilbert's collectivist account of so-called collective guilt feelings (Sect. 3.3). I closed the chapter by discussing a fundamental objection that has been repeatedly leveled against this account. This objection does not directly address Gilbert's idea of a sort of plural subject of feeling, but rather the phenomenological inadequacy of her account. I interpreted Gilbert's critics to be protesting that, having endorsed the judgmentalist view of emotions, Gilbert has offered an account of a collective belief or evaluation (or, at best, an account of a collective feeling rule), but not an account of a collective affective intentional episode. Following this line of criticism, I suggested that a theory of collective affective intentionality able to capture the affective, the intentional, and the collective nature of the phenomenon at issue has to take as its point of departure the idea that collective affective intentionality is a matter of joint actualizations of our human faculty to feel-towards together.

Seeking to further recommend this general suggestion and prepare a more specific proposal, in the present chapter I shall discuss Hans Bernhard Schmid's account of shared feelings. Schmid's account could be understood as an attempt to, in the context of the incipient debate on collective affective intentionality, elaborate on the central insight of the 'phenomenological turn in the philosophy of emotions': the idea that affective intentionality is a matter of world-directed feelings. Aiming at a commented exposition of Schmid's proposal, in a first move (Sect. 4.2) I shall reconstruct the concrete philosophical problem Schmid is seeking to solve. This problem concerns the conflict between two deep-seated intuitions: the intuition that we human beings can share at least some of our emotional experiences—in the sense that we can come to feel together—and the intuition that only individuals (and not groups) can be understood as legitimate subjects of feeling. By reconstructing Schmid's exposition of this problem, I shall try to explain in how far the recent philosophical response to the cognitivist view of emotions—the phenomenologically inspired approach to affective intentionality defended above (in Sect. 2.4)— could be thought to render the notion of collective affective intentionality absolutely puzzling. Subsequently, I shall present Schmid's solution to the exposed riddle. This is a solution by means of which Schmid attempts to show, firstly, that feelings can be shared in a non-metaphorical sense of 'sharing', and secondly, that collective affective intentionality can, accordingly, be claimed to be a matter of shared feelings (Sect. 4.3). Finally, and seeking to motivate a particular suggestion concerning the terms in which we should conceive of collective affective intentionality, I shall try to articulate a concrete question which Schmid's proposal may be argued to leave unanswered (Sect. 4.4). The idea is that the formulation of this question may indicate the direction we could take in order to spell out a phenomenologically adequate account of collective affective intentionality, i.e. an account along the lines of the general view proposed at the end of Chap. 3.

4.2   One and the Same Emotional Feeling: The Problem of Shared Feelings

In the context of the current debate on collective intentionality, Hans Bernhard Schmid's work on shared feelings (2008, 2009) can be regarded as the only attempt so far to elaborate on the thought that the intentionality of an emotion and its specific phenomenology are inextricably intertwined (cf. the discussion in Sect. 2.4).[1] As we have seen (in Sect. 3.3), other philosophers have also criticized Gilbert's account of collective guilt feelings for its failure to respect the idea that feelings are fundamental constituents (as opposed to being accessory components) of genuine occurrent emotions. None of them has, however, made a comparable effort to provide an account of collective affective intentionality that takes seriously this idea.[2]

Schmid motivates his account of shared feelings by formulating a concrete philosophical problem. This is a problem that, in his view, has to be solved if we are to show that feelings are at the heart of collective affective intentionality, too. This problem, which I shall call *The Problem of Shared Feelings*, concerns the conflict

---

[1] The arguments I am going to discuss in what follows appeared for the first time in English in Schmid's paper 'Shared Feelings: Towards a Phenomenology of Collective Affective Intentionality' (2008). A modified version of this analysis has been published in the fourth chapter of Schmid's book *Plural Action* (2009). This latest version contains some additional observations that are fundamental for the view of collective affective intentionality I shall develop in this book. For this reason, I am going to systematically quote from the latest version of Schmid's analysis, unless the referred to passages have been omitted in this later text. To be sure, there is an earlier German version of this analysis which appeared as part of Schmid's contribution to the sixth Conference of the German Society of Analytic Philosophy (Berlin, September 2006). The argument developed in the present chapter makes use of a number of ideas and formulations I originally articulated in two papers that began with a review of Schmid's proposal (cf. Sánchez Guerrero 2011, 2014).

[2] My claim that Schmid's account of shared feelings stands as the unique attempt to elaborate on the idea that the intentionality of an emotion is inextricably intertwined with its phenomenology is restricted to the current (analytic philosophical) debate on collective intentionality. As we shall immediately see, Schmid takes himself to be elaborating on some suggestions made by Max Scheler ([1913] 2008). These are suggestions we briefly discussed above (in Sect. 1.1).

between two apparently incompatible intuitions (cf. the discussion in Sect. 1.2): the intuition that we humans can share at least some of our emotions and the intuition that only individuals, and not groups, can experience (or be in) an affective state and, what is more, that they can only experience their own affective states; the issue being that the subjective nature of feelings precludes us from really participating in the affective life of another individual.

Although, as we shall see, The Problem of Shared Feelings exhibits a variety of aspects, it might be regarded as a problem that is broadly metaphysical in nature, as Schmid himself observes.[3] In what follows immediately I shall try to reconstruct this philosophical riddle. My aim in so doing is to clarify what, in Schmid's view, an account apt to extend the 'phenomenological turn in the philosophy of emotions' (2009, p. 64) to the collective level has to be able to offer.

Schmid's formulation of The Problem of Shared Feelings begins with an analysis of the uses of the expression 'sharing a feeling'. By means of this analysis Schmid seeks, first, to show that in the contexts that are relevant here the term 'shared' is quite frequently used in what he takes to be a rather non-literal way, and second, to determine the main condition a clearly non-metaphorical use of this term has to meet.

Schmid begins this discussion by observing that, according to the less demanding use of the expression 'sharing a feeling with someone else', the feelings of a number of individuals could be said to be shared, if these feelings were '*qualitatively similar*, and converge[d] on one object or on one type of object' (2008, p. 65).[4] This is an understanding of what it is to share a feeling with someone else which Schmid takes to be too unspecific to serve as a conceptual basis for the notion of a collective affective intentional episode. The problem is that, if we were to elaborate on this meaning of the expression 'to share a feeling', we would have to accept situations in which the alleged emotional sharing could be said to, first, be completely *accidental*, and second, not be accompanied by *any sense of togetherness* as cases of collective affective intentionality. Schmid illustrates the problem by writing: 'In this sense, fear of dogs might be said to be widely shared even though people are afraid of different dogs, and might not even be aware of each other's feelings towards dogs' (2008, p. 66).

Schmid's example is certainly extreme. As he concedes, 'this way of speaking [clearly] borders on the metaphorical' (2009, p. 65). Moreover, one could object

---

[3] Having discussed the neglect of affective phenomena in the context of the debate on collective intentionality, Schmid begins his problematization of the notion of a shared feeling as follows: 'With this result, let me now turn to a metaphysical question. It is this: in what sense of the word are feelings to be genuinely *shared*? What does the term *sharing* really mean in this context?' (2009, p. 69). Some pages before he tells us that, after having examined the structure of feelings towards, he is going to defend 'the *metaphysical* claim that, when people genuinely share a feeling, there is a sort of phenomenological fusion between the consciousness of the participating individuals' (p. 64; my emphasis).

[4] There is a sense of the expression 'to share a feeling' which is irrelevant for the present discussion. We often use this expression in order to refer to the act by means of which we communicate or make public our feelings.

that the assertion 'fear of dogs is widely shared among the members of this population' refers to a shared affective *disposition*, and not to an *occurrent* emotion that is
shared by a number of individuals. In other words, one sees immediately that such
an assertion does not refer to a collective affective intentional *episode*. But the
remark is definitely not a trivial one. We could reinforce the central insight of this
remark by appealing to a slightly different example in which the intentional target
of the involved (occurrent) emotions would amount to one and the same
occurrence.

Imagine two persons who are two kilometers apart and are not aware of each
other's existence. Suppose that at a given point they are simultaneously, but independently, beginning to engage in some outdoor activity. All of a sudden they both
hear a thunder that announces the beginning of a storm and become profoundly
upset because this means that they are not going to complete the planned activity.
Let us assume that they are experiencing exactly the same sort of emotional
feeling.

There certainly is a clear sense in which we could assert that these individuals are
sharing a feeling towards. The intentional object of their emotions is one and the
same occurrence (the thunder), their emotions have the same formal object, and
both of them are related to this occurrence by means of an intentional state that has
a determinate phenomenology which is the same in both cases. I take it to be uncontroversial, however, that this sense of 'sharing a feeling towards one and the same
occurrence' does not exhaust the meaning of what we are trying to say when we, for
instance, assert that, having won the cup again, the members of the Spanish football
team are sharing a feeling of enormous pride.[5]

In the latest version of his analysis, Schmid makes explicit why such a notion of
shared feelings does not serve as a conceptual foundation for the notion of a collective affective intentional episode. Touching on an issue we have already discussed
above (in Sect. 3.2), Schmid writes: 'For a feeling to be *genuinely* shared one person's being in an affective state of a certain mode cannot be entirely *independent* of
the other person's being in the same affective mode. There have to be *connections*
of some sort' (2009, pp. 65–66). This unspecific, but extremely relevant, appeal to
certain 'connections of some sort' is clearly intended to exclude what I have called
mere affective parallelisms (cf. our discussion in Sect. 1.1). In other words, this
remark aims at telling apart those situations in which the involved individuals are
actualizing their ability to feel-towards together from situations in which they are
just experiencing similar (or even qualitatively identical) emotions as a result of a
sheer convergence of individual emotions. The latter, I have pointed out, are situations in which the involved individuals can be said to merely be feeling alongside
each other.

One could think that, in arguing that the affective states of the individuals
involved in a case of collective affective intentionality cannot be entirely independent from one another, Schmid is basically claiming that the fact that they are having

---

[5] I have already made thematic this unspecificity of the verb 'to share' while discussing the idea of
a shared intention above (in Sect. 3.2).

similar affective experiences has to be common knowledge among the participants. While discussing Max Scheler's notion of an immediate feeling-together, Schmid writes, however: 'There needn't be any *interaction* or even *intercognition* between the [involved individuals] for their feeling to be genuinely shared' (p. 66). A number of questions arise in this context. Does Schmid understand by the term 'intercognition' the mutual conscious awareness of the involved individuals to the effect that they are having the same sort of experience? If so, is Schmid pointing to a 'connection' that is, so to say, cognitively less demanding than what we may call an act of intercognition? Is Schmid, moreover, suggesting that any kind of 'connection' could bring two or more individuals who have a similar emotional experience in response to some particular occurrence to share this feeling in the sense that is relevant here?

I think that we can positively answer the second question. The third one has, on the contrary, to be answered negatively.[6] One could get the impression that Schmid takes a cognitively rather undemanding phenomenon like emotional contagion, which, as we have seen, does normally not involve conscious awareness of the shared character of the affective state at issue, to be a connection valid enough. For he writes that emotional contagion is '[o]ne way in which a person's affective state may account for another person's being in a state of the same kind' (ibid.). Following Scheler, he immediately remarks, however, that 'affective contagion *per se* does not mean that there is anything shared about those affective states' (ibid.; my emphasis). So it is safe to conclude that Schmid does not take any sort of connection—not even any sort of *affective* connection—between two or more individuals who are experiencing a similar emotion at a given point to be sufficient for us to assert that they are sharing a feeling in the sense that is relevant here. As we shall see, however, he has in mind a kind of connection that may be said to, in some sense, be cognitively undemanding. This is a kind of connection that, being intentional through and through, is non-thematic and pre-reflective.

Trying to merge the notion of something being common knowledge among the participants—a notion that plays an important role in the analytic debate on collective intentionality, but which seems to involve conscious awareness concerning that which is said to be common knowledge—and the Heideggerian idea concerning the pre-articulate understanding that precedes any thematic interpretation (cf. the discussion in Sect. 2.4), we could assert something along the following lines: in a genuine case of collective affective intentionality the fact that they are feeling towards in a joint manner has to (at least) be *common understanding* among the involved individuals. That is to say, the participants have to at least pre-thematically understand themselves as individuals who are responding together in an affective manner to the requirements of the world. We will have time to discuss in detail what this sort of connection amounts to. For the moment let me emphasize that, whatever exactly Schmid means by 'connections of some sort', his remark should be taken to

---

[6] There is no clue in the texts I am discussing to an answer to the first question. This, however, has no consequence for our discussion, since the second question assumes that by the term 'intercognition' Schmid does understand the mutual conscious awareness of the participants to the effect that they are having the same sort of affective experience.

be absolutely fundamental for a reason I have already mentioned: it is in reference to this connection that we can distinguish between cases of collective affective intentionality and cases of mere affective parallelism.

The expression 'sharing a feeling with somebody', Schmid continues, is often used in the sense of sympathizing with another person (or with the feelings of this other person). Following Scheler again, Schmid remarks that in such a situation the target of the emotion of person B, who sympathizes with person A, is the feeling of A (or perhaps person A), and not the object towards which the feeling of A is directed. In such a situation, thus, the affective states in question cannot be said to share their target. Schmid seems to be suggesting here that in such a situation it would be rather inaccurate to speak of a collective intentional state *in general*, despite the fact that, first, the affective experiences of the involved individuals may be said to be qualitatively similar, and second, B's feelings could be said to be dependent on A's feelings, i.e. despite the fact that there is some (asymmetric) intentional connection between the feelings of the individuals involved.[7]

A third and, in Schmid's view, more demanding use of the expression 'sharing a feeling with somebody' refers to some circumstances in which a number of individuals 'have feelings towards the same object or object type, [...] *know* about each other's feelings, and the feelings of the individuals participating [...] [can be said to] be causally connected in one or the other way' (2008, p. 66). Schmid appeals in this context to Robert Sugden's reconstruction of Adam Smith's ([1759] 2000) notion of a *fellow-feeling*. Let us take a brief look at Sugden's/Smith's notion of a fellow-feeling.

In his paper 'Beyond Sympathy and Empathy: Adam Smith's Concept of Fellow-Feeling' (2002), Robert Sugden tries to offer an alternative to Philippe Fontaine's (1997) view of the role that different forms of sympathy and empathy play in Adam Smith's work on 'moral sentiments'. Sugden's main claim is that Smith's understanding of the ways in which the affective state of an individual may have an effect on the affective state of another individual is based on the notion of a fellow-feeling; a notion that, according to Sugden, can be clearly differentiated from both the concept of sympathy and the concept of empathy to which the contemporary debate that elaborates on Smith's thoughts repeatedly appeals.[8] According to Sugden, by

---

[7] This interpretation is supported by a claim Schmid makes in a different passage in which he considers the fear 'shared' by a group of schoolchildren who are playing hooky. He writes: 'The children might be enjoying their affective attunement in their fear, and even reach some affective agreement [i.e. a generally shared idea about the level of affective attunement expected to be reached in the relevant situation], but there is a sense in which these children's fear isn't genuinely shared, because the children's feelings have different targets: each child is afraid of *his or her own* parent's reaction' (2009, p. 66). However, if this is really what Schmid is trying to suggest, this remark may be taken to contradict a claim he makes in the latest version of his analysis. This claim, which he articulates in analyzing a passage of Homer's *Iliad*, concerns the idea that in order to constitute a shared feeling, the feelings of the involved individuals do not have to have the same target (not even the same focus). We shall come back to this point below (in Sect. 4.4).

[8] Sugden makes a diagnosis concerning the reason why the notion of a fellow-feeling has been neglected in the contemporary debate that draws on Smith. He contends that the reason is simply that this notion does not fit well into the frame of rational choice theory.

'fellow-feeling' Smith means a kind of second-order feeling that arises in situations in which there is some sort of emotional harmony based on the qualitative identity of the (first-order) feelings of the involved individuals. Sugden argues that Smith has conceived of this higher-order feeling as a feeling that, independently of the valence of the primary feelings, always has a positive hedonic valence. Sugden writes: 'I suggest that the best reading of Smith is that our awareness of *any* correspondence of our sentiments with those of others is a potential source of pleasure, and that our awareness of *any* dissonance is a potential source of pain' (2002, pp. 72–73). The idea is that a fellow-feeling experientially expresses the psychological fact that, as Schmid writes, 'people *enjoy* being in the same affective state as those around them' (2009, p. 66).

In the earlier version of his paper, Schmid points to a theoretical possibility opened up by this notion of a fellow-feeling. Appealing to Adam Smith's picture of what it is to share a feeling, one could hypothesize that '[the k]nowledge of sharedness might deeply transform the way we feel' (Schmid 2008, p. 66). This idea that the intensity and/or the phenomenal character of a feeling could be modified by the knowledge of its being shared could allow for a rather literal interpretation of the popular saying, according to which a sorrow shared is a sorrow halved and a joy shared is a joy doubled. Schmid observes, more generally, that, according to this view, we could take the sharing of a feeling to involve a 'feeling of sharedness' (ibid.).[9] So one could take the expression 'sharing a feeling with somebody' to refer to a structurally complex multipersonal affective condition which is based on a qualitative correspondence between the (first-order) feelings of the involved individuals that gives rise to a hedonically positive (second-order) feeling. Schmid prefers the term 'affective attunement' to refer to these sorts of situations.[10]

Having discussed these three possible interpretations of the notion of a shared feeling, Schmid argues that they all fail to conform to the most straightforward meaning of the expression 'sharing something with someone else'. The problem is, however, not—as one could expect—that all the discussed meanings fail to make understandable in how far, in those cases in which we can speak of a genuinely shared feeling, the collective *itself* may be understood as the subject of the relevant feeling.[11] Rather, the point is that none of the three meanings of 'sharing a feeling'

---

[9] This idea of a feeling of sharedness is clearly akin to what I call a sense of togetherness. However, I shall not try to explain this sense of togetherness by invoking a second-order feeling. On the contrary, I am going to appeal to something that is more fundamental than a first-order intentional feeling: a pre-intentional structure of experience (cf. the discussion in Sect. 6.4).

[10] The reason for doing so is presumably because calling such a complex *state of affairs* a (shared) feeling would be unacceptable for some philosophers. We have touched on a similar issue above (in Sect. 3.2) while discussing Michael Bratman's account of a shared intention. In the next chapter (particularly in Sect. 5.4) I shall use the term 'affective attunement' to refer to a completely different phenomenon; a phenomenon that concerns our affective situatedness in a particular world.

[11] Recall that, according to Margaret Gilbert (2002) and Bryce Huebner (2011), this is a requirement any adequate account of a collective affective intentional attitude has to fulfill (cf. the discussion in Sects. 1.1, 3.2, and 3.3).

we have considered manages to elucidate in how far individuals can be said to share a feeling *in a non-metaphorical sense of 'sharing'*.

In order to spell out what we usually mean when we use the expression 'sharing something with somebody', Schmid suggests considering situations in which one proposes sharing a bottle of wine or sharing a car. He writes:

> Certainly, I do not thereby suggest that you and I each open a bottle, the two bottles being of the same vintage, or brand. Rather, I suggest that we enjoy *one and the same (token) bottle*. Similarly, the idea of sharing a car is not that of each one driving his or her own car, the cars being of the same brand. The point is to use *one and the same (token)* car *together*. The idea is this: one car, many users, one cake, many pieces, one apartment, many inhabitants, and so on, and so forth. This is what I will call the straightforward sense of sharing (2009, p. 69).

The reason, hence, why Schmid considers the discussed notions of shared feelings to be inadequate (at least as a conceptual basis for the notion of a collective affective intentional episode) is because they all draw too heavily on the idea that the involved affective states have to be *qualitatively similar* or *type-identical*, thereby neglecting a crucial point: if we are to understand these feelings as feelings the individuals involved experience *together* we have to conceive of them as affective experiences that, in some sense, constitute *one and the same feeling*. Schmid writes: 'In the straightforward sense, sharing is not a matter of type, or of qualitative identity (i.e. of having different things that are somehow similar), but a matter of token, or *numerical identity*' (ibid.).

One could certainly find questionable the basic assumption that is operative here: the assumption that this, as one could argue, very specific notion of sharedness corresponds to the *sole* non-metaphorical use of the verb 'to share'. Putting aside the discussion as to what it is for a word to be used in a literal sense, one may wonder whether this paradigm of a shared bottle of wine manages to capture the intensional definition of the most common *correct uses* of the verb 'to share'. In this vein, Anita Konzelmann Ziv observes that 'the term "sharing" does not imply part-whole ontology' (2009, p. 88). She attenuates the claim by writing that '[the] weaker sister [of this assertion] would consist in saying that "sharing" has a basic meaning which implies part-whole ontology, and that the meaning of "sharing" in certain uses is derived or parasitic on this basic meaning' (ibid.). This, however, does not prevent her from concluding that 'the term "sharing" is a good example for a term whose wide array of application cannot be accounted for in terms of primary and secondary, or literal and metaphorical meaning' (p. 89). As Konzelmann Ziv puts it, '[e]motions just are not the kind of things that—in order to be shared—can be cut to pieces like a cake, or split into time-intervals like the use of a car' (ibid.).

The claim that a non-metaphorical use of the expression 'sharing a feeling' necessarily implies the numerical identity of the feelings at issue—whatever exactly this turns out to mean—may be argued to be too strong. It is important, however, not to overlook the motivation behind this attempt to spell out the condition a non-metaphorical use of the expression 'to share a feeling' has to fulfill. This motivation is strongly related to a point I have repeatedly underscored: if we are to develop a theory of *collective* affective intentionality we have to, at a minimum, be able to differentiate in a principled way those situations in which some individuals are feeling in a genuinely joint manner from those other situations in which they merely are feeling alongside each other. As far as this crucial point is concerned, Schmid's claim is neat: we can assert that the involved individuals are sharing a feeling in a sufficiently demanding sense of 'sharing', i.e. in a sense that allows us to speak of a genuinely collective affective intentional episode, just in case they can be thought to be experiencing one and the same feeling.

As we have seen (in Sect. 1.2), the idea that there is something like a unitary state of consciousness somehow constituted by the feelings of the involved individuals sounds strange enough to most contemporary ears.[12] Schmid, however, makes an effort to provide a differentiated problematization. This problematization aims to explicate the reasons contemporary philosophers have to find unattractive the idea of a unitary feeling in which the involved individuals participate. Let me try to reconstruct Schmid's diagnosis.

As already mentioned, The Problem of Shared Feelings boils down to the, at least apparent, incompatibility of two strong intuitions: the intuition concerning the shareability of at least some of our affective states and the intuition concerning the subjective nature of feelings, which prevents us from understanding a group as an entity capable of feeling. In order to bring this incompatibility to the fore, Schmid examines an intuitively plausible position he calls 'individualism about feelings' (cf. 2009, pp. 69ff.). This is a position based on two tenets I have already mentioned: that only individuals can have feelings and that they can only have their own feelings. Schmid begins this problematization by observing that there are at least three senses in which feelings are normally claimed to be states of singular subjects of experience. In other words, one could differentiate at least three versions of the mentioned position.

The first version of this position relies on the idea that feelings are conscious states. Qua conscious states, feelings are *ontologically subjective* in the sense that their existence presupposes the existence of the experiencing subject. As most contemporary philosophers would agree, the relevant subject is always a particular individual that possesses certain capacities. Put another way, feelings are always the feelings of some particular subject of experience and at the moment we have no grounds to accept the idea that something different from an individual organism capable of consciousness could be seen as a genuine subject of experience.

Now, one could feel urged to observe that this ontological dependence on a subject of experience characterizes most psychological states. Furthermore, one could wonder whether Schmid's conclusion concerning what it means to share a feeling in a non-metaphorical sense does not render problematic the idea that we can share other mental states which are also ontologically dependent on some bearer of mentality. As we have seen (in Sect. 3.2), however, philosophers have little reservations

---

[12] As he tells us, it is precisely the prima facie implausibility of the idea that feelings can be shared in the strong sense of 'sharing', which he calls the straightforward sense, that motivates Schmid to examine Scheler's notion of immediate feeling-together in the context of the debate on collective intentionality (see 2009, p. 70).

about talking of a shared belief or of a shared intention. Moreover, there are a number of plausible accounts that spell out what a shared belief or a shared intention amounts to.[13] So what exactly does the problem amount to?

The key to understanding why in the case of a shared emotional experience this ontological dependence on a subject becomes a real problem is to recognize that what renders the issue pressing is precisely the insight that the intentionality of an emotion is inextricably intertwined with its phenomenology. In the case of a shared intention or of a shared belief it is what Montague (2009) calls the 'thin content' (i.e. the that-clause) of this intentional attitude that is normally taken to be shared. Accordingly, philosophers seldom feel compelled to defend the idea that a shared intention or a shared belief could be understood as *one and the same experiential state*. To participate in a common emotional experience, on the contrary, is clearly more than sharing some evaluative view of a given occurrence. Particularly, it is more than being in an intentional state the 'thin content' of which exactly corresponds with the that-clause of the evaluative state in which the other involved individuals are. For, as we have seen (cf. the discussion in Sect. 3.3), to share an occurrent emotion means to participate in some joint act of feeling towards. The idea that some individuals are sharing an affective state can, thus, be argued to essentially be the idea that they are taking part in some common experience. Given that, according to a widely shared assumption, only individual subjects of consciousness can be seen as legitimate subjects of emotional feeling, it is unclear what it could mean for a number of individuals to participate in one and the same experiential state.

The second version of the position we are examining is based on the idea that feelings are *epistemologically subjective* in the sense that only the experiencing subject can access them in the particular way she or he does. There is an ongoing debate that focuses on the issue as to whether the experiences of another person can be *directly perceived*, as opposed to being inferred. Furthermore, there probably are philosophers who are prepared to argue that there is a sense in which we can perceive the experiences of another person (as opposed to merely perceiving *that* this person is having these experiences).[14] But even if we were to accept this claim, we

---

[13] Mikko Salmela does, in fact, raise an objection along these lines. He writes: 'The ontological individuality of emotions […] is beyond doubt: only individual subjects feel emotions, as Schmid observes. However, this is not a problem for collective intentionality, for shared beliefs and intentions are also realized in the minds of individuals, and there is a considerable consensus that it is the content or mode of having those mental states that is collective rather than their ontological subject' (2012, p. 37). As we have seen, even if we can speak of a 'considerable consensus', we cannot speak of unanimity in this respect (cf. Gilbert's [2002] and Huebner's [2011] view).

[14] For a recent defense of the idea that a direct perceptual grasp of other person's intentions, feelings, etc. plays a role in social cognition, see Gallagher (2008). Already in Max Scheler we find this idea concerning a sort of direct perception of the affectedness of others. Scheler writes: 'that "experiences" occur there ["in a subject"] is given for us *in* expressive phenomena—again, not by inference, but directly, as a sort of primary "perception". It is *in* the blush that we perceive shame, *in* the laughter joy' ([1913] 2008, p. 10). However, Scheler seems to be committed to the view that *it is the fact that* they occur (that they are being experienced by the relevant other), and not these experiences themselves, that are directly given to us in expressive phenomena.

should recognize that we have, at best, only second- or third-person access to the experiences of other persons. In other words, there is a clear sense in which it can be claimed that 'individuals can have *only their own feelings*' (Schmid 2009, p. 70).

Finally, Schmid observes that feelings can be claimed to be *physically individual*. What Schmid has in mind seems to be the intuition that feelings are always *individually embodied*, since he does not only address the physical body, but also the phenomenal body. In this respect, Schmid writes:

> In the normal case, phenomenal bodies are *individual* in a twofold sense. They are individual *in themselves*, and they are individual in that they are related to our physical bodies, because normally, physical bodies are individual. In themselves, phenomenal bodies are individualized by their *mode of access*: nobody feels a twinge in somebody else's stomach, let alone a throbbing feeling in some collective *Leviathan*'s breastbone. [...] [And they] are individual in their relation to physical bodies, because in the standard case (i.e. if we disregard for the moment phenomena such as phantom pains, which are parasitic in that their very possibility depends on the normal case), phenomenal bodies are co-extensive with physical bodies (2008, pp. 69–70).[15]

We are now in a position to appreciate the extent to which the idea that there is a distinct form of world-relatedness that deserves to be called collective affective intentionality becomes profoundly puzzling in light of the claim that the intentional and the phenomenal aspects of an emotion cannot be disentangled from each other. The problem can be stated as follows. It seems that a philosophical account of collective affective intentionality grounded in the thought that affective intentionality is a matter of the world-directedness of our emotional feelings must be able to show that at least certain feelings (namely our feelings towards) can be shared in a non-metaphorical sense of 'sharing'. It must be able to show that there is a sense in which we can speak of one and the same feeling towards. Given, however, that feelings are ontologically and epistemologically subjective, and that they can be said to be individualized by both the feeling and the felt body, there seems to be no room whatsoever for a non-metaphorical notion of a shared feeling. The uncomfortable conclusion is that something like a *genuinely* collective affective intentional episode is impossible, not merely in the sense of being absolutely unlikely, but in the sense of being unthinkable.

By means of the proposal we are going to discuss shortly (in Sect. 4.3), Schmid, who evidently finds this conclusion counterintuitive, illustrates the popular philosophical saying according to which one philosopher's modus ponens is another philosopher's modus tollens. He interprets the problem just exposed as an indication

---

[15] Schmid observes that Scheler, in a way, anticipated the distinction between bodily feelings on the one hand—here we should probably include what Scheler calls 'sensible feelings' and what he calls 'vital feelings'—, and psychic feelings on the other. Scheler limits the phenomenon of immediate feeling-together to psychic feelings (cf. Schmid 2009, pp. 71–72). The reference here is to the taxonomy of feelings offered by Scheler in his *Formalism in Ethics and Non-Formal Ethics of Values* ([1913–1916] 1973, pp. 328ff.) under the title 'The Stratification of the Emotional Life'. This remark is crucial, since it makes clear that, in order to follow Scheler, one 'only' has to show that feelings towards can be shared in a strong sense of 'sharing'. This is important given the very limited prospect of success of an endeavor aimed at showing that we can experience the bodily feelings of other persons.

that the set of assumptions and premises on which this conclusion draws requires a second look. Schmid's intuition seems to be that this second look could make understandable in how far the phenomenological perspective that has rendered puzzling the idea of a collective affective intentional episode may also explain in how far the pre-theoretical intuition concerning the shareability of our emotions is compatible with the intuition concerning the subjective nature of our feelings. In this context, Schmid makes it his philosophical business to defend the idea that emotional feelings can be shared in something of the straightforward sense of 'sharing'. He finds here a motive to appeal to Scheler's debated notion of an immediate feeling-together. Specifically, Schmid makes an effort to take seriously Scheler's claim that there is a sense in which the individuals who are participating in some joint emotional response can be said to be participating in one and the very same feeling.[16]

4.3   Schmid's Phenomenologically Inspired Solution

In order to solve The Problem of Shared Feelings, Schmid appeals to an idea that, in his view, has not received sufficient attention by analytic philosophers. He articulates the point by observing that '[t]o be in a conscious state [...] means to have some pre-reflective *awareness* of one's being in a conscious state' (2009, p. 77). Schmid begins to explicate this idea as follows:

> Conscious states are—pre-reflectively and un-thematically—*conceived* and *interpreted* by the subjects who have them. To be in a conscious state means to *conceive of this state* in some or another way. In the case of intentional states of consciousness, this concerns the intentional *content* as well as the *mode* and the *subject* of the intention (ibid.).

By pointing to these different aspects of a conscious intentional state, namely its content, its mode, and its subject, Schmid tries to make room for a distinction that, as we shall see, will serve as the central piece of his solution to the riddle just exposed. This distinction pertains to an ambiguity of the expression 'subject of experience'. Schmid succinctly states the issue by writing: 'The subject of a conscious state can mean either of the following: (a) the subject who has the conscious state in question; (b) the subject *as who* the subject takes himself or herself to have the state in question' (ibid.).

Schmid proposes disambiguating the expression 'subject of a conscious state' by distinguishing between the *ontic* and the *phenomenal* subject of an experience (cf. p. 65). The same point could be stated by differentiating between the subject *of* experience and the subject *in* experience (or, alternatively, between the experienc*ing*

---

[16] Schmid rejects Stan van Hooft's (1994) interpretation of Scheler's notion of an immediate feeling-together; an interpretation based on the idea that feeling together is a matter of the numerical identity of the intentional object of the emotions in question. Schmid stresses that Scheler has expressis verbis argued for the idea that the phenomenon of immediate feeling-together is a matter of *experiencing together* [*Miteinandererleben*] (cf. Schmid 2009, p. 69); as Schmid puts it, '[it is] a matter of the identity of the feeling *as an emotional impulse* (*Gefühlsregung*)' (p. 72).

and the experienc*ed* subject). Regardless of the preferred terminology, what is important here is to understand that this distinction allows for a completely different view of the issue. This view is based on the following consideration: even if we were to agree that only individuals can have feelings (and that they can only have their own feelings), the question would remain open as to who appears *in* the relevant affective experience as its subject. In other words, by distinguishing between the actual individual who has the relevant feeling and the self-concept implicit *in* this affective experience, Schmid makes room for the idea that, under certain conditions, the involved individuals may be correct in *pre-reflectively and un-thematically understanding themselves* as individuals that constitute a sort of community of affective experience, as I have put it above.[17] Before we proceed to discuss this solution in detail, let me briefly comment on the basic suggestion that permits Schmid to articulate such a proposal: the suggestion that to be in a conscious state means to interpret this state as the experiential state of some particular subject.

To begin with, one could certainly be puzzled by the general claim that to have an experience means to interpret this experience in some way or another. To be in an experiential state, one could object, means to conceive of (or interpret) a particular *situation* as being a certain way. In other words, someone who is in a conscious state is normally aware *of the worldly entities and occurrences she or he is dealing with*, and not of the conscious state she or he is in.

I believe that Schmid's point can be restated in such a way as to begin to respond to this sensible objection by claiming something along the following lines: in consciously dealing with the world, a mature human individual is normally at least pre-thematically aware that she or he is dealing with the world *as it is experienced by her or him*. That is to say, one's being in an experiential state is normally accompanied by some sense to the effect that one is having *a particular experience of an aspect of the world*. This sense that one has the world in view from one's particular perspective (or point of view) permits one to, for instance, consider the possibility that the circumstances one is facing may not really correspond to one's experience of the situation. This sense permits us, as we say, to take a step back from our own experiences. To be pre-reflectively and pre-thematically aware (in the sense of having some non-verbalized sense) that one is having a particular experience of the circumstance at issue is to interpret this experience (and not only this situation) as being a certain way. Let me try to further clarify the point by addressing the view I take Schmid to be drawing on when he suggests that an experience (a conscious sate) is typically structured by an implicit self-concept.

As far as this point is concerned, Schmid is presumably appealing to a view that is widely shared among phenomenologist. According to this view any intentional act of consciousness could be claimed to refer not only to an object of consciousness (this is something it does *qua intentional state*), but also to the particular 'stream of consciousness' it co-constitutes and, to this extent, to a particular subject

---

[17] According to Schmid, the solution he is offering to what I have called The Problem of Shared Feelings has already been outlined in the frame of the philosophical debate that followed Scheler's analysis of the phenomenon of immediate feeling-together.

(this is something it does *qua experiential act*). It is particularly important to understand that the point is not that every intentional state *has to have* a subject in the sense that it has to have *a bearer* whose necessary existence could be reflectively inferred or deduced (or who could be somehow introspectively encountered). In fact, when phenomenologists claim that all conscious states involve a sort of pre-reflective self-awareness, they are not claiming that our conscious acts invariantly involve an awareness of some additional intentional *object* we could call 'the self'. They are not claiming that our experiential acts involve an awareness of some transcendental entity that, to put it in the words of Dan Zahavi, '[exists] apart from, or above, the experience and [...] might be encountered in separation from the experience [at issue]' (2005, p. 126). As Zahavi stresses, in invoking this pre-reflective self-awareness, phenomenologists are rather pointing to *a quality* that is constant across all experiences one can have: they always *feel like* one's own experiences. My experiences, Zahavi writes, '[are] given immediately, noninferentially and noncritically as *mine*' (p. 124). This self-referential aspect, he submits, is a matter of the *first-personal mode* in which our experiences are given to us. Zahavi goes so far as to claim, drawing on Michel Henry, that what philosophers usually call the self is nothing more (and nothing less) than the very first-personal mode of givenness of the experiential phenomena (cf. p. 106).[18]

I believe that one could interpret Schmid's proposal as a proposal that, at the same time, elaborates on and questions the view just presented. Although the phenomenological account just sketched manages to spell out the intuition concerning some pre-reflective self-awareness that can be said to accompany every act of consciousness, this way of framing the issue in terms of a *sense of mineness* has the problem of making us blind to an important possibility—the possibility Schmid is after. Let me begin to state the point in a negative way by making the following observation: even if we were to agree that all our experiences involve a tacit self-reference and that this self-referential aspect is a matter of the first-personal mode in which an experience is given to the relevant subject, one could reject the idea that this self-reference is *necessarily* a matter of a sense of *mine*ness. The point is a rather simple one: the first-person perspective can be either singular or plural. So, at least in certain situations, the self-referential aspect of our experiences may be said to be a matter of a sense of *our*ness. This, I think, is the basic intuition on which Schmid's account is founded. But let us see how Schmid fleshes out the proposal just sketched.

As already mentioned, Schmid is exploring the idea that, at least in certain situations, the (phenomenal) subject may appear *in* the experience of an individual (better: of a number of individuals) in the form of a plural self-awareness.[19] Schmid

---

[18] Zahavi writes: 'An effective way to capture this basic point is to replace the traditional phrase "subject of experience" with the phrase "subjectivity of experience"' (p. 126). If I understand Zahavi correctly, the proposed term 'subjectivity of experience' refers to what Schmid calls the phenomenal subject.

[19] In a later paper, Schmid (2014a) coins the expression 'plural self-awareness' to refer to what I am calling here a sense of ourness. He is eager to differentiate this *pre-reflective* form of self-

captures this thought by means of a formula that is intended to describe the structure of every intentional feeling qua experiential act that (as such) involves some oblique reference to its subject. The formula runs as follows: 'S_A feels x *as had by* S_B' (2009, p. 78). The crucial point here is that S_A, the ontic subject, and S_B, the phenomenal subject, have the possibility to differ.

At this point, one could be absolutely puzzled by the implicit suggestion that drawing such a distinction could illuminate the idea of a genuinely joint feeling. Why is it that as soon as we distinguish between two possible senses of the expression 'subject of a feeling' the Problem of Shared Feelings becomes tractable?

Schmid's point is that we could safely assume that in at least some of those cases in which the (phenomenal) subject appears as a 'we-subject' *in* the affective experiences of a number of individuals—as a *subject-we*, as Schmid, drawing on Sartre, prefers to call it (cf. 2009, pp. 173ff.)—the conditions could be met under which these individuals would not be mistaken in taking their feelings to be shared by the other members of the relevant group of individuals. So the proposal is that we could begin to understand what is the case in a situation that merits being called a collective affective intentional episode by recognizing that we would be correct in asserting that the individuals involved in the relevant situation are sharing a feeling just in case *each of them* were to experience her or his feeling as had by *all of them together*. In other words, the way in which Schmid reveals the compatibility between the intuitions at issue—the intuition concerning the subjective nature of feelings and the intuition that emotions can be shared—is by pointing to the possibility of what we could call a *non-misleading sense of plural selfhood*.[20]

---

awareness from what is usually called self-reflection, 'an attitude in which a subject makes itself the object of its cognitive, affective, or practical considerations' (Schmid 2014a, p. 13). Self-awareness, Schmid writes, 'is not a proper intentional "act" that is directed towards the subject, but rather a feature, or component, of an intentional act that is directed towards whatever it is the subject happens to have in mind' (ibid.). Schmid argues that the sort of plural pre-reflective self-awareness that is at issue in a genuinely collective intentional act fulfills at the level of the group mind three roles self-awareness plays in the individual mind in unifying the mind and constituting selfhood. First, '[s]elf-awareness is the feature by which any of our occurrent beliefs, desires, feelings, or intentions present themselves to us *as ours*' (p. 15). Second, '[i]t introduces the distinction between what is "self" and what is not' (ibid.). Third, 'self-awareness is the driving force behind the *normatively unified mind* and thus constitutes proper beliefs and goal-directed attitudes in terms of commitments, and thus *our* kind of agency' (p. 16). Schmid summarizes by writing: 'Self-awareness is being aware of one's attitudes *as one's own*, as attitudes that are one's own perspective *on* something, and as one's own *commitments*' (pp. 16–17). The point is that at the level of the group mind plural self-awareness allows for *common* ownership, *shared* perspective, and *joint* commitment. In his book *Wir-Intentionalität* (2005), Schmid suggests that some ideas articulated in the context of the phenomenological tradition of thought may be read as pointing towards this idea of a plural pre-reflective self-awareness; an idea that, as he argues, may neutralize some of the central problems of plural subject theories (cf. the discussion in Sects. 3.2, 3.3 and 8.2). In Chap. 6 (particularly in Sect. 6.4), I shall tackle the issue of a pre-intentional structure of experience that might serve as a background for a participation in collective intentional episodes in terms of what, elaborating on Matthew Ratcliffe (2005, 2008), I shall call a feeling of being-together.

[20] It is by arguing for the possibility of what I am calling here a *sense of plural selfhood* (or a *sense of we-selfhood*)—and this is a notion that has to be differentiated from Gilbert's notion of a *plural*

Against this background, Schmid eventually proposes conceiving of those situations in which the mentioned conditions are met—the conditions under which the involved individuals would not be misguided by the sense of ourness that structures their feelings—as situations in which, in virtue of what he calls a 'phenomenological fusion of feelings' (cf. pp. 77ff.), the individuals' feelings come to constitute *a unique shared feeling*, as is required by a straightforward notion of a shared feeling.

Despite Schmid's attempts to defend it from a number of anticipated objections, the idea of a phenomenological fusion of feelings remains relatively obscure throughout the texts discussed here.[21] This should, however, not prevent us from appreciating the fundamental virtue of Schmid's proposal, which relies on its capacity to relieve us of the burden of having to determine (in advance) whether or not the idea of a plural subject *of* experience is a viable one. Independently of whether or not there can be something like a plural subject *of* feeling, at first sight at least, nothing speaks against the idea that a sense of plural selfhood can be episodically given *in* the experiences of a number of individuals who, under certain conditions, could be said to *really* be feeling something together (and not merely alongside each other).

In this order of ideas, one could read Schmid's proposal as an invitation to take the metaphysical problem he has carefully described less seriously—a problem which poses a challenge particularly to someone who believes that we have to conceive of a collective experience as a collective's experience. His insistence, however, that we have to understand a genuinely shared feeling as a unitary (token identical) experience could bring one to suspect that, by means of his notion of a phenomenological fusion of feelings, Schmid is seeking to calm the metaphysical worries of those who feel urged to show that in a collective affective intentional episode the group itself (understood as a supraindividual centre of intentionality) can be conceived as the bearer of the relevant affective experience. As already mentioned (at the end of the preceding chapter), I am inclined to accept this invitation I am attributing to Schmid—the invitation to avoid taking too seriously the metaphysical anxieties to which The Problem of Shared Feelings may be taken to point. Indeed, the proposal I am to develop in the second part of this book aims at showing that we can make sense of the idea of an authentically affective and, at the same time, genuinely joint response, without having to make plausible the idea of a unitary state of consciousness somehow constituted by the 'fused' feelings of the participants. But let me for the moment continue to reconstruct Schmid's proposal.

---

subject, which refers to the ontic subject of an experience—that Schmid is, in my view, extending the idea of a character of mineness that, according to Zahavi, *invariantly* accompanies my experiences and pointing to the possibility of a sense of ourness that can structure *some* of my experiences (and, in veridical cases, *does* structure *our* experiences).

[21] As far as I can see, Schmid does not spell out this notion of a phenomenological fusion of feelings in later texts, either. In a brief response to a remark along these lines I articulated in a paper (cf. Sánchez Guerrero 2014), Schmid (cf. 2014b, p. 10) states in reference to this notion of a phenomenological fusion of feelings that it simply captures the idea that the participants are pre-reflectively aware of their emotionally expressed concern *as theirs*.

In a next move, Schmid assesses the plausibility of his proposal concerning what a genuinely shared feeling amounts to. He does so by determining four conditions of adequacy any valid notion of a shared conscious states, in his view, has to meet.[22] He aims at showing that these are all conditions a notion of shared feelings based on the idea of a phenomenological fusion of feelings could conform to. In what follows I shall briefly describe the first three conditions of adequacy and devote some attention only to the fourth one.[23]

According to the first condition, any valid notion of shared feelings should be compatible with individual and 'veridical' forms of self-awareness; the point being that a plausible notion of shared feelings cannot require of the involved individuals to confound themselves with the other participating individuals or to feel dissolved in some sort of 'group consciousness'. Schmid makes this point concrete by arguing that in genuine cases of shared feelings the involved individuals are aware of the difference between the ontic and the phenomenal subject (cf. p. 80). In the texts I am discussing, Schmid does not tell us whether he takes this awareness of the difference between the ontic and the phenomenal subject to be a matter of one's having, *at the same time*, a sense that the experienced feeling is one we (the participants) share (in the relevant sense of the verb 'to share') *and* a sense that the feeling I am experiencing is a feeling of mine. An alternative would be to take the awareness of this difference to be a matter of one's *experiencing* this sharedness, i.e. of one's experiencing the relevant feeling as a feeling had by us (the participants), and *knowing* (in a way that does not involve immediate experiential givenness) that the feeling I directly experience can only be my own experience.[24] At a minimum, one could argue, each of the participants in a collective affective intentional episode should be able to *reflectively* understand her or his experience as an experience to which she or he 'serves' as its ontic subject, if the first condition of adequacy is to be fulfilled. It is important to note, however, that the possibility a person has to do

---

[22] Schmid declares to have taken up these conditions of adequacy from the debate immediately generated by Scheler's suggestion in the German-speaking philosophical scene.

[23] The reason for doing so is not only because Schmid himself explicates this fourth condition in a more detailed way, thereby anticipating some sensible objections to the idea of a phenomenological fusion of feelings. Rather, the reason to focus on the last condition is because in the next section (Sect. 4.4) I shall try to point to a question related to this fourth condition Schmid's proposal does not answer.

[24] This unclarity is presumably at the heart of Salmela's criticism of Schmid's argument. Salmela seems to think that one can only in an alternating (and mutually exclusive) way understand an experience either as my experience or as our experience. He writes: 'The first problem with Schmid's account concerns the phenomenological fusion of feelings. I believe that it is a contingent rather than a necessary condition of shared emotions. The main reason is phenomenological, namely the elusiveness of this experience. True enough, people may *pre-reflectively* interpret and experience their feelings as *your* or *our*, but such experience vanishes as soon as the ontological individual becomes *reflexively* aware of the feeling as *her* or *his*. This may happen any time during a fused experience, for, however initially interpreted as to its subject, I can always step back from my experience and recognize it as *mine*' (2012, p. 38). I cannot see a reason why we should exclude the possibility of having a sense that one's feeling that some worldly occurrence merits a response of a certain sort is part of *our* feeling that it does.

so is not necessarily based on her capacity to infer that the experience at issue 'belongs' to her. For it may be based on her having always already understood this experience (in a non-thematic way) as an experience of hers.[25] In other words, I think that Schmid would be inclined to argue for the idea that in a case of collective affective intentionality both senses just mentioned are *simultaneously* given in the experiences of the involved individuals. Indeed, one could argue that Schmid ought to be prepared to defend such a view, were he, in this point, too, to follow Scheler.[26]

The second condition of adequacy concerns the idea that any plausible notion of a shared feeling has to be compatible with the fact that a person who understands her feelings as feelings she shares with certain other individuals can always be mistaken. As Schmid points out, '[n]o feeling, however strongly felt, and however intimately connected one believes it to be to another person's life, provides infallible information about other people's feelings. In other words: no feeling is in itself the criterion of its being shared' (p. 78). Schmid emphasizes, however, that this fact concerning the capacity the sense of togetherness at issue has to mislead the subject of experience 'does not preclude [...] strong sharedness in cases where [the relevant] conditions (whatever they might be) are met' (p. 80). Schmid does not specify the conditions that have to be fulfilled, if one's sense of ourness can be claimed to be warranted. He writes:

> I expect that an analysis of the structure and presuppositions of these episodes [of phenomenological fusion of feelings] should also yield some insights into the independent truth conditions to which a feeling has to conform in order to count as shared in the straightforward sense. This is an issue not to be pursued further here (p. 80).

As we have seen, however, he clearly suggests that there definitively are (thinkable) situations in which these conditions could be fulfilled, i.e. situations in which one would not be misled by the sense one has to the effect that one is really sharing one's feeling with the other members of the relevant group.[27,28]

The third condition of adequacy mentioned by Schmid requires of a notion of shared feelings 'to leave room for the experience of (partial) separateness of our conscious lives' (p. 79). The point here is that the individuals involved cannot be required to share their *whole* stream of consciousness in order to share a feeling. Schmid appeals in this context to the notion of an *episode of consciousness*, which

---

[25] This interpretation is supported by Schmid's claim that '[s]elf-reflection only serves to make explicit the peculiar pre-reflective awareness characteristic of any kind of consciousness' (p. 77).

[26] Although in the relevant passage Scheler is speaking of love, and more precisely of a particular phase of love 'as it gradually re-emerges from the state of identification' ([1913] 2008, p. 71), he claims that 'there is built in, within the phenomenon itself, a clear-cut consciousness of two *distinct* persons' (ibid.).

[27] In Chap. 6 (particularly in Sects. 6.2 and 6.3), I shall address the issue as to what may be said to warrant our felt conviction, as I shall call it, that we are feeling in a joint manner.

[28] In response to a previous formulation of this critical review of his account (cf. Sánchez Guerrero 2011, 2014), Schmid (personal communication) has made me aware that I have erroneously asked for criteria that permit us to determine whether in a concrete case such a sense of ourness is warranted; the point being that we are not required to specify *empirical* criteria, but only truth conditions.

has to be differentiated from both a *state* and a *stream* of consciousness. He stresses that '[i]t is within shared intentional *episodes* that these phenomenological fusions of feelings occur' (p. 80).

Finally, Schmid submits that any plausible concept of shared feelings 'has to conform to the experience that very often (if not always), the sharedness of a feeling is a matter of the qualitative difference between the individual contributions' (p. 79). Schmid illustrates this point by considering the shared feeling of joy at the success of the first performance of a symphony. He writes:

> If the man at the triangle, the composer, some member of the audience and the stage manager take themselves to share a single feeling of joy, this is because in their perception of the situation, their individual feelings 'match' with that of the others rather than being qualitatively or even numerically identical. In order to be taken as 'matching', these feelings have to be taken as *different from each other* according to the different roles the participants play in the joint activity (ibid.).

In a last step, Schmid defends this picture of a collective affective intentional episode by anticipating, and responding to, two objections related to this image of 'matching feelings'. Let me close this section by briefly exposing Schmid's response to these objections.

The first objection Schmid considers could be stated as follows: if the feelings of the participating individuals are conceived of as 'matching' parts, which qua parts are *necessarily numerically different from each other*, it is hard to see in which sense these states could be said to amount to *one and the same* feeling.

Appealing to his distinction between the ontic and the phenomenal subject of a feeling, Schmid contends that there are two ways in which one could count the feelings involved in a case of collective affective intentionality. 'With regard to subject$_B$ [the phenomenal subject] (which is a "we"), the number is *one*. With regard to subject$_A$ [the ontic subject], the number is *two* (in the dyadic case)' (p. 81). There is no reason, Schmid argues, to consider one way of counting more legitimate than the other. He emphasizes, furthermore, that 'there is no legitimate way of counting that yields *three*' (ibid.); the point being that the shared feeling cannot be regarded as something that exists in addition to the individuals' feelings: this shared feeling is *constituted* by the feelings of the individuals involved. Schmid stresses this point by writing: 'The individuals' feelings *are* the one shared feeling insofar as the conditions under which individuals are not mistaken in experiencing their feelings as being shared by the other participants are met' (p. 81).

The second objection Schmid anticipates concerns the apparent incompatibility between the claim that the participants' feelings constitute a single shared feeling and the requirement established by Schmid's fourth condition of adequacy: the requirement concerning some awareness of the qualitative differences between the feelings involved. The problem is that, if there is only one feeling (constituted in the way just explained by the individuals' feelings), this feeling should be *the same feeling* for all the participating individuals. This sameness, so the objection goes, would preclude qualitative differences between the individuals' feelings.

Schmid replies to this objection in a succinct way by observing that the idea that a feeling can be shared in a non-metaphorical sense of 'sharing' leaves ample room for qualitative differences which may be understood as *aspects* of the whole (cf. p. 82). This suggestion might sound strange at first. But one could argue that, in claiming this, Schmid is just extending an intuition most philosophers involved in the debate on collective intentionality share: a joint action is quite often constituted by a number of individuals' actions (contributions) that are different in character.

By means of this remark, on which he does not elaborate further, Schmid concludes his account of shared feelings. We can, thus, sum up the main points of the proposal as follows. Schmid dissolves the apparent clash of intuitions to which The Problem of Shared Feelings boils down by showing that, at least in certain situations, feelings can be said to be shared in quite a strong sense of the verb 'to share'. He does so by developing an argument based on three considerations. First, qua intentional acts of consciousness, our emotional feelings exhibit a built-in self-referential aspect. Contrary to what is normally assumed (even by certain phenomenologists), this implicit self-reference is not always a matter of a sense of mineness. It is sometimes a matter of a sense of ourness; it is a matter of what Schmid (2014a) calls *plural self-awareness*. That is to say, in certain situations the phenomenal subject appears as a we-subject *in* the emotional experiences of a number of individuals who are feeling towards something. Second, there are situations, namely genuine cases of collective affective intentionality, in which the conditions are met under which the experiencing subjects are not mistaken in experiencing their feelings as feelings that are had by them (the participants in the relevant situation) together. Third, the sense of togetherness that characterizes the affective experiences of the individuals involved in a case of collective affective intentionality—a sense of togetherness that, as just mentioned is based on a plural form of self-awareness—is, up to some point at least, not disturbed by conceivable differences concerning the experiential quality of their respective feelings.

Schmid closes his 2008 paper by making the following concluding remark: 'there is no reason not to take the phenomenological turn in the philosophy of emotions to the collective level. Collective affective intentionality is a matter of shared feelings' (p. 84). Against the background of the argument just reconstructed, we can take this conclusion to involve at least two related, but differentiable, suggestions. These are suggestions that could both be argued to require some additional clarificatory efforts.

On the one hand, Schmid is explicitly claiming that collective affective intentionality is a matter of shared feelings. As straightforward as it might sound at this point of the discussion, this claim is not unequivocal. The problem is that the term 'feeling' is an ambiguous one—indeed, as we have seen above (particularly in Sect. 2.4), it involves a number of ambiguities. For, it can refer to the act of feelingly understanding a situation as being a certain way and meriting a certain sort of response, but it can also refer to a psychological state with a certain intentional content and a certain phenomenal quality. As I shall discuss at the end of the next section (Sect. 4.4), I believe that we can take a collective affective intentional episode to be a matter of a shared feeling in the former, but not in the latter, sense of 'feeling'. That is to say, I think that we can feel comfortable with the idea that at the heart of a collective affective intentional episode we always find a *joint act of feeling towards*, but not with the idea that the feelings of the individuals involved constitute a *unique experiential state* the relevant group (as a suprapersonal centre of sentience) can be said to be in. To be sure, I doubt that Schmid wants us to understand the 'result' of the alleged phenomenological fusion of feelings to be a single (emergent) supraindividual experiential state. He explicitly observes: 'Without doubt, the parents in Scheler's example are two different persons *each of whom has his or her own feelings*' (2009, p. 77; my emphasis). But as far as the distinction I am referring to is concerned, it seems to me that Schmid is not clear enough. He is certainly right in suggesting (along with Scheler) that there is a sense in which the intentional act of two individuals who are jointly actualizing what I call our capacity to feel-towards together can be understood as a single fact (cf. p. 74). In my view, however, he does not make sufficiently clear that what can be said to be a single fact is the joint emotional response, and not the experiential state.

On the other hand, Schmid's conclusion that we can take the phenomenological turn in the philosophy of emotions to the collective level could be argued to result 'sufficiently interesting' only against the background of a claim he makes concerning the philosophical duty of someone who aims at offering a phenomenologically adequate account of collective affective intentionality. I am referring to the claim that, in order to show that feelings are at the heart of collective affective intentionality, too, we are compelled to show that some of our affective experiences can be shared in a non-metaphorical sense of the verb 'to share'. I think that we should accept a particular interpretation of this requirement. We could agree that it is necessary to show that in a collective affective intentional episode the participants are taking part in one and the same moment of affective intentional community. But this challenge should be understood as the challenge to show that the participants' emotional responses can be taken to constitute one and the same joint act of feeling towards; a joint affective response to the demands posed by the world. For, as we have seen, it is doubtful enough that there is some plausible sense in which the participants' experiential states could be taken to constitute a single feeling experienced by the relevant collective as a supraindividual centre of sentience.

The conviction, however, that it is rather implausible to speak of a feeling that is experienced by the collective itself is not a reason to refrain from characterizing a situation in which the participants are emotionally responding to some worldly occurrence in a properly joint manner—and we, of course, have to clarify in the course of this inquiry what exactly this means—as a *genuinely collective* affective intentional response. Put another way, without having to make plausible the idea that certain groups can as such be understood as legitimate bearers of experiential states, we can defend the central picture of some individuals participating in *one and the very same* episode of collective affective intentionality.

Against this background, my general aim in the remainder of the present work is to show that in order to make room for the idea that feelings are at the core of collective affective intentionality, too, we are not required to 'finally' solve a particular *metaphysical* problem to which Schmid's discussion could be—erroneously—taken to ultimately point. Concretely, we are not urged to show that the feelings of the participants in a case of collective affective intentionality somehow come to constitute a unique experiential state that can be attributed to the relevant group as a particular entity.[29]

In order to motivate the view on collective affective intentionality that I am going to develop and defend in the second part of this book, in the last section of this chapter I shall formulate an, in my view, pressing question that could lead the next steps of our inquiry. Following a suggestion made by Schmid, in closing this last section I shall try to rearticulate the task to be accomplished in order to bring to light the fundamental role feelings play in collective affective intentionality.

4.4 Feeling Together that It Matters: An Attempt to Recast Our Philosophical Task

My intention in what follows is to reshape the philosophical task that has to be accomplished in order to provide a phenomenologically adequate account of collective affective intentionality. I shall do so by developing a discussion that intends to progressively crystallize a question apt to lead the rest of the present inquiry. This is a question to which Schmid's illuminating account of shared feelings does not offer a clear answer. The answer to this question can, however, be claimed to be fundamental for us to understand what it means for a number of individuals to participate in *one and the same* episode of collective affective intentionality.

I shall begin this discussion by trying to cast doubt on a common and prima facie plausible assumption. The assumption is that the emotions of the participants in a collective affective intentional episode are necessarily instances of the same kind of emotion. It is due to the fact, I believe, that he, in the end, uncritically accepts this assumption that, in the texts I have been discussing, Schmid does not come to pose (and try to answer) the question I shall try to articulate in this section.

As we have just seen, Schmid claims that the fact that we can assume some qualitative differences between the feelings of the participants in a case of collective affective intentionality does not threaten the idea of a phenomenological fusion of feelings. He argues that these qualitative differences may be understood as aspects of a whole, i.e. as different expressions of a singular shared feeling constituted by a number of individuals' experiences, which, as Schmid puts it, 'match' one another. I believe that it is this image of 'matching feelings' to which we should turn our attention. For, in order to get a clear grasp of what Schmid's proposal finally amounts

---

[29] I have been pointing to some unclarity in Schmid's account. I believe, however, that it is clear enough that Schmid is not after the idea that in a collective affective intentional episode there is some 'fused' feeling which is experienced by the relevant group *as a supraindividual centre of sentience*. As pointed out, the appeal to the idea of a plural *self-awareness* is intended to resist the pressure to, in order to account for the idea of a *genuinely collective* affective response, invoke a plural *subject* of emotion. If there is some sense in which Schmid could take the feelings that are at the heart of a collective affective intentional episode to be experienced by the collective *as such*, it presumably would amount to a thought along the following lines: an emotion experienced by a collective is an emotion experienced by the participants *as a collective*.

to, one needs to understand what it means for two or more qualitatively different affective states to 'match' one another.

Coming back to Schmid's example of the first performance of a symphony, imagine that Adrian, who is in the audience, is focused on his daughter, Beatrice, who is the composer of the symphony performed this night. He is not mistaken in considering that he shares with Beatrice a feeling which both of them would characterize as a joyful feeling of pride. That is to say, each of them (at least pre-reflectively and non-thematically) understands her or his affective experience as a feeling of joyful pride that is *experienced by both of them*. Moreover, each of them (at least pre-reflectively and non-thematically) understands her or his emotion as an experience that *non-accidentally* exhibits the same qualitative character she or he is taking the experience of the other to exhibit.[30] Thus, they both understand their joyful pride as an emotion that is *jointly felt by them*.

Imagine further that Cornelius, the conductor, has an affective experience he would characterize as a feeling of joyful satisfaction. This is a feeling he correctly takes himself to be sharing with the musician members of the orchestra, in the sense that, at the relevant moment, each of them is taking this feeling of joyful satisfaction to be an experience that is *jointly had by them*. Adrian, Beatrice, Cornelius, and the other members of the orchestra they all register the blissful atmosphere that reigns that night at the theatre, and are (at least unreflectively and non-thematically) aware of their *taking part in* and *contributing to* this emotionally rich situation.[31]

Now, in such a situation one might certainly be tempted to talk of a moment of affective community, i.e. of an episode in which the participants' feelings 'match' one another. One could wonder, however, whether it is justified to assert that all the involved individuals are participating in one and the same episode *of collective joy* (and not in one and the same episode *of collective pride* or *satisfaction*, for instance). On which grounds should one determine this? If each of the participants' feelings 'matches' with the feelings of all other individuals involved, how is one to decide which of them serves as the 'standard feeling' in relation to which the other feelings may be understood as varieties (or as aspects, as Schmid puts it)? What is more important, if the feelings at issue are understandable as experiences that instantiate emotions of different kinds, what is it exactly that brings them to 'match' one another?

---

[30] By 'non-accidentally' I mean that Adrian and Beatrice do not understand their experiences as experiences that *merely happen to converge*. We still have to elucidate (in the second part of this book) what characterizes such experiences—experiences structured by what I call a sense of togetherness.

[31] Here, I am elaborating on Schmid's example. Seeking to illustrate the idea of qualitative differences that can be assumed to exist between the feelings of the involved individuals—differences of which the involved individuals are aware—, Schmid writes: 'If the composer takes the man at the triangle and the member of the audience to share her joy, she will not, in her right mind, take them to experience her exuberant exaltation; rather, she will take the shared feeling to entail her own exuberant elation together with, for example, the audience member's delight, and the man at the triangle's silent satisfaction' (2009, p. 79).

Postponing the answer to these central questions, what in the course of this reflection seems to become clear is that qualitatively different affective states that 'match' one another are not necessarily comprehensible as instances of the same type of emotion. Indeed, it is relatively easy, I think, to imagine a situation in which the clearly non-type-identical emotions of two (or more) individuals may be plausibly said to 'match' one another in such a way as to emotionally connect these individuals to one another in the context of the relevant situation.

Suppose that someone is playing with a ball in the vicinity of a fragile object that Adrian and Beatrice particularly value. Both Adrian and Beatrice emotionally respond to the threat posed to the valued object by the flying ball. They do so, however, in completely different ways. Adrian turns in anger towards the person who is carelessly playing with the ball and shouts at her loudly, while Beatrice turns back in fear and closes her eyes.[32] Not only would we, in such a situation, probably assume some substantial qualitative differences between Adrian's and Beatrice's feelings. What is more, it would be utterly inaccurate to speak of a shared emotion here. But the significant fact is that both of them are responding emotionally and at least simultaneously to the threat posed to the integrity of one and the same object. Their individual emotional responses, one could say, make visible that this object has some value for both of them. So one could easily understand this situation as a situation in which the participants are *feeling together that the object or occurrence in question matters to them*. For this reason alone, I think, we could understand such a situation as a possible case of collective affective intentionality.[33]

The image of 'matching feelings'—an image to which Schmid appeals in order to defend the view that the feelings of the individuals involved in a collective affective intentional episode can be said to constitute a singular affective experience—can, thus, be argued to be evocative, but just too vague for us to understand what it is that brings the participants to (at least non-thematically) understand their affective experiences as experiences they have together. It seems that, in order to decide whether or not collective affective intentionality can be said to be a matter of shared feelings—and in order to understand what exactly this could mean—, we need an independent characterization of the idea of 'matching affective states'. Presumably because of the intuitive appeal of this image of 'matching feelings', however, in his initial proposal Schmid makes no effort whatsoever to explicate what it means for two or more qualitatively different emotional feelings to 'match' one another.

In the later version of his analysis of shared feelings, Schmid makes a remark that one could consider particularly illuminating in this respect. He articulates the relevant point in the course of a discussion of Bennett Helm's notion of an emotion's focus (cf. the discussion in Sect. 2.3). Interestingly enough, he does not argue,

---

[32] Here, I am extending an example offered by Bennett Helm (2001, p. 69).

[33] Let me emphasize that an additional condition is met in those situations in which the individuals involved can be taken to be feeling in a *genuinely joint* manner. For, *independently* valuing the object in question, Adrian and Beatrice could show the simultaneous affective response just described. This is the reason why I talk here of a *possible* case of collective affective intentionality. (I shall spell out the condition at issue in the second part of this book.)

as one might expect, that the different emotional feelings involved in what one could intuitively understand as a collective affective intentional episode may be said to 'match' one another just in case they could be understood as emotional feelings that have the same target, formal object, *and* focus. Schmid suggests that the sharing of the target, the formal object, and the focus may be understood as a sufficient condition for us to say that the individuals' feelings at issue constitute a unique shared feeling, but definitively not as a necessary one. Schmid supports this suggestion by analyzing what he takes to be a shared feeling of grief described at the end of Homer's *Iliad*. In the short extract Schmid is referring to, Homer describes Achilles' emotional response to an appeal made by King Priam. The passage is as follows:

> 'Respect the gods, Achilles, and take pity on me, remembering your own father. I am more piteous far than he, and have endured what no other mortal on the face of earth has yet endured, to reach out my hand to the face of the man who has slain my sons'. So [Priam] spoke, and in Achilles he roused desire to weep for his father; and he took the old man by the hand, and gently pushed him away from him. So the two remembered—the one remembered man-slaying Hector and wept loudly, collapsed at Achilles' feet, but Achilles wept for his own father, and now again for Patroclus; and the sound of their moaning went up through the house (Iliad, Book 24, 503–512; as quoted by Schmid 2009, p. 67).

Schmid observes that this simultaneous feeling of grief may be intuitively said to connect Achilles and King Priam to one another, despite the fact that Priam's feeling is directed towards his son, Hector, and Achilles' emotion towards both his father, Pelleas, and his friend, Patroclus. That is to say, despite the fact that the participants' emotions do clearly not have the same target. Schmid contends further that Priam's and Achilles' emotions cannot be said to have the same focus, either. In this context, he eventually makes an important suggestion concerning what probably brings us to take these feelings to constitute a shared feeling of grief; a feeling of grief that connects the individuals involved in the situation at issue. Schmid writes: 'If the feeling of grief connects the two, it is rather by means of the *concern* behind the target-focus relation' (2009, p. 68).[34]

The proposal I shall develop in the second part of this book heavily draws on what one could take to be an implicit claim of Schmid's analysis: that the individuals

---

[34] We are going to come back (in Sect. 5.2) to this important point concerning the role a particular concern plays in relating the target of an emotion to what Helm (2001) calls its focus; a point we already touched on (in Sect. 2.3). Let me recall the main idea by pointing out that what ultimately grounds the intelligibility of a particular emotion is the significance or worthiness the focus of this emotion has for the relevant subject—who has, correspondingly, to be understood as a being able to care about the particular background object that constitutes the focus of this emotion. Schmid makes the point as follows: 'For a focus-target relation to rationalize the mode of a feeling [...] there has to be an additional feature in place: the subject has to have some *concern* that serves to make the relation between focus and target *relevant* to the subject. If a person simply doesn't *care* about her own well-being, or about the safety of children, the fact that a dog might attack her, or the children, does not rationalize her feeling of fear. Insofar as they involve a concern, [emotional] feelings are an indicator of what *matters* to us' (p. 65). As we shall see (in Sect. 5.2), according to Helm, emotional feelings are not merely an indicator of the worthiness certain things have for the subject of emotion. Rather, they co-constitute this significance.

involved in a case of collective affective intentionality can always be said to share a particular concern. As for the example offered by Schmid, however, I have to admit that I am puzzled by the suggestion that the scene narrated by Homer could be understood as a situation in which the participants are affectively linked to one another in the way captured by Scheler's notion of an immediate feeling-together. I agree that this scene can be easily understood, as Schmid puts it, as an 'affective meeting of minds' (p. 67), but this is much too unspecific. Schmid analyzes the sort of affective connectedness that is at issue here as follows:

> Priam's grief for his son combines with Achilles' grief for his father's abandonment so as to move Achilles to an act of goodwill towards Priam *because Achilles recognizes his own concern with Pelleas' being deprived of Achilles in Priam's grief for the loss of Hector.* In order to do so, however, Achilles has to move from Pelleas to fathers *in general.* This involves reconceiving of himself *as a son* rather than as Achilles, and that means a shift in the phenomenal subject of his affective attitude. This fits nicely with the usual interpretation that is given of the Iliad, according to which the whole epos is about Achilles' affective withdrawal from his community in wrath in books 1–17, his acting out of purely *individual feelings* in books 18–23, and his finally being able to feel *as a human being* again in his sympathy with Priam in book 24 (p. 68).

But if this is what brings Achilles and Priam to feel connected to one another, the connectedness at issue here turns out to be a matter of Achilles' capacity to (by means of a series of abstractions) 'put himself in the shoes of Priam'. At best, we can speak here, thus, of a case of sympathy 'about something' (cf. the discussion in Sect. 1.1). As Schmid emphasizes, there is, at any rate, no object that can be understood as the shared focus of both Priam's and Achilles' emotions. So Priam and Achilles cannot be taken to, by means of their emotions, express that some particular object is valuable for both of them.[35] That is to say, their affective responses are, at best, motivated by extremely similar concerns. To put it briefly, although their emotions have the same formal object, it is not clear that we can assert that Priam and Achilles are responding to some worldly occurrence in a genuinely joint, and not merely in a sympathetic or merely concordant, manner. Schmid seems to think that what ultimately connects them is the fact that they understand each other as beings that can be deeply concerned about the wellbeing of a beloved person. However, if this is what connects them, then King Priam and Achilles can be claimed to be sharing a concern in a very weak sense of the verb 'to share'. Their connectedness waters down to their being aware that they are experiencing the same *type* of care-expressive-suffering, as we may call it, or to their being aware that they share a care-defined mode of being, as I shall put it below (cf. the discussion in Sect. 5.3). Their affective connectedness, to put it another way, is exhausted by their being aware that they can both, as Schmid writes, feel *as a human being* and care about certain sorts of things or occurrences.

---

[35] At this point of the discussion we cannot agree (yet) that this is a requirement a situation has to fulfill in order to be understandable as a collective affective intentional episode. Schmid explicitly—but, in my view, erroneously—claims that it is not. At any rate, a shared concern about some particular object cannot be what, in this situation, brings the participants' minds to 'affectively meet'.

But even if, as I have just argued, there are some reasons to doubt that this scene of the Iliad depicts a situation in which two individuals are actualizing their ability to feel-towards together, one could be tempted to read Schmid's proposal as an attempt to answer the pressing question I have been trying to articulate throughout this section. In other words, one could think that Schmid's intention in pointing to a shared concern is to explicate what it means for two (or more) qualitatively different affective states to be understandable as 'matching feelings'. It is, however, important to be aware that Schmid simply does not have to look for such an explication. We can begin to understand the reason why he does not feel urged to do so by specifying the aim of the argument just exposed. Schmid is trying to show that there is no need for a collective affective intentional state to be constituted by feelings that have the same target (and the same focus) as long as the involved individuals are connected by the concern behind the target-focus relation of their emotions. In claiming so, Schmid is casting doubt on a plausible intuition: that the feelings that are part of a collective affective intentional response are always directed towards one and the same worldly object or occurrence. Observe, however, that he at no point questions a second intuition concerning what is required for us to talk of a case of collective affective intentionality. This is an intuition we have already become suspicious of above, namely that the feelings of the individuals involved have necessarily to have the same formal object. So the reason why Schmid does not feel compelled to spell out the idea of two qualitatively different feelings that 'match' one another, one could think, is because he, in the end, accepts an assumption that makes such an effort redundant. He seems to believe that we would be justified in speaking of 'matching feelings' just in case the affective states of the involved individuals could be regarded as instances of the same *sort* of emotion. Put another way, Schmid may be accused of assuming that only a case of shared emotion can be understood as a case of collective affective intentionality.

This view that every single case of collective affective intentionality amounts to a situation in which an emotion of a particular kind comes to be shared by a number of individuals is definitively supported by the way we usually talk about the affective interpersonal connections that concern us here. We normally say that we are, for instance, feeling joy together or feeling sorrow together, and not simply that we are feeling together (unless it is already clear what sort of emotion it is that we are feeling together). Moreover, the intuition that two or more individuals that participate in an episode of collective affective intentionality are necessarily experiencing emotions that have the same (or a sufficiently similar) character certainly amounts to an idea most philosophers interested in the topic would not even find worth debating. As we have seen (in Sect. 3.3), Konzelmann Ziv takes this idea to amount to a 'seemingly trivial' condition. In light, however, of the findings of the short analysis offered above—the analysis concerning a situation in which two individuals are responding in emotionally different ways to the threat faced by an object they both value—, we should consider the possibility of at least having to suspend the intuition that 'matching' affective states have to have the same formal object. Furthermore, seeking to meet the challenge posed by this finding, we could appeal to Schmid's suggestion and try to elaborate on the idea that what we find at the root of any genuine case of collective affective intentionality is a shared concern (or set of concerns).

I believe that, by elaborating on this motive of a shared concern, we could bypass the assumption that collective affective intentionality is necessarily a matter of sharing feelings of the very same emotional sort. Moreover, we could do so in such a way as to avoid having to deny that there is a sense in which those cases of collective affective intentionality that can also be understood as cases of a shared emotion (of a particular kind) could be seen as exemplary (or, if you prefer, ideal) cases of collective affective intentionality. In other words, by elaborating on the suggestion that at the root of a collective affective intentional act we always find a shared concern, it is possible to explain why *not every single instance* of the phenomenon of collective affective intentionality has to correspond to a case of shared emotion. In particular, it is possible to specify the condition under which a number of individuals who, in virtue of affective states that do not instantiate the same type of emotion, are intentionally directed towards a given occurrence can be taken to participate in one and the same moment of affective intentional community.

Seeking to exploit the thought that what a number of individuals ultimately share, when they come to jointly actualize their ability to feel-towards together, is the significance a given object, occurrence, or situation has for them, in the remainder of this book I shall defend the view that collective affective intentionality may be understood in terms of interrelated acts of feeling that are directed towards something the individuals involved *jointly care about*. By these means I shall show that, in order to take the phenomenological turn in the philosophy of emotions to the collective level, we do not have to make plausible the idea that the feelings of the participants in a collective affective intentional episode could be taken to constitute a single experiential state. In order to develop a phenomenologically adequate account of collective affective intentionality, I shall try to show, it is sufficient to elucidate the sense in which a collective affective intentional episode may be claimed to be a matter of some *joint act* of feeling-towards. In closing this chapter, I would like to clarify what the proposal just outlined aims at showing and how it is related to—what, in my view, differentiates it from—the analysis we have discussed in this chapter.

In this section I have tried to motivate my approach to the phenomenon of collective affective intentionality by pointing to a particular question Schmid does not answer in his inspiring analysis of shared feelings. As I have argued, this is a question he presumably does not even deem it necessary to pose. The question is: what does it mean for two or more emotional feelings to 'match' one another in such a way as to bring the bearers of these feeling to participate in one and the same moment of affective intentional community? I believe that only after having answered a further question we will be in a position to differentiate in a principled way a set of feelings that, in the sense that is relevant here, 'match' one another from a set of feelings that do not. This further question can now be articulated as follows: what does it mean for two (or more) individuals to, by means of their acts of feeling towards, bring to light that they share a concern in a sufficiently demanding sense of the verb 'to share'?

Although these are questions that do not guide Schmid's account of shared feelings, there definitively is much more in common than there are differences between the account just reviewed and the suggestions I am going to articulate in the remainder of this book. If there really is some fundamental disagreement, it probably waters down to a point I have already touched on. Schmid seems to think that his phenomenologically inspired solution is able to calm the philosophical anxieties of someone who is profoundly puzzled by a metaphysical issue the Problem of Shared Feelings may be taken to ultimately point to: the idea that there is some 'fused' experiential state that can be understood as the feeling of the group as such.

This is something I doubt. My goal, however, is not to calm these metaphysical worries by other means. My way of elaborating on (and radicalizing) Schmid's insight is rather based on the idea that something we can learn from Schmid's account is precisely that, in order to make room for the intuition that is central here, we do not have to *finally* calm these metaphysical anxieties. I am referring to the intuition that at the heart of a collective affective intentional episode we find feelings towards that can be argued to be shared in a strong sense of 'sharing'.[36] This is the reason why I am not going to discuss the extent to which the image of a phenomenological fusion of feelings may be taken to clarify the status of groups as legitimate subjects of feeling. Moreover, this is an image I shall completely abandon in my attempt to elaborate on Schmid's proposal. I shall rather try to show that, leaving aside the image of a fused emotional experience, it is possible to offer an account of collective affective intentionality that fulfills two basic conditions of adequacy we have repeatedly touched on throughout this discussion. Concretely, it is possible to, firstly, offer an account apt to show that acts of feeling-towards are central to the phenomenon of collective affective intentionality, and secondly, formulate a condition by reference to which we could tell apart those situations in which the individuals involved are jointly actualizing their ability to feel-towards together from those other situations in which they merely are feeling alongside each other.[37]

---

[36] It seems to me that those philosophers who, like Huebner and Gilbert, maintain that we can speak of a genuinely collective intentional state just in case the collective *itself* can be understood as the ontic subject of the intentional state at issue—and these are the philosophers I am alluding to when I talk of someone who is profoundly puzzled by the metaphysical problem posed by the idea of a genuinely collective feeling—would only be satisfied with a proposal that shows that the intuition concerning the profoundly subjective character of feelings is compatible with the idea of a plural subject of emotion (as opposed to merely being compatible with the phenomenological idea of a non-misleading sense of plural selfhood that structures some of our emotional experiences). This is what I mean by 'finally' solving the metaphysical problem of collective emotions. One of the reasons why we could feel comfortable with a strategy that 'continues to suspend' the mentioned metaphysical issue is because it is an open issue—one which will probably not be settled soon—whether or not we, in general, necessarily have to conceive of a collective intentional state as a collective's intentional state.

[37] Any theory of collective affective intentionality should, for reasons discussed throughout the first part of this book, be able to explain in which sense the involved individuals may be taken to participate in a *joint* emotional response, in a *joint* act of felt understanding. To avoid some problematic implications of the idea that the involved individuals participate in one and the same *emotional experience*—an idea that could be taken to suggest that there is some feeling at the group level, which could be experienced by the group as a supraindividual centre of sentience—it is advisable to talk of one and the same *episode* of collective affective intentionality. We can, thus, articulate the idea concerning the token-identity of the relevant act of feeling, which is fundamental for us to differentiate situations in which a number of individuals are feeling together from situations in which they are feeling alongside each other, in terms of a participation in *one and the same moment of affective intentional community*.

In the remainder of this work I shall, as just mentioned, basically elaborate on Schmid's insight concerning the fundamental role the sharing of a particular concern plays in the situations we are interested in. I shall do so, however, by developing a suggestion I believe to find in the work of Bennett Helm (2008). The suggestion is that collective affective intentionality could be understood in terms of *interdependent acts of feeling towards* that disclose and co-constitute the significance a given occurrence has for the involved individuals *qua members of a group*. In this context, I shall show that we can elucidate the sense in which feelings can be claimed to be at the heart of a collective affective intentional episode by conceiving of collective affective intentionality as a phenomenon grounded in our human ability to share an evaluative perspective.

Part II
Caring with One Another: A Proposal Concerning Our Ability to Feel Together

Chapter 5
Affectively-Enabled Shared Belongingness to the World

Abstract This chapter articulates a proposal concerning what it means for a number of individuals to respond in an authentically affective and properly joint manner. It does so by elaborating on Schmid's insight pertaining to the fundamental role the sharing of a concern plays in situations in which two or more individuals come to jointly actualize their ability to feel-towards together. By discussing Bennett Helm's account of emotions as felt evaluations, I lay down some theoretical foundations needed to develop the following idea: collective affective intentionality could be understood in terms of interdependent acts of feeling that disclose and co-constitute the significance a given occurrence has for the participants qua members of a particular group, i.e. in terms of interdependent acts of feeling that disclose a shared evaluative perspective. Against this background, I begin to anchor the notion of collective affective intentionality in Martin Heidegger's theme of a care-defined human mode of being by arguing that human intentionality may be understood in terms of an essentially shareable (but not necessarily collective) openness to the world. Appealing to another set of Heideggerian themes rearticulated by Matthew Ratcliffe, I discuss the role certain feelings play in setting up this essentially shareable relatedness to the world. This allows me to characterize our human openness to the world as an affectively enabled and essentially shareable world-belongingness. By means of this argument I prepare a claim that is central to the spirit of my proposal: the affective acts that actualize our ability to feel-towards together express in an outstanding manner our human nature.

Keywords Affective attunement • Affectively enabled world-belongingness • Care-defined existence • Collective emotional response • Existential feelings • Feeling-towards together • Felt Evaluation • For-the-sake-of-which • Import • Shareable world-belongingness • Shared concern • Shared evaluative perspective

5.1 Introduction

In the first part of this book I addressed the philosophical challenge posed by an idea that in pre-theoretical thought may appear unproblematic. I am referring to the idea of a number of individuals responding in a properly affective and, at the same time, genuinely joint manner. We saw in this first part that the main difficulty one faces

© Springer International Publishing Switzerland 2016
H.A. Sánchez Guerrero, *Feeling Together and Caring with One Another*,
Studies in the Philosophy of Sociality 7, DOI 10.1007/978-3-319-33735-7_5

while explicating what it means for two or more individuals to feel *together*, and not merely alongside each other, consists in elucidating what it means for the participants to really *feel* together—as opposed to jointly understanding in a purely cognitive manner—that something is a particular way and merits a response of a certain sort. This first part ended with a chapter that addressed a very specific philosophical problem which, according to Hans Bernhard Schmid, has to be solved if we are to offer a phenomenologically adequate account of collective affective intentionality: The Problem of Shared Feelings (Sect. 4.2). Having gone over the main points of Schmid's attempt to solve this problem (Sect. 4.3), I pointed to a pressing question that arises with regard to his proposal (Sect. 4.4). This is the question as to what exactly it means for two (or more) qualitatively different feelings to 'match' one another. In a diagnostic spirit, I argued that the reason why Schmid does not feel urged to pose and answer this question in his original contribution is because he, in the end, accepts a common assumption. The assumption is that we can speak of a collective affective intentional episode just in case the involved individuals' emotional feelings can be taken to have the same formal object; the point being that it is this concordance of their formal object that in a case of collective affective intentionality brings the participating individuals' feelings to 'match' one another. In other words, Schmid points to the possibility that feelings of phenomenologically different qualities have to be understood as constituents of one and the same collective affective intentional act. However, he could be accused of taking for granted that only an episode of shared emotion, i.e. an episode in which an emotion of some particular kind is shared, can be understood as an episode of collective affective intentionality. Having called into question this assumption, I maintained that, in order to come to offer a qualified answer to the question I pointed to, we could appeal to a suggestion Schmid may be taken to himself make in a later version of his analysis of shared feelings: at the heart of a collective affective intentional episode we always find a shared concern; the idea being that this is what ultimately brings the participants' feelings to 'match' one another.

The second part of the book articulates a proposal concerning what it means for a number of individuals to respond in an authentically affective and properly joint manner. In this chapter and the next one I shall begin to do so by elaborating on Schmid's insight pertaining to the fundamental role the sharing of a concern may be taken to play in those situations in which two or more individuals come to jointly actualize their ability to feel-towards together. I shall frame this proposal by laying down some theoretical foundations needed to develop, in the next chapters of this book, the following idea: collective affective intentionality could be understood in terms of interdependent acts of feeling that disclose and co-constitute the significance a given occurrence has for the participants qua members of a particular group. In the course of my attempt to develop this view, I shall show that, in order to make room for the idea that feelings are at the heart of collective affective intentionality, too, we are not required to finally solve the metaphysical issue Schmid's Problem of Shared Feelings may be (mistakenly) argued to point to. As I shall show, it is possible to advance our understanding of the basic nature of our ability to participate in moments of affective intentional community, without having to explicate the sense in which the feelings involved in a case of collective affective intentionality may be taken to constitute a token-identical experiential state. In particular, we do not have to make sense of the idea of a sort of suprapersonal centre of sentience that could be understood as the bearer of such an experiential state.

The structure of this chapter is as follows. In a first step (Sect. 5.2), I shall discuss Bennett Helm's analysis of the double role emotions play in disclosing and co-constituting the significance something has for us. Thereby I shall prepare the claim that in a collective affective intentional episode the emotional responses of the involved individuals may be taken to make visible that these individuals share an evaluative perspective. In a second move (Sect. 5.3), I shall begin to anchor the notion of collective affective intentionality in Martin Heidegger's theme of a care-defined human mode of being. I shall do so by trying to make plausible the idea that human intentionality, in general, may be understood in terms of an essentially share-able (but not necessarily collective) openness to the world. Appealing to another set of Heideggerian themes recently rearticulated by Matthew Ratcliffe, in a third step (Sect. 5.4), I shall discuss the fundamental role certain feelings may be said to play in setting up this essentially shareable relatedness to the world. This last move will allow me to characterize our human openness to the world as an affectively enabled and essentially shareable world-belongingness. By means of this argument I shall prepare a claim that is central to the spirit of the present proposal. The claim is that the affective acts that actualize our ability to feel-towards together express in an outstanding manner our human nature.[1]

5.2 Coming to Be Affected by Some Occurrence and Caring About Something

In this section I shall try to lay down some theoretical foundations needed to expli-cate the sense in which it can be asserted that actualizing one's ability to feel-towards together is a matter of expressing in an emotional way that one shares certain concerns with concrete others. The central aim of this discussion is to pre-pare a suggestion on which I shall elaborate in the remainder of this work. This is a suggestion I take Bennett Helm (2008) to be making in his account of *plural robust agents*. The proposal is that in an episode of collective affective intentionality the participants' emotions may be argued to make visible that these individuals share an evaluative perspective on something. The way in which I am going to lead up to this preliminary conclusion is by discussing some ideas that Helm (2001) develops in the context of his illuminating work on emotional reason. These are ideas that per-tain to the dual role feelings can be said to play in *disclosing* and *co-constituting* the significance something has.

---

[1] The argument developed in this chapter makes use of a number of ideas and formulations I origi-nally articulated in Sánchez Guerrero (2011, 2014).

In his book *Emotional Reason: Deliberation, Motivation and the Nature of Value* (2001), Helm aims at solving two problems of practical reason he respectively calls the *motivational problem* and the *deliberative problem*.[2] His analysis begins with a diagnosis that concerns the sui generis character of affective intentionality.[3] Helm suggests that these two problems are based on the assumption that every intentional state may be said to have one (and only one) of two possible directions of fit. He calls this assumption 'the cognitive-conative divide' (cf. 2001, pp. 4ff.).

Helm makes an effort to solve the targeted problems by showing that our emotions could, in a sense, be conceived of as intentional states that have *both* directions of fit.[4] He does so by arguing for the idea that human emotions are best understood as kinds of *evaluative feelings*; the point being that qua evaluative feelings our emotions may be understood as 'unitary states of assent and motivation' (p. 60).

Helm begins to explicate this claim that we should conceive of our emotions as evaluative feelings by suggesting that 'to feel an emotion is to be pleased or pained by the import of one's situation' (p. 62).[5] This way of understanding human emotions, Helm argues, allows us to accommodate the common view that emotions typically have a distinct phenomenal character. In so doing, it permits us to account for *the emotionality of emotions*. In other words, appealing to this characterization of our emotions, we can begin to elucidate 'what is distinctive of emotions as the kind of mental state they are' (p. 38). Furthermore, this way of conceiving of emotions allows us to understand in which sense our emotional feelings may be said to be acts that passively actualize a receptive capacity. Helm writes: 'in feeling an emotion, the import of one's situation *impresses itself upon one*, pleasing or paining one' (p. 60; my emphasis). Finally, this view permits us to conceive of an emotion as an experiential state that involves a particular sort of *evaluative content*, without having to construe our emotions as essentially cognitive states. In conceiving of human emotions as kinds of pleasures and pains, we begin to explicate the idea that an emotion is neither merely a reaction to certain worldly occurrences nor a cognitive evaluation, but an intentional act proper, which as such can be said to have some world-related evaluative content, the nature of which, however, is eminently affective. Put another way, this idea that emotions are sorts of pleasures and pains allows us to elucidate the extent to which our emotions can be claimed to be feelings that typically are about some particular situation.

---

[2] Helm is interested in elucidating the relation that holds between a person's choosing something in a deliberative way and her being motivated to pursue it (*the motivational problem*). Helm finds it puzzling how deliberation about value is possible at all, given that, as he puts it, 'our concept of value is pulled in seemingly opposed directions of objectivity and subjectivity' (2001, p. 200) (*the deliberative problem*). I am not going to deal with these problems here. For a review of how Helm tackles these issues, see Hursthouse (2002).

[3] For a brief exposition of the view of affective intentionality developed in the book just mentioned, see Helm (2002).

[4] To be sure, Helm appears to be rather skeptical about the very idea of a direction of fit.

[5] The technical term 'import' is intended to denote any 'worthiness imparted by a subject's concern for something' (Helm 2001, p. 49). This is a term Charles Taylor (cf. 1985, p. 48) introduced to the contemporary philosophical discussion on emotions.

Now, one certainly could take Helm to merely be articulating an ancient intuition in a new format: the intuition that the intentional content of an emotion is essentially evaluative in nature (cf. the discussion in Sects. 2.2 and 2.3). In the course of his defense of the view just outlined, however, Helm comes to make an absolutely original suggestion concerning the sense in which our emotions may be claimed to typically involve some evaluative content. He suggests that qua pleasures and pains of different sorts, our emotions could be said to involve evaluative content in a twofold way: first, as *responsive to*, and second, as *constitutive of* import.

This crucial thought that our emotions cannot be understood as mere responses to, but have to be seen as states that constitute the value, significance, or worthiness something has—a worthiness which, as Helm emphasizes, is 'imparted by a subject's concern for something' (p. 49)—allows us to clarify an issue which I have claimed above to be absolutely fundamental. This issue concerns the idea that our emotions may be said to be grounded in, and to express, what we could call *a personal view of the world* (cf. the discussion in Sect. 2.2). In this respect, Helm is eager to emphasize that any question concerning the *real* import of something has to be understood as a question concerning the import this object or occurrence *really has to someone*—a concrete subject of concern.

A first difficulty arises soon in this context. This is a difficulty that could be stated in such a way as to articulate a boundary condition of the idea of a subject responding to something in an emotional way. The issue is as follows: if we are to make sense of the idea that our emotions are responsive to the worthiness something has (in the sense of being apt to disclose the import some particular object or project has), we have to understand this import as something that exhibits an objective character.

Helm solves this critical issue by showing that the import something has can be said to be *at the same time subjective and objective*. He does so by defending the following thought: although the idea of something having import only makes sense in reference to the perspective of a concrete subject of concern, the import a particular object or project has is something about which this subject can be right or wrong. Helm's argument is based on an analogy he draws between the ontological statuses of import on the one hand and secondary qualities on the other.[6] Helm begins this argument by observing that, although secondary qualities are not objective in the way primary qualities are—for, as he writes, 'their existence is intelligible only in terms of their being the objects of a certain sort of awareness, a certain perspective on the world' (p. 52)—, we normally do not understand them as qualities that have been *merely projected* onto the world by a particular intentional state. As he remarks, it would be misleading to assert that secondary qualities do not really exist, although it is plausible to suggest that 'if we were to transcend the perspective afforded by our experiences we would be unable to make sense of their existence' (ibid.). The reason is because, given the possibility of the relevant perceptual experiences, we can take secondary qualities to be something that 'we might discover, or mistakenly seem to discover, *in the world*' (ibid.; my emphasis). Secondary qualities, hence, are

---

[6] Helm's solution draws on an argument developed by John McDowell (1985).

properties that are subjectively *ascribed* to objects, but these properties can be *correctly* or *incorrectly* ascribed to these objects on the basis of the object's disposition to present certain perceptual appearances. Helm suggests that the import something has to us is akin to secondary qualities in that it is, on the one hand, *perspectivally subjective*, and on the other, *objectively discoverable*.

One could certainly be inclined to object at this point that we tend to understand the value something has (for someone) as something that is *entirely* relative to the individual at issue and, in this sense, more subjective, as it were, than secondary qualities are. Helm replies to this sensible objection by arguing that we can conceive of the import things have as something that has an objective character in a very concrete sense: the import things have normally serves as a 'standard of warrant' for our assent to the view of the world our emotions present. This is an idea that requires some clarificatory efforts.

The first thing I find worth remarking is that Helm's claim that import has the sort of objective character just mentioned can be said to be related to a point I have emphasized above (in Sects. 2.2 and 2.3): we normally conceive of our emotions as responses that in light of concrete circumstances (in the context of which they have come to be elicited) can be said to be either appropriate or inappropriate, proportionate or disproportionate, or, as Helm prefers to write, warranted or unwarranted. The point is that the objective character of the significance something has for a given person becomes visible when one reflects on the role an appeal to this import can play in those situations in which one is trying to make sense of some of this person's behaviors as genuine emotional responses or actions out of emotion. Helm develops this idea by reframing the notion of a formal object in terms of what defines the kind of import to which an emotion is responsive. He writes: 'What makes an emotion be the kind of emotion it is and so distinguishes it from other kinds of emotion is the way in which the emotion construes the target as having a kind of import' (p. 34). It is important to understand that Helm's suggestion is not simply that we can define the formal object of a particular emotion in terms of the kind of import to which this particular emotion can be argued to respond. Rather, the point is that we can *assess the warrant of an emotion* by considering the kind of import to which it is responsive. Helm writes: 'an emotion is *warranted* just in case the target of the emotion has, or intelligibly seems to have, the import defined by the emotion's formal object' (p. 64).[7]

---

[7] In this context, Helm makes an important observation concerning the circular foundational relation that holds between the claim that a particular emotion has this or that formal object and the claim that it instantiates a particular kind of emotion. This circularity, he observes, is of a non-vicious sort. We simply cannot take our understanding of the formal object of an emotion to be prior to our understanding of this emotion as instantiating a particular kind of emotion. Nor can we take our understanding of what it is to experience an emotion of a particular kind to be prior to our understanding of the formal object that defines this kind of emotion. Helm makes the point as follows: 'one cannot have a prior understanding of what it is to be afraid (or embarrassed) and only subsequently come to understand what it is for something to be dangerous (or embarrassing); conversely one cannot have a prior understanding of what it is for something to be dangerous (or embarrassing) and only subsequently come to understand what it is to be afraid (or embarrassed).

Observe that, in line with the view of affective intentionality I recommended above (in Sects. 2.2, 2.3 and 2.4), Helm is conceiving of our emotional responses not as mere reactions to worldly events, but as ways of *tacitly assenting* to a particular view of the world. Indeed—and this brings us to the second point I find worth emphasizing—, the key to understanding Helm's idea of import serving as a standard of warrant is to understand that it is *the assent to the view of the world* a particular emotion presents, and *not the mere appearance of the world*, that can be evaluated as warranted or unwarranted. A particular emotion can only be said to be warranted (given the concrete circumstances in the context of which it arises) if this emotional assent can be said to *reflect* the import things really have to the subject in question.

Helm suggests that this notion of an emotional assent is 'thinner' than the notion of a judgment. He highlights two fundamental differences between judgments and emotional assents. The first difference could be articulated by pointing out that judgments are normally understood as *active exercises* of what Kant calls our spontaneity. This is so to the extent to which '[t]o make a judgment is to do something *actively*, consciously, and (for the most part) freely' (Helm 2001, p. 65). On the contrary, we should conceive of emotional assents as *passive actualizations* of the spontaneity that is operative in our receptive capacities—to use a McDowellian expression. Emotional assents are 'states of consciousness that for the most part come over us in a way very much like that of perception' (p. 66). The second difference Helm stresses pertains to the idea that ordinary judgments involve cognitive assents, which are assents to the existence of certain features of concrete objects or occurrences. This is an existence that is normally thought to be independent of the subject's pattern of assents. As we have seen, the kind of assent that is proper to human emotions is, in contrast, disclosive of the import things have to the subject of experience. An emotional assent brings to light the subject's evaluative point of view of the occurrences at issue. This point of view is not independent, but, on the contrary, partially constituted by those very emotional assents that disclose it.

But one could certainly wonder in which sense exactly our emotions may be said to constitute the import they are responsive to. Moreover, in the face of the thoughts just discussed one could find this idea profoundly puzzling. For it seems that in order to serve as a standard of warrant to our emotional assents, the import things have has to exist *independently* of the particular emotions that disclose it. Furthermore, if it makes sense to suggest that, in experiencing an emotion, the import of an object 'impresses itself on us', then this import must be *prior* to our emotional responses to the relevant occurrences.

Helm dismantles this sensible objection by distinguishing between the import-assenting role *a particular emotional response* may be said to play and the import-constituting role *a number of emotions* could be taken to play in virtue of their constituting a coherent ensemble of evaluative attitudes. Taken alone, he observes,

---

Rather, an understanding of the formal object and the emotion can only come simultaneously *if either is possible*. Such a circularity is not vicious but is rather a feature of the kind of perspectival subjectivity import, and so the formal object of an emotion, have' (pp. 63–64; my emphasis).

a particular emotion can often be understood as a response to the specific kind of import something, in a sense, already has. But in order to make sense of the idea that our emotions constitute this very import to which they are responsive, we have to look at them in a different way, namely as constituents of a coherent pattern of evaluative attitudes tied together by rational connections. Let me begin to explicate this important claim by making explicit the theoretical background of Helm's view of affective intentionality, namely Donald Davidson's holistic view of the realm of the mental.

At the very beginning of his analysis, Helm brings into play a well-known Davidsonian theme, according to which the psychological explanation of a mental phenomenon normally proceeds by embedding this phenomenon within a broader context of other mental phenomena *in such a way as to reveal their rational connections*.[8] Endorsing the idea that rationality can be said to be constitutive of the mental *as such*, Helm maintains that 'mental phenomena are intelligible only as located within a broader pattern of rationality in terms of which they can be explained' (p. 3).

Central to this way of conceiving of the realm of the affective (and of the realm of the mental more generally) is the idea that our everyday explanations of human actions—explanations that make use of mentalistic vocabulary—are essentially *normative* in nature. As Helm writes, '[a] psychological explanation reveals the explanandum as what rationally ought to happen' (p. 3). This way of understanding what a psychological explanation amounts to has an implication that may be found counterintuitive. Helm, who clearly does not find this implication problematic, states the point as follows: 'a creature is intelligible as an agent, as having various mental capacities, only if its exercise of those capacities is for the most part rational' (p. 3). Here, it is fundamental to appreciate that the claim is not that *every single actualization* of an agent's mental capacities has to be rational. The point is, rather, that the accumulation of too much irrationality would render the agency of this being questionable by rendering unintelligible the mental acts under consideration.

In the context of his particular interest in emotional reason, Helm elaborates on this view by introducing the notion of an *emotional commitment*. This notion seeks to capture the following idea: given certain conceptual relations that hold between the emotions that constitute one of the mentioned patterns, a particular emotional response could be said to commit one to continue to have certain other emotions. If you, for instance, take the dog of your neighbor to be worth being frightened, you not only *ought to* be disposed to react in some self-protective way, if you all of a sudden see this dog coming towards you. Rather, you also *ought to* feel relieved, if the dog suddenly turns around and begins to run in the opposite direction. Helm articulates the point by claiming that a particular emotion 'exerts *rational pressure*

---

[8] What Davidson calls 'psychology' is something clearly different from the empirical discipline usually called psychology. Davidson has in view our *everyday practice* of making sense of our human acts by invoking 'psychological phenomena'.

on one to have subsequent emotions that conform to [the pattern in question] in the relevant circumstances' (p. 67).[9]

Against this background, Helm introduces the already explained notion of an emotion's *focus* in order to refer to the background object of import that 'makes intelligible the evaluation implicit in the emotion' (p. 69); the point being that this focus may be said to define the range of emotions to which a particular emotion commits one.[10] The introduction of this term allows Helm to refine the suggestion that the specific kind of import an emotion is responsive to corresponds to the formal object of this type of emotion. Helm writes: 'we can understand the specific kind of import at issue in each emotion's formal object in terms of a relation between its target and focus' (ibid.). He illustrates this point by writing that 'we can understand danger, the formal object of fear, in terms of the target being *a threat to the focus of the emotion* such that it is the import of the focus that makes intelligible the resulting import of the target' (ibid.; my emphasis). In this context, he eventually comes to claim that any warranted emotional response presupposes a commitment to the import of that emotion's focus. In other words, what a particular emotional response should be taken to ultimately disclose is the import its focus (the focus of the whole pattern of emotions of which this emotion is a constitutive element) has to the relevant subject.

As hinted at above, what is fundamental for my account of collective affective intentionality is the thought that our emotional responses disclose our evaluative perspective, and not merely the significance something has for us. This thought has not been supported up to now. Helm begins to do so by observing that the idea of an *internal* coherence exhibited by the mentioned patterns of emotions cannot be seen as a sufficient ground for our understanding of an emotion as a response to the

---

[9] Helm elaborates on this idea of an emotional commitment by introducing two further terms. He coins the term 'transitional commitments' to refer to those commitments that concern the temporal transitions from one emotion to another (cf. pp. 67–68). In order to understand this notion, we have to differentiate two basic sorts of emotions: forward-looking and backward-looking emotions. Forward-looking emotions, such as hope and fear, anticipate good or bad things that may come to occur, whereas backward-looking emotions, such as relief and disappointment, are responses to something good or bad that has already happened. The idea is that, depending on whether or not the anticipated occurrence comes to take place, a forward-looking emotion of a certain sort *ought to* become a backward-looking emotion of a corresponding sort. If you are, for instance, hoping to get a grant for a project you are very interested in, you *ought to* feel disappointed if you are informed that you are not going to receive the expected financial support. Otherwise it would be questionable that this project was really significant to you. The second term Helm coins in this context is the term 'tonal commitments' (cf. p. 68). This term refers to those commitments that concern the valence of particular emotions. In this case, we have to distinguish between positively- and negatively-valenced emotions. To say that our emotions involve tonal commitments is to say that, if one experiences a positively-valenced emotion in response to something that has happened, then one *ought to* have experienced a corresponding negatively-valenced emotion if instead what happened had been the contrary. These normative expectations are, of course, subject to ceteris paribus conditions.

[10] It is to the extent to which certain forward- and backward-looking emotions and certain positively- and negatively-valenced emotions can be said to have *a common focus* that we can understand them as imposing transitional and tonal commitments on each other.

import something has. Rather, we have to understand such a pattern of emotions as something that *for the most part* coheres with other patterns of evaluative attitudes of different kinds (e.g. desires or evaluative judgments) that have the same focus. Otherwise, Helm observes, we could not make sense of the idea that an emotion is a response to the significance something *really* has for the subject at issue. Put another way, we have to understand our general capacity to respond emotionally as a capacity that is grounded in our being disposed both actually and counterfactually to respond in certain ways 'when rationally required and not when rationally prohibited' (p. 70).

In this context, Helm comes to claim that the postulated patterns of emotions are in general *projectible*; the idea being that a given pattern of emotions may be said to exert rational pressure on one to evaluate a number of occurrences in certain particular manners, not only in an affective, but also in different non-affective ways. If a particular emotion is warranted, one ought to be disposed to, for instance, judging particular situations to be a certain way and meriting certain responses that are rationally coherent with the emotional response at issue. In the same vein, one ought to be disposed to, for instance, desiring certain things in a way that is rationally coherent with this emotion.

Helm construes this general disposition to respond in certain ways as a disposition to, first, attend to the focus of the felt evaluations in question[11], and second, act appropriately on behalf of that focus. In this context, he submits that the import something has '*enthralls* us by moving us to act' (p. 79). The point is that, in conceiving of our emotions in terms of such a complex of dispositions, we begin to conceive of them as *conceptually indivisible* states that *at the same time evaluate and motivate* in a way that casts doubt on the assumption of the cognitive-conative divide.[12]

Helm completes this train of thought to the effect that our emotions disclose and constitute our unified evaluative perspective by addressing our capacity to prefer one thing to another. He appeals to a very simple thought: if a given project has more significance for us than another, then we have reasons to pursue this first project more strenuously than the second one. In this order of ideas, he contends that we are compelled to construe the strength of our motivation to pursue something in terms of the *relative* import different things have. The point is that we have to take for granted the possibility of something like a tacit comparison of the import different things have. This means that we have to presuppose some rational connections to also hold between patterns *with different foci* (cf. p. 112).

In this context, Helm eventually comes to suggest that the intensity of an emotion, which may, in principle, be taken to be warranted in a particular situation, can sometimes be 'properly dampened because of the way in which preferences are

---

[11] The claim is not that we are always *actively* vigilant of those occurrences which could affect the objects that have import to us. Rather, the idea is that, in virtue of some sort of *attunement* of one's sensibilities to the import something has, one's attention is *effortlessly drawn* to the relevant kinds of situations (cf. pp. 71ff.).

[12] At this point, Helm offers the following preliminary summary: 'In short, emotions are *felt evaluations* in the sense that (a) by virtue of their mutual focal commitments they form projectible, rational patterns that constitute import, and (b) they are nonetheless individually responsive to that import impressing itself on us in such a way that (c) we are enthralled by its practical import and so motivated to act' (p. 80).

involved in defining the circumstances' (p. 112). Accordingly, he proposes to understand a felt evaluation as a commitment, not only to have other felt evaluations with the same focus in the relevant circumstances, but also to dampen felt evaluations the import of whose foci is of a lesser degree (cf. p. 113).

Helm elaborates on this last observation by pointing out that, in order to be intelligible *at all*, the commitments in question 'must impose rational pressure on subsequent felt evaluations with various foci to conform in a way that is generally *transitive* and *asymmetric*' (ibid.; my emphasis); the result being 'a pattern of responsiveness not merely to the import of a particular focus but to the broader circumstances in a way that defines the dampening relations among various foci' (ibid.). He closes this thought by asserting that 'to prefer one thing to another [...] just is to be committed to such transitive and asymmetrical dampening relations, other things being equal' (ibid.). So we cannot understand our general receptivity to the significance that certain things and occurrences have in terms of a series of *independent* concerns. 'Rather, given the sensitivity to *relative* import required by the dampening effect, we must understand these distinct cares and values to be *unified into a single evaluative perspective*—as both a commitment and receptivity to import in general' (p. 115; my emphasis).

This last consideration allows us to finally articulate a fundamental condition of intelligibility of the idea of someone's reaction to a given occurrence amounting to a *genuinely emotional response*. This condition may be stated as follows: if we are to understand a given comportment as an emotional response, i.e. as an act that reveals and, at the same time, determines the import something has to the subject of some felt evaluation, we have to take for granted that the subject at issue is the subject of a unified and, for the most part, coherent evaluative perspective.

It is important to note that the idea of a unitary evaluative perspective that can be disclosed by someone's emotional responses does not merely amount to an ideal abstraction: the image of an ultimate rationally coherent pattern constituted by *all possible* patterns of evaluative responses of the subject at issue. Furthermore—and this is the reason why we can talk of a fundamental condition of intelligibility—, it amounts to a basic presupposition, i.e. to something that opens up the possibility of understanding a given comportment as an emotion or an action out of emotion.[13]

---

[13] Let me try to get rid of a particular aura of implausibility that surrounds this claim by reinforcing a point made above. It is important to note that coherence is *not* meant here as *lack of conflict*. Not only because *absolute* lack of conflict is not to be expected, but because lack of conflict, in general, is not required. What is required is only that our evaluative conflicts remain *isolated*; that is to say, that they do not become the rule. So when we talk in this context of coherence we mean coherence in the sense of mutual support and defensibility of the attitudes that constitute and express an evaluative pattern. Seeking to offer a sketch of what seems to me to be a very similar view of coherence, Laura Ekstrom draws our attention to Keith Lehrer's (1990) theory of epistemic justification. Ekstrom writes: 'Lehrer's theory [...] provides a useful model of this coherence, as it envisions justification centrally as a contest with a skeptical interlocutor who challenges one's beliefs. On the account, roughly, a state of acceptance is justified just in case it coheres with whatever else the believer accepts, and an acceptance coheres just in case it can be defended against skeptical challenges by the believer's other acceptances' (2010, p. 284, footnote 17). Helm would probably not accept the claim that an emotion is warranted just in case its 'evaluative content' coheres with *whatever else* the relevant subject accepts. But this picture captures the idea of coherence that is at issue here well.

One could certainly wonder what is the point of revealing this necessity to presuppose a coherent evaluative perspective in the context of an attempt to explicate what collective affective intentionality consists in. The arguments I am going to develop in the remainder of this book are all based on the idea that, in pointing to a unified evaluative perspective, Helm is pointing to the foundation our affective life has in *the unity of our care-defined personal existence*, in the unity of our *particular* Dasein. In this context, I shall develop a proposal that aims at connecting Helm's view of affective intentionality to a series of themes articulated by the early Martin Heidegger.[14]

Concretely, the proposal aims at anchoring the notion of collective affective intentionality to the claim that our human mode of being is essentially defined by what Heidegger calls care [*Sorge*]. The underlying intuition is that by articulating such a view we could come to see the extent to which emotionally responding to something in a genuinely joint manner may be said to constitute an eminently human ability, not merely in the sense of being something we can without doubt do, but in the more demanding sense of being something that in an outstanding manner expresses our human nature.

Before I begin to develop this proposal, I would like to spend some words on the basic idea that motivates the argument to be developed in the remainder of this book. I would like to do so by providing a very brief excursus that pertains to a notion that will be central to my account: the Heideggerian notion of an emotion's

---

[14] This aim to connect Helm's thought that, if we are to understand an emotional response as an act apt to bring to light what we care about, we have to assume that the relevant person's evaluative perspective exhibits a unitary character and Heidegger's central idea that our human mode of existence is defined by what he calls care [*Sorge*] might sound too adventurous. In particular, one could wonder whether Helm's notion of caring and Heidegger's notion of *Sorge* are commensurate with each other, given that they seem to address two completely different things. As we shall see in detail (in Sects. 7.2 and 7.3), Heidegger's notion of care is seeking to capture the very structure that defines our human existence. Helm, on the other side, seems to 'merely' be pointing to a class of attitudes towards intentional objects. He writes: 'To care about something or value it is to make it be central to our lives as a worthy object of our attention and action and therefore to be the proper source of desires and emotions that are genuinely one's own' (2001, p. 128). In the course of our discussion (particularly in Sect. 5.3, 5.4, 7.2, and 7.3), it should become clearer that there are important overlaps between Helm's idea that our emotional reason makes visible what we really care about (and take ourselves to be) and Heidegger's understanding of our affective attunement to the world [*Befindlichkeit*] as a structural moment of *Sorge*. Slaby points to two important similarities of these two views of affectivity. First, Helm's and Heidegger's view of human affectivity may both be said to be guided by the intuition that 'a well-conceived philosophy of emotion inevitably snowballs into a philosophy of personhood' (Slaby 2012, p. 56). Second, Helm's and Heidegger's understanding of human emotional life both describe affectivity as a unity of world-disclosure and world-constitution that challenges the notion of a direction of fit. Slaby writes: 'Helm's view is similar to Heidegger's in that it operates on a level of a world-disclosure prior to the level on which it makes sense to distinguish between beliefs, desires and sensations' (2012, p. 58). In a paper in which Helm (forthcoming) stresses that he is not a Heidegger scholar, we are made aware of an indirect connection between the centrality that the idea of caring about something—in the sense of having a concern for its wellbeing—plays in Helm's theory of emotions and a particular reading of Heidegger's thoughts concerning Dasein's affective attunement to the world. This connection goes through Helm's PhD adviser John Haugeland.

for-the-sake-of-which. I expect this discussion to complement Helm's illuminating view of our emotional life by drawing our attention to a particular aspect on which Helm's analysis of the structure of affective intentionality does not put much emphasis. It is in reference to this aspect, I shall argue in the next chapter, that we can characterize those emotions by means of which we participate in a moment of affective intentional community.

In §30 of *Being and Time*, Heidegger begins his analysis of what he calls *fear* [*Furcht*] by asserting that there are three points of view from which (or aspects in reference to which) this affective phenomenon could be analyzed (cf. [1927] 1962, pp. 179ff.). The first aspect pertains to *that in the face of which* we fear, namely *the fearsome* [*das Furchtbare*]. The other two aspects concern *the act of fearing as such* [*das Fürchten selbst*] and *the for-the-sake-of-which* of fear [*das Worum*]. It is rather clear that with the compound technical term 'in-the-face-of-which' Heidegger is referring to what contemporary philosophers call the formal object of an emotion.[15] The term 'for-the-sake-of-which', on the contrary, does not correspond to any of the technical notions we have discussed above. However, and as we shall immediately see, it is clear enough that, in this context, Heidegger is employing this term to point to an aspect we have also thematized above, namely the self-referential aspect of the emotional act of fearing.

I think that it promotes our understanding of what is at issue here to observe that Heidegger does not introduce the term 'for-the-sake-of-which' in the context of his analysis of fear. Rather, this is a term around which Heidegger's discussion on 'the worldhood of the world' (cf. particularly §§14–18 of *Being and Time*) takes a radical turn.[16] Indeed, this is the term that finally reveals the transcendental nature of Heidegger's notion of 'world'. But how can this remark bring us to understand what is meant by the expression 'the for-the-sake-of-which of an emotion'?

In the context of this transcendental-philosophical discussion on the worldhood of the world, Heidegger prepares the idea that our emotional acts can be analyzed in respect to their for-the-sake-of-which by pointing to the way in which certain entities normally appear to us as entities that are *available* [*zuhanden*], i.e. as entities that can be used in specific ways in the context of certain activities we are already involved in. Heidegger submits that our encounters with these sorts of entities are phenomenologically defined by the following particularity: in so far as they appear in the relevant circumstances as something that can be used *in order to do or achieve something*, these entities can be said to make some sort of tacit reference to a more or less concrete *for-which* [*das Wozu*]—in fact, to a series of them.[17] In the course of this analysis, Heidegger eventually comes to explain the idea of the for-the-sake-of-which of an act in terms of the ultimate (or primary) for-which of this act. In so

---

[15] For a discussion of Heidegger's analysis of fear, see Slaby (2007).

[16] Romano Pocai (2007, p. 60) speaks of a change of perspective in Heidegger's analysis.

[17] In the next section (Sect. 5.3) we are going to deal with this idea concerning some references (or 'involvements') that can be said to tacitly constitute our understanding of something as having a particular nature; as exhibiting a particular way of being, as Heidegger writes.

doing, he connects the notion of an act's for-the-sake-of-which to a recurrent and central theme of *Being and Time*: the idea that for Dasein its own being is an issue.[18] It is in this order of ideas that, in the mentioned analysis of fear, Heidegger comes to make the following claim: '*That which* fear fears *about* is that very entity which is afraid' ([1927] 1962, p. 180). In closing this section, let me elucidate the relevance this thought has for us by briefly explaining how I intend to connect this claim to the insight that our emotions disclose and co-constitute our evaluative perspective.

In the remainder of this work I shall account for the sense of togetherness that characterizes the emotional experiences that are at the heart of a collective affective intentional act in terms of a peculiar for-the-sake-of-which that may be argued to phenomenologically define these affective experiences: a concrete group the participants take themselves to be a part of. As mentioned at the beginning of this section, I shall do so in such a way as to elaborate on a suggestion I take Helm (2008) to be making in his account of plural robust agents. The suggestion is that a collective affective intentional episode may be said to disclose an evaluative perspective that is shared by the participants in a strong sense of the verb 'to share'.[19] In particular, I shall try to show that an account of collective affective intentionality based on the idea that at the core of any joint emotional response we find a shared evaluative perspective can make visible that acts of felt understanding are also at the heart of those episodes I call moments of affective intentional community. In the following section I shall begin to develop an account along these lines by discussing a condition of intelligibility of the idea that emotionally responding in a joint manner is a matter of actualizing in an affective way some shared evaluative perspective. The condition of intelligibility I am going to discuss concerns the apparently trivial thought that we humans normally share (to a considerable extent) the world we are in. I shall cash out this idea of normally being in the same world in terms of the thought that things and occurrences usually matter to us in particular ways (and not in others), so as to bring us to understand our world as an, in a weak sense, shared world; as a world that is share*able* in a number of stronger senses of the verb 'to share'. The point is that we can begin to elucidate the nature of our ability to participate in moments of affective intentional community by explicating the sense in which human intentionality can be said to essentially be shareable intentionality.

---

[18] For a discussion of this point, see Pocai (2007, pp. 60ff.).

[19] Just to anticipate, the main difficulty faced by this attempt to connect Helm's view of affective intentionality to Heidegger's theme of a care-defined mode of being (in order to develop an account of *collective* affective intentionality) lies in the fact that the mere idea of a unified evaluative perspective may be taken to point to what Heidegger calls the *in-each-case-mine* character [*Jemeinigkeit*] of our *personal* existence (cf. [1927] 1962, §9).

5.3 Being-in-the-Same-World: Sharing Our Care-Defined Mode of Being

My aim in this section is a double one: first, to explicate the sense in which human intentionality can be said to *essentially* be shareable intentionality, and second, to begin to make plausible the suggestion that collective affective intentionality should be regarded as a phenomenon that in an outstanding manner expresses our human nature. The argument to be developed here aims at supporting the following thought: if we are to make sense of the idea that participating in an episode of collective affective intentionality presupposes being able to share some evaluative perspective, we have to explicate the sense in which our acts of feeling-towards together can be understood as acts that bring the fundamental fact to light that we humans share a mode of being that is defined by the structure Heidegger calls care. In order to prepare this conclusion, in what follows I shall address a claim I take to be central to Heidegger's view of the grounds of our human sociality, and particularly, to his notion of *being-with* [*Mitsein*].[20] The claim is that our fundamental sense of being-in-the-world is normally the sense of being in a world we always already share with other human individuals in an at least weak sense of the verb 'to share'. It is the sense of being in a world that is shareable in a number of ways that are much more demanding. The upshot of the argument is that it is only because human intentionality *characteristically* involves this sense of being in an essentially shareable world that we can come to participate in *genuinely collective* (affective) intentional episodes. So, as just hinted at, in what follows I shall elucidate the sense in which it

---

[20] 'Being-with' is the term of art Macquarrie and Robinson (1962) use to translate Heidegger's compound verbal noun *das Mitsein*. This translation has become customary. Here, I shall adhere to this custom. Although there are passages in which he prefers to use the term 'Miteinandersein' to refer to the *factual* being-with-one-another of two or more individuals, Heidegger normally uses 'Mitsein' in an ambiguous way to refer, on some occasions, to the phenomenon just mentioned, and on others, to what he, drawing on Kant, calls the *inner possibility* [*innere Möglichkeit*] of this phenomenon—and what we may call the condition of the possibility of any factual being-with-one-another. Moreover, Heidegger does not systematically distinguish between demanding and relatively undemanding forms of *Miteinandersein*. In other words, he does not differentiate between *genuine being-together* (with concrete others) and what I call *mere being-alongside-each-other*. In a number of passages, Heidegger uses the term 'Mitdasein' (which is often translated as 'Dasein-with') in order to refer to the mode of being or to the concrete existence of other human individuals. But it seems to me that this use is not systematic, either. So the term 'being-with' is a murky one, and this certainly adds difficulty to the interpretation of Heidegger's claims. (For a very brief explication of Heidegger's term 'Mitsein' and its cognates, see Inwood [1999, pp. 31ff.].) In what follows I am going to discuss exclusively the view of the grounds of our human communal life [*Gemeinschaft*] Heidegger articulates during the so-called Being and Time period. What he, in his later work—and in the context of an attempt to answer the question 'Who are we ourselves?'—, writes about *the people* [*das Volk*] or *the We-Ourselves* [*das Wir-Selbst*] will not be my topic (cf. Heidegger [1934] 1998, §§10–15). Moreover, a number of issues that are more directly connected to this early notion of being-with will remain untouched. I mean issues related to the distinction between *authentic* [*eigentliches*] and *inauthentic* [*uneigentliches*] being-with and issues that pertain to Heidegger's famous notion of *the One* [*das Man*], which Macquarrie and Robinson translate as the 'they' (cf. Heidegger [1927] 1962, §§25–27).

could be non-trivially asserted that we human individuals are, by and large, in the same world. The ultimate point in so doing will be to bring to the fore some fundamental continuity that may be taken to hold between non-cooperatively marked forms of intentionality—what I shall call, for lack of a better term, 'ordinary' intentionality—and those forms of intentionality that deserve to be characterized as collective. A crucial thought here will be that this sense of being-in-the-same-world could be taken to be a matter of our *having always already pre-thematically understood that we share a care-defined mode of being.*

I believe that we can begin to explicate this suggestion concerning a sense to the effect that we are in an essentially shareable world in terms of the (perhaps more familiar) idea that *certain ways of making sense* of the situations in which we encounter, or at least could encounter, one another *are common to us.* Let me commence to do so by briefly discussing a view that is widely shared among phenomenologists.

According to the mentioned view which is condensed in Edmund Husserl's notion of an *intentional horizon*, our perceptual experiences of concrete objects could be claimed to normally involve a number of tacit references of at least two different kinds. On the one hand, human perceptual experiences may be said to usually involve some references to *further aspects* of the object at issue. As David Smith puts it, '[e]very individual perception necessarily has the sense of being but a particular "view" on one segment of the world' (2003, p. 75). Husserl groups together the references of this sort under the notion of the *inner horizon* of an object. The second kind of tacit references phenomenologists point to constitute what Husserl calls the *outer horizon* of the object. In this case, the claim is that our perceptual experiences of concrete objects usually involve a number of references to further objects, practices, and purposes (among other things). The idea is that these two types of 'involvements' that constitute the intentional horizon of an object may be argued to be *presupposed by any meaningful experience* of this object. In other words, the suggestion is that some sort of interplay normally occurs between what may be said to be *explicitly given* in a concrete experience and what can be said to be 'meant' by it in the sense of being only *tacitly given* in this concrete experience. Suggesting that we can understand our experiences as usually involving a sort of *anticipation* of the intentional content of some possible future experiences, Husserl characterizes this intentional horizon as a 'predelineated potentiality' (see [1929] 1999, p. 45).

It is important to note that the references or anticipations at issue here are not the result of certain optional conscious inferential processes. For Husserl, the horizon is a *perceptual* fact and a necessary condition for the experiential understanding of an object or situation. The idea is that a particular experience would not be the experience of the sort of object or situation it is, were it not to involve (to tacitly refer to) some further possible experiences. In other words, the mentioned anticipations may be said to be *essential* to an object's *being the sort of object it is* (for us). In this context, Husserl eventually comes to conceive of the world (of human experience) as the *ultimate* intentional horizon; as the condition of the possibility of any intelligible experience.

As mentioned at the end of the previous section, Heidegger elaborates on this view by pointing to the way in which most of the entities we encounter in everyday life usually 'show up' as something that is available to be used in the context of some project we are involved in; as an item of 'equipment', or as something that, as he writes, is *ready-to-hand* [*zuhanden*].[21] He suggests that our immediate (and pre-thematic) understanding of certain *possibilities for dealing with these entities* is constituted by references of the second sort mentioned above that involve, among other things, further entities, practices, activities, and, specially, purposes. The idea is that it is only because we, in an immediate and usually non-thematic way, understand some *practical possibilities* we have in the frame of particular *contexts of involvements* [*Bewandtniszusammenhänge*]—as Heidegger comes to call these horizons of references—that most of our experiences exhibit the character we may call meaningfulness. Put another way, Heidegger suggests that the sufficiently intelligible quality of the majority of encounters with other entities is grounded in the immediate practical significance these entities exhibit in the specific context in which the encounter takes place. The point is that this is a significance these entities exhibit *in virtue of their being part of a particular functional whole integrated by certain purposes and projects we have.*

In line with Husserl's suggestion that our human *lived world* [*Lebenswelt*] should be understood as the ultimate intentional horizon, Heidegger ([1927] 1962, §§15–17) makes use of the idea of a context of involvements to characterize our human world. His claim is that we can conceive of the pre-thematically understood world we are always already in when we come to encounter some entity as a sort of ultimate context of involvements. That is to say, we can understand the world as a realm of practical relations we inhabit; as a context that enables our meaningful encounters with other entities.

Against the background of this understanding of what it is to be in a (human) world, in what follows I shall try to specify the relation that holds between three ideas I have introduced in this section: the idea that we are, by and large, in the same world; the idea that we share certain ways of making sense of the situations in which we encounter one another; and the idea that, in being with others, we have always already understood that we human individuals share a care-defined mode of being. I shall try to do so in such a way as to eventually come to explicate what is meant by the suggestion that human intentionality is essentially shareable intentionality.

---

[21] In *Being and Time*, Heidegger famously distinguishes three ways in which worldly entities can appear to us. We can encounter an entity: as something that is available or *ready-to-hand* [*zuhanden*]; as something that is occurrent or *present-at-hand* [*vorhanden*]; or as something that has the same mode of being we have, i.e. as another *Dasein* (cf. Heidegger [1927] 1962, §§15–17). Heidegger is aware that those entities we usually encounter as ready-to-hand (and this holds true for those entities we immediately understand as another Dasein) can also come to be regarded as something occurrent. But, as he points out, this is precisely *not* the way these entities are *usually* (or, as he prefers to say, *firstly and mostly* [*zunächst und zumeist*]) encountered; they can *come to be regarded* as something present-at-hand. In his lecture *Die Grundbegriffe der Metaphysik*, Heidegger addresses a fourth mode of being (a fourth way in which something can appear to us): an entity can appear as an organism (cf. [1929/30] 1983, §§45–63).

This will require me, however, to deal with an issue that pertains to the co-originality of two experiential structures that may be said to organize our fundamental sense of being-in-the-world: our usual sense that the situations we are in exhibit an objective character and our sense of mutual openness qua Dasein. I shall deal with this issue by reconstructing the main points of an argument offered by Heidegger in the context of an attempt to characterize 'the essence of truth' [*das Wesen der Wahrheit*].[22]

In his lecture *Einleitung in die Philosophie*, Heidegger begins to develop the idea concerning the *equiprimordiality of being-alongside-things and being-with* [*die Gleichursprünglichkeit von Sein-bei... und Miteinandersein*] (cf. [1928/29] 1996, pp. 117ff.) by contrasting two, in his view, extremely different forms of co-presence: the simultaneous presence-at-hand that is proper to things [*Zusammenvorhandensein der Dinge*] and Dasein's being-with-one-another [*Miteinandersein von Menschen*]. His reflection builds upon a simple observation: we usually do not express our co-presence by making thematic our mutual vicinity. Rather, we normally say that we are *with one another*.

According to Heidegger, the possibility we have to differentiate these two forms of co-presence reflects our understanding of some fundamental differences in the mode of being [*Seinsart*] of the entities we can encounter in the world. Concretely, this way of thematizing our simultaneous presence, by using the expression 'with one another', indicates that we do not understand our encounters with other human individuals as encounters with certain entities that are spatially close to us and *additionally* share our human nature. Rather, one could argue that it is our having already understood that we share a particular mode of being that enables us to use the word 'with' in a meaningful way while describing the kind of co-presence in question. The preposition 'with', Heidegger submits, does not indicate in this case a particular spatiotemporal relation, but a sort of *participation* (see p. 85).[23]

In the course of his attempt to elucidate what this participation consists in, Heidegger comes to reject two prima facie plausible answers to the question about the ground of the mentioned difference concerning two varieties of co-presence. The first answer he rejects is based on the idea that the difference between simultaneous presence-at-hand and being-with-one-another could be grounded in the fact that we human beings *consciously apprehend* each other. Heidegger contends that our being-with-one-another cannot be reduced to a *conscious presence-at-hand* [*bewusstes Zusammenvorhandensein*] (cf. p. 86). The reason is as follows: even if we agree that such a characterization of being-with-one-another manages to capture a fundamental particularity of the entities that can come to be involved in the sort of

---

[22] To be sure, at the beginning of the passage I am going to reconstruct, Heidegger asserts that he wants to postpone the issue concerning the essence of truth and devote his attention to the problem concerning the differences between the varied modes of being [*Seinsarten*] (cf. [1928/29] 1996, p. 84).

[23] One could object that there are situations in which one is *only* spatially close to another human individual. The key to understanding the claim that the preposition 'with' does not point to a particular spatiotemporal relation is to recognize that the participation at issue here—and I shall, of course, spell out what this participation amounts to—can be said to be presupposed by every single (human) being-spatially-close-to-one-another.

relationship at issue—namely the capacity we human beings have to become consciously aware of our co-presence—, we have to accept that it fails to explain certain situations of a very familiar sort.

Concretely, the idea of a mutual conscious awareness fails to explain those situations in which one can assert that two or more individuals are with one another, despite the fact that their intentional acts are not directed towards each other. Heidegger illustrates this point by considering a situation in which two hikers come to be carried away by a landscape that opens itself in front of their eyes (cf. p. 86). The point of this example is that even though these individuals are focused on the fascinating landscape (and not on each other), they can be said to be with one another in this situation.[24] Heidegger explicitly draws the conclusion that mutual conscious awareness cannot be a necessary condition for being with one another. On the contrary, the possibility we have to be aware of one another has to be said to have its foundation in our being-with.[25] Dasein necessarily has to be *already* disclosed qua Dasein for Dasein, if something like mutual awareness is to be possible.[26]

We could, I think, rearticulate this crucial point by stating something along the following lines: if we are to make sense of the claim that two individuals are, on a given occasion, with one another, we have to presuppose that they are open to one another *qua beings that can share in the situation at issue*. That is to say, we have to presuppose that they have already understood each other as an entity that can also respond to the specific demands posed by the situation at issue; as an entity that is a possible partner of some joint response.[27] But what is it exactly that two individuals who can be said to be with one another have to already have understood?

---

[24] There is a particular respect in which Heidegger's example should be said to be absolutely unspecific. Heidegger does not tell us whether the two hikers just happen to meet at this point or whether they are hiking *together*. In a later passage, which we are going to discuss below, Heidegger elaborates on this example in such a way as to give the impression that these hikers belong together, as we often say; that they constitute a sort of group.

[25] Heidegger writes: 'Gegenseitiges Sicherfassen ist fundiert im Miteinandersein' (p. 87).

[26] Heidegger writes: 'Dasein muß zuvor schon für Dasein offenbar sein, damit gegenseitiges Erfassen möglich wird' (p. 88).

[27] It seems to me that John Searle is trying to articulate a similar intuition when he claims that '[c]ollective intentionality presupposes a Background sense of the other as a candidate for cooperative agency' ([1990] 2002, p. 104). Indeed, while preparing this conclusion, Searle makes a number of observations that come close to Heidegger's idea of a fundamental mutual openness qua Dasein. Searle talks of features of what he calls the Background 'that are general or pervasive [...] for collective behavior' (p. 103), and which amount to 'the sorts of things that old-time philosophers were driving at when they said things like "Man is a social animal" or "Man is a political animal"' (ibid.). He asserts that besides the 'biological capacity to recognize other people as importantly like us, in a way that waterfalls, trees, and stones are not like us' (ibid.), we have to presuppose 'a preintentional sense of "the other" as an actual or potential agent like oneself in cooperative activities' (ibid.). Searle is emphatic in asserting that this sense of the others as candidates for cooperative agency is *not* the result of some collective intentionality. On the contrary, 'collective intentionality seems to presuppose some level of sense of community before it can ever function' (ibid.).

We can begin to answer this question by addressing the second proposal concerning the nature of the difference between simultaneous presence-at-hand and being-with Heidegger rejects. I believe that in coming to understand the reasons he has for rejecting this suggestion, we come to recognize that Heidegger is after the following condition of intelligibility of the idea of being with one another: we have to assume that two individuals who, in the context of a given situation, can be said to be with one another have *already* understood (at least in a pre-thematic way) that they share a care-defined mode of being. Let us see how Heidegger leads us to this conclusion. The second suggestion Heidegger comes to discard concerns the idea that the difference between simultaneous presence-at-hand and being-with has its root in the fact that two (or more) human individuals could exhibit the *same sort of behavior* in a given circumstance. Heidegger observes that there is an obvious problem with this answer: this holds true even for inanimate entities, such as stones. Heidegger does, however, not abandon the suggestion under consideration. Rather, he continues his reflection by considering the idea that something that, in this respect, could probably be thought to be specific to us humans is that in certain situations two or more human individuals exhibit the same *comportment towards other entities* [*Verhalten zu...*] (cf. p. 89).[28]

Heidegger immediately points to a new problem that arises in this context. Given that any concrete comportment-towards presupposes a *particular* point of view (namely the point of view of the concrete individual who in the context of the relevant situation is comporting itself towards something), strictly speaking, we can never talk of the *same* comportment-towards. At best we can assert that two or more individuals are behaving in an identical way towards something. Hence, were we to accept the suggestion that being with one another is a matter of the sameness of the participants' comportment-towards, Heidegger observes, we would be forced to conclude that being with one another is impossible.

The solution Heidegger offers to this rather strange problem is, at least at first sight, a too trivial one. Heidegger observes that the *sameness* [*Selbigkeit*] at issue here is not the sameness of our comportment-towards, but the sameness of the particular entity towards which we are oriented in a particular circumstance. In other words, it seems that it is our comporting ourselves *in a certain way* towards *one and the same* object that allows us to assert that we (the involved individuals) are with

---

[28] It could be objected that this comporting-oneself-towards-other-entities cannot be said to be specific to us humans. For, as a matter of fact, a number of nonhuman animals exhibit some sort of behavior-towards. Heidegger does not ignore this fact. In the already mentioned lecture *Die Grundbegriffe der Metaphysik*, he addresses the issue of animal intentionality, as we may call it. In this context, he acknowledges that nonhuman animals exhibit some sort of openness [*Offenheit*] to what we understand as worldly occurrences. But he makes an elaborate effort to show that nonhuman animals are not open to beings *qua beings*. (For an overview of this argument, see Cerbone [2000, pp. 223ff.].) I do not want to enter this discussion here, not only because this would lead us astray from the argument I am seeking to reconstruct, but because I think that, although the dichotomy Dasein/Non-Dasein is worth being defended, it is a mistake to, in the context of this debate on nonhuman intentionality, group *all* the varied forms of animal life (and of animal world-relatedness) in a single category. (For a criticism along these lines, see Glendinning 1998.)

one another in the relevant situation, and not merely co-occurring (cf. pp. 89ff.). This solution becomes less trivial when Heidegger, subsequently, addresses a peculiar difficulty. The problem is that we apparently lack the conceptual tools required to understand in which sense the sameness of some entity towards which two or more individuals are intentionally directed may be taken to reveal that the very being of these individuals is characterized by the sense we have called being-with-one-another. Heidegger suggests that, on the basis of the received view of intentionality—understood as a relation that holds between a self-enclosed subject and a worldly object this subject reaches by somehow transcending its sphere of immanence—, we cannot spell out what it means for two subjects to comport themselves towards one and the same entity, as opposed to comporting themselves towards two exactly similar (but numerically different) objects of consciousness.[29]

Heidegger does not tackle this issue in a direct way. Rather, he continues the argument by observing that there are situations in which even extreme differences in the comportment exhibited by the involved individuals are unable to prevent us from asserting that they are with one another in this situation. In order to support this suggestion, he elaborates on the example of the two hikers. Heidegger asks us to imagine that, after having hiked the whole day, these hikers are, at a given moment, preparing dinner together. Although one is focused on chopping wood and the other on peeling potatoes, they can be said to be with one another, and not only (not mainly) because they are close to each other.

Heidegger concludes that the possibility we have to understand a particular situation as a situation in which the participants are comporting themselves *in purpose towards the same thing* [*in Absicht auf Selbiges*] ultimately discloses a pervasive—an existence-defining—sense of being-with-one-another (cf. p. 92). The sort of participation that is at issue is, hence, intimately related to our usual non-thematic understanding of the worldly entities or occurrences towards which we are intentionally directed as entities or occurrences towards which another human individual (or a number of them) may also be directed *in one intentional mode or another.*[30]

Although the argument I have been reconstructing heavily draws on the idea that worldly entities exhibit an objective character, Heidegger completes this train of

---

[29] This is the reason why Heidegger finds it so relevant to emphasize that, in asserting that the entity towards which we are directed in a given circumstance is one and the same entity, we are not asserting that we are intentionally directed towards objects that are *exactly similar*. The point is that the notion of exact similarity [*Gleichheit*] presupposes the numerical difference of those things that are said to be exactly similar. He writes: 'Wir sehen also nicht jeder von uns die gleiche Kreide, sondern alle miteinander dieselbe' (p. 90).

[30] There are two points I would like to stress here. Anticipating an issue that will be absolutely central to my account of collective affective intentionality, I would like to note that, following Gilbert (cf. our discussion in Sects. 3.2 and 3.3), we may affirm that, at least in the context of this concrete situation, the two hikers of the example constitute a sort of group. For one could say, for instance, that they are jointly committed to cooking the soup together. We shall come back to this important idea below (in Sect. 8.2). The second remark I would like to make concerns the fact that Heidegger's suggestion is in line with the insight that we can come to participate in a moment of affective intentional community even in those situations in which our emotional responses cannot be taken to instantiate the same kind of emotion (cf. the discussion in Sect. 4.4).

thought by claiming that we have to understand the *sameness* [*Selbigkeit*] at issue here as something that is *relative to us* (cf. p. 96). This argumentative move is extraordinarily important, since it allows him to, finally, tackle the issue mentioned above. To recall, the issue is that those philosophical notions we would likely appeal to in order to explicate the idea that worldly entities typically exhibit the quality Heidegger calls sameness are unable to elucidate the sense in which the objective condition of an entity towards which two or more individuals are intentionally directed can be argued to reveal their essential being-with-one-another.[31] Heidegger argues that the only way we have to relate these two thoughts to one another is by accepting that the sameness at issue here, *being a feature of the encountered entities*, cannot be an *intrinsic* feature of these entities.[32] He eventually claims that the sameness of those entities towards which two or more individuals, on a given occasion, comport themselves ultimately brings to light the shared character of their fundamental 'being-alongside-things' [*Sein bei Vorhandenem*].[33] Let me try to clarify this claim—and the relevance it has for the argument I am reconstructing—by briefly explicating an expression Heidegger repeatedly employs throughout this discussion.

Heidegger appeals to the expression 'the unconcealment of entities', which he presents as the literal translation of the Greek term 'aletheia', in order to condense a thought along the following lines: worldly entities are such that, in virtue of their very (objective) nature, they are able to 'show themselves to us' in one way or another. Worldly entities, to put it in a slightly different way, are *essentially discoverable* by creatures that like us understand the mode of being of different beings.

It is important to note that Heidegger is not claiming that we have immediate unrestricted access to all existing things. He is definitively aware that sometimes a given entity has to be *brought to show itself* by, for instance, defining and setting up certain very special experimental conditions. These are conditions in the context of which this entity can become manifest. But even in these cases the relevant entity can be said to (under the specified conditions) reveal itself. Moreover, only something that is essentially discoverable can remain under certain conditions really undiscovered. Heidegger observes that there is, furthermore, a dynamic interplay between disclosure and concealment that is constitutive of the *specific* mode of

---

[31] Heidegger addresses the notion of formal identity, the notion of a non-altered permanence, and the notion of substantial persistence (cf. pp. 92ff.).

[32] Heidegger writes: 'Wir können jetzt sagen, Selbigkeit kann sehr wohl eine Bestimmung des Gegenstands selbst sein, aber dieses mit sich selbst identische Seiende steht dazu noch in einer Beziehung des Erfaßtwerdens. Diese Beziehung macht das vorhandene Seiende eben dann noch relativ auf mehrere andere Seiende vom Charakter des Daseins' (p. 97).

[33] Heidegger comes to make this claim in the context of a criticism of the notion of subject he takes to be characteristic of modern philosophy. This is a notion that is based on the, in his view, misleading idea of a worldless subject who has to go out of itself, as it were, in order to reach the world. Heidegger asserts that the idea of being-alongside-things is part of the idea of being a subject. He writes: 'Dieses Sein bei Vorhandenem gehört zum Begriff des Subjekts' (p. 115). To be a subject means, among other things, to normally have a sense that one is amidst worldly entities. It means to have a sense that one is in a world that, as I have put it, exhibits an objective character.

unconcealment of particular entities. Depending on the circumstances, entities reveal themselves to us in certain ways and not in others; they exhibit a particular mode of being and not another.

One way in which we could approach this idea concerning the unconcealment of entities is by conceiving of it as the counterpart of an image that has been central to our discussion on the topic of affective intentionality: the image of an openness to the world that is essential to our human nature. Indeed, to say that we humans are essentially open to the world is to say that the existence of worldly entities is fundamentally unconcealed to creatures like us (who are able to understand the diverse mode of being of different entities).

At any rate, appealing to this idea of some sort of openness to the world that determines our human mode of being, we can finally specify the nature of the basic form of participation that is at issue here—a fundamental form of participation that permits more specific (less pervasive, bur more demanding) forms of participation. Moreover, we can do so in such a way as to come back to the idea that being a human subject means, among other things, being alongside-things. The point can be stated as follows: in virtue of our shared openness to the world, we human individuals ineluctably participate in the unconcealment of those entities we are qua Dasein amidst.[34] So the claim that our human existence is structured by the sense of being-with is the claim that our existence is defined by a sense of being in a world that is essentially shareable.

Seeking to support the idea that our sense of being-alongside-things (our sense of being in a world that exhibits an objective character) is not the sense of being in a world that is sometimes (or usually) shared, but the sense of being in an *essentially* shareable world—that is to say, in a world that is *always already* shared in some way—, Heidegger discusses the situation of an individual who discovers something, but tries to keep the discovery completely to himself (cf. p. 127). Heidegger observes that keeping a discovery secret is something that usually requires arduous efforts. For the sheer fact of one's discovery proves that the entity at issue can (in principle) be discovered by human individuals. Moreover, in such a situation one is normally compelled to hide from view, not only the encountered entity, but also the fact that one is open to the unconcealment of this entity. Heidegger asserts that in such a situation one shares with others the unconcealment of the encountered entity *in the mode of a withholding disclosure* [*im Modus des Vorenthaltens*] (cf. pp. 127–128).

The last claim is not only a bold one, but also one which may be understood as the complement of another risky suggestion Heidegger articulates some pages above, namely that there is a sense in which even in those situations in which one is *factually* alone one can be said to be with others. Solitude, he suggests, can be understood as a mode of being-with (cf. p. 119).[35] Let me try to briefly explain not only the sense in which Heidegger wants this claim to be understood, but also the

---

[34] Heidegger writes: 'Wir teilen uns in die Unverborgenheit des Seienden' (p. 105).

[35] Our fundamental being-with, Heidegger claims, is experienced during an episode of aloneness, for instance, in the form of a sense that someone is missing. Heidegger writes: 'im Alleinsein ist ein Ohneeinandersein; das Ohneeinander aber ist ein spezifisches Miteinandersein' (p. 118).

relation that holds between this claim and the idea that there is a sense in which we, in principle, *inevitably* share the unconcealment of entities.

The key to understanding the suggestion that aloneness is a mode of being-with— as well as its relation to the idea that qua Dasein we are in a world that always exhibits some character of sharedness—is to appreciate that, in this context, Heidegger is using the term 'being-with' to refer to the condition of possibility of any *factual* being-with-one-another. We can spell out what this condition of possibility amounts to by slightly modifying a suggestion we are already too familiar with: not only in order to come to understand a given situation as a situation in which we are with another person (or with certain other persons), but also in order to come to understand it as a situation in which we are *not* with one another (as a situation in which certain persons are missing or absent), we have to already have understood this situation as a shareable situation; we have to already have understood the world we are in as an *essentially* shareable world. In other words, the term 'being-with', as used in this context, refers not only to the condition of possibility of any factual being-with-one-another, but also of any factual being-*without*-one-another.

To understand the world one is in as an essentially shareable world—as a world we in some sense already share—does not basically mean to understand it as a physical world to which we all are causally related. Insofar as the shared unconcealment at issue here is not only the unconcealment of the encountered entities, but also (and fundamentally) the unconcealment of their *respective mode of being*, to understand the world one is in as an essentially shareable world means to understand the sense of familiarity that accompanies our daily engagement with a number of worldly entities as a sense one shares (or at least could share) with other human beings.[36] This is the sense in which, as suggested at the beginning of this section, the idea of being-in-the-same-world may be said to be intimately related to the idea that we share some practical possibilities for dealing with the worldly entities we encounter.

Indeed, although Heidegger does not employ the expression 'practical possibilities', he begins to develop the idea concerning a participation in the unconcealment of entities and their mode of being by suggesting that we participate in the usability of those entities we encounter as ready-to-hand (cf. pp. 100ff.).[37] One could, hence, take him to intuit some strong relation between our sense of being in an essentially shareable world and a sort of tacit conviction we often have: the conviction to the effect that we share many of the possibilities we have to deal with the entities encountered in the world. It is important, however, to note that, according to Heidegger, we do not only share the world in those situations in which we are

---

[36] Seeking to stress the idea of some sense of familiarity that usually underlies our engagement with other worldly beings, William Blattner (2006, p. 15) recommends translating Heidegger's 'Sein-bei…' as 'being-amidst' (and not as 'being-alongside', as Macquarrie and Robinson [1962] propose).

[37] Heidegger writes: 'Sich in etwas teilen, ohne es dabei zu zerteilen in Stücke, heißt: etwas für den Gebrauch und im Gebrauch sich gegenseitig überlassen' (p. 100).

making use of certain worldly entities.[38] Moreover, in the passages I have been referring to, Heidegger is heading towards the conclusion that we participate in the unconcealment of entities precisely to the extent to which we can *let them be what and how they are* by, for instance, adopting what we may call a (broadly) theoretical attitude towards them.[39] What is more, Heidegger thinks that what ultimately reveals the ground of the participation at issue is precisely the fact that we can at every moment let an entity show itself *the way it is in itself* [*so, wie sie an ihr selbst ist*] by allowing it to appear in a context that is *not* structured by a given concernful-circumspective comportment; the point being that we seem to, in the end, share their sheer occurrentness.[40]

But if this is so, it may be objected, Heidegger's argument does not support a claim I made at the beginning of this section. The claim is that being-in-the-same-world is a matter of having always already understood that we human individuals share a mode of being that is defined by care. For, according to the view just sketched, we can have a sense of being with one another even in situations in which no concernful-circumspective comportment brings to light this care-defined mode of being.

This objection misfires, however. The reason is that letting an entity be what and how it is does not imply ceasing to engage oneself with it; it does not mean to adopt an absolutely passive and concernless attitude towards this entity, as it were. Michael Inwood stresses this point by writing:

> *Seinlassen* usually means 'leave alone, drop, stop doing'. But Heidegger's *Sein-lassen* involves *Sicheinlassen*, 'getting into, engaging with, getting involved with' beings [...]. We open up a space in which beings can be themselves. We enter that open space and there engage with beings *as beings,* as independent entities that are not simply appendages of ourselves (1999, p. 117).

Indeed, Heidegger explicitly observes that the letting-be at issue here should be seen as an *act of a very fundamental sort.*[41] What is more, he asserts, that we do not only let an entity be what and how it is when we refrain from making use of it. On the

---

[38] Heidegger explicitly answers the question as to whether this participation in the usability of the encountered entities *primarily* constitutes our being-with by asserting that in order to be shareable in this practical respect an entity has to already be present for us (cf. p. 101). Schmid (2009, p. 170) puts a particular emphasis on this claim of the non-priority of some shared sense of usability (as far as our fundamental being-with is concerned).

[39] Heidegger writes: 'Gerade in diesem unserem Liegen-lassen der Kreide, in dem, was und wie sie als dieses Gebrauchsding *ist*, muß das zu finden sein, was wir suchen: nämlich das Teilhaben an der Kreide, dieses ursprüngliche Sichteilen in die Kreide, gemäß dem sie ein Gemeinsames ist und unser Sein bei ihr ein Miteinander' (p. 101).

[40] Heidegger writes: 'Es stellte sich aber heraus, daß wir schon ohne daß wir von etwas Gebrauch machen, Seiendes, Vorhandenes, Vorliegendes in gewisser Weise gemeinsam vor uns haben, so daß also dieses Sichteilen in etwas im Miteinandersein bei einem Vorhandenen nicht im Vollzug des Gebrauchens selbst liegen kann, sondern in einer Seinsweise des Daseins, die schon vor allem Gebrauchen liegt und die das gemeinsame Gebrauchmachen von etwas allererst ermöglicht' (p. 108).

[41] Heidegger writes: 'Seinlassen [ist] ein "Tun" der höchsten und ursprünglichen Art' (p. 103).

contrary, particularly in those situations in which we come to employ them in the context of a given *projection* [*Entwurf*], we let things be what they are.[42] This last remark, I am aware, does not help me to get rid of an aura of puzzlement that surrounds the claim that there is a strong relation between our sense of being in an essentially shareable world and our sense of sharing some practical possibilities; an aura of puzzlement that motivates the objection just considered. Two basic and pressing questions arise in this context. What can letting-be mean here? What is it that is special about letting an entity be what it is in such a way as to let it *show itself the way it is in itself*?

To begin with, to let an entity be what and how it is, in general, means to engage with this entity in such a way *as to not seek to make out of it something different*. This is something we do not only do in those situations in which we engage theoretically with the entity at issue, but also in those situations in which we engage practically with it in such a way as to, for instance, make 'appropriate' use of it (i.e. in such a way as to allow it to appear in the context of one's activities as the particular sort of 'equipment' it *is*).[43] So what is special about the cases in which we let something be what it is *by allowing it to show itself as it is in itself* is only that we abstract from certain purposes in the context of which we normally encounter it, as something that can be employed in order to achieve this or that end. Put another way, in this context, the expression 'as it is in itself' indeed means: not in the context of some concernful-circumspective comportment. But, if this is so, one could find the suggestion puzzling that we can speak in this context, too, of an act that expresses our care-defined mode of being.

The crucial point is as follows: independently of whether one has encountered an entity in the context of a concernful-circumspective comportment or in the context of an attempt to determine what it is in itself, one has always *brought this entity to show itself in the way it is*. One has done so by allowing it to be encountered *in a particular respect (and not in others)*; in the case of a (broadly) theoretical letting-be, as we may call it, in a respect that does not concern its usability for the purpose of achieving this or that end.[44]

In order to refer to this letting-things-be-encountered-in-a-particular-respect, Heidegger appeals to the notion of *transcendence*. In this context, he talks of a 'metaphysical indifference to things' that is *prior* to any purpose-driven interest in

---

[42] Heidegger writes: 'Wir lassen die Dinge sein, wie sie sind, überlassen sie ihnen selbst, auch dann *und gerade dann*, wenn wir uns so intensiv wie immer beschäftigen. Ja, gerade in dem und für den Gebrauch muß ich das Ding sein lassen, was es ist' (p. 102; my emphasis).

[43] Heidegger writes: 'Ließe ich die Kreide nicht Kreide sein, würde ich sie etwa im Mörser zerstampfen, dann würde ich sie nicht gebrauchen' (p. 102).

[44] Physicists, for instance, always encounter (and study) entities *qua constituents of nature* (e.g. as material entities that occupy particular spatiotemporal positions and are subject to certain laws of nature). So Heidegger's suggestion that we always let things be what and how they are is related to the classical claim that we always encounter something *as something* (cf. the Aristotelian language of *legein ti kata tinos*). Put another way, letting-be basically means letting something be encountered *as* something. (For a very brief discussion on this issue, see Inwood 1999, p. 116.)

something.[45] Interestingly, Heidegger immediately remarks that this 'indifference' is only possible in care (cf. p. 102). The point, as I understand it, is that this sort of indifference can only be exhibited by a being for whom, as Heidegger repeatedly says, the mode of being of entities—entities it *ineluctably* is amidst—is an issue. The claim seems to be that letting things be, and particularly, letting them be *in certain respects* is required if we are to 'share in them'.

One could probably articulate in a different way this very same point concerning a care-expressing act that is at the root of any theoretical attitude towards something by observing that a (broadly) theoretical engagement always (and necessarily) takes place in terms of a particular manner of understanding the entity at issue. To this extent any theoretical engagement with a given entity could be taken to imply an (at least non-thematic) interpretative act that brings the encountered entity to *in advance* have certain sorts of significance (and not others).[46] In other words, in those situations in which we let something be what it is, by refraining from some practical purposes, we are expressing our care-defined mode of being in a particular mode. This is a mode that is not *circum*-spective (that is not a matter of 'looking around'), but *in*-spective (a matter of 'looking at' *in a certain respect*). Being 'only' in-spective, however, our theoretical letting-something-be-what-it-is is concern-driven through and through; it is an expression of our being there in such a way as to come to, in advance and in light of certain projections, understand the entities we are amidst as having a particular mode of being.

There is, however, an important point we have not touched upon yet. This point concerns a suggestion I have promised to elucidate in order to finally explicate the sense in which human intentionality can be said to always exhibit some character of sharedness. I am referring to the suggestion concerning the equiprimordiality of being-alongside-things and being-with. Reconstructing Heidegger's argument to this effect would require us to dig deep into a number of complicated issues. I think that we can avoid having to do so here by contextualizing the argument just presented in such a way as to bring to light a particular problem. This is a problem that may be said to call for the idea of an equiprimordiality of being-alongside-things and being-with.

As already mentioned, Heidegger develops the argument just exposed within an attempt to determine what he calls the essence of truth. In this context, he eventually comes to argue that the whole matter comes down to the following issue: the unconcealment of entities is something that can be attributed to the them—since it is the

---

[45] Heidegger writes: 'Dieses Seinlassen der Dinge im weitesten Sinne liegt grundsätzlich noch vor jeder besonderen Interessiertheit bzw. bestimmten Gleichgültigkeit. Dieses unser Seinlassen, unser Überlassen der Dinge an sie selbst und ihr Sein ist eine eigene Gleichgültigkeit unsererseits, eine Gleichgültigkeit des Daseins, die zu seinem metaphysischen Wesen gehört' (p. 102).

[46] In order to refer to this previously determined (and determining) respect in which an entity is encountered in the context of a given situation, in the text I am quoting from, Heidegger appeals to the notion of a *projection* [*Entwurf*] (cf. pp. 185ff.). 'Projection' is, however, a term he uses in *Being and Time* to refer to a certainly related, but definitively richer, topic that pertains to our forward-looking mode of existence. We will come to discuss this notion of a projection below (in Sect. 7.3).

entities themselves that come to 'show up' in this or that way—, but has to be taken to be grounded in our care-defined mode of being (cf. pp. 110ff.). Let me tackle this issue by means of a brief reflection that, close in spirit to Heidegger's argument, does not correspond exactly to anything Heidegger claims in the relevant passages.

Our factual being-with-one-another in the context of some concrete encounter often plays an objectifying role with respect to other worldly entities encountered in this situation.[47] If one sees another person comporting herself in an intelligible way towards a particular entity—an entity towards which one could oneself intelligibly behave in a number of ways—, one may feel reassured that there *really* is a particular being calling for certain sorts of comportment. Moreover, a factual being-with-one-another of a relatively undemanding sort could fulfill this objectifying function. To come to understand something as *really being the case* we (the involved individuals) are not required to be cooperatively oriented towards some goal. We just need to be aware that there is another being who like me is open to entities as entities of particular sorts. We can, thus, characterize our mutual openness qua Dasein as a *world-objectifying mutual openness*.

Indeed, one could argue that our intuitive image of something really being the case is basically the image of something being *at least in principle* also accessible to other individuals who share our openness to these sorts of things or occurrences. Suppose that Robinson Crusoe has lost count of the passing days and has begun to ask himself whether he really has spent several weeks on this island or just a couple of days. What is it exactly that he is asking himself? A possible answer to this question could be that he is wondering what someone else—a being that understands things in a similar way—would say, were she or he to be asked about the number of days (or weeks) Robinson has spent on the island. So even a *non-factual* being-with could be said to play the world-objectifying role at issue here.

Now, this consideration, which I take to be in line with Heidegger's picture of what he calls the essence of truth, seems to be at odds with the argument reconstructed in this section. The problem is as follows: our last reflection suggests that the objective character the world (as world) normally exhibits presupposes a sense that in this very same world we could encounter other human beings for whom entities are also unconcealed as entities. The argument exposed above, however, seems to aim at showing precisely the contrary: that the structural sense Heidegger calls being-with could be said to be grounded in the objective character exhibited by the world we are amidst; in the character of sameness exhibited by the entities towards which we humans behave. To put it bluntly, were one interested in integrating the two trains of thought just condensed in a unitary account of the relationship that holds between the fundamental sense Heidegger calls being-with and the equally basic sense of being in a world that exhibits an objective character, one would probably end up offering a perfectly circular account.

---

[47] I think that this is in line with what Donald Davidson thematizes under the heading of triangulation. For an interesting discussion on the relation between triangulation and shared experience, see Hutto (2002).

This is the context in which the notion of equiprimordiality comes to play a role. Heidegger's claim concerning the equiprimordiality of being-alongside-things and being-with does, however, not amount to a sort of ad hoc solution to the problem just outlined. Indeed, Heidegger does not regard this circularity as a problem of his argument. On the contrary, one could argue that it is precisely this circularity that he is seeking to bring to light by means of the argument I have been exposing throughout this section.

So the conclusion Heidegger is driving at may finally be stated as follows: as far as our existence-defining sense of being-in-the-world is concerned, being-alongside-things and being-with have no priority over each other.[48] To the extent to which our sense of being-in-the-world (a world that normally exhibits an objective character) can be said to be grounded in the sense Heidegger calls being-with and this sense of being-with can, in turn, be said to be grounded in our sense of being in a world that is essentially shareable, being-there [*da-sein*] (or being a subject) could be said to be a matter of *being-with-alongside-things*.[49] In other words, to exist as a human being means to normally have a sense of being in a world that one can share with other beings who, in virtue of their care-defined mode of being, *also* participate in the unconcealment not only of the occurrentness of entities, but furthermore (and fundamentally), of certain sorts of significance these entities can exhibit in concrete situations—in the unconcealment of their mode of being.[50]

It is worth noting in this context that we do not normally have to come to the *conclusion* that the comportment of another human expresses some view of a world we share. On the contrary, our interpretation of some segment of human behavior (and our interaction with other individuals) is normally based on the *assumption* that the relevant segment of behavior amounts to an act that expresses a particular view of this shared world. In the course of our observation of (or of our interaction with) other individuals we may come to feel limited in our capacity to make sense of the view of the world that the acts at issue express. In a foreign land, for instance, we could come to conclude that, coming from a completely different cultural background, it is extremely difficult (for us) to understand what the natives are doing. But even in such a situation we would probably not come to conclude that there is no intelligible context whatsoever in which these acts may make perfect sense—a context we could in principle come to understand. Even certain pieces of 'extremely bizarre' comportment exhibited by individuals affected by what we call mental

---

[48] To be sure, in a further move Heidegger develops this point in such a way as to come to elucidate the equiprimordiality of being-alongside-things, being-with, and being-one's-self [*Selbstsein*] (cf. p. 148). In order to make plausible the idea that human intentionality can be said to always exhibit some character of sharedness, I do not have to enter this further discussion though.

[49] Heidegger explicitly makes this claim: 'Dasein ist Miteinandersein bei…' (p. 141).

[50] Seeking to capture Heidegger's suggestion in terms that are less technical, we could affirm that Heidegger is pointing to a pervasive, but rather inconspicuous, sense we normally have: the sense that we move in realms of significance in which other humans also move (or at least could also move). Normally inconspicuous, this is a sense that becomes notorious in those situations in which it comes to a break-down of the system of factors on which it relies. In general terms, I believe, we could take this sense to be dependent on shared mental capacities and common practices.

disorders may come to be seen as acts that make sense against the background of certain ways of understanding we do not share with these individuals. The point is that we can understand these behaviors as puzzling acts, as it were, only on the condition of having already presupposed that there is a more encompassing realm of significance we share with the behaving individuals.[51] This is the sense in which our human relation to the world can be taken to be essentially shareable in nature.[52] Our human openness to the world can to this extent be argued to presuppose an, at least non-thematic, understanding of the situations we are in as situations we (may come to) share with other beings with whom we always already share a (significance-disclosing) care-defined mode of being.

As mentioned at the beginning of this section, by means of the argument just developed, I have aimed at supporting a conclusion which seeks to make plausible the suggestion that the phenomenon of collective affective intentionality, in a particularly rich manner, expresses our human nature: it is only because human intentionality is a matter of an *essentially* shareable world-relatedness that we can come to emotionally respond to certain occurrences in a genuinely joint manner.[53] In the following section, I shall further develop this suggestion by discussing the phenomenologically foundational role certain feelings play with regard to the care-defined mode of being we, as argued in this section, have always already taken ourselves to share when we come to actualize our ability to feel-towards together. My goal in so doing is to clarify the sense in which 'ordinary' human intentionality may be taken to, furthermore, be *affectively enabled* shareable (and often factually shared) intentionality.

5.4 Feelings of Being: On Our Affectively Grounded World-Belongingness

Seeking to overcome an excessive emphasis on emotional feelings in the contemporary philosophical discussion on affectivity, Matthew Ratcliffe (2005, 2008) has recently rearticulated Heidegger's suggestion that any particular experience occurs

---

[51] In the remainder of this inquiry, I shall come to explicate and elaborate on the idea that certain affective states situate us in *particular* worlds; the idea being that they situate us in *relatively specific sub-realms of significance*. This idea of coming to be situated in certain worlds presupposes, however, the idea that we share certain wide-ranging ways of making sense of worldly occurrences.

[52] It is important to understand that 'essentially' does not mean always. Under certain (often pathological) conditions human beings can come to experience their world as a radically non-shareable one.

[53] Heidegger is making a very similar point, I think, when he writes: 'Nur weil jedes Dasein als solches von Hause aus – wie, wurde in einer Hinsicht gezeigt – ein Mitsein ist, d.h. Miteinander, nur deshalb ist menschliche Gemeinschaft und Gesellschaft möglich, in den verschiedenen Abwandlungen, Stufen und Graden der Echtheit und Unechtheit, Dauerhaftigkeit und Flüchtigkeit' (p. 141).

against the background of what may be called our *affective attunement* to the world—Heidegger calls it *Befindlichkeit*.[54] In this section I shall reconstruct the main points of Ratcliffe's argument to the effect that the existence-defining sense to which Heidegger refers with the compound term 'being-in-the-world' is basically a modifiable feeling of belongingness to the world.

Ratcliffe begins his discussion by pointing to a series of affective states that are frequently alluded to in everyday discourse. These are states that are usually referred to as 'feelings' and characterized, for instance, as a sense of 'belonging', 'familiarity', 'completeness', 'estrangement', 'distance', 'separation', or 'homeliness' (cf. 2008, p. 56).[55] According to Ratcliffe, the fundamental commonality of all these feelings—and by feelings he means 'bodily states of which we have at least some awareness' (p. 2)—is that they cannot be properly understood as emotional experiences of particular objects or occurrences. Rather, Ratcliffe argues, they have to be regarded as 'ways of finding oneself in a world' (ibid.). Accordingly, he proposes to conceive of these affective states as 'background orientations', i.e. as states that shape all our particular object-directed experiences, and claims that these sorts of feelings neglected in the philosophical debate should be taken to constitute a phenomenological category of their own: the class of *existential feelings*. In what follows I shall try to clarify what is special about these feelings from a phenomenological point of view.

Ratcliffe comes to qualify the feelings just listed as 'existential' in the context of an attempt to develop the idea that the affective states at issue convey a sense of reality to the situations in which we encounter other worldly entities. He suggests that this sense of reality 'is inextricable from a changeable *feeling* of relatedness between body and world' (ibid.).[56] One could certainly find this very first proposal that there is a relation between the sense of reality alleged to normally accompany our perceptual experiences and a class of feelings puzzling enough. After all, one could be tempted to object, we usually take an intentional object (or a situation) to

---

[54] Macquarrie and Robinson (1962) translate Heidegger's term 'Befindlichkeit' as 'state of mind'. Ratcliffe observes that this translation is misleading, since what Heidegger is pointing to is not a 'perception of one's internal mental states' (Ratcliffe 2005, p. 51, footnote 8). Ratcliffe prefers the term 'attunement', which is the one proposed by Joan Stambaugh in her translation of *Being and Time* ([1927] 1996). Taylor Carman (2003) proposes the term 'disposedness', which, as we shall see, aptly captures the role the affective states we are going to focus on in this section may be said to play. In my view, Ratcliffe's expression 'ways of finding oneself (in the world)' comes particularly close to the intension of Heidegger's 'Befindlichkeit'.

[55] In his paper 'The Feeling of Being', in which he introduces most of the ideas we are going to discuss in this section, Ratcliffe offers a longer list. He mentions there: 'The feeling of being: "complete", "flawed and diminished", "unworthy", "humble", "separate and in limitation", "at home", "a fraud", "slightly lost", "over-whelmed", "abandoned", "stared at", "torn", "disconnected from the world", "invulnerable", "unloved", "watched", "empty", "in control", "powerful", "completely helpless", "part of the real world again", "trapped and weighed down", "part of a larger machine", "at one with life", "at one with nature", "there", "familiar", "real"' (2005, p. 45). Ratcliffe states that he obtained all of these examples by typing 'the feeling of being' into the search engine Google on 12th February 2005.

[56] This is an idea Ratcliffe claims to have taken from William James' late work (see 2005, p. 56).

be either real or not. If the sense of reality at issue here were a matter of feelings, the class of existential feelings would be constituted by exactly two types of feelings: feelings to the effect that things are real and feelings to the effect that they are not. In other words, one could wonder what Ratcliffe's reasons could be for conceiving of what he calls a sense of reality as something that may suffer *nuanced qualitative modifications*.

I believe that we can begin to make sense of this suggestion by pointing out that Ratcliffe is conceiving of what he calls a sense of reality basically as what we may call a *sense of world-belongingness*.[57] He writes: 'The world can seem close or distant and our relationship with it can involve a general sense of belonging or estrangement' (p. 3). This suggestion is based on the observation that dramatic modifications of this sense of belongingness (for instance, in psychopathological cases) are often accompanied by complaints that things, people, or the world as a whole seem unreal (cf. Ratcliffe 2008, pp. 61ff. and Part II). This common association, Ratcliffe seems to think, allows us to identify the experiential structure I am calling here a feeling of world-belongingness with the sense of reality that normally accompanies our perceptual experiences as experiences of worldly entities. In other words, the sense of reality at issue here is basically a *modifiable sense of situatedness*. It is a matter of a dynamic feeling of being, to a greater or a lesser extent, part of a particular worldly situation. The point of the argument is that such a sense can be argued to be presupposed by our capacity to have particular experiences of worldly entities or occurrences or think about them.

Referring to Husserl's notion of a *natural attitude*, Ratcliffe characterizes this sense of reality as a 'pre-articulate conviction that is already in place before we explicitly assent to anything in the form of a propositional attitude' (p. 4). Drawing on Merleau-Ponty (1964, pp. 163–164), he elaborates on this idea of a pre-articulate conviction by writing that the sense of reality alluded to 'is not a body of conceptual knowledge [...], but an "opening" onto the world—an existential orientation that operates as a background to experience and thought, rather than an explicit content of experience or thought' (ibid.). Ratcliffe's original suggestion here concerns the claim that, contrary to what Husserl's idea of a natural attitude takes for granted, this 'opening' onto the world is not categorical and invariant; it can (and does normally) suffer a series of gradual modifications.

Now, although this pre-articulate conviction that one is part of some worldly situation can exhibit a series of (often unattended) variations, it always plays the very same phenomenological role. Whatever experiential character this *felt conviction*, as we may call it, exhibits at a given moment, it always *situates one in a specific world*—in a specific realm of relations of significance, we could say.

As we shall immediately see, this idea concerning the capacity existential feelings have to locate us in *specific* regions of import, as we may put it, allows Ratcliffe to flesh out the claim that there is a relation that holds between the affective states listed above and a modifiable sense of reality that structures our experiences of

---

[57] Ratcliffe does not use the term 'world-belongingness', but he repeatedly appeals to the idea of some sense of belonging to this or that situation or of being part of the world.

particular objects. In order to clarify this relation, let us try to get a first grasp of what it could mean for a feeling to situate us in a world. In the course of my attempt to explicate this thought, I shall come to spell out the particularity of the experiential role existential feelings may be said to play.

Elaborating on Heidegger's challenge of what he takes to be the commonplace view of experience, Ratcliffe sets up his discussion of the phenomenological role existential feelings play by criticizing a view that is widely shared among philosophers and scientists interested in affective phenomena. According to this view we can understand our whole affective life in terms of feelings that result from our having come to be 'touched' by particular (real or imagined) occurrences that take place in a world we are in contact with, but separated from. Ratcliffe writes that this picture draws on 'a tendency to construe experience as the standoffish, spectatorial contemplation of objects by a curiously detached subject, who is set apart from the world that she somehow experiences' (p. 41).

In order to oppose this view, Ratcliffe appeals to an apparently trivial observation made by Heidegger: 'we already *find ourselves in a world* when we encounter something' (Ratcliffe 2008, p. 41). In this context, Ratcliffe suggests that existential feelings should be understood as states that, in a sense, antecede and make possible any *experiential* distinction between us (subjects) and the (objective) world we are in.[58] The point is that this phenomenological particularity of existential feelings may be understood as the feature in virtue of which they can situate us in specific worlds, as suggested by the idea of a modifiable world-belongingness.

In a footnote that is particularly relevant in this context Ratcliffe refers to a remark made by Stephan Strasser. According to Strasser (cf. 1977, p. 188), our sense of being-in-the-world may be said to be phenomenologically prior to any distinction between subject and object (see Ratcliffe 2008, p. 48, footnote 4). This reference makes clear that Ratcliffe is driving at the conclusion that existential feelings should be regarded as the experiential foundation of what, according to Heidegger, amounts to the central phenomenological particularity of our human mode of being: our sense of being-in-the-world. Ratcliffe's novel claim is, as already hinted at, that we should understand this sense as a *changeable* sense of being-in-the-world.

Ratcliffe comes to explicitly invoke Heidegger's notion of *Befindlichkeit* in the course of an attempt to spell out this idea concerning the foundational role existential feelings play with regard to our normal sense of being-*in* (of belonging to the world). In this context, he furthermore makes evident that he wants us to understand existential feelings as affective states that basically play the role Heidegger attributes to what he calls 'mood' [*Stimmung*]. Ratcliffe writes: 'Even when an experience does incorporate a contrast between oneself and something else, that experience continues to presuppose a unitary structure of belonging and it is *Befindlichkeit* that makes this structure possible' (p. 47).

---

[58] Of course, existential feelings are feelings of concrete ontic subjects (individualized worldly entities). What is at issue here is the distinction between world and self which, from a phenomenological point of view, can be said to structure any intentional experience.

Ratcliffe continues to develop this thought by appealing to an observation made by Heidegger. This observation, which we have already discussed above (in Sects. 5.2 and 5.3), concerns the idea that worldly entities always already exhibit some sorts of significance when we come to encounter them (usually in the context of some project or ongoing purposeful activity we are involved in). The appeal to this phenomenological insight permits him to promote the thought at issue by suggesting that existential feelings situate us in a world *by serving as a meaning-giving background*. Ratcliffe writes: 'The possibilities of purposively engaging with anything, of striving towards a goal, of valuing something, of registering something as practically salient and of pursuing a project all *presuppose* a sense of things "mattering" to us' (p. 47; my emphasis).[59] Ratcliffe's claim is that it is a pre-intentional feeling of the above-listed sort that allows things to always already have some sorts of significance (and not others) when we come to encounter them.

Now, it is important to note that the point Ratcliffe is making here, by appealing to the idea that entities often appear as already having some sort of practical significance, is different from the one made above (in Sect. 5.3) in relation to this idea. In the previous section, the reference to this thought sought to support the suggestion that intentionality is primarily a matter of our immersed engagement with the world, and not of some basically thematic-observational relation to it. The point Ratcliffe is making here rather concerns the idea that there is a form of world-relatedness that is prior to (i.e. that is presupposed by) any object-directed experiential relation to some worldly entity or occurrence, but which is already experiential in nature. This is a form of *presentational* world-relatedness, as we may call it, that could be characterized as a pre-intentional relation to the world.

Since, as pointed out, Ratcliffe is elaborating here on Heidegger's claim that it is our 'mood' that situates us in specific domains of significance, a brief look at Heidegger's view of the relation between 'mood' and the experience-structuring sense he calls being-in could be enlightening. The basic idea, we have just seen, is that the affective states at issue may be said to *open up* a particular domain of significance 'by revealing the world as a realm of practical purposes, values and goals' (Ratcliffe 2008, p. 47). Heidegger begins to make plausible this idea of a feeling situating us in some particular domain of significance by emphasizing that a 'mood' is something one finds oneself *in*. He observes—and Ratcliffe emphasizes this remark—that one does not experience a 'mood' as an internal (subjective) state. One does, however, not experience it as something that comes from 'the outside', either.[60] Moreover, we do normally not affirm that we *have* a particular 'mood'; rather, we say that we *are* in this or that 'mood', as Ratcliffe remarks (cf. p. 48).

Now, these loose observations broadly elucidate the sense in which certain affective states could be taken to ground our fundamental sense of being *in* a specific world. Moreover, on the basis of this observation it is possible to spell out a central difference between existential feelings and emotions. This difference relies on the

---

[59] Ratcliffe refers here to Heidegger ([1927] 1962, p. 176).
[60] Heidegger writes: 'A mood assails us. It comes neither from "outside" nor from "inside", but arises out of Being-in-the-world, as a way of such Being' ([1927] 1962, p. 176).

capacity existential feelings, but not emotions, have to *set up* the world we are in at a given moment; the world in which we can come to have specific and meaningful object-directed (affective and non-affective) experiences. But the observations just exposed clearly fail to clarify the sense in which the affective states at issue may be taken to allow things to always already matter to us in certain ways when we come to encounter them. This is a thought we have to illuminate if we are to get a sufficiently clear idea of the specific phenomenological role existential feelings play.

I believe that the claim that existential feelings allow things to always already matter to us (in specific ways) when we come to encounter them could be explicated by developing the idea of a *felt preparedness* to have certain sorts of experiences. The suggestion is that existential feelings may be understood as (occurrent) disposing states of a particular kind. Indeed, it seems to me that this notion of a felt preparedness is quite close to a suggestion Ratcliffe comes to articulate in more recent papers (2010, 2012). The suggestion concerns the idea that the phenomenological role existential feelings play could be understood in terms of a modifiable sense of one's space of possibilities. The idea seems to be that this space of possibilities is determined by those *specific* categories of mattering under which something can come to be experienced in a concrete situation.

Moreover, already in his original proposal Ratcliffe seems to be conceiving of existential feelings in terms of such a sort of preparedness, since he deems it important to refer to a remark Heidegger makes in his analysis of fear ([1927] 1962, §30). This is a remark which may be taken to suggest that certain affective states *of a non-emotional kind* dispose us to have certain sorts of *emotional* experiences. In the relevant extract, Heidegger writes that fear 'has already disclosed the world, in that out of it something like the fearsome may come close' (p. 180; as quoted by Ratcliffe 2008, p. 49).

The key to understanding this claim is to realize that, as Ratcliffe observes, Heidegger is not always referring to an object-directed affective state when, in *Being and Time,* he employs the term 'fear'. In other words, the *emotion* we usually call fear is not always what Heidegger has in mind when he makes a series of claims pertaining to the phenomenological role of some affective condition he names 'fear'. Rather, and as we shall see, there are passages in which he seems to be pointing to something he takes to *ground the very possibility* of having the emotion we call fear (cf. Ratcliffe 2008, p. 49). Following a suggestion made by Jan Slaby, in what follows I shall begin to develop the notion of a felt preparedness by explicating the claim that fear (as a mood) has already disclosed a world in which something like the fearsome may come close.

In the passage of his paper 'Emotionaler Weltbezug: Ein Strukturschema im Anschluss an Heidegger' (2007) that is pertinent here, Slaby tries to respond to an objection against the view that typical emotions are intentional states. This objection is based on the fact that people often allude to emotions that have no clear intentional object. Slaby replies to this sensible objection by appealing to the fragment of *Being and Time* I have just quoted. He begins his rejoinder by observing that Heidegger anticipates a number of ideas that are central to the cognitivist view of affective intentionality (cf. the discussion in Sect. 2.3). Particularly, Heidegger conceives of the act of fearing as an act that, as I have put it, presents its target as being a certain way and therefore meriting a response of a certain sort; as exhibiting a particular feature defined by the formal object of this emotion.[61]

Slaby points out that, according to Heidegger, the feeling of fear presents its target not only as something that can be detrimental [*abträglich*] for us (i.e. as something that is able to cause some damage or to adversely affect us in one way or another), but furthermore, as something the detrimentality of which 'is not yet within striking distance' (Heidegger [1927] 1962, pp. 179–180). The point is that the feeling of fear presents the harm in question as a *possibility*. Slaby completes this thought by observing that worldly occurrences that may *in principle* be regarded as harmful are usually not experienced as fearsome if they are not understood by the relevant person as occurrences that have the possibility to, in one way or another, 'touch' her *in her personal existence* (cf. Slaby 2007, p. 97). In this context, Slaby recalls an observation made by Heidegger, according to which the feeling of fear ultimately reveals our *fearfulness* [*Furchtsamkeit*] as a capacity to be threatened. Heidegger's point here is that our acts of fearing can be taken to disclose a prior openness to *the fearsome* as such [*das Furchtbare*] (cf. [1927] 1962, p. 180); an openness that, in turn, expresses the fact that Dasein, as Heidegger repeatedly claims, is the being for whom its own being is an issue. Appealing to this idea of a prior openness to the fearsome, Slaby provides a simple analysis of those situations in which we are in an affective state that lacks an identifiable intentional target, but can be argued to nevertheless exhibit the experiential quality of fear. He suggests that these are situations in which the very possibility of being adversely affected by what one could encounter in the world becomes experientially actual in the form of an awareness of our capacity to be hurt, damaged, or otherwise negatively affected. This is a suggestion that has an important implication for the idea that the distinct phenomenological role that existential feelings play may be understood in terms of a sort of preparedness to have certain affective experiences (and not others). For what Slaby's argument brings us to see is that our preparedness to have emotional experiences of certain sorts should not be understood as a mere disposition to enter, under relevant conditions, into certain states that exhibit a particular experiential character. That is to say, the preparedness at issue here should not be understood, to use Helm's terminology, as a mere emotional commitment to the import the circumstances at issue have to us. Rather, this preparedness should be conceived of in terms of an *occurrent* affective state, which as such already has some experiential character; i.e. not as a disposedness (simpliciter), but as a sort of *disposing condition that is already experiential in nature*.

On this basis, we can finally explicate the sense in which existential feelings may be said to allow worldly entities to always already have some sort of significance when we come to encounter them—to always already matter to us in some more or less specific ways. In virtue of their being occurrent conditions that have a *determinate* experiential character, the pre-intentional affective states at issue here could be said to prepare us to *feelingly* understand the encountered entities as being a certain

---

[61] Of course, Heidegger does not use this terminology.

way by, in a way, calling *in an anticipated manner* for certain sorts of 'responses', and not for others.[62]

Now, according to the view just exposed, our attunement to the world is a matter of feelings of a certain sort. Feelings—whatever sort they instantiate—are, as discussed above (cf. the discussion in Sect. 4.2), not only ontologically, but also epistemologically subjective. So one could wonder whether this subjective nature of existential feelings does not constitute a serious problem to the claim that, when we come to encounter one another, we have always already understood that we share an affectively enabled import-disclosing mode of being (cf. the discussion in Sect. 5.3).

No one else can experience one's feelings in the very same way one does. The fundamental fact, however, that one is affectively attuned to the world in some particular way—that things tend to matter to one in determinate ways—normally becomes evident to other persons. It does so in one's being ready to comport in certain ways (and not in others) towards worldly entities. It becomes particularly patent in one's readiness to emotionally respond in particular ways to the requirements of the world.[63] So the idea that we have always already understood that we share a care-defined mode of being, when we come to encounter one another, can be taken to be related to the idea that we are at least non-thematically aware that the fundamental affectiveness we experience—in the form of a preparedness to consider certain events significant—is something that is common to us (human individuals). Before I come to close this chapter, let me make a remark aimed at clarifying this point.

It is important to note that, as far as our mere mutual openness qua Dasein is concerned, we do not have to assume that we normally share some specific background feeling.[64] All we have to assume to be sharing (insofar as we are in a shareable world) is our being always affectively attuned *in one mode or another* to this world; our being able to encounter things as already mattering to us in certain ways. In other words, in order to be in an essentially shareable world, we only have to assume that the fundamental affectiveness we experience in the form of a felt preparedness to attribute certain sorts of significance to particular kinds of worldly occurrences amounts to an essential trait of the way of being of those beings with which we can come to share in some particular situation.

This being-affectively-attuned-to-the-world is not simply something that determines the mode of being of each of us (potential participants in some shared experience). As we have seen (in Sect. 5.3), it is something we share in a stronger sense of the verb 'to share': in a sense that implies some at least tacit common knowledge

---

[62] The reason for putting the term 'responses' in quotation marks is because we are talking here of responses to question the world has not posed yet.

[63] Things are, of course, more complicated. For one's specific temperament is to a great extent responsible for the sorts of moods (or existential feelings) one is disposed to be in. For an interesting discussion on this topic, see Deonna and Teroni (2009).

[64] This remark is in line with Ratcliffe's rejection of the idea that there is a unique 'natural attitude' that is at the bottom of the sense of everydayness that normally structures our quotidian experiences.

concerning that which is shared by us. Concretely, our being-affectively-attuned-to-the-world is something we share in the sense of *having always already understood*, when we come to encounter one another, that this (affectively enabled) import-disclosing mode of being is something we have in common.

As just pointed out, we (humans and potential participants in some joint affective experience) are not necessarily *jointly* attuned to the world in some specific way. So, on the basis of the considerations articulated so far, we are definitively not allowed to conclude that there is some sense in which 'ordinary' human intentionality may be claimed to always be collective affective intentionality. As I shall try to show below (particularly in Sect. 6.4), however, the view just exposed could be exploited in such a way as to support the idea that certain pre-intentional feelings may play a fundamental role in making out of our humanity-defining, affectively enabled being-with (i.e. of our basic sense of being in an essentially shareable world) a situation-specific being-*together*-in-the-same-world. In closing this discussion, I would like to briefly characterize the approach I have begun to develop here, in order to delineate the next step of this argument.

Against the background of a particular understanding of what affective intentionality amounts to, I have tried to bring to light a sort of continuum that may be taken to exist between what I have called 'ordinary' human intentionality and the phenomenon we are interested in: the phenomenon of collective affective intentionality. I have done so by focusing, first, on our usual sense of being in an essentially shareable world, and second, on the affective foundation of our (in a relatively weak sense of the verb 'to share') shared human openness to the world. My ultimate goal has been to ground the claim that our acts of feeling-towards together in an outstanding manner express our human nature; the point being that they do so to the extent to which they, as I shall continue to elucidate throughout this book, in a very rich manner reveal that we exist in a way that is defined by what Heidegger calls care. My approach to the phenomenon of collective affective intentionality is, hence, based on the intuition that we can begin to understand our ability to feel-towards together by explicating the sense in which, independently of the type of intentional relationship it instantiates, a world-directed experience can normally be said to (at least minimally) express the two features that characterize the phenomenon we are concerned with: its affective character and its character of sharedness. In the course of my initial attempt to support this idea, I have established a theoretical framework that, as I shall try to show in the remainder of this work, allows us to develop Schmid's suggestion that at the heart of a collective affective intentional episode we always find a shared concern.

Since, as just pointed out, most of our experiences do not exhibit the features in question to an extent that permits us to characterize them as collective affective intentional experiences, in a next move I shall make an effort to spell out what is special about those experiences that can be taken to actualize our human ability to feel-towards together. Specifically, I shall argue for the idea that our acts of feeling-towards together ultimately disclose a distinct mode of caring. In the course of this argument, I shall, furthermore, suggest that certain pre-intentional feelings of the sort discussed in this section may be said to set up, in the very same motion, the world we are in (in a given situation) and the character of togetherness some, and only some, of our world-directed (affective) experiences exhibit.

Chapter 6
Being Together and Caring-With

Abstract This chapter spells out what is special about our joint acts of feeling-towards together. It does so by pointing to a distinct felt conviction that phenomeno-logically defines the experiences that are at the heart of a collective affective intentional episode: the conviction that we (the participants) are jointly caring about something. The chapter elucidates what, in two different respects, grounds this felt conviction: what justifies this conviction and what, from a phenomenological point of view, serves as an experiential foundation for it. This allows me to, first, bring to light a distinctive mode of caring-about disclosed by our joint acts of feeling-towards together, and second, argue that certain pre-intentional feelings prepare us to feelingly understand certain circumstances as situations in which we (the partici-pants) are caring about something as a group. In the course of this discussion, I introduce two notions: the notion of caring-with and the notion of feelings of being-together. I show that, leaving aside the image of some 'fused feelings', it is possible to develop an account of the phenomenon of collective affective intentionality that satisfies the two basic conditions of adequacy determined in the first part of this book. That is, an account that, first, makes visible that acts of felt understanding are at the heart of collective affective intentionality, and second, permits us to tell apart in a principled way the situations in which the involved individuals are feeling together from the situations in which they merely are feeling alongside each other.

Keywords Caring as a group • Caring-with • Collective affective intentional epi-sode • Feelings of being-together • Feeling-towards together • Felt conviction • Import-assenting position

6.1 Introduction

Chapter 5 offered a characterization of our human openness to the world in terms of an affectively enabled belongingness to an essentially shareable world. This charac-terization condensed the following thought: we can find in non-affective and non-collective forms of world-relatedness the features that centrally define those acts by means of which we participate in a collective affective intentional episode. The point in stressing this commonality has been to suggest that our inquiry into the

© Springer International Publishing Switzerland 2016   169
H.A. Sánchez Guerrero, *Feeling Together and Caring with One Another*,
Studies in the Philosophy of Sociality 7, DOI 10.1007/978-3-319-33735-7_6

nature of the phenomenon of collective affective intentionality necessarily touches on the issue concerning our particularly human way of being—a way of being that according to Heidegger is defined by care.

Having pointed to the continuity that holds between 'ordinary' intentionality and collective affective intentionality, in what follows I shall spell out what is special about our joint acts of feeling-towards together. I shall do so by pointing to a distinct felt conviction, as I shall call it, that may be claimed to phenomenologically define the experiences that are at the heart of a collective affective intentional act: the conviction that we (the participants) are jointly caring about something.[1] The discussion will consist in an elucidation of what, in two different respects, can be said to *ground* this distinct felt conviction. In a first step I shall address what could be said to *justify* this conviction, while in a second move I shall make thematic what, from a phenomenological point of view, may be taken to *serve as an experiential foundation* for it. Concretely, I am going to discuss two different roles affective states (of different sorts) may be said to play in cases of genuinely collective affective intentionality. In doing this, I shall, first, bring to light a distinctive mode of caring-about that may be claimed to be at the core of our joint acts of feeling-towards together (Sects. 6.2 and 6.3), and second, suggest that certain pre-intentional feelings may prepare us to feelingly understand certain circumstances as situations in which we (the participants) are caring about something as a group (Sect. 6.4). In the course of this discussion, I shall introduce two notions: the notion of *caring-with* and the notion of *feelings of being-together*. By means of this discussion I shall begin to show that, leaving aside the image of some 'fused feelings', it is possible to develop an account of the phenomenon of collective affective intentionality that satisfies the two basic conditions of adequacy determined in the first part of this book. That is, an account that, firstly, makes visible that acts of felt understanding are at the heart of collective affective intentionality, and secondly, permits us to tell apart in a principled way the situations in which the involved individuals are feeling together from the situations in which they merely are feeling alongside each other. By extending in the manner just sketched Schmid's suggestion that at the heart of a collective affective intentional episode we always find a shared concern (cf. our discussion in Sect. 4.4), I aim at developing a conceptual framework for a phenomenologically adequate view of collective affective intentionality apt to endow this phenomenon with existential significance. Specifically, the account to be developed in the remainder of this book aims at making plausible the idea that our joint actualizations of our ability to feel-towards together express our human nature in an exemplary manner.

---

[1] My reader might be irritated by the unidiomatic use of the verb 'to care' in its continuous form. The reason for systematically doing so is that I want to emphasize the temporal aspect—the episodic character—of those acts that bring to light that the relevant subject is guided by the import something has to her.

6.2   Emotions Which Reveal that We Jointly Care About Something

What is special about those emotions by means of which a number of individuals participate in a collective affective intentional episode is that they disclose the fact that these individuals are jointly caring about something.[2] In order to support this claim, I shall examine emotions that arise against a particular experiential background. Here I mean the background of an at least tacit understanding of the situation one finds oneself in as a situation in which one is contributing to some collective endeavor. Thus, my methodological assumption is that we can begin to determine the phenomenological specificum of the affective experiences that are at the heart of *any* collective affective intentional act by focusing on certain emotions a number of individuals can have in the context of ongoing activities in which they are participating *as members of some concrete group they, at the relevant moment, take themselves to jointly constitute.* I am referring to emotions which the participants understand as contributions to some emotional response of their group.[3]

I believe that the key to grasping the nature of the experiences mentioned is to understand the following issue: someone's failure to have the emotional experiences I am pointing to in those situations that normatively require them could bring this person (and other persons also) to suspect that, despite her participation in the relevant activities, at this point, she did not *really* understand herself as a member of the group at issue. The idea is that she (and other persons also) could be inclined to conclude that what brings her to fail to respond in the expected manner is the fact that, at the relevant moment, she was not concerned with the occurrence at issue *as an occurrence that is relevant to the 'wellbeing' and 'flourishing' of this group.*

It is on the basis of this consideration that I would like to explore the idea that the experiences we are interested in are phenomenologically determined—in a way to be specified in the course of this discussion—by a sort of felt conviction to the effect that we (the involved individuals) are *caring together about something.* In order to begin to clarify this idea, I would like to come back to a suggestion I made above (in Sect. 4.4) in discussing the case of Adrian's and Beatrice's simultaneous emotional response to the threat posed to an object they value. In the relevant passage, I suggested that we could take Adrian's and Beatrice's simultaneous emotional responses

---

[2] I have argued for this idea in Sánchez Guerrero (2011, 2014). The argument developed in this chapter makes use of a number of formulations originally articulated in these two papers.

[3] I shall refer in my examples mostly to groups of people who are at least partially held together by certain institutional frames and relatively long-term (shared) goals (i.e. a volleyball team or an orchestra). I do not believe, however, that groups that are occasionally constituted as a function of a momentary impulse (and quickly dissolved once the relevant joint act has been accomplished) do not offer the conditions necessary for the participants to come to have an emotional experience of the sort we are interested in. The thoughts I am to articulate in what follows could, thus, be tested by appealing to John Searle's ([1990] 2002, p. 91) example of a person who, having seen a man pushing a car in an evident effort to get it started, without any explicit agreement, simply begins to push with him.

to bring to the fore that they *both* care about the 'wellbeing' of the relevant object. I pointed out that we could do so, even if their individual affective states had to be understood as instances of different types of emotions. Given that we could plausibly take Adrian and Beatrice to feel affectively connected to one another in virtue of their having responded in a particular way to one and the same occurrence, I argued, we could take their simultaneous affective response to constitute a possible case of collective affective intentionality. The reason why we could only speak of a *possible* case of collective affective intentionality in this context can now be articulated as follows: the fact that Adrian and Beatrice have both responded in an emotional manner to the threat posed to the valued object does not imply that they are caring *as a group* about the 'wellbeing' of this object. The point is that the situation of our example would deserve to be regarded as a case of collective affective intentionality just in case Adrian and Beatrice were to (at least non-thematically) understand themselves as individuals who are caring about this object *in a joint manner*. But what exactly does it mean for two or more individuals to have a sense that they are jointly caring about something, as opposed to having a sense that they are doing so alongside each other?

A possible way of identifying what is at the heart of the sorts of experiences that concern us consists in trying to understand what could justify the participant's felt conviction concerning the collective character of their caring about something. In other words, we could begin to answer the question just posed by trying to specify what could serve as a *rational* foundation for this conviction.

Appealing to some of the ideas discussed above (in Sect. 5.2), it may be maintained that the participants could in principle *give reasons for* such a conviction by invoking some emotional responses of the relevant others, i.e. of those individuals with whom they take themselves to be sharing in the pertinent moment of affective intentional community. They could do so because, under the presupposition of a unified and for the most part rationally coherent evaluative perspective, some of the behaviors of these other individuals would be intelligible (considering some circumstances in which they may be explanatorily embedded) as emotional responses or actions out of emotion, i.e. as behaviors prompted by their emotional assent to the import something has to them. So these individuals' emotional responses may be said to make some of their concerns *publicly evident*. In other words, the key to understanding the extent to which a felt conviction of the sort alluded to here could, if required, be shown to be warranted is to appreciate that, in coming to understand a behavioral segment as an emotional response, we often come to experience what the person at issue is caring about.[4]

---

[4] In suggesting that the significance something has *for a particular subject* can have a public character, I do not mean to suggest that other persons can experience this significance *in the very same way the person at issue does*. For the other individuals can come to experience the significance the relevant occurrence has for this person only from a second- or third-person point of view. But it is important to observe that this idea that other individuals could have second- or third-personal experiential access to the significance something has for someone is at the heart of the idea that, in virtue of our ability to adopt *a personal perspective*, we are in principle open to the import disclosed by human emotions. (For a similar claim, see Goldie 2000, p. 16.) I am pointing here to the

The capacity we have to recognize—often in an immediate experiential way—the object of care of another individual or of a number of individuals permits us to justify our conviction that we (the participants) are caring together about something in particular sorts of cases. The cases I am referring to are those in which a group we (the involved individuals) take ourselves to constitute can be understood as the for-the-sake-of-which of our (perhaps qualitatively very different) emotions, i.e. as that on behalf of which we are, in the end, caring when we respond in a concernful-affective manner to a given occurrence. In order to elaborate on this thought, I would like to appeal to a distinction made by Bennett Helm. This distinction concerns two qualitatively different sorts of emotional reactions someone can exhibit.

In *Emotional Reason*, Helm discusses two kinds of behavioral effects a particular emotion can have. He observes that there are, on the one hand, some emotional reactions we normally take to be purposeless. These are behavioral effects that do not have a point or end in terms of which the notions of success or failure could be used intelligibly (cf. Helm 2001, p. 75). Take, as an example, someone's crying in response to some sad or distressful (or perhaps to some extremely joyful) event. If someone's crying is genuine, in the sense of not being pretended, this crying cannot be a means to a further end.[5] Accordingly, in everyday talk it does not make much sense to speak of a successful genuine crying.[6] Helm maintains that there is nothing about these emotional expressions that makes them an *essential* part of the emotions they express. The reason is because it is possible to experience a particular emotion (grief or joy) without ever expressing one's feeling in this characteristic way (cf. p. 75). According to Helm, the second class of behavioral effects emotions can have is constituted by actions proper which as such are aimed at some end—what Peter Goldie calls actions out of emotion. In these cases the appeal to certain emotional feelings is intended to make intelligible a concrete action, not merely by pointing to what has caused it, but by referring to what *(rationally) motivates* it. Helm observes that, in the case of an action out of emotion, the evaluation implicit in the formal object of the relevant emotion is normally able to justify the pertinent action by presenting its end as something that is *worth pursuing* in the relevant circumstance (see p. 75).[7]

---

fact that this ability to grasp the import the emotions of other persons disclose is fundamental to our ability to participate in moments of affective intentional community.

[5] Goldie explicitly observes: 'An expression of emotion is genuine only if it is not done as a means to some further end' (2000, p. 125).

[6] Against the background of an understanding of our emotions informed by evolutionary *theory*, one could argue that crying serves a purpose and that a genuine act of crying can, correspondingly, be said to be either successful or not. But needless to say, this is not the stance from which we *in everyday life* make sense of our interpersonal affective exchanges.

[7] Helm contends furthermore that we could spell out the idea that our emotions involve an implicit evaluation by specifying the formal object of each emotion in terms of a particular sort of action, thereby making explicit the way in which this emotion may be said to justify the comportment in question. We can, for instance, specify the formal object of the emotion we call fear by characterizing the object affectively experienced as dangerous as something that is worth avoiding (cf. 2001, p. 76).

But why is this important here? In particular, how is this consideration related to the claim that we can justify our felt conviction to the effect that we (the participating individuals) are caring about something in a joint manner? The crucial point is to recognize that some of our actions out of emotion are intelligible—and sometimes exclusively so—as responses that express our finding something worth pursuing (or worth avoiding) *for the sake of a particular group we constitute*.

In this order of ideas, I would like to propose the notion of *caring-with* in order to refer to the distinct mode of caring-about that grounds the type of emotionally motivated comportment we have begun to explore in this section. As already pointed out, it is a peculiar ultimate for-which that characterizes these sorts of comportment: a concrete group the involved individuals take themselves to jointly constitute.[8]

It is possible to begin to develop this notion of caring-with by contrasting it with Heidegger's notion of being-with (cf. the discussion in Sect. 5.3). To begin with, my notion of caring-with differs from Heidegger's notion of being-with in that it refers to a *merely possible* and, in this sense, *circumstantially determined* way of being-in-the-world. Concretely, it refers to the situation-specific possibility of experiencing some togetherness *while caring about something*. This sense of togetherness, I am arguing, amounts to a sense to the effect that we (the participants) are, at the relevant moment, jointly disclosing the import something has.

As already hinted at, something that justifies the introduction of a further technical term here—the term 'caring-with'—is the difference between our fundamental sense of being-in-the-same-world, i.e. the sense of being-alongside-each-other-in-an-essentially-shareable-world (cf. the discussion in Sect. 5.3), and our circumstantially specific sense of being-*together*-in-the-same-world.[9] To draw this first distinction is important for the following reason. The strategy I have been pursuing so far consists, as already mentioned, in elucidating the nature of the phenomenon of collective affective intentionality by revealing some continuity to exist between our 'ordinary' (affectively enabled and essentially shareable) world-belongingness and genuine cases of collective affective intentionality. But revealing this continuity will advance our understanding of the relevant matter only if we are also able to specify *the main difference* that holds between our 'ordinary' world-belongingness and gen-

---

[8] This proposal is in line, I think, with a suggestion Helm made in a presentation entitled 'Joint Caring, Respect, and Submission to Norms'; a presentation delivered in the context of the seventh Conference on Collective Intentionality (held from August 23rd through 26th, 2010, at the University of Basel, Switzerland). Helm claimed that the focus of certain collective emotions amounts to what he calls a *community of respect*. (For a development of this idea in the context of an attempt to show that our ability to take responsibility is not intelligible apart from our having a place in such a community—a community in which others hold us accountable—, see Helm 2012.) As already mentioned, in my view, it is not the sameness of the focus, but the peculiar plural character of the for-the-sake-of-which of the relevant emotional responses that determines those emotions by means of which one can participate in a moment of affective intentional community.

[9] My notion of *caring-with* (in German: *Mitsorge*) is the result of merging two Heideggerian notions: the already discussed notion of *being-with* [*Mitsein*] and the notion of *caring-for* [*Fürsorge*]. I shall contrast the mode of caring-about I call caring-with with the form of concernful circumspection Heidegger calls caring-for below.

uine cases of collective affective intentionality. So we have to specify the difference that holds between being-in-the-same-world and being-together-in-the-same-world.

At least in part the relevant difference can be cashed out in terms of a difference we have already touched on: the difference between merely *sharing our care-defined mode of being* and *sharing a number of concrete concerns that determine a specific way of being-in-the-world*. But it is particularly important to be clear about the fact that not only the sense in which an emotion may be said to be shared can be more or less demanding. Also the sense in which one can take a concern to be shared in a concrete situation can be stronger or weaker, as Mikko Salmela (2012) points out.

Drawing on Tuomela (2007), Salmela offers an interesting typology of shared emotions grounded in this basic idea of different ways of sharing a concern. He suggests that emotions that are shared in the weakest possible form 'emerge when individuals with *overlapping private concerns* appraise the emotion-eliciting situation similarly from their *personal points of view*' (Salmela 2012, p. 43; my emphasis). He offers the following example: 'panic in the stock market is an intense weakly shared fear that each shareholder feels for his or her own well-being' (ibid.).[10] He continues his classification by proposing that 'moderately shared emotions are responses to reasons that emerge from people's *private commitment* to a concern that is shared with other individuals who have similarly committed themselves to the same concern' (ibid.; my emphasis). As an example of a moderately shared emotion, he mentions 'the joy of random fans over a goal scored by their favorite team' (ibid.). Salmela finally proposes that emotions which are shared in the most demanding way 'are responsive to group reasons that emerge from individuals' *collective commitment* to a concern as a group' (ibid.; my emphasis). In this last case, he illustrates the point by appealing to the emotions of the members of a team. He observes that '[the] team members do not rejoice merely in winning the championship but instead in "*our* winning the championship"' (ibid.).

Concerning the idea that being-together in the manner we are seeking to understand is a matter of sharing a number of concerns *that determine a circumstantially-specific way of being-in-the-world*, this typology is relevant in that it allows us to arrive at a crucial thought: if we are to make sense of the idea that the participants in a particular situation are caring about something *in a genuinely joint manner*, we have to understand their shared concerns as concerns that determine their circumstantially-specific being-in-the-world as an *interdependent* way of being-oriented-towards. In other words, at the root of a joint actualization of our ability to feel-towards together we do not merely find a set of shared concerns, but furthermore, *a particular mode of caring—one which merits being called genuinely joint caring.*[11]

---

[10] Salmela has probably taken up this example from Konzelmann Ziv (2009, p. 101). (Cf. Chap. 3, footnote 45 above.)

[11] In Chap. 5, I emphasized the continuity that holds between 'ordinary' intentionality and collective affective intentionality. There is another continuity that has to be stressed here: that between non-affective forms of collective intentionality and collective affective intentionality. Put another way, while specifying here the central difference that holds between being-in-the-same-world and

In order to develop this crucial point, I would like to continue to explicate the notion of caring-with by discussing a specific kind of situations that could be taken to provide a counterexample to the idea I am beginning to develop. The idea is that, in order to emotionally respond to a given occurrence in a genuinely joint manner, a number of individuals have to be able to understand themselves as individuals who, in the relevant situation, are *caring about something as a group*. By contrasting the form of caring-about I call caring-with with another modality of multipersonal concern-driven orientation-towards, in what follows I shall try to support the following claim: we can understand a multipersonal affective response as a collective affective intentional act just in case we can understand it as a multipersonal act that makes visible that the participants are caring about something for the sake of a particular group they together constitute. The discussion that follows will also allow me to determine the specific manner in which the relevant others are backwardly referred to in those emotions through which a number of individuals participate in a moment of affective intentional community. The point to be made is that these others are referentially included in the intentional structure of the emotions at issue by way of a tacit plural self-reference, and not by way of a second- or third-personal indication.

Hans Bernhard Schmid (2014a), we have seen (in Sect. 4.3), argues that a peculiar form of tacit (pre-reflective) self-reference characterizes *all* intentional acts by means of which a number of individuals participate in a collective intentional state, and coins the term 'plural self-awareness'. Regarding the specific case of those emotions that allow us to participate in a collective affective intentional episode, I am defending a similar intuition here. Seeking to connect the discussion on collective affective intentionality to Heidegger's motive of a care-defined way of being, I have spelt out the idea of a plural self-reference in terms of a particular for-the-sake-of-which that can be argued to characterize the emotions at issue. I shall claim below that the emotions through which a number of individuals come to participate in a moment of affective intentional community characteristically refer back to a

being-together-in-the-same-world, it is important to be aware that *emotionally* responding to some occurrence in an joint manner is *not* the only way we humans have to be *together* in the world we share. Moreover, it is not accidental that the sorts of groups I usually refer to, in order to illustrate some of my claims, are, as I pointed out, in part held together by institutional frames and long-term shared goals. I suggested (cf. footnote 3 above) that episodes of collective affective intentionality could also emerge spontaneously, as it were. However, even in these 'spontaneous' cases it is normally possible to describe some institutional frames and shared goals, principles, and/or believes. This points to a further relationship between collective affective intentionality and other forms of collective intentionality to which I made aware above (in Chap. 3, footnote 46) in suggesting that there normally are *historical preconditions* of collective affective intentionality. In this chapter, I have been claiming that our capacity to participate in moments of affective intentional community is grounded in a *circumstantially specific* sense of being-together-in-the-same-world. In so claiming, I am not denying that moments of collective affective intentionality *usually* occur on the ground of preexistent social structures. My focus on the circumstantial nature of our emotionally expressed acts of joint caring should not obscure the fact that collective affective intentional phenomena are typically recurrent in several areas of social life, as an anonymous reviewer of the manuscript of this book has emphasized. I am grateful to this reviewer for pushing me to make a remark on this important issue, to which I unfortunately cannot offer enough attention in this study.

concrete plurality *as constituting a particular unity that is understandable as the ultimate for-which of the relevant act of caring-about*. But before I come to do so, let us contrast the mode of caring-about I call caring-with with a different form of concernful orientation-towards to which, drawing on Heidegger, we could refer by use of the term caring-for (or solicitude [*Fürsorge*]).

In his analysis of what he calls *plural robust agents*, Bennett Helm (2008) exploits his fundamental insight concerning the role our emotions play in disclosing and co-constituting the import things have in such a way as to develop an image that is central to my account of collective affective intentionality: the image of a shared evaluative perspective. He begins to do so by addressing situations of a rather familiar sort. These are situations in which one comes to *subsidiarily* care about something while *primarily* caring about someone else. Helm sets up this discussion by observing that to care about another person *as a person* essentially means to care about the wellbeing and flourishing of another being *as a being who is able to care about things* (cf. Helm 2008, pp. 29ff.).[12] Put in the terms I have employed above (in Sect. 5.3), the situations we are beginning to characterize are situations in which one's concerns about the wellbeing and flourishing of another person are informed by one's having already understood this person *as a being with whom one shares a care-defined mode of being*, i.e. *as a being to whom certain (and only certain) things always already have some import*.[13]

This simple reflection concerning what it means to care about another person as a person allows us to understand why, while caring about someone else, one becomes prone to share certain concerns with this person. Insofar as the wellbeing and flourishing of a person can plausibly be taken to be related to the 'wellbeing' of the objects (or to the fulfillment of the projects) she cares about, one could easily come to care about some of the objects (and projects) a person cares about while caring about her.[14]

---

[12] There are situations in which we are caring about another person, but we are not caring about this person *as a person* (cf. Helm 2008, p. 30).

[13] Heidegger writes that in the cases we are dealing with the beings one cares about are not really objects of concern, but rather objects of *solicitude* (cf. [1927] 1962, p. 157). He writes: 'Dieses Seiende wird nicht besorgt, sondern steht in der *Fürsorge*' ([1927] 2006, p. 121). I believe that something that motivates Heidegger to make this distinction is precisely the fact that a usual way in which one cares about another person as a person is by caring *for* her about something one takes to be relevant to her wellbeing and flourishing.

[14] I do not mean to suggest that in order to come to share a concern with someone else we have to, in a first move, come to care about the wellbeing and flourishing of this person. Indeed, although Helm does not touch on this issue, we could add to the picture of the 'mechanisms' by means of which we come to share some concerns with certain other individuals those cases in which, as a consequence of our being involved (as objects of care or solicitude) in normal child rearing practices, we come to respond emotionally in certain manners (and not in others) to some occurrences that have, either in themselves or in view of further possible occurrences, import to those other individuals who care about us. Salmela, I think, is partially addressing these sorts of shared concerns when he points to *socially grounded but only moderately collective concerns* (cf. 2012, p. 40). In some cases, we can exclusively from a third-person perspective speak of a concern shared by the involved individuals. Moreover, we can do so only because a number of individuals do not have to understand a concern they have as a shared concern in order to share it *in an undemanding sense of 'sharing'*.

Caring about the wellbeing of another person (as a person) is probably one of the most common ways in which, in the course of one's repeated encounters with another individual, one comes to simultaneously respond with her to certain occurrences that can positively or negatively affect some particular objects of concern. Thus, we have here a very rough picture of one of the usual interindividual processes by means of which a number of beings that, in virtue of their nature, share a care-defined mode of being can begin to share *what* they care about. In other words, we have here a description of one of the ways in which two human individuals can come to share an evaluative perspective on something.[15] Moreover, we have here a picture of one of the ways in which two persons can come to share a concern in what could be taken to be a relatively strong sense of 'sharing'. For the sense in which these persons can be said to have come to share a concern (or an evaluative view of something) clearly differs from the sense in which a set of individuals, who have *coincidentally* taken the same train, may, for instance, come to share a concern about the possibility of (not) reaching their *respective* train connections in the face of a concrete occurrence that happens to affect them all (the train they are in has left the last station with a delay of about twenty minutes).

The crucial fact here—the fact that invites us to speak of a concern that is shared in a relatively strong sense of the word—concerns the issue that the outcome of the process just sketched does not simply amount to the establishment of a common object of care; an object of care that *happens to be* the same for the involved individuals. If we are to make sense of the idea that Beatrice, who cares about the wellbeing of her son, Claude, has come to share with him some concrete concerns *as a result of the fact that her son has (as a person) import to her*, Claude (Beatrice's original object of concern) cannot disappear from the structure of some of her concern-driven engagements with the world. For what allows us to assert that Beatrice's relevant acts of emotionally motivated circumspection make visible that she shares a concern with Claude *in a way that goes beyond a mere accidental convergence of purely individual concerns* is the fact that Claude conserves a particular position—as the primary object of care—in the structure of Beatrice's concern about the 'wellbeing' of the object (or about the fulfillment of the project) at issue.

Appealing to the notion of instrumental rationality, Helm addresses a similar point. He does so in the context of an attempt to discard a (precipitated) conclusion which might seem warranted at first sight. The conclusion can be articulated as follows: what seems to occur in the situations of the sort just portrayed is that the import of the person towards whom one's primary concern is directed comes to be ascribed (by one's emotions) to the object of care one has come to share with this person as a result of one's caring about her. Helm explains why this conclusion does not hold by emphasizing the difference between something's having import *for its own sake* and its having import *merely for the sake of something else* (cf. 2008, pp. 31–32). As far as the sorts of situations we are dealing with are concerned, if one

---

[15] I cannot address here the specific 'mechanisms' by means of which we learn to respond emotionally in particular ways (and not in others) to certain occurrences. This is an issue Goldie, to some extent, discusses under the heading of the 'recognition-response tie' (cf. 2000, pp. 28ff.).

confounded these two forms of import, one would undermine any claim concerning the significance the other person (one's original object of concern) has for one. This confusion, Helm argues, would profoundly affect the coherence of the pattern of evaluative attitudes that is constitutive of the import this person has.[16]

The sort of multipersonal caring-about we have just considered is, hence, akin to the modality of caring-about I call caring-with in that it amounts to a relatively demanding manner of sharing a concern-driven orientation-towards. But in another respect it clearly differs from the kind of joint concernful orientation-towards that becomes expressed in the emotionally motivated comportment of a number of individuals who are, for instance, playing a crucial game with a volleyball team they take themselves to be a part of. Moreover, these two modes of pluripersonal caring-about can be claimed to differ in a fundamental respect. One key to understanding the extent to which this is so is to recognize the asymmetry that characterizes the interpersonal relation that holds between the individuals involved in a case of solicitude. To illustrate the point let me come back to Beatrice and Claude.

The situation is as follows: on a particular occasion Beatrice comes to respond in a properly emotional manner to some occurrence that affects a project that is primarily important to her son Claude. Her response coincides with Claude's emotional response. On a purely intuitive basis, one could certainly feel allowed to assert that Beatrice is expressing in an emotional way that, in the relevant situation, she is caring *with* Claude about the project at issue. Note, however, that we cannot assume that Claude understands his emotionally expressed concern about this project as a concern he shares with his mother; let alone as a concern he shares with her in a rather demanding sense of the verb 'to share'. There is, hence, a clear sense in which one could argue that Beatrice and Claude are not necessarily caring *with one another* about this project.

It is this fact that Claude is (as a matter of necessity) part of the intentional structure of Beatrice's emotion, but Beatrice is not necessarily in some way part of the intentional structure of Claude's emotion, that brings us to classify the situation just considered as an instance of the form of caring-about which Heidegger calls *caring-for* (cf. [1927] 1962, p. 157), and not as an example of the one I call caring-with.[17] But what have we understood by marking this contrast?

---

[16] In *Emotional Reason*, Helm generalizes this point concerning the importance of recognizing that the significance something has can exhibit an instrumental character. He writes: 'The instrumental principle […] is not a one-way directive, imposing a requirement merely on the necessary means having import for the sake of that end […]. Rather, a failure of the means to have this merely instrumental import is a failure of the coherence of the broader pattern constitutive of the import of the end, and such a failure itself may begin to undermine the import of that end' (2001, p. 119).

[17] Heidegger differentiates two forms of solicitude (or caring-for). He writes that an act of solicitude 'can, as it were, take away "care" from the Other and put itself in his position in concern: it can *leap in* for him. […] In contrast to this, there is also the possibility of a kind of solicitude which does not so much leap in for the Other as *leap ahead* of him [ihm *vorausspringt*] in his existentiell potentiality-for-Being, not in order to take away his "care" but rather to give it back to him authentically as such for the first time' ([1927] 1962, pp. 158–159). None of these two forms of solicitude corresponds necessarily to what I call caring-with, but there probably are acts which are at the same time comprehensible as acts of caring-for and as acts of caring-with.

We have seen, in a previous move, that, in order to participate in a collective affective intentional episode, it is not sufficient for the involved individuals to take their emotions to express that they share an evaluative perspective on something. Related to this insight, the upshot of our last reflection was a completely different one: it is not sufficient for an emotion to be comprehensible as an affective act that expresses that its subject is caring about something in the mode I call caring-with to tacitly refer to the relevant others, i.e. to those other persons with whom this subject takes herself to be sharing some concern. The point is that it has to refer to these others in a particular way. Let me flesh out the idea.

An emotion that expresses the mode of caring-about we have been referring to by the term 'solicitude' characteristically integrates in its intentional structure (as its background object of import) *another person for the sake of which the subject of emotion is responding to some occurrence*. On the contrary, the specificum of those emotions that permit one to jointly actualize (with certain others) one's ability to feel-towards together should, rather, be articulated along the following lines: these emotions characteristically express that one is caring about something *for one's own sake, insofar as one is a part of some particular group that is immediately understood by us (the participants) as a unitary pluripersonal centre of concernful orientation-towards*.

But in coming to understand this crucial point we have come to understand something else. Instead of *tacitly referring to one and the same background object of import* the emotions that allow a number of individuals to participate in a collective affective intentional episode *tacitly refer back to a particular subject of care*.

In the following section I shall elaborate on the insights arrived at in this section in terms of a suggestion we have already touched on above: the suggestion that the emotions that permit a number of individuals to participate in a moment of affective intentional community express the fact that they are caring about something *on behalf of* a particular group they together constitute.

6.3   Emotionally Expressing that We Care About It on Behalf of Our Group

In the last part of the preceding section I contrasted two modes of multipersonal concernful orientation-towards: caring-for and caring-with. I argued that, in order to differentiate shared emotions that arise when someone is caring about something for someone else from emotions that express that the participants are oriented towards something in the mode I call caring-with, we have to address what Heidegger calls the for-the-sake-of-which of our emotionally disclosed concerns. In so doing, I began to explicate a claim I articulated for the fist time in Chap. 5: in order to specify what is special about those emotions through which a number of individuals participate in a moment of affective intentional community, we have to address that on behalf of which the emotional responses at issue are evoked.

In this section I shall continue to flesh out this claim by arguing that a number of individuals who are jointly actualizing their ability to feel-towards together are responding to some occurrence that, *as it is understood by them*, positively or negatively affects the 'wellbeing' and 'flourishing' of a concrete group they together constitute. The point is that the participants in a collective affective intentional episode are not merely sharing some concrete concerns that bring them to emotionally respond to certain occurrences in ways that are sufficiently concordant. Furthermore, they are *affectively engaged with the world in a very specific manner*. Concretely, they are affectively engaged with the world in such a way as to emotionally disclose that they care about something on behalf of this specific group they jointly constitute.

Take, as a first example, a number of individuals who are playing a decisive game with a volleyball team of which they take themselves to be a part. Note that in such a situation the participants could reasonably expect from one another to express by means of some of their emotionally motivated comportments that they can be affected by certain sorts of occurrences *in their quality of members of this team which they jointly constitute*.

Now, the idea that an emotion could express that one is *qua member of some group* affectively directed towards something may appear absolutely obscure at this point. I shall immediately try to make this idea plausible. But at this point this simple remark allows me to provide a characterization of the referent of the term 'caring-with'. As pointed out above (in Sect. 6.2), the term 'caring-with' aims at capturing a modality of concernful orientation-towards that is characterized by the *symmetric interdependence of the participants' acts of care*. The idea is, however, not that the participants in such a response have to take their concern-driven acts to be sufficiently coordinated, whatever this turns out to mean.[18] Nor do their acts of care have to be directed towards the acts of care of the relevant others. Rather, the term 'caring-with' aims at capturing the idea of a modality of multipersonal concernful orientation-towards that is phenomenologically structured by a backward implicit reference to a certain group the participants take themselves to be a part of. So the point is that those individuals who, in the context of a particular situation, come to care about something in the mode I am trying to characterize can be said to be caring about this thing in a properly joint manner to the extent to which they are not mistaken in (tacitly) presupposing that the relevant others also care about this thing *on behalf of this group which they jointly constitute*.

---

[18] In particular, I do not believe that behavioral, experiential, or neurophysiologic *synchrony* of the participants can be seen as a sufficient and/or necessary condition for collective affective intentionality. As to the non-sufficient character of this condition, it may be argued that an alignment of bodily feelings, behavioral segments, and/or neuronal activity is also thinkable in situations in which the involved individuals are experiencing a similar emotion *in a merely parallel way*. Concerning the non-necessary character of this condition, one could appeal to the case of a number of individuals (e.g. the members of a revolutionary party) who, on the basis of a shared attitude (e.g. rage against the oppressing system of a country), on different occasions, i.e. in a non-synchronous way, emotionally respond to certain worldly events as members of this party, thereby contributing to *their* emotional response to certain occurrences that have significance to *them*.

But at this point we touch again on a puzzlement that has, from the very beginning, surrounded the argument developed in this chapter. This puzzlement concerns the idea that, if required, one could show that one's conviction that we (the participants) are jointly caring about something *as members of a group we together constitute* is warranted. We can, I think, begin to make this idea plausible by considering a situation in which someone is inclined to understand a certain behavioral segment as an emotional response, but unable to make sense of this behavior as a *genuine* emotional response by assessing the situation at issue from the purely individual evaluative perspective of the behaving person. The point is that a way in which this interpreting person could render intelligible the behavioral segment in question is by, alternatively, making reference to a concrete group as that on behalf of which the behaving individual has emotionally disclosed the import of something—a group of which the behaving person can be said to be a constitutive part.[19] To illustrate this point, let me elaborate on Hans Bernhard Schmid's example of the successful first performance of a symphony.

Suppose that for Dania, who plays the oboe in the orchestra, this performance has a particular personal significance, for Professor Emerson, with whom Dania is hoping to continue her musical studies, is going to be in the audience. So the success of this concert is particularly important for her *with regard to the future actualization of certain personal possibilities*. In fact, she is not only concerned with the success of the orchestral performance in general, but also with achieving a more than satisfactory interpretation of a short solo passage she is going to play. By means of this performance she expects to draw Professor Emerson's attention to her. This is, at least, the answer she gives when Frederic, another member of the orchestra, who knows Dania sufficiently well, asks her why she looks so nervous.

For an unclear reason, Professor Emerson abandons the theatre before Dania has come to play the solo passage. This is something every member of the orchestra registers. After the concert, however, Dania looks satisfied with the general success of the performance. It is hard to doubt that she is participating in the joyful satisfaction that connects most members of the orchestra in this situation. And she definitively contributes with her expressed satisfaction to the joyful atmosphere that reigns this night at the theatre. Moreover, she credibly describes her own state as 'a sort of joyful satisfaction' when Frederic, who knows how important it was for Dania to impress Professor Emerson, asks her how she is doing. What motivates Frederic to pose this question is, of course, the fact that he is not able to recognize Dania's *expectable* disappointment.

I believe that in such a situation someone who, like Frederic, knows Dania sufficiently well would be justified in interpreting her emotional response as a response that makes evident that Dania is concerned with the success of this performance *as*

---

[19] The point is not that the mode of caring-about I call caring-with has a for-the-sake-of-which that goes beyond the relevant subject of concern, as it were. As already pointed out, while caring with certain others about something we are not caring about this thing *for the sake of someone or something else*, but *for our own sake insofar as we understand ourselves as members of the relevant group*; for the sake of a group *we constitute*.

something that is important for the 'wellbeing' and 'flourishing' of the orchestra. Specifically, Dania's emotional response may be said to make visible—not only to her, but also to certain others—the relatively higher import the success of this concert has to her *as a member of this group.*[20] What is more, someone who, like Frederic, takes himself to care about the 'wellbeing' and 'flourishing' of this very same orchestra could understand Dania's emotional response as a response that expresses not only an evaluative perspective they have come to share in the course of their having come to conceive of themselves as members of this group, but furthermore, as a mode of caring-about whose ultimate for-which is given by this concrete group they jointly constitute.

Of course, Dania could just be pretending to be satisfied. Moreover, even assuming that her affective response is genuine, one could be inclined to understand it as the result merely of emotional contagion. This is precisely the reason why I am appealing here to someone who knows Dania sufficiently well; the point being that, depending on the rational consistency between this particular emotional response and other evaluative responses of Dania, this well-informed interpreter could feel entitled to rule out these two alternative interpretations.[21] So it seems fair to conclude that, at least in certain cases, we clearly have the possibility to show that our felt conviction concerning the collective nature of our caring about something is warranted. But why is this important here?

By means of an elucidation of the ground of justifiability of the felt conviction that phenomenologically characterizes those emotions by means of which a number of individuals participate in a collective affective intentional episode, I have been

---

[20] Here, I am illustrating the point by appealing to a case of collective affective intentionality that is at the same time understandable as a case of shared emotion. But, as we shall come to see, I could have offered an example that involves emotions of different kinds—provided these emotions were understandable as affective acts that express a mode of caring-about whose for-the-sake-of-which corresponds to the group at issue.

[21] The thought just developed allows us to begin to dismantle an epistemological worry which is related to the suggestion that at the bottom of our acts of feeling-towards together we find a felt conviction to the effect that we (the involved individuals) are, in the circumstances at issue, caring about something together. The worry concerns the insight that one could always be mistaken in taking the relevant others to also be experiencing the sort of felt conviction that is at issue here. It is undeniable that one's felt conviction to the effect that we (the participating individuals) are, in a given circumstance, caring about something together can always be misleading. And this is definitively not a minor point. For participating in an episode of collective affective intentionality, as mentioned above (at the end of Chap. 3, footnote 46), cannot simply be a matter of experiencing some affectively based togetherness in the presence of certain others (and in relation to a given occurrence). At a minimum, it has to mean to experience this togetherness *together* with these others. But it is important to note that the suggestion that we can, if required, justify this felt conviction is not a puzzling one. The reason is because this suggestion is not based on the idea that we can somehow compare our feelings with the feelings of the relevant others. Rather, it is based on the idea that there are situations in which the responses of the relevant others *are best understood as* acts that express that they are caring about something on behalf of the group we (the participants) jointly constitute. This is not a mere consolation. For not every behavior can be said to be best understood in this way. Indeed, a number of behaviors do not allow for such an interpretation.

trying to defend the following view: what is distinctive about those emotions that actualize our ability to feel-towards together is that they are understandable as affective acts that express a mode of caring-about whose for-the-sake-of-which is defined by a particular group we (the participants) take ourselves to jointly constitute. The point is that the fact that we can at least in certain situations show that this felt conviction is rationally warranted supports the proposal that the emotional acts at issue here are able to disclose a situationally specific and genuinely collective manner of being-in-the-world. To put it in a slightly different way, the mode of being-oriented-towards I referred to above by means of the term 'being-together-in-the-same-world' comes into view when trying to show the rational character of certain emotions that can be argued to have a common ultimate for-which: a group of which the participants take themselves to be a part.[22]

Before I come to address in a next step (Sect. 6.4) the phenomenological (instead of the rational) foundation of the felt conviction at issue, I would like to show that the idea I have been trying to support throughout this chapter is of great help while trying to differentiate *in a principled way* cases we intuitively take to be dissimilar in the respect that concerns us in this inquiry. I shall do so by telling apart a number of situations in which we could be inclined to assert that the involved individuals are experiencing some sort of togetherness related to their momentary affective condition.

Following Schmid and Scheler (cf. the discussion in Sects. 1.1 and 4.2), in a first move we should rule out a number of forms of shared affectivity that are not understandable as collective affective intentional responses.[23] Let us begin with cases of emotional contagion. As we have seen, as far as the involved individuals' intentional relation to a particular occurrence is concerned, in a case of sheer emotional contagion there is nothing the participants necessarily share. In a case of sympathy 'about something', the intentional object of the involved individuals' emotions is a com-

---

[22] This suggestion to the effect that the ultimate for-which of a collective affective intentional act is always a group—a group the participants take themselves to constitute—amounts to an elaboration on a number of ideas developed (in different terms) by Helm in a series of contributions to which the present proposal, as it has been repeatedly acknowledged, owes much. Elaborating on Schmid (2014a), I am developing these thoughts by claiming that it is not the focus of the relevant emotions, but their for-the-sake-of-which (which only sometimes corresponds to the focus of these emotions) that is ultimately shared. This suggestion that the emotions of the participants in an episode of collective affective intentionality do not *necessarily* have the same focus, but, *as a matter of necessity*, refer back to the same pluripersonal subject of concern is probably the only important respect in which the picture of collective affective intentionality developed in this book departs from the inspiring view of shared emotions developed by Helm (2008, 2010).

[23] This is not to suggest that these forms of shared affectivity are less common or that they play a less important role in our everyday life. The point is only that they are not understandable as forms of collective affective intentionality. The reason is because they do not fit to the basic definition of a collective affective intentional episode offered at the beginning of our inquiry. Just to recall, I have proposed in a first move (and drawing on Scheler) that in a collective affective intentional episode the involved individuals can be taken to feel affectively connected to one another as an immediate result of their being emotionally related to one and the same worldly occurrence in a particular way.

pletely different one. So there is no point in talking in this context of a form of collective intentionality. In cases that involve what Adam Smith calls fellow-feelings the problem is that the togetherness experienced by the involved individuals is not an *immediate result* of their being emotionally related to a concrete occurrence. Rather, it is the result of a second order intentional act directed towards the emotional responses at issue—or, as one could even argue, towards the similarity of these responses. In other words, two individuals that come to experience fellow-feelings do not feel affectively connected to one another in relation to a concrete occurrence towards which they are intentionally directed at the relevant moment, but in relation to their being in a similar affective state at this moment. But we should also rule out cases of pure convergence of formally individual emotions. As our example of the passengers who have begun to worry about the possibility of not reaching their respective train connections shows, we can rule out cases of sheer emotional parallelism as examples of collective affective intentionality, even though in these cases we can, in some sense, speak of a shared concern. The reason is simply because in an exemplary (or pure) case of emotional parallelism there is no sense of togetherness at all.[24]

So it may seem that those cases in which someone is caring about something for someone else represent the first interesting cases. But as we have seen, even in such a case we have to be careful not to inadequately use the preposition 'with' (cf. our discussion in Sect. 6.2). We cannot assert that the involved individuals are caring *with one another* unless the person who serves as an object of solicitude has already realized that the other person is caring *for* her about that about which she is, at the relevant moment, also caring.[25] Beatrice could be said to be caring with her son about the project at issue—a project that primarily concerns Claude's existence— just in case Claude had recognized that his mother is caring for him about this project.

Now, one could think that at least these very specific sorts of situations call into question my claim that what characterizes those emotions by means of which a number of individuals participate in a moment of affective intentional community is their oblique and implicit reference to a particular group the participants, at the relevant moment, take themselves to constitute. But it is important to note—con-

---

[24] There probably are 'less exemplary' cases of emotional convergence in which the involved individuals come to experience some togetherness. But I think that what makes them to be less exemplary is precisely the fact that in these cases one could allege either that the involved individuals have some understanding of themselves as members of a sort of social group or that an additional intentional act of another sort has brought them to understand themselves as individuals who are affectively close to one another.

[25] To be sure, there are certain forms of caring-for we can also immediately rule out as candidates of collective affective intentionality. I mean those forms of solicitude that are related to situations in which in the context of a concrete occurrence we come to care about the wellbeing of another person precisely *because this person is not able to care about this wellbeing*. This is a common experience among parents (or caregivers more generally) of infants, children, and even adolescents, who seem to not yet be able to 'see' some risks associated with a number of situations and behaviors. Indeed, one could say that the less the (beloved) person for whom one is caring is able to care about her own wellbeing, the more one tends to care about it (and for this person).

tinuing with our example—that Beatrice and Claude would begin to have a justified sense that they are caring with one another about Claude's project at the moment at which they both came to understand themselves as being jointly committed to doing certain things aimed at ensuring the fulfillment of Claude's project. As soon as they were to do so, we could, following Gilbert, take Beatrice and Claude to constitute a group on behalf of which they are, at the relevant point, caring about the project at issue.[26]

But it could be objected that the claim I am *necessarily* trying to make plausible here (on pain of otherwise not touching on the relevant matter)—the claim that in the case of a multipersonal emotional response that expresses a simple caring-for the involved individuals cannot experience their emotional responses as constituting a genuinely joint emotional act—just begs the question. Even if we assumed that Claude does not recognize that his mother is caring for him about the fulfillment of his project, we could easily imagine a situation in which Beatrice and Claude could come to feel affectively connected to one another in relation to an occurrence that positively or negatively affects Claude's project. This would be the case, were Beatrice to, for instance, emotionally respond to an occurrence able to affect Claude's project in a way that is sufficiently similar to the one in which Claude is responding.

It is true that in such a situation Beatrice and Claude could come to feel affectively close to one another. But there is no possibility whatsoever to construe the example as a case of collective affective intentionality that, contrary to what I have been proposing, does not imply a concernful orientation towards the project at issue in the mode I call caring-with. For as soon as Claude came to understand his response as an emotion which *immediately*, and not in virtue of a second order intentional act, connects him to Beatrice in an affective manner, he would be forced to understand Beatrice's emotion as a response to the import the project at issue has to both of them.

Even so, my objector may insist, Claude could understand Beatrice's emotion in two different ways; one of them would not imply understanding their simultaneous affective responses as an expression of their caring about the project at issue for the sake of some group they jointly constitute. Claude could, as I have been suggesting, understand Beatrice's emotion as a response to the import this project primarily has to *him* and in a derived way to *them as a group*. In this case he would take her to primarily be caring *for* him and derivatively *with* him about the fulfillment of this project. He would understand his concern-driven orientation towards this project as an attitude he shares with Beatrice in a quite strong sense of 'sharing'; as an attitude that, as I have argued, makes out of them a sort of community. But he could also take her to be caring about this project for reasons that do not involve them as a group—say, because the success of the project is, in itself, important to her—and still feel affectively close to her. In this case, so my objector could conclude, Beatrice and Claude could be said to be actualizing their ability to feel-towards together,

---

[26] Note that it is utterly irrelevant that the project at issue is one that primarily concerns Claude's existence.

despite the fact that they are not caring about the project at issue on behalf of some group they together constitute.

But this is not true. While examining above the case of the train passengers who have come to worry in a parallel way about a possible outcome we saw that we would not expect the involved individuals to feel immediately connected to one another because of their weakly shared concern—not even if they became aware of the similitude of each other's *formally individual* preoccupation. In the same vein, we should not expect Claude to feel immediately connected to Beatrice, were he to understand her emotion as a response to the import the project at issue has to *her*. In the situation my imaginary objector is seeking to construe—in order to offer a counterexample to the claim that emotionally responding to something in a genuinely joint manner presupposes caring about something in the mode I call caring-with—, the 'affective connectedness' experienced by Beatrice and Claude would not be the immediate result of their emotional response to some occurrence. Rather, it would be a matter of certain fellow-feelings based on the recognition of the similitude of their responses. The alleged counterexample, thus, completely misses its intended target. But let us consider now a completely different scenario.

Imagine a disaster. An airplane has crashed. Hoping to hear about survivors, the relatives of the missing passengers have gathered at the desk of the operating airline. Each of them shows signs of profound distress. One would probably not hesitate to talk of a shared concern. But are all these persons worrying with one another about something?

Intuitively, one could say that they are, at any rate, not necessarily worrying together. But what is the condition they would have to fulfill in order to *necessarily* be doing so? My claim is that in this case, too, we could, in a principled way, tell apart cases we pre-theoretically take to be of a different nature by answering the question as to whether or not the individuals involved may be argued to constitute some group on behalf of which they are responding in an affective manner in the face of the relevant occurrence. Let me undertake this exercise.

Imagine that each of the individuals congregated at the desk of the airline is so deeply concerned about the wellbeing of one of the missing passengers that they all fail to recognize that the other involved persons are in the same situation. In this case, we would be disinclined to assert that the individuals at issue are worrying in a joint manner, and not merely in parallel. The central problem is, however, not the possible divergence concerning the target of the involved individuals' emotions. As long as we were to see the participants as individuals who are worrying about a particular person, *individually*, nothing would change, were we to recognize that they were all worrying about the wellbeing of one and the very same person. Our impression that we are facing a sheer convergence of individual emotions would not vary, unless we could come to see the participants as individuals that are responding to the relevant occurrence on behalf of some group they constitute. What is more, the participants would not have a sense that they are responding in a joint manner if they were not to (at least pre-thematically) conceive of themselves as responding on behalf of some group which they constitute. So to have a sense that they are, in the relevant situation, caring about something in the mode I call caring-with is necessary for a number of individuals to understand their emotions as constituting a joint emotional response. But is it sufficient?

Imagine now that, in the context of this tragic situation, the individuals involved have rapidly come to understand themselves as constituting a group interested in the rescue of all the survivors. In this case the announcement, for instance, that the rescue crew has not yet been able to find the airplane would be feelingly understood by them as an announcement that concerns *them* (as a group). The mere fact that they have come to conceive of themselves as members of a particular group on behalf of which they are prepared to respond *as one* to certain occurrences brings the participants to understand their emotions as constituents of a joint emotional response. So it seems to also be sufficient for a number of individuals to understand their feelings as contributions to a joint emotional response to take these feelings to express the fact that, in the relevant situation, they are caring with one another about something.[27]

This possibility we have to, in the context of some multipersonal affective orientation-towards, emotionally respond in ways that radically differ in their nature is something that becomes recognizable in situations in which some (usually repeated) occurrences that have affected (or are still affecting) a great number of individuals give birth to a sustained emotional attitude able to motivate a series of collective and individual actions of different sorts. Take, as an example, the case of the relatives of the victims of forced disappearance in Argentina. As is well known, a number of Argentineans share the misfortune of having lost relatives during the so-called Dirty War of the dictatorship, between 1976 and 1983. Although not few of them have been protesting for years, and have been taking numerous legal actions aimed at achieving truth, justice, and reparation, only some of them have come to do so in a properly collective manner by, for instance, taking part in actions as members of associations such as the well-known group of activists 'Mothers of the Plaza de Mayo' [*Asociación Madres de Plaza de Mayo*].[28]

We could agree here, too, that the multipersonal fight for reparation is, at any rate, understandable as a more or les cooperative response based on a shared attitude of indignation, anger, and/or resentment. But, like in the case of the crashed airplane, we can take the experiences of those individuals who are jointly responding to the import of the pertinent events as members of some group to differ in character from the experiences of those other individuals who are responding to them on the basis of their formally individual concerns.

In a similar vein, we could explicate what is special about at least some of the situations which Gilbert understands as cases of genuinely collective guilt feelings

---

[27] In a real-life case one would probably encounter a mixed picture. On the one hand, one would encounter persons who are jointly responding as members of a 'freshly constituted' group to the significance of this disaster (and of a number of related events). On the other hand, one would encounter sets of individuals who are feeling alongside each other in the face of this occurrence; an occurrence that certainly affects them all, but to which they are not responding in a joint manner—we should prefer to say that this occurrence affects 'each of them'.

[28] I am grateful to Fanny Gómez for drawing my attention to these sorts of cases.

(cf. the discussion in Sect. 3.3) by asserting something along the following lines: those individuals who come to *feel* guilt over a wrongdoing committed by other members of a group they take themselves to constitute can understand this feeling as a feeling that immediately connects them to certain other individuals (namely the other members of this group) *precisely* on the condition of always already conceiving of themselves as members of some collective on behalf of which they are prepared to affectively respond to certain occurrences.[29]

But what about the case that serves as a point of departure for the philosophical debate the present inquiry is seeking to contribute to? Can Max Scheler's example of the parents' shared grief at the deathbed of their beloved child be explicated by appealing to the notion of caring-with? I believe that this can be done. Moreover, a way in which we could come to terms with Scheler's bold claim concerning the token-identity of the emotions that constitute the pluripersonal act of feeling described in his example is by pointing to the following fact[30]: unless more information is provided, in this context one would be inclined to take these individuals to understand their respective feelings of grief as feelings *they* are experiencing qua members of a family, couple, or partnership they constitute. So, and as I have maintained above, in order to take seriously Scheler's claim, we are not forced to elucidate the extent to which the affective states of the individuals at issue can be said to constitute one and the same experiential state.[31] We are not forced to do so because, by appealing to the difference between caring about something in the mode I call caring-with and caring about this thing alongside each other, we could explicate what sets apart the affective condition of the individuals in Scheler's example from the condition of two individuals who in a similar situation have come to share their

---

[29] Gilbert would probably take this account to be unsatisfactory as an account of a collective guilt feeling. The reason is because, as we have seen, in her view, we can talk of a genuinely collective feeling of guilt just in case we can attribute this emotional attitude to the group itself (to the plural subject). But, as I have been trying to show, appealing to a clear criterion—namely whether or not the involved individuals can be said to be caring with one another (or as members of a group)—, my account allows us to tell apart in a principled way those cases we would on an intuitive basis classify as belonging to two different categories. I believe that to this extent, my account should be taken to be 'clarifying enough'. There is a point, however, Gilbert could wish to stress in order to show that her view has more explanatory power: her account, she could argue, permits us to explain why we are inclined to speak of a shared guilt feeling in cases in which most of the individuals alluded to do not really *feel* guilt. Personally, I think that we do not have grounds to speak in these cases of a collective guilt *feeling*. It is just a common way of talking.

[30] Recall that, according to Scheler, the feelings of grief of the individuals involved in the situation he describes constitute one and the same feeling-act [*dieselbe Gefühlsregung*], in the sense of constituting an act of feeling-together [*Miteinanderfühlen*] (cf. the discussion in Sect. 1.1).

[31] I believe that this is in line with Schmid's proposal that the solution to the Problem of Shared Feelings is phenomenological, and not metaphysical, in nature. As already mentioned, the problem I see is that Schmid's phenomenological solution is probably not able to calm the philosophical anxieties of someone who expects the solution of a metaphysical problem to also be metaphysical. This is why, in an attempt to take seriously Scheler's suggestion, I have preferred to develop an argument that indirectly shows that, in order to offer a phenomenologically adequate account of collective affective intentionality, we do not have to neutralize some metaphysical worries the Problem of Shared Feelings may be (erroneously) taken to point out.

grief in a less demanding sense of 'sharing'; in a sense that does not invite us to talk of a *Miteinanderfühlen*.

Suppose, to illustrate the point, that the dead child was the happy, but unintended, result of an affair between two persons who never came to understand themselves as constituting a family (or a couple). However, each of them has separately developed a very strong relation to the child. Let us assume that the import this child has to each of them is, as far as its degree is concerned, comparable to the import the child of Scheler's original example has to his parents. I argue that in the case of the modified example we would be less inclined to understand the, in some sense, shared grief of the parents as a joint emotional response. Moreover, the individuals involved would not necessarily feel affectively connected to one another in the context of this situation. This would not necessarily be the case, even if they were aware of the import the child *also* has to the other grieving person. In the context of this tragedy they may eventually *come to* feel affectively connected to one another. But again, their having come to feel so would be best understood as something that is grounded in their *finally* having come to understand themselves as constituting some sort of group.

In closing this point, let me emphasize again that as soon as a number of individuals came to, in the context of a particular situation, take themselves to constitute some sort of group, the question concerning whether or not these individuals' emotional responses may be said to instantiate the same kind of emotion would become irrelevant (as far as the question whether they are responding in a genuinely joint manner is concerned). We can reinforce this point by appealing once more to Schmid's example of the first performance of a symphony. Schmid, we have seen (in Sect. 4.3), tells us that the individuals involved in the success of this performance could come to feel affectively connected to one another, even in case they were aware that their emotions exhibit qualitative differences. It is just a radicalization of this thought to assert that they could come to feel affectively connected to one another, even in case they were aware that they were experiencing emotions of different sorts.

Suppose that Mrs. Harnett, a wealthy widow who has been sponsoring the orchestra for years, is aware that Cornelius, the conductor, is proud of his orchestra's performance. Cornelius, in turn, takes Mrs. Harnett to be profoundly satisfied with this success. We certainly could imagine that, in the context of this situation, Cornelius and Mrs. Harnett come to feel affectively connected to one another. Assuming that this affective togetherness is not the result of a second-order intentional act—that is to say, assuming that Cornelius and Mrs. Harnett feel *immediately* connected to one another in the context of this situation—, we could hardly find a better explanation for their sense of affective connectedness than the fact that they understand themselves as individuals who have been caring about the success of this concert, *in different ways, but in a joint manner*.

Moreover, it is worth noting that we could imagine them feeling affectively connected to one another in the immediate mode we are interested in, even if we assumed that they were perfectly aware that their relation to the orchestra was a completely different one, and that the reasons each of them has for finding this success important diverge. But how are we supposed to make sense of this insight in the context of an account based on the idea that the individuals involved in a case of collective affective intentionality share an evaluative perspective on the occurrences at issue?

The key to understanding how this is possible is to realize that, although the involved individuals could be said to, in a very strong sense of the verb, share an evaluative perspective,[32] they could be thought to be responding to the import the occurrence at issue has from what we may call *their respective import-assenting position*; from the different positions they occupy at this very moment in the frame of a joint caring-about. This thought, I think, is completely in line with Schmid's claim that, depending on the role they played in the situation, the involved individuals would come to experience their joy for the success of this performance in a different way (cf. the discussion in Sect. 4.3). Moreover, this is a thought that just extends the unproblematic idea that, in different situations, one could come to exhibit different emotional responses to the import one and the same thing has to one.

Having discussed in this section (and the previous one) the rational ground of justification of the felt conviction I have claimed to structure the emotional experiences that are at the heart of a collective affective intentional episode—the felt conviction to the effect that we (the participating individuals) are caring about something in a properly joint manner—, let us turn our attention to a complementary issue. This issue pertains to that which, from a (genetic/generative) phenomenological perspective, may be said to serve as a foundation of the conviction at issue here.

6.4   Becoming Prepared to Feel Concern-Based Togetherness

I have been arguing that the emotional responses of the participants in a case of collective affective intentionality are able to disclose that these individuals are jointly caring about something. In this context, I have made the following claim: non-mistakenly taking their emotional feelings to manifest that they are caring about something in the mode I call caring-with, i.e. as one, is necessary and sufficient for a number of individuals to *correctly* understand their emotional reactions as contributions to one and the same joint act of felt understanding. In what follows, I shall argue that the role affective states can play in cases of collective affective intentionality is not exhausted by this capacity intelligible emotional responses have to reveal that the participants are caring with one another about something. Appealing to the thought that some of our emotional responses point to a sort of felt preparedness to understand particular circumstances as situations of a certain sort (cf. the discussion in Sect. 5.4), in this last section of the chapter I shall introduce, and briefly explicate, a second notion: the notion of *feelings of being-together*.

---

[32] As I have been arguing, they could be said to do so to the extent to which some group they constitute may be taken to amount to the shared for-the-sake-of-which of their emotions.

What motivates me to introduce this notion of feelings of being-together is the intuition that some of the affective states listed by Mathew Ratcliffe may be had in certain situations on the condition of already having come to share certain concerns with concrete others. Take, for instance, the sense of 'familiarity', the sense of 'being at home', or the sense of 'belonging' one tends to experience in the presence of certain human constellations (and not of others). The possibility I want to submit for consideration concerns the idea that some subspecies of existential feelings, as we could conceive of the affective states I am pointing to, may serve *in a situation-specific manner* as experiential background structures that prepare us to immediately understand certain circumstances as situations in which what goes on has import to us (the participants) as a group.

Here, I am building, thus, on Ratcliffe's proposal that the phenomenological role of certain affective states consists in situating us in particular worlds. I am doing so by suggesting that some of our 'feelings of being' are understandable as dynamic structures of experience the emergence of which is related to the fact that in the course of varied interactions with other people we come to share particular concerns with them. The idea is that the feelings I am referring to could be conceived of as background orientations that, in the presence of certain others, facilitate our caring about something in the specific modality I call caring-with.[33] So many of the experiences that are part of a joint emotional response could be argued to be *phenomenologically* grounded in a class of feelings the distinctive role of which consists in defining certain circumstances as situations in which what goes on may positively or negatively affect us as a group. In other words, the idea is that there is a class of non-emotional affective states that is constituted by pre-intentional feelings that, on specific occasions, *open up the possibility* of *immediately* experiencing an occurrence as one that can affect us (the participants) *collectively*.

I am well aware that the argumentative move I am making is particularly difficult to follow. The difficulty, I think, lies in part in the fact that, in endorsing this genetic/generative phenomenological view, I am changing our theoretical perspective and adopting a completely different approach. This is an approach that does not focus on the grounds of intelligibility of our experiences, but requests us to consider the issue in terms of a series of experience-constituting acts that frame and constrain the world (the ultimate intentional horizon) in which we always already find ourselves when we come to encounter other worldly entities. In his illuminating treatment of

---

[33] There is a difficulty one faces while trying to philosophically make a strong case for the *existence* of the feelings I call feelings of being-together. Given the non-intentional (i.e. merely pre-intentional) nature of existential feelings, it is difficult to recognize from a first-person perspective whether a background feeling of familiarity, for instance, has its root in our sharing some concerns with the other participants or in other conditions that define the situation at issue. Put another way, a pre-intentional feeling of familiarity just is a feeling of familiarity (and not a feeling of familiarity concerning this or that particular occurrence). It should be possible, however, to determine empirically whether or not such a sense of familiarity is related in a sufficiently consistent way to the presence of a particular group of individuals who share a series of concerns. This empirical work still has to be conducted. Here, I only argue for the conceivability of the sorts of existential feelings I call feelings of being-together.

affective intentionality, Bennett Helm (2001) discusses a role played by affective states that are not properly emotional in character. But Helm's (cf. 2001, §5.4) appeal to the idea of *being in the mood* to do something cannot offer a view of the matter that is comparable to the one I am recommending here. For the suggestion I am trying to make plausible is not that the feelings in question *modulate* some of our emotional experiences. The idea is, rather, that certain pre-intentional affective states may be argued to *open up a given space of experiential possibilities marked by a sense of togetherness*. It may be helpful for the purpose of explicating this idea to make explicit the additional theoretical consideration that invites me to propose the existence of this subclass of existential feelings.

In the context of the phenomenological tradition a view has been defended according to which certain experiences may be argued to make possible and even prompt some sorts of forthcoming experiential states. The idea is that particular ways of making sense of determinate circumstances may be taken to mold future experiences in virtue of their being 'pre-given' in these forthcoming acts of consciousness.[34] These frames of meaning may be understood as 'sedimented' structures of experience (cf. Thompson 2007, pp. 33ff.). This is an idea Emanuele Caminada (2014) explicates in his discussion of Gerda Walther's (1923) notion of a *habitual joining* (*habituelle Einigung*). In the context of a discussion of Husserl's view of intentional habits—one of the views Walther builds upon—Caminada begins to elucidate the idea we are concerned with by arguing that '[e]very act [...] tends to leave behind meaningful marks of its execution in the form of *habitus*' (2014, p. 200). As he writes a few lines earlier, this '"*background*" of experience [...] produces intentional habits and provides the frames through which every new experience of the same type can be anticipated' (p. 199).

Caminada is eager to emphasize that '[t]his *background* is [...] not a hypothesis about some non-intentional functions, [but] an intentional structure articulated according to an intentional modality (*habituality*) that we can directly experience' (p. 201). This observation touches on an idea semantically condensed in my talk of (occurrent) disposing states (cf. the discussion in Sect. 5.4). The point is that the disposing states referred to by the term 'existential feelings' already have an experiential character. As I have put it above, they amount to a felt preparedness to understand certain situations as being a particular way. The theoretical possibility opened up by this genetic/generative phenomenological approach basically concerns, thus, the possibility of conceiving of some of these occurrent pre-intentional feelings as disposing states that have been laid down in the course of a particular history of experiences.

Based on this thought, I would like to suggest that some of the situations in which we repeatedly encounter certain other people, as responding (in a rationally consistent manner) to the import some occurrences have, lead us to passively associate a number of feelings with certain sorts of circumstances that involve these others. As a result of such an association, some pre-intentional feelings can come to

---

[34] This idea is at the root of what Husserl calls 'genetic phenomenology' as well as of a late development of Husserl's philosophy Anthony Steinbock (1995) calls 'generative phenomenology'.

be elicited by certain forthcoming conditions in a circumstance-specific, but not object-directed, manner. These feelings can then operate as dynamic background orientations that situate us in a world in which a number of events are likely to be understood as occurrences that, as I have put it, affect us as a group.

This suggestion is compatible with and, as I think, extends an argument Caminada thinks to find in Walther's (1923) work. The argument, as I understand it, basically concerns that which may be argued to make possible a collective intentional act.[35] According to Caminada, '[t]he solution that Walther's approach to we-intentionality proposes [...] lies in the following intuition: beyond our active, actual conscious life, we carry in the background something like "others in me"' (p. 205). The idea seems to be that in situations related to persons who, in virtue of some shared enculturation processes and previous interactions, are 'on the same wavelength' we are, certain *relational* (anticipatory) frames of experience become effective.[36] Caminada

---

[35] Antonio Calcagno offers a different picture of what Walther is ultimately after. He takes Walther to be pointing to 'a deep psychological structure of habit that allows us [the members of some group] to continue to experience ourselves as a community [...] *even though we are not always conscious of [being a community]*' (Calcagno 2012, p. 89). To point to this possibility is relevant against the background of the view Calcagno attributes to Walther, according to which 'any full and real experience of community must be defined in terms of [a] conscious, lived experience of being one with others, being similar to them and feeling together as one' (p. 91).

[36] This image of people who are on the same wavelength could serve as an entry into a certainly important topic with which I do not deal in this study. This topic concerns some of the psychological and neurophysiologic mechanisms that, as it has been argued, correlate with situations in which feelings of solidarity, rapport, affiliation, and/or interpersonal liking arise. Salmela suggests that the study of these mechanisms is required 'to explain the collectivity of [shared] emotional experience' (2012, p. 41). In line with this suggestion, an anonymous reviewer of the manuscript of this book has invited me to revise the existing body of empirical evidence concerning the association of some of the feelings just mentioned with different types of synchrony of the interacting individuals, such as synchronized motor representations (Rizzolatti and Craighero 2004), body postures and gaze patterns (Shockley et al. 2009), facial expressions (Chartrand and Bargh 1999; Bourgois and Hess 2008), and/or heart rate (Vikhoff et al. 2013). This reviewer seems to take this literature to be central to the present discussion; the point being that, on the basis of this body of empirical evidence, one could argue that physiological and behavioral synchrony between individuals *is experienced as mutual feelings of togetherness*. The study of these sorts of mechanisms could definitively *complement* the present discussion on the experiential background structures of collective affective intentionality. But a *phenomenological* elucidation of that which serves as a ground for certain sorts of experiences is, as discussed above (cf. the discussion in Sect. 1.3), *not* the study of certain causes, mechanisms, and/or processes that might be argued to correlate with or even 'underlie' these experiences. I furthermore disagree that the existing empirical evidence to the effect that we mimic facial, vocal, and postural expressions of emotion more with those with whom we affiliate by virtue of a shared group membership than with out-group members (cf. Hess et al. 2014) could be taken to show that the synchronization of the participants' emotions is an *essential* aspect of typical instances of collective emotions, as this reviewer has objected to my claim that synchronization is neither a necessary nor a sufficient condition for collective affective intentionality (cf. footnote 18 above). I believe, however, that this literature could support the idea that there are certain feelings *properly so called*, i.e. somatosensorically based felt manners of understanding a situation, that are at the core of our circumstantially specific sense that we are a part of some community. Moreover, in line with the suggestion that there typically are historical preconditions of collective affective intentionality, it would be interesting, as proposed by this

puts the point as follows: 'The Self is attuned to other subjects because it has sedimented its relations with them. These counterparts are *typificated* in the background as *relational types* that can be aroused in relevant situations thrown into similar forms of affective relief' (pp. 205–206). Caminada quotes the following passage in order to support the proposal that Walther's claim to the effect that our conscious life carries in the background 'others in me' touches on the idea of a (*pre-intentional*) *plural first-person perspective*:

> I live and experience at the same time through myself *and* through *them in me*, through 'Us'. Well *before* these experiences come to the fore of the I-point, before they are actualized, they are lived experiences of the community, because they already arise as motions from me *and* the others *in* me (Walther 1923, p. 71; as quoted by Caminada 2014, p. 208).

It is important to stress that, in this fragment, Walther is not offering a characterization of those experiences by means of which a number of individuals participate in a collective experiential act (we-experiences). Rather, she is pointing to the experiential background against which we-experiences *can* arise. Caminada calls it the us-background.

Now, Walther's/Caminada's argument for the existence of a community-enabling us-background draws on Husserl's reflections concerning the existence of some sedimented structures of experience. But Caminada does not explicitly make the point I am articulating here: that there are some affective structures of experience that bring us to immediately understand certain situations as situations that are pertinent to us as a group. One could think that the reason is because he intuits that to postulate such affective structures may be explanatorily redundant. It is important to note, however, that the us-background, as Caminada seems to understand it, is a background against which not only joint experiences, but also merely parallel acts of consciousness, can arise. Caminada makes this point clear by noting that one can, on the basis of the us-background, remain in a sheer mutual recognition or go beyond to a joint intentional act. He writes:

> Against [a concrete background that already joins some typical intentional structures that relate to the object they are experiencing], [two individuals may] realize that they are both directed to the same object. They could remain in this situation of mutual recognition: in the rush of daily life we habitually notice that we are with other people doing similar things, waiting for the train or shopping, and so on. This usually happens without commitment: everybody gets off the train when they have to, without deliberating it with their fellow travelers, mutually knowing that they were plausibly all waiting for the same train. […] On the other hand, fighting for workers' rights cannot be successful if the workers do not join together as a group and do not recognize themselves as part of it' (pp. 207–208).

One gets the impression that the us-background pointed to here basically corresponds to the sense of being in an essentially shareable (and always to some extent

---

reviewer, to take a look, for instance, at the processes of synchrony that operate in small-scale, egalitarian joint action with little specialization of roles and high stability of the co-agents (cf. Pacherie 2014). For these processes may be argued to *facilitate* instances of collective emotions. Such a discussion could give some flesh to the claim that it is normally in virtue of their having taken part in shared enculturation processes and previous interactions that people come to be prepared to actualize in particular situations their natural ability to feel-towards together.

already shared) world I discussed above (in Sect. 5.3). This us-background defini-tively amounts to a basic foundation of the sense of being-*together*-in-the-same-world which we are interested in. But it does not explicate why it is that in certain situations we tend to immediately have a sense to the effect that we (the partici-pants) are experiencing something together (i.e. as one), while in other situations we are inclined to understand some common experience as an experience we (the indi-viduals involved) merely have alongside each other. The claim is, hence, that the background structures of experience I call feelings of being-together facilitate the crucial step from a sheer being-in-the-same-world to a situationally specific being-together-in-the-same-world by facilitating an understanding of the relevant situa-tion as one in which we (the participants) are caring about something in the mode I call caring-with.

The key to understanding why the proposed notion of feelings of being-together is not redundant is, hence, to realize that Caminada is pointing to a distinction that is absolutely relevant to our discussion—the distinction between actual we-experiences and what Caminada calls the us-background—, but he is not addressing exactly the same structures of experience I am interested in. The sense of possible community Caminada is pointing to here is at the heart of any sense of actual com-munity we can come to develop, but also at the heart of any sense of merely parallel intentional relatedness to something. The noetic structures I call feelings of being-together, on the contrary, *exclusively* mold those experiences that are marked by a sense that we are experiencing something *as one*. So we can differentiate those intentional acts that actualize our ability to feel-towards together (we-emotions), not only from the affective structures of experience for which I coined the term 'feel-ings of being-together', but also from the affectively enabled sense of being in an essentially shareable world. The point is that this idea of some background feelings of being-together allows us to explicate something the idea of a joining of habitual frames does not: the fact that in certain situations we are liable to immediately (i.e. without any conscious inferential process) understand our emotions as feelings that are part of some joint feeling, as opposed to experiencing them as feelings we (the involved individuals) merely have alongside each other.

But even having granted that there is an important explanatory role the postu-lated feelings may be argued to play, one could be puzzled by the suggestion that coming to have a disposition to have certain feelings in the presence of particular others could affect what philosophers usually call the content of our experiences (by 'bringing' them to be the experiences of something that is worthwhile for the group). There are two keys to understanding this complicated issue.

The first key consists in appreciating that two different types of dispositions are involved here: first, the disposition to be attuned to the world in certain ways (and not in others) in the presence of a particular group, and second, the disposition that these background affective states one is disposed to be in (in the presence of the relevant group) *in themselves amount to*. The latter is a disposition I have discussed above by appealing to the idea of a preparedness to have certain experiences that already has an experiential character. The sorts of experiences facilitated by the feel-ings in question should, thus, not be understood as experiences that merely have a peculiar phenomenal character, so to say. For, as I have insisted, the phenomenological role of the background structures I am appealing to here consists in situating us in determinate worlds in which certain sorts of experiences are likely, and others not.

The second key is to recognize that, as argued above (in Sects. 6.2 and 6.3), it is not some content which refers to the relevant group that distinguishes those emotional experiences by means of which a number of persons participate in a collective affective intentional episode. What is characteristic of those emotions that are at the root of a moment of affective intentional community is rather that they bring the participants to understand themselves as having the pertinent feelings on behalf of some particular group which they jointly constitute.[37] To put it in the terminology suggested by Schmid (2014a), what is characteristic of the emotions that concern us here is the plural self-awareness they integrate. According to the view I am recommending, in a number of situations, it is in virtue of some (sedimented) affective structures of experience of the sort described by Ratcliffe that we are prone to have emotions that integrate such a plural self-awareness in the face of certain human constellations (and not of others).

The claim is, hence, that the situations I call moments of affective intentional community are experienced in a particular way, namely as situations in which what is going on has significance for us (the individuals involved) as members of a particular group on behalf of which we are able to jointly care about certain things. And I am proposing that, at least in certain cases, this may be thought to occur on the basis of a number of background orientations that in the course of different processes, by means of which we have come to share particular concerns with certain other individuals, have come to be part of the structure of some of our experiences.

So I am pointing to a conceivable variety of background feelings that may prepare us to experience and make sense of some circumstances as situations that are connected to something that has import to us (the participants) as a group. The idea is that these feelings of being-together could be at the heart of a particular sort of affective connectedness between creatures that, in virtue of their nature, share a care-defined mode of being, and in virtue of their having taken part in different socialization and enculturation processes, have additionally come to share a number of concerns that constitute a sufficiently coherent shared evaluative perspective.

In the remainder of this book, I shall develop the main suggestions introduced in this chapter. Particularly, I shall flesh out and further recommend the idea that at the heart of a collective affective intentional episode we always find a particular mode of caring. In so doing, I shall try to further support the claim that our acts of feeling-towards together are to be understood as actualizations of a distinctively human ability; not merely in the sense of being something we humans can do, but in the sense of being acts that express in a particularly rich manner our care-defined mode of being. In order to do so, in the remainder of this book I shall address what is special about this care-defined mode of being and subsequently explain what caring-with amounts to. The discussion to be developed in what follows could hence be regarded as an attempt to clarify the relationship that holds between Heidegger's notion of care and my notion of caring-with.

---

[37] This is in line with Calcagno's claim that Walther is pointing to the fact that 'there are noetic and noematic sides to the oneness, which ultimately determine the quality of communal consciousness' (2012, p. 93).

Chapter 7
Caring (with One Another) and Existing as (Our Group)

Abstract In this chapter I argue that the mode of affective togetherness we are interested in discloses an essential character of our human nature: we are beings that can exist as some particular group we (together with certain others) constitute. I begin by explicating Heidegger's proposal that Dasein essentially is its possibilities. This discussion results in the following suggestion: to care about something in a particular situation presupposes being able to exist as such-and-such in the context of this situation. Pulling together a number of thoughts articulated in different parts of this book, I discuss the sense in which the idea of an affective attunement to the world is related to the claim that a person essentially is her existential possibilities. A central thought of this discussion is that only against the background of certain already defined ways of valuing the occurrences one faces, one can come to press ahead into the actualization of some concrete possibility, thereby coming to project oneself into this specific possibility—thereby coming to be this possibility. On this basis, I come back to the claim that the emotional responses by means of which a number of individuals participate in a moment of affective intentional community characteristically have a for-the-sake-of-which that encompasses a plurality in some particular unity. I reformulate this claim by arguing that our capacity to participate in episodes of collective affective intentionality is grounded in our ability to exist as some specific group in the context of particular situations.

Keywords Ability-to-be • Affective attunement • Affective intentional community • Dasein's determinacy • Existential possibilities • Existing as a group • For-the-sake-of-which • Projection

7.1 Introduction

In the first part of this book I discussed some significant difficulties one faces when trying to offer a phenomenologically adequate account of collective affective intentionality (Chaps. 2, 3, and 4). On the basis of this mainly diagnostic discussion, in the previous two chapters I began to delineate a view of the phenomenon at issue (Chaps. 5 and 6). This view is based on the idea that our faculty to share specific concerns with certain other people, in such a way as to *jointly care with them about*

© Springer International Publishing Switzerland 2016
H.A. Sánchez Guerrero, *Feeling Together and Caring with One Another*,
Studies in the Philosophy of Sociality 7, DOI 10.1007/978-3-319-33735-7_7

particular things, is central to our ability to participate in moments of affective intentional community. In particular, I recommended conceiving of an episode of collective affective intentionality as a situation in which a *shared evaluative perspective* comes to be expressed by the participants' emotional responses to some occurrence. I suggested that the manner in which, in a particular situation, this shared perspective comes to be actualized by the (diverse) emotional responses of the participants could be taken to depend on their respective import-assenting position. By means of this idea that one and the same evaluative perspective could be actualized from different import-assenting positions I accounted for an insight we arrived at in Chap. 4: contrary to what one may be initially inclined to assume, a collective affective intentional episode is not necessarily constituted by emotions that have the same formal object (Sect. 4.4).

After discussing some preliminaries that pertain to the relationship between the import things have to us and the specific manner in which we come to be affected by certain occurrences (Sect. 5.2), I articulated a condition of intelligibility of the idea of a number of individuals expressing in an emotional manner some evaluative perspective they share. This condition of intelligibility concerns the following issue: we cannot make sense of the picture of a number of people emotionally expressing some shared evaluative view of something if we do not conceive of human individuals as beings that always already share some openness to the import things can have. That is to say, we cannot understand our ability to emotionally respond in a genuinely joint manner if we do not clarify the sense in which we (humans) can be said to, with respect to the import things can have, be in an essentially shareable world (Sects. 5.3 and 5.4). By discussing an argument offered by Martin Heidegger, I cashed out the idea that we humans are in an *essentially* shareable world in terms of the following thought: we normally experience the situations we are in as situations other human individuals are in principle also able to understand due to the fact that they share with us a care-defined way of being. To this extent, our way of being can be characterized as being-alongside-each-other-in-a-shareable-world. Drawing further on Heidegger, I pointed out that this idea that our way of being is being-alongside-each-other-in-a-shareable-world flows into the idea of a world-objectifying mutual openness qua Dasein. I extended this consideration by arguing that we do not merely experience our everyday encounters with other entities as encounters that occur in a world we humans always already share in an at least weak sense of 'sharing'. We furthermore experience them as encounters that take place in a world we may, under certain conditions, come to share *with concrete other individuals* in a much more demanding sense of the verb 'to share'.

Seeking to tell apart these two ways in which we can participate in a situation that is essentially disclosable by others—the demanding and the undemanding sense of 'sharing the world'—, I contrasted the mentioned sense of being in a fundamentally shareable world with the ability normal human individuals have to, in a circumstance-specific manner, experientially understand the situation they are in as a situation in which they are responding to some occurrence *together with certain others* (Sects. 6.2 and 6.3). In order to refer to the particular mode of caring-about expressed by those forms of multipersonal emotional engagement with the world that are experienced by the participants as a genuine being-together (as opposed to being experienced as a mere being-alongside-each-other), I coined and began to develop the notion of caring-with. This line of reasoning aimed at supporting the proposal that the situations we are trying to understand—the situations I call moments of affective intentional community—may be regarded as situations in which our essential concern-driven openness to the world becomes manifest in a distinctive mode. It is, thus, our human way of being, and not a mere capacity or set of capacities, I argued, that in the situations at issue becomes expressed in a unique and pretty demanding manner. By means of the argument just summarized I elaborated on Bennett Helm's suggestion that our emotions may disclose the significance something has for us (not only individually, but also as members of a group) and began to anchor the notion of collective affective intentionality in the Heideggerian theme of a human care-defined mode of being.

In the remainder of this study I shall make out of this proposal a solid philosophical account of the phenomenon of collective affective intentionality by specifying the relationship that holds between the structure Heidegger calls care and the mode of caring-about I call caring-with. The suggestion I aim at supporting in this chapter concerns the idea that the specific modality of affective togetherness we are interested in may be taken to disclose an essential character of our human nature: we are beings that can (and often do) *exist as some particular group we (together with certain others) constitute.*

The structure of the present chapter is as follows. In a first step, I shall begin to explicate an, at first glance, strange proposal. The proposal is that Dasein essentially *is* its possibilities (Sect. 7.2). I shall do so by clarifying Heidegger's idea of an eminently practical form of self-understanding which may be argued to define the acts that constitute a personal existence. The point to be made is that existing at a given moment in the form a person characteristically does is a matter of being able to, in the relevant situation, press ahead towards the actualization of certain possibilities. These are possibilities in terms of which the person at issue at the relevant moment understands herself. This discussion will result in the following suggestion: to care about something in a particular situation presupposes being able to exist as such-and-such in the context of this situation. In a second step, I shall pull together a number of thoughts articulated in different parts of this book in order to interrelate, extend, and clarify them. In particular, I shall discuss the sense in which the idea of an affective attunement to the world—an idea I have begun to explicate in Sect. 5.4—is related to the claim that a person essentially *is* her existential possibilities (Sect. 7.3). A central thought of this discussion will be that only against the background of certain already defined ways of valuing the occurrences one faces, one can come to press ahead into the actualization of some concrete possibility, thereby coming to project oneself into *this specific* existential possibility—thereby coming to *be* this possibility. The point is that our affectivity reveals these ways of valuing which may be argued to, at the same time, determine us and open us to certain possible ways of existing. In a third step, I shall come back to the claim that the emotional responses by means of which a number of individuals participate in a moment of affective intentional community can be said to characteristically have a for-the-sake-of-which that encompasses a plurality in some particular unity. Against the background of the discussion developed in the first two sections of this chapter, I shall reformulate this claim by arguing that our capacity to participate in concrete episodes of collective affective intentionality is grounded in our ability to exist as some specific group in the context of particular situations (Sect. 7.4). By means of this discussion I shall prepare a proposal which I shall really argue for in the next chapter (particularly in Sect. 8.3). The proposal is that the faculty we human individuals have to emotionally respond to certain occurrences in a genuinely joint manner is grounded in the ability we have to exist in certain situations in terms of some possibilities we share with concrete others—the ability we humans have to jointly *be* our (shared) possibilities.

7.2 Caring About Something: A Matter of Being Able to Exist as Such-and-Such

I have been suggesting that to care with one another about something, as opposed to just caring alongside each other about this thing, essentially means to care about it for the sake of a group we (the involved individuals) constitute. But what exactly does this mean? In particular, how is one to bring the idea of a number of individuals caring about something *ultimately* for the sake of some group they jointly constitute to harmonize with Heidegger's claim that what we care about is, in the end, always our *personal* existence?

In the next chapter I shall offer an answer to this question based on the suggestion that we humans can, in certain situations, exist in terms of *our* (shared) possibilities (Sect. 8.3).[1,2] In order to prepare this suggestion, in this section and the next one I shall explicate Heidegger's proposal that Dasein essentially is its (existential)

---

[1] In this chapter (and in the next one), I am going to make use of a convention in order to differentiate two uses of the first-person plural possessive adjective 'our'. With the word '*our*' (italicized) I will qualify something as belonging to (or possessed by) a particular multipersonal unity we (the involved individuals) take ourselves to constitute. That is, I shall use the italicized form to refer to something we *together* possess or own. In contrast, I shall employ the word 'our' (non-italicized) to refer to something that may be said to be *merely common* to us (the involved individuals), in the sense of being something each of us *individually* (i.e. in a non-necessarily interrelated way) possesses. In the same vein, I shall differentiate between *we* and we, *us* and us, *they* and they, and *them* and them—whenever I deem it necessary. (Margaret Gilbert [1989, Chapter 4] prefers to indicate this difference, or a similar one, by means of an asterisk [we* vs. we].) My use of this convention will not be absolutely systematic. I will make explicit the difference at issue only in those passages in which ambiguity may be expected to arise.

[2] Schmid (2001; 2009, Chapter 9) argues for the possibility of a genuinely joint [gemeinsames] Dasein. In this context, he touches on the idea that we humans can exist in terms of certain possibilities we share with others. Schmid is particularly concerned, however, with the issue of the authenticity/inauthenticity of such a shared existence. He does, in my view, not offer an elucidation of what it is to exist in terms of *our* (shared) possibilities comparable to the one I shall prepare in this chapter and articulate in Chap. 8 below.

possibilities. This discussion will heavily draw on an interpretation of some passages of *Being and Time* that William Blattner offers in his clarifying *Heidegger's Temporal Idealism* (1999).[3] Blattner's reconstruction of Heidegger's view of what it is to exist as a Dasein—of what it is to exhibit a care-defined mode of being—will allow me to articulate an idea I shall exploit in the last part of this chapter: to care about something presupposes being able to exist as such-and-such in the context of the relevant situation.

As pointed out in previous sections, Heidegger uses the term 'care' to refer to the unitary structure that defines the way of being that is specific to Dasein. As Blattner observes, in the passage of *Being and Time* in which Heidegger begins to explain this notion, the term 'care' is employed to merely re-label what up to this point has been called *existence* (cf. Heidegger [1927] 1962, §39). Blattner writes: '"care" [is] the term that replaces "existence" as a more specific and developed name for the being of Dasein' (p. 31).

This remark does not seem to bring us much closer to understanding Heidegger's notion of care. But it is informative in that it allows us to appreciate the profoundly technical character of this notion. Moreover, drawing on this remark, we could take the term 'care' to, at least initially, serve as a mere place-holder for an explanation of the claim that our human way of being *in fundamental-ontological respects* stands out from all other ways of being.[4] This is convenient, since, given this role of place-holder, in order to get a first grasp of what Heidegger's notion of care is intended to capture, we could try to answer the question concerning those concrete

---

[3] I do not aim at an exhaustive elucidation of the structure Heidegger calls care. A number of important issues are, thus, going to linger untouched, for instance, the issue concerning the equiprimordiality of the constituents of the 'structural moment' Heidegger calls *being-in as such* [das *In-Sein als solches*] (i.e. attunement [*Befindlichkeit*], understanding [*Verstehen*], and discourse [*Rede*]) and their relation to the *falling* [*Verfallenheit*] of Dasein (cf. Heidegger [1927] 1962, §§28–38). The very notion of discourse is going to remain completely unthematized here. An introductory, though very detailed, discussion of some of these issues and their relation to the care-structure can be found in Blattner's already mentioned book (1999, pp. 31–88). (For a somewhat shorter version of this discussion, see Blattner 1996.) For those who read German, I recommend Barbara Merker's (2007) interpretation of §§39–44 of *Being and Time*. To the extent to which I am able to make the points that are pertinent to my own proposal, without having to compare divergent views concerning Heidegger's suggestions, I shall avoid exegetical discussions. The reason is simply that the present proposal is not conceived as an exercise in Heidegger-scholarship, but as an attempt to make certain of his ideas fruitful for thinking about the phenomenon of collective affectivity intentionality.

[4] In §9 of *Being and Time*, Heidegger makes a strange claim we shall come to understand in the course of this discussion. He writes: '*The "essence" of Dasein lies in its existence*. Accordingly those characteristics which can be exhibited in this entity are not "properties" present-at-hand of some entity which "looks" so and so and is itself present-at-hand; they are in each case possible ways for it to be, and no more than that. All the Being-as-it-is [So-sein] which this entity possesses is primarily Being. So when we designate this entity with the term "Dasein", we are expressing not its "what" (as if it were a table, house or tree) but its Being' ([1927] 1962, p. 67).

peculiarities of our human way of being that bring Heidegger to make the surprising claim that only Dasein 'exists'.[5]

The first particularity that, according to Heidegger, distinguishes our human existence as a very special mode of being is one we have already touched on: we are beings whose being is distinctively marked by the character of *mineness*. As Heidegger puts it at the very beginning of what he calls 'the preparatory analytic of Dasein', what is special about our human way of being is that '[t]he Being of any such entity is *in each case mine* [*je meines*]' ([1927] 1962, p. 67; original German term added).

Heidegger begins to elucidate this idea concerning a way of being that is defined by what he calls an in-each-case-mine character [*Jemeinigkeit*] by claiming that Dasein is an entity that has a very unique kind of relation to its own being. He articulates the point as follows: 'These entities [human persons], in their Being, comport themselves towards their Being' (ibid.).

Although Heidegger's point is not immediately clear, something we can easily appreciate here is that the in-each-case-mine character Heidegger takes to be definitional for our way of being is not a matter of our having some cognitive capacities that allow us to *reflectively* and *thematically* make out of ourselves a suitable object of our thoughts—capacities that amount to what we may call explicit self-consciousness. For it is, first, *in its being* (and not in its thinking) that Dasein comports itself to its being, and it is, second, in its being that Dasein *comports itself to* [*verhält sich zu*] its being (and not that Dasein comes to reflect about its being). But what could it mean for an entity to, in its being, comport itself to its being?

Heidegger provides a first answer to this question by specifying that 'Dasein is an entity which, in its very Being, comports itself *understandingly* towards that Being' (p. 78; my emphasis). This specification might seem to be at odds with the claim that what defines our way of being is not the set of capacities we refer to by use of the expression 'explicit self-consciousness'. It is important, hence, to recall that Heidegger does not use the term 'understanding' to refer to an explicit and cognitively demanding form of awareness (cf. the discussion in Sect. 2.4). As Heidegger is eager to emphasize, in the context of his fundamental-ontological inquiry, '[w]ith the term "understanding" we have in mind a fundamental *existentiale*, which is neither a definite *species of cognition* distinguished, let us say, from explaining and conceiving, nor any cognition at all in the sense of grasping something thematically' (p. 385).[6]

---

[5] As we shall immediately see, Heidegger's notion of existence also exhibits a profoundly technical character.

[6] '*Existentialia*' is the term Heidegger introduces to refer to those characteristics of Dasein that come into view in the course of an analysis of its way of being. An *existentiale*, hence, is a character *of the particular way of being* that, according to Heidegger, deserves to be called 'existence', as opposed to being a property *of the sort of entity* an individual human is. That is to say, we touch on existentialia when trying to give an answer to the question as to *what it is like to be* (or to exist as) a person. Heidegger writes: 'All *explicata* to which the analytic of Dasein gives rise are obtained by considering Dasein's existence-structure. Because Dasein's characters of Being are defined in terms of existentiality, we call them "*existentialia*"' ([1927] 1962, p. 70). Heidegger wants *existentialia* to be systematically distinguished from *categories*, which, as he argues, capture characteristics of the way of being of those entities the character of which is *not* that of Dasein. It is important to note, however, that an *existentiale* is also to be determined on an *a priori* basis.

The point here is not merely that the self-understanding at issue is not a matter of an intellectual and fundamentally spectatorial self-awareness. In asserting that understanding is a 'fundamental *existentiale*', Heidegger is seeking to convey the idea that in just comporting itself in a particular way in the context of the concrete situation it finds itself in, Dasein is *ineluctably* relating itself to its own being. As Blattner puts it, 'Dasein is the being whose being is always at issue *in what it does*' (1999, p. 32; my emphasis). And we may certainly add that Dasein is the being whose being is always at issue *in the particular way it does* what it does. We shall come to understand the extent to which this thought could be taken to structure Heidegger's picture of what it is to exist as a human being. For the moment, it is sufficient to observe that Heidegger is not claiming that Dasein is an entity that is (normally) able to comprehend its own existence, whatever exactly this turns out to mean. As Blattner puts it, Heidegger is rather after the idea that Dasein is the entity 'whose self-understanding is constitutive of its "being-so," its being what or who it is' (ibid.).

But leaving the latter interpretative claim aside for the moment, one may be already puzzled by the very idea of a (non-cognitive) *practical* self-understanding. In particular, if by 'understanding' Heidegger means something like 'knowing how to deal with other worldly entities in the context of particular situations', one may wonder what the prefix 'self' could refer to here.

We can begin to clarify this idea of an eminently practical mode of self-understanding by way of a suggestion along the following lines: by means of our absorbed engagement with other entities in everyday life we make visible that we take ourselves to be such-and-such. So a way in which we could provisionally spell out the idea of a practical self-understanding that can be argued to define our human existence as a distinct way of being is by pointing out that *the specific manners in which we deal with other worldly entities* in the context of those situations that constitute our life *bring to light what kind of person we are seeking to be.*[7]

To be sure, a more precise—though more artificial—phrase would be 'constantly brings to light *what kind of person we have come to seek to (continue to) be*'. For, as we shall see, Heidegger can be taken to be claiming that Dasein's existence characteristically exhibits what we may call a *grounded projective* nature. The point can be explicated as follows. One's existence is, as just suggested, temporally constituted by a number of situations in which, by dealing with other entities (in the specific way one does), *one is 'living out' a particular understanding of oneself* as a person of a particular sort. Correspondingly, in the diverse situations that constitute one's life the acts one carries out *allow one to become or continue to exist as* a person of this particular sort. Being diachronically constituted by her (more or less) intelligible acts, the existence of a person can, thus, be said to typically exhibit a *self-riveted anticipatory* makeup.[8] Let me explicate further this idea by coming back

---

[7] I am aware that this suggestion may lead us too far away from what Heidegger is *explicitly* asserting in the considered passages—i.e. it could mislead us.

[8] In an attempt to explain what he calls a 'metaphysically "light" sense of self', Peter Goldie introduces the expression '[being] riveted to one's past' (2012, p. 109). In so doing, he elaborates on the

to Blattner's interpretation of the claim that Dasein is the entity that, in its being, comports itself understandingly towards its being.

Blattner seems to also understand Heidegger's claim as an attempt to call attention to a strong relation between the (more or less intelligible) acts that constitute one's life and the kind of person one takes oneself to be. He introduces, however, a crucial element to the interpretation by suggesting that what is at issue is the kind of person one takes oneself *to be able to be*. He addresses the issue by discussing what he calls *The Existentiality Thesis*. Blattner articulates the point as follows: '*If Dasein is A, then it is A because it understands itself as A*' (1999, p. 32).

In order to explicate The Existentiality Thesis, Blattner refers to the following passage of *Being and Time*:

> If we Interpret understanding as a fundamental *existentiale*, this indicates that this phenomenon is conceived as a basic mode of Dasein's *Being*. On the other hand, 'understanding' in the sense of *one* possible kind of cognizing among others (as distinguished, for instance, from 'explaining'), must, like explaining, be Interpreted as an existential derivative of that primary understanding which is one of the constituents of the Being of the 'there' in general (Heidegger [1927] 1962, p. 182).

This passage is relevant here to the extent to which it touches on the issue concerning the relation between Heidegger's notion of understanding [*Verstehen*] and expressions such as 'being able to manage something', 'being a match for it', or 'being competent to do something' (cf. our discussion in Sect. 2.4). On this basis, Blattner spells out Heidegger's claim that *primary* understanding amounts to an existentiale, i.e. to a central feature of Dasein's way of being, by writing: 'The more basic phenomenon is competence, capability' (1999, p. 33).[9] The claim is that a person at every point exists *in terms of certain capabilities she takes herself to be able to actualize* in the context of the situation she, at the relevant moment, finds herself in.

This way of cashing out the claim that a person at every point exists understandingly is of extraordinary help in the elucidation of the suggestion that what is at stake is the grounded anticipatory nature of our existence. Moreover, a brief discussion concerning a particular subtype of personal capabilities may allow us to, on the basis of the discussion just developed, begin to understand the claim that Dasein essentially *is* its possibilities. What I have in mind are those capabilities that have to be 'brought to form and fruition'. These are capabilities that could be said to have a sort of ambiguous teleological structure.

The point could be initially stated as follows. Exercises of capabilities are always teleologically structured in the sense that they are always actualizations of concrete

---

following thought Emmanuel Lévinas has developed in the context of a discussion on shame: 'What appears in shame is [...] precisely the fact of being riveted to oneself, the radical impossibility of fleeing oneself to hide from oneself, the unalterably binding presence of the I to itself [*du moi à soi-même*]' ([1935] 2003, p. 64).

[9] Blattner refers to Hubert Dreyfus (1991), Charles Guignon (1983), and Richard Schmitt (1969) as commentators who have already pointed out that there is a strong relation between what Heidegger calls (primary) understanding and what we usually call a capability.

abilities to do this or that *in order to achieve such-and-such*; where that which can be achieved by (actively) exercising or (rather passively) actualizing the abilities at issue partly determines what sort of capabilities these capabilities are. The capabilities of a surgeon, for instance, do not exhaust themselves in her or his knowing how to handle certain items of surgical equipment. In order to be understandable as an exercise of a surgical capability someone's skillful dealing with the relevant items of equipment should be understandable as an act intended to promote the health and wellbeing of a patient.

At least some of our capabilities, however, are such that they can be understood as *ends* of some of our strivings. I mean those capabilities that have to undergo a process of maturation in which we are more or less actively involved. Being in a sense part of our potentialities, these capabilities come to be capabilities *we really possess* only in the course of some acts by means of which we *press forward towards coming to systematically respond in certain ways* in the context of particular situations we often find (or expect to find) ourselves in. These acts are easily understandable as acts by means of which we are pressing forward towards *coming to exist in a particular way*. But why are these capabilities of interest here?

Note that besides being understandable as means and at the same time as ends, the actualizations of the capabilities we are considering may be said to have a clear self-referential character. For, being understandable as the result of some deeds by means of which the individual at issue has been pressing forward towards coming (or continuing) to systematically respond in a particular way, the actualizations of these capabilities are understandable as the product of a number of acts by means of which this individual has been pressing forward towards *becoming (or continuing to be) a person of some particular sort*.

Now, the self-referential character of those deeds that are understandable as actualizations of some of our capabilities is more evident in the case of the actualization of those abilities that, as I have put it, have to undergo a process of maturation. But it is not a peculiarity of them. So we still have to understand the sense in which it can be claimed that, in conceiving of someone's deeds as exercises or actualizations of some of her or his capabilities, we are *generally* bringing to light an implicit self-referential aspect of the comportment at issue.

Blattner tackles the issue by appealing to a usual and normally inconspicuous way of talking. The fact that we are and feel competent to cope with some situation can be expressed by saying that we 'are capable of handling ourselves [in these circumstances]' (Blattner 1999, p. 34).

The phrase 'handling *oneself* in a given circumstance' beautifully captures the non-thematic self-reference one's absorbed and skillful engagement with other worldly entities can be said to entail. The point is that we can speak of an *eminently practical* self-understanding precisely to the extent to which, in the course of our absorbed engagement with other entities in the context of the different situations that constitute our personal existence—situations in which we feel able to handle ourselves in certain ways—, as acting persons we do normally not figure as an object of our own attention.[10]

Now, we have been talking of capabilities a person possesses in the sense of having a founded sense that she can deal with the pertinent circumstances. It is important to note, however, that the self-referential aspect of someone's actualized capabilities we are interested in could be brought to light regardless of whether or not the person at issue may be taken to, at the relevant moment, have been guided by an *explicit* view of what kind of person she is seeking to become or continue to be.[11] But we probably only come to understand this thesis concerning the relationship between a person's capabilities an Dasein's mode of being when addressing a simple relation that holds between *veridical* self-understanding and those capabilities *one really possesses*. This is a relation that, in a sense, is inverse to the one we have been thematizing: one cannot understand oneself as a person of a certain kind (i.e. as someone that exists in a certain way) if one does not take oneself to be able to do certain things and to actualize certain possibilities. This, I think, is what allows Blattner to make the following assertion: 'To say [...] that [a given person] understands herself as being (or, to be) *A*, is to say that she is capable of being *A*' (p. 34).

This remark, which is intended to clarify Heidegger's claim that '*Understanding is the existential being of Dasein's own ability-to-be* [Seinkönnen]' ([1927] 2006,

---

[10] The phrase 'handling oneself in a given circumstance' makes, thus, clear that we can speak of an implicit understanding of one's situation both in the sense of a non-thematic understanding of the circumstances *one is facing* and in the sense of an understanding of oneself as being able to handle *oneself* in these concrete circumstances.

[11] I have warned my reader about the potentially misleading character of my suggestion that Heidegger is committed to the following view: in our encounters with other worldly entities, by revealing that we know how to deal with them in certain ways, we bring to light what kind of person we are, at this moment, seeking to (continue to) be. My last remark should serve as a first measure to avoid that my reader is misled by this proposal. As we shall see, existing in the projected way Dasein does is not essentially a matter of having some concrete and explicit goals in life. As discussed in detail by Theodore Kisiel (1993), Heidegger began to develop many of the motives that are central to his 'analytic of Dasein' in the context of the lectures he held (in Freiburg and Marburg) during the early 20s. These lectures were devoted to a particular reading of certain texts of Aristotle. Particularly the discussion developed in his *Phenomenological Interpretations of Aristotle* allows us to see that Heidegger's notion of care is not only based on some considerations related to Aristotle's notion of *phronesis* (and on the intuition that our *practical knowledge* is prior to the form of knowledge we qualify as theoretical), but also on Aristotle's notion of *energeia*—a notion that captures a number of ideas to which Heidegger devotes particular attention when seeking to determine what he calls 'the basic categories of life' (cf. [1921/22] [1985] 2001, pp. 64ff.). We shall come to better understand the claim that our human way of being exhibits a projected nature in discussing Heidegger's notion of an *Entwurf*. The point I am trying to stress here is that the claim that our way of being is *teleologically* structured by care (i.e. that we live in a grounded forward-regarding manner) is not based on the intuition that we possess the ability to make explicit some 'ultimate goals of our life'. Rather, it is based on the idea that we human beings are, in a way, 'always on the move'. Indeed, the notion of care we are seeking to elucidate is related to the Aristotelian thought that the way of being of those entities that are always on the move is *intranquility*. Heidegger writes: 'The movedness [*Bewegtheit*] of factical life can be provisionally interpreted and described as *unrest*' ([1921/22] [1985] 2001, p. 70). (For those who read Spanish, I recommend Gutiérrez Alemán [2002, pp. 98ff.].)

p. 144; as translated by Blattner 1999, p. 34),[12] allows us to get a first glimpse of the sense in which someone could be said to *be* her or his possibilities (as opposed to just *having* some possibilities). But there are a number of issues we still have to elucidate in order to get a robust grasp on this claim. Blattner begins to clarify the idea by differentiating between the 'state-characteristics' of a person, i.e. characteristics such as 'being six feet tall', and what he calls the 'ability-characteristics' of this person, where he has in mind characteristics such as 'being able to run ten miles per hour' (see, p. 34). By 'state-characteristics of a person' he seems to mean *all* those properties of an individual in respect to which it makes *no* sense to affirm that this person is able to *be* them; the point being that *there are* certain characteristics of an individual in relation to which one could straightforwardly assert that this person is able to be them. But what could this distinction point to?

Blattner illustrates the point by distinguishing the physical height of a person (which he understands as a state-characteristic of this individual) from her stature (which he takes to be an ability-characteristic of this person). As far as the sheer physical fact is concerned, Blattner observes, nobody is '*capable* of being, or *competent* at being six feet tall' (ibid.). This, however, does not mean that there is no sense whatsoever in which a person may be said to be capable of being six feet tall. The sense that is relevant here is related to the fact that one could straightforwardly affirm that this person is *able to comport herself as* a six feet tall person.

As Blattner observes the comportment a person exhibits in a given situation (or in a number of situations) could unproblematically be said to embody this person's self-understanding of, in this case, her physical height. Blattner underscores the idea that we are dealing here with features of two completely different kinds by writing that '[s]tature, in this sense, is not purely physical, [it] is not the sort of characteristic a tree of the same physical height can have' (p. 35). In the same way, he continues, for a person 'being feminine is her way of interpreting [the corresponding] biological fact' (ibid.).

Now, it could be objected that the last remark makes visible that we are confronted with a category mistake. Under the heading 'ability-characteristics' we are referring to *mere interpretations* of some facts, of some characteristics proper. Strictly speaking, it may be argued further, an individual's ability to behave as someone who has a certain stature or to behave in a feminine way should not be understood as a primary feature of this individual as the sort of entity it is.

The problem with this objection is that, as a matter of fact, we understand what Blattner calls ability-characteristics as features that are apt to characterize an individual *as the sort of entity she or he is: a person of some particular kind*. Were one asked to describe a particular individual, one might be inclined to assert that she is a very feminine person. Here, the 'very' would betray that one is not referring to the

---

[12] Here, I am quoting from Blattner's translation of the relevant passage of *Being and Time* (and not from Macquarrie and Robinson's [1962] 'standard' translation) for terminological reasons. Blattner translates Heidegger's 'Seinkönnen' as 'ability-to-be', which Macquarrie and Robinson translate as 'potentiality-for-Being'. I have no view concerning whether Blattner's translation is more accurate, but in the rest of this study I will be making use of his term 'ability-to-be'.

sheer biological fact that she has an XX chromosomal pair. Moreover, one's conversational partner would probably not get the impression that one is evading the question as to the features that characterize this person.

As soon as we agree that those comportments of an individual that can be thought to express her taking herself to be a certain way are *essential characteristics of this individual as a person of a certain sort*, we begin to understand the suggestion that there are a number of abilities someone can, in a particular sense, *be*, as opposed to merely possessing them. At any rate, Blattner's suggestion here is only that 'self-interpretative characteristics are abilities' (p. 35). He claims that we can understand self-interpretative characteristics as abilities to the extent to which '[o]ne must *know how* to be them' (ibid.). Blattner adds force to the point by making the following observation: 'Being tall is learned, sometimes mastered, and can be done better and worse' (ibid.).

But it may be rejoined that the *primary* feature is the physical property at issue in each case. That is to say, even if we were to agree that the ability-characteristics of an individual are features that define this individual as a person of a certain sort, one could argue that those features Blattner calls ability-characteristics have a *merely derivative* nature. Thus, they cannot *primarily determine* what a human individual is.

Such a rejoinder would only reveal the source of the discomfort: the commitment to a materialistic outlook of what a person is. Given that the ultimate intuition that is operative in the picture I am trying to portray concerns Heidegger's idea that our personal existence differs in certain *essential* respects from the way of being of other entities, particularly of those entities that are *merely physically occurrent*, such an objection could be taken to beg the question.[13] The point is that, as should be uncontroversial, being does not clearly mean 'occurring in a physical world and therefore exhibiting some specific physical features'. Put another way, the fundamental disagreement here seems to concern the very idea that the diverse senses of 'being' correspond to *metaphysically relevant* differences in the manner of existence of entities we are not inclined to group in the same ontological category.

Putting this fundamental disagreement aside, one could try to respond to the objection we are considering by claiming something along the following lines: what is at issue here is one's living the *determinate* existence one ineluctably has to lead as long as one exists as a particular Dasein. For this allows us to restate the claim concerning the character of mineness that is alleged to centrally define our human

---

[13] Heidegger's point of departure in his 'analytic of Dasein' is the conviction that, in order to determine what a human being is, we have to answer the question concerning what it is like *for us* to be (to exist as) determinate persons. In other words, Heidegger is committed to the idea that an *onto-logical* account of our human way of being amounts to a *phenomenology* of what we may call a personal existence. To be sure, Heidegger systematically avoids the term 'person' and its cognates. As Andreas Luckner (2007, p. 154) observes, this is due to the fact that Heidegger wants to distance himself from the philosophical notions of a person developed by Edmund Husserl and Max Scheler in the context of their 'personalistic' accounts of man; accounts that, in Heidegger's view, exclusively address the 'what', and systematically neglect the 'how', of a personal being (cf. Heidegger [1927] 1962, pp. 72ff.).

way of being in the following terms: to exist as a person is to be at least non-thematically aware that one inevitably exists as *this particular person* one is. So a person's understanding of herself as being such-and-such cannot be regarded as something that *is posterior to, or derived from, the pertinent facts* (the facts that are relevant to her being what or who she is).[14] In particular, a person's self-understanding as being such-and-such cannot be regarded as something that is derived from the pertinent facts when it is supported by her (really possessed) ability to, under certain circumstances, actualize those specific possibilities in terms of which she can understand herself as being such-and-such.

As far as this point is concerned, however, Heidegger seems to be committed to a much more radical view, which might at first sight appear utterly implausible. Blattner articulates this view by means of the following claim, which he labels *The Ability Thesis*: '*All of Dasein's characteristics are ability-characteristics*' (p. 34). There are two keys to correctly assessing the plausibility of this proposal.

First, in claiming that, as far as our existence qua Dasein is concerned, the features that centrally determine our being are *exclusively* ability-characteristics, Heidegger is not denying that some of our state-characteristics can easily be regarded as that which makes a number of (self-interpretative) ability-characteristics *factually* possible. It would be extremely difficult, to say the least, for an individual very far below the average height of the population of which she is a part to comport as a tall person in the different situations that constitute her life.

Second, it is important to note that the distinction at issue here is not the one between the physical properties of an individual and her self-interpretative characteristics. The relevant distinction is the one between state-characteristics and ability-characteristics. The point is that the characteristics in terms of which a person understands herself as the sort of person she is are *not* characteristics that arise from her having come to *reflectively* recognize that she has certain physical features. The suggestion that Dasein exclusively is its ability-characteristics is rather related to the idea that a person *begins to come into view for herself* as the sort of person she

---

[14] This response certainly involves a sort of dualism. This dualism pertains to a difference that is assumed to hold between the physical individual and the person one is. To this extent it could fail to satisfy our materialistically-minded imagined objector. It is important to note, however, that in accepting this sort of dualism one is not denying that there is a clear sense in which a person is determined by the physical characteristics she or he *as a concrete individual* exhibits. The idea is, hence, not that we are *qua persons radically open* to all thinkable possibilities. Rather, the point is that, even though our individual possibilities are always determined, among other things, by a number of state-characteristics we possess, this form of determinacy does not define what the specific possibilities are *in terms of which we (are able to) exist at a given moment*. Anticipating myself, I would like to remark that the dualism at issue here is related to the difference that can be taken to hold between what we may call our being *simpliciter* (what is usually called existence) and our *qualified* being. (Only the latter corresponds to what Heidegger calls existence.) This dualism could also be thought to be related to an ambiguity of our modern notion of life to which both Giorgio Agamben ([1995] 1998) and Heidegger ([1928/29] 1996, p. 168) point by observing that the ancient Greeks had two words for what we call life: '*zoë*, which expressed the simple fact of living common to all living beings (animals, men, or gods), and *bios*, which indicated the form or way of living proper to an individual or a group' (Agamben [1995] 1998, p. 1).

is in light of certain possibilities which she is able to actualize (or at least to begin to actualize) in the situations she finds herself in. Blattner makes the point by claiming that Dasein *primarily occurs to itself* as certain ability-characteristics (see pp. 36ff.). This is the sense in which existing in a care-defined way means to be able to exist as such-an-such.

Against the background of this initial elucidation of Heidegger's notion of care (as the central structure of a personal existence), it is now possible to articulate a crucial thought on which I shall elaborate in the last part of this chapter: to care on a particular occasion about something presupposes being able to exist as such-and-such in the context of the relevant situation.

In the course of an attempt to further clarify this idea, in the following section we shall come to understand what Heidegger means by the notion of *facticity*. That is, we shall come to understand the extent to which, as Blattner puts it, Heidegger is seeking to bring to light a specific form of determinacy he takes to be proper to Dasein as such.[15]

7.3   Care, Facticity, and Projection: On the Sense in Which Our Affectivity Situates Us

At this point, we could come back to an idea that has been central to our earlier discussion (in Sect. 5.4), namely the idea that we are always affectively situated in some particular world. For, as we shall see, we could come to understand the proposal that Dasein primarily occurs to itself as certain ability-characteristics by clarifying the extent to which—playing with the assonance of the German words—*Stimmung* can be said to be *Bestimmung* (attunement can be said to be determinacy). I shall begin to do so by addressing an issue Blattner articulates as follows: 'Heidegger suggests that there is a special notion of possibility that applies to Dasein, one quite unlike that that applies to, say, a tree' (p. 37). Here is the passage of *Being and Time* Blattner has in view in making this claim:

> The Being-possible which Dasein is existentially in every case, is to be sharply distinguished both from empty logical possibility and from the contingency of something present-at-hand, so far as with the present-at-hand this or that can 'come to pass'. As a modal category of presence-at-hand, possibility signifies what is *not yet* actual and what is *not at any* time necessary. It characterizes the *merely* possible. Ontologically it is on a lower level than actuality and necessity. On the other hand, possibility as an *existentiale* is the most primordial and ultimate positive way in which Dasein is characterized ontologically (Heidegger [1927] 1962, p. 183).

---

[15] Blattner observes that in conceiving of a person *factually* (as opposed to conceiving of her *factically*), i.e. by focusing on her state-characteristics (and abstracting away from her ability-characteristics), one is grasping an aspect of this being that does not correspond to its 'proper occurrence' (p. 36). That is to say, one is grasping an aspect of this being that is irrelevant to its being what it is *qua Dasein*.

In this, in different respects, obscure passage, Heidegger manages to make clear that, in claiming that Dasein essentially is its 'being-possible' [*Seinkönnen*], he is not pointing to what we may call sheer in-principle possibilities—what Heidegger here calls 'empty logical possibilities'. Heidegger is not concerned with the fact that certain occurrences or states of affairs are *thinkable* (in the sense of being conceivable in certain ways that do not involve contradiction). Nor does he have in mind a notion of possibility that basically pertains to the opportunity or prospect something has to come to obtain, given that it does not have to do so as a matter of necessity— what is usually called an empirical possibility. In short, he is not concerned with the contingency of those thinkable states of affairs that may or may not occur. The question is thus: what is the notion of possibility at issue here?

Seeking to oppose both the notion of logical possibility and the notion of empirical possibility, Heidegger elaborates on Søren Kierkegaard's notion of an *existential possibility*.[16] According to Blattner, who in this point follows Richard Schmitt (cf. 1969, pp. 178ff.), he does so precisely by developing the idea that 'Dasein's possibilities are abilities' (Blattner 1999, p. 38). In order to get a first grasp of what is meant by the suggestion that Dasein's possibilities basically are abilities, we have to try to understand Heidegger's notion of *projection* [*Entwurf*]. An initial negative characterization of this notion may be helpful at this point.

Although Heidegger's claim that Dasein at every point exists in terms of certain projections is related to the idea that we are normally involved in a number of projects able to guide our quotidian deeds, there are at least two reasons why we should avoid equating an *Entwurf* with what we ordinarily call a project. The first reason is one Blattner is eager to underscore: when Heidegger speaks of a projection, he does not have in mind an *explicit* 'plan, sketch, or blueprint' (Blattner 1999, p. 39).[17] Existing, in the sense of unavoidably being-projected into certain possibilities which one takes oneself to have, is not a matter of having previously thematized some central aims of the undertakings that constitute one's life—although being able to do so is something that differentiates us from other creatures that seem to have a similar way of being, i.e. other animals.[18]

---

[16] George Stack (1972) argues that Kierkegaard's notion of existential possibility may be traced back to Hegel and, indirectly, to Aristotle.

[17] Heidegger writes: 'Projecting has nothing to do with comporting oneself towards a plan that has been thought out, and in accordance with which Dasein arranges its Being' ([1927] 1962, p. 185). In this context, and following John Caputo (1986), Blattner observes that the German word '*ent-werfen*' can be literally translated as 'to throw or cast forth' (1999, p. 39).

[18] In a very influential paper Robert Brandom (1997) argues that Heidegger is committed to a view of Dasein as the being that thematizes. Besides arguably being something that partially amounts to the so-called 'anthropological difference', this capacity to make thematic—and in this case, particularly, to make thematic what we are seeking to (continue to) be—could be claimed to be central to our human capacity to exist *in the mode of authenticity* [*Eigentlichkeit*]. That is, our capacity to exist in such a way that our manner of comporting ourselves may be said to express our having assumed our personal possibilities; our 'having taken these possibilities into our hands', as we often say.

The second reason concerns the fact that we often cannot claim full authorship over a given projection that becomes expressed in our acts. As Carlos Gutiérrez Alemán puts it, 'our projections are not at our disposition; rather, it is we who are thrown into, inserted in, them' (2002, p. 107; my translation). Our existence is in each case determined by the particular ways in which, in understanding our own situation, we (actively or passively) *come to be* projected into certain possibilities.

It is now possible to offer a positive picture of what Heidegger means by the term 'projection' by elaborating on a thought I have just touched on when specifying that it is *in understanding our situation* that we project ourselves into certain possibilities. The idea that is central to Heidegger's notion of a projection may be spelled out in the following terms: our having always already understood in a particular way the situation we are in is a matter of our having always already begun to *press forward into* the actualization of certain possibilities [*in Möglichkeiten dringen*] in the context of the relevant circumstance (cf. Heidegger [1927] 1962, pp. 184ff.). This seems to be what Heidegger has in mind when he claims that 'understanding has in itself the existential structure which we call "projection"' (pp. 184–185). This claim could be explicated further in such a way as to elaborate on the idea that to understand the situation one is in basically means to understand how to handle oneself in a particular context.

As repeatedly pointed out, by 'understanding' Heidegger means our primary and essentially practical understanding of the situation one finds oneself in, our capacity to meaningfully deal with other worldly entities in particular contexts. In this order of ideas, to understand one's own situation basically means to, at least non-thematically, understand a given state of affairs as one in which *this or that possibility* can, in virtue of one's acts, (begin to) become actualized. It means to understand a particular context as one in which one can *comport oneself* in a certain way in order to achieve something. So one's understanding of the situation one is in can be said to be a matter of one's having always already *taken oneself to be capable* of doing certain things in order to (begin to) actualize some particular possibility (or possibilities).

The upshot of this reflection is as follows: at every point in her existence, a person's understanding of her *particular being-there* [*jeweiliges Da-sein*] can be argued to be a matter of her having always already thrown herself (or having always already been thrown) into certain possibilities that seem to be actualizable (by her) in the context of the relevant circumstances. It is important to note that the point is not merely that in understanding her own situation a person always gets a basis for projecting herself into certain possibilities. For the relation between understandingly being-there and projection is such that it could be expressed the other way around: it is in virtue of her having always already begun to press ahead into the actualization of certain possibilities that a person comes to be understandingly situated in a particular 'there'.

Our last consideration allows us to get a more thorough grasp of the sense in which Dasein, as we have seen at the beginning of this chapter, can be claimed to be the being who in its being understandingly comports itself to its being; the being for whom its own being is an issue, as Heidegger claims (see [1927] 1962, p. 32).

Indeed, having understood the intricate relation that holds between being-there, understanding, and projection, we can begin to explicate the suggestion that there is a particular form of determinacy that is proper to Dasein by clarifying the idea that *Stimmung*, in a particular sense, is *Bestimmung*. What is more, in explaining the relation between the idea that we are always affectively situated in a particular world and the idea that there is a particular form of determinacy that is proper to Dasein—namely its factical being delivered over to its 'there'—, we should be able to complete the elucidation of the sense in which a person may be said to *be* her possibilities.

The crucial point here is to recognize that in the varied situations that constitute our respective temporally extended existence we can only press ahead into *certain* possibilities, thereby *necessarily* leaving unrealized other possibilities we, at the relevant point, may also take ourselves to have. Blattner makes the point by writing that 'projection has as its object that (those) *definite* possibility(ies) for the sake of which [the person at issue] is *now* acting' (p. 40; my emphasis). It is important to note that what is at issue here is precisely the moment of *actuality* that is central to a serious notion of being (or of existence).[19] For it is in view of this character of actuality certain (and only certain) conceivable possibilities *at a given moment* exhibit that we can finally make sense of the idea we are trying to elucidate: that there are some possibilities one, in a sense, *is*. Let me make the point as follows: a person can be said to, at a given moment, *be* a possibility she, as we normally say, *has* to the extent to which she, at this very moment, has already begun to press ahead into the actualization of *this concrete possibility*.[20]

Something we come to see here is that the suggestion that we always exist in terms of certain possibilities does not involve the idea of some radical openness or absolute freedom. As Blattner observes, on the one hand, this suggestion may be taken to imply that we human beings exist in such a way as to constantly be 'opening up the range of possibilities' (p. 41). But on the other hand, it may be taken to mean that we exist in such a way as to at every moment be 'pressing ahead into one of [these possibilities]' (ibid.). Blattner remarks that Heidegger 'seems to subsume both [ideas] under the notion of projection' (ibid.).[21]

This observation allows us to understand the relation between the notion of an existential possibility and the claim that there is a distinct form of determinacy that exclusively concerns Dasein as such. It also allows us to concretize the claim that there are some possibilities one *is*. What is at issue are those *concrete possibilities in terms of which one is really able to exist*. But in order to round out this thought,

---

[19] Blattner emphasizes, however, that actuality in the sense of factual occurrence is not attributable to Dasein *qua Dasein* (cf. p. 43).

[20] In the relevant passage Heidegger writes: 'Dasein is its basis existently—that is, in such a manner that it understands itself in terms of possibilities, and, as so understanding itself, is that entity which has been thrown. But this implies that in having a potentiality-for-Being [an ability-to-be] it always stands in one possibility or another: it constantly is *not* other possibilities, and it has waived these in its existentiell projection' ([1927] 1962, p. 331).

[21] Blattner speaks of two *functions* projections have.

we still have to clarify the extent to which the fact that we exist in terms of certain projections is related to our fundamental affectivity. In the course of an attempt to do so, we shall come to understand why Heidegger takes our affective attunement to the world [*Befindlichkeit*] to be constitutive of the structure he calls care. There are, however, three points I would like to briefly make before I come to close this section in the way just delineated.

The first point concerns an impression probably left by the last move of the argument. Here I mean the impression that our possibilities are, in a sense, always competing with each other in order to become actualities. Although in pressing ahead into a given possibility we are necessarily leaving a number of possibilities unrealized, there are situations in which we are pressing ahead into more than one possibility *at the same time*. Moreover, there are situations in which we can only press ahead into a given possibility by pressing ahead into another possibility. I shall come to illustrate this point in the next chapter, when discussing the sense in which we can be *our* possibilities.

The second point pertains to a completely different issue. Every single act of a person could be said to express a particular projection of hers.[22] Certain abilities-to-be that become actualized in one's acts, however, can be said to determine the person one is in a more consistent way than others. These are abilities-to-be that, to borrow an expression from Laura Ekstrom (2010), one could claim to be relatively 'central to one's psychological identity'.

One could think that it is possible to address these abilities-to-be by pointing to those possibilities in terms of which (or in terms of whose actualized consequences) one, if required, would *explicitly* characterize oneself as the person one is (or is seeking to become). But there is a problem: the fact that one is inclined to explicitly characterize oneself as the person one is in terms of a particular possibility does not necessarily imply that this ability in a consistent way determines what kind of person one *really* is. One may be mistaken about the possibilities in terms of which one is living at a given point.

Take the case of a person who explicitly conceives of herself as someone for whom her family has priority over her professional career. Not only has she repeatedly expressed (in a verbal way) her commitment to this priority, but suppose that it is furthermore the case that she sincerely thinks that she is 'living out' this, as she calls it, 'self-imposed principle'. Whenever there is some conflicting situation that concerns both what we may call her family-oriented-possibilities and her career-oriented-possibilities, however, she clearly and consistently 'throws herself'—or perhaps we should say, assuming that she is not aware of this, that she 'is thrown' by a certain projection—into activities directed towards the actualization of those possibilities that more directly concern her professional career.

So there is a clear sense in which we can speak of abilities-to-be in terms of which one would *correctly* characterize oneself as the person one is seeking to

---

[22] This claim does not hold true for those behavioral expressions that cannot be understood as *genuine* acts, but have to be understood as mere (mechanical) reactions that do not presuppose an understanding of some situation.

(continue to) be. Moreover, we should say that, strictly speaking, even if the person of our example has all the physical, biological, psychological, and social resources that would be required in order to really 'live out' the family-oriented life she has in mind (whatever this means and whatever these resources are), *at least at this point* she does not have the relevant ability-to-be.

The third remark I would like to make in this context is aimed at avoiding that a notion that is central to my account, namely the notion of a coherent evaluative perspective, becomes implausible against the background of the claim that some projections are, in a way, more central to what we are than others. It is important to take into account the fact that a particular projection that *at a given point* in someone's existence may be taken to be central to this person's psychological identity could, in the course of her life, become peripheral to this identity (to this existence). As we all know, there are a number of aspects in respect to which we can just cease to take ourselves to exist in this or that way (to be this or that kind of person).

Take, as an example, a young man who, not really seeking to become a professional pianist—in fact he has never given a thought to the issue of becoming a professional of some sort—, understands himself as (and consistently presses ahead into the possibility of becoming) a good pianist. He, for instance, does not lose any opportunity to play piano in public, thereby not only showing that he is really good, but furthermore, becoming increasingly more able to, for instance, perform in front of an audience and musically share something with others. Being a pianist, or being a good pianist, may thus at this point (or during this period) of his life be said to be central to his psychological identity. That this is so is something that could become manifest, for instance, in the fact that in those situations in which he is confronted with non-constructive critical comments concerning his performances, or even worse, concerning his pianistic and musical capacities, he consistently responds in a way that betrays *profound* frustration.

Some years later, having not only devoted his life, as we often say, to something entirely different, but furthermore, not having been able for years to find the time to play the piano seriously, he on an occasion faces a number of critical remarks concerning his musical capacities. Despite coming from someone who has significance to him, and who has an authorized opinion on this matter, these remarks leave him untouched. Being a good pianist is no longer central to his understanding of himself as the person he is. At this point, and in spite of not having practiced for a long time, he definitely knows how to handle a piano. As far as the basic capacities are concerned, he does this more or less the way he did it twenty years ago. But there is an important difference. The difference lies in the fact that, not being particularly interested in making evident and further developing his musical capacities, he, in a sense, does no longer know how to handle *himself* as a good pianist in the relevant situations. He, for instance, is no longer disposed to *see in certain situations opportunities* to musically share something with others.

Now, being clear about this fact of our human existence—the fact that the abilities-to-be in terms of which we understand ourselves can vary in more or less dramatic ways in the course of our life—is important for us to come to clarify an issue that concerns the interpretability of our emotional comportment: the coherence taken to hold between the different emotions of a particular person has to be understood as something that has certain (perhaps non-clearly defined) temporal limits. We just cannot expect that an evaluative pattern which at a given moment can be said to be central to the intelligibility of someone's emotional (and, in general, evaluative) responses necessarily serves as a standard of warrant for this person's assent to a number of other evaluations that concern 'sufficiently remote' (whatever this means in each case) past or future periods of this person's life. This is something we know perfectly well; something we manifest to be clear about when we, seeking to explain some of our acts, for instance, assert that our interests or our motives have changed. This having been remarked, let us finally address the suggestion that, for us human beings, affectivity can be said to be determinacy, in the sense of being what at every moment situates us in a particular world.

In the context of his discussion on fear as a mode of attunement, Heidegger makes the following claim: '[primarily] and for the most part, Dasein *is* in terms of *what* it is concerned with' ([1927] 1962, pp. 180–181). I believe that the key to finally understanding the idea that our affectivity always situates us in some particular world (and the relation between our fundamental affectiveness and the structure Heidegger calls care) is to recognize that Heidegger is pointing here to a strong relation that can be taken to hold, not only between motivation and affectivity, but between motivation, affectivity, and existence as the way of being that is proper to Dasein. Let me try to clarify this relation.

The claim that Dasein is the being that, in its being, understandingly relates to itself could now be cashed out in the following terms: existing as a person is a matter of always finding oneself in some situation in the context of which one has already begun to press ahead into the actualization of this or that *determinate* possibility.[23] There is, however, a suggestion in the claim that as a being that 'exists', and does not merely occur, Dasein has always already begun to press forward towards the actualization of this or that particular possibility which we have not thematized yet. This suggestion concerns what we usually call our motivation. It may be articulated in the following terms: we always, though certainly to variable degrees, find ourselves in a situation as being *already inclined* to either pursue or avoid this or that. In virtue of our very way of being, we can never be *completely* indifferent to the possibilities 'offered' by our respective situation (cf. Blattner 1999, pp. 44–45).[24]

---

[23] Someone could be inclined to object that this formulation does not allow us to make thematic those situations in which we are not able to decide which project we should pursue. It is important to note that in those situations in which we have difficulties in choosing between two mutually exclusive possibilities our indecision is articulated in certain terms (and not in others). The point is that the terms in which the indecision at issue is formulated are defined by a particular projection, i.e. by a particular understanding of one's own situation as one in which this or that possibility (but not both possibilities at the same time) can (begin to) be actualized.

[24] Moreover, there are circumstances in which one cannot be indifferent to the fact that one's situation is *not* offering a given possibility (yet). To see a possibility as one that *is lacking* in one's actual situation does not only mean to understand this possibility, but furthermore, to understand oneself in terms of this *extremely remote* possibility. What is more, even an extremely remote possibility could be seen as one that is central to what one is seeking to (continue to) be.

As discussed above (in Chap. 5), affective states of different sorts may be thought to be at the heart of a person's inclination to either pursue or avoid certain things in the context of concrete situations. Not only because emotions can easily be seen as motivational forces, but also because, as we have seen, pre-intentional affective states (i.e. affective states of a non-emotional type) may be thought to allow things to already have some particular sort of import when we come to encounter them. Our *Befindlichkeit* could, thus, be easily conceived as that which allows a concrete circumstance *to call for the actualization of a particular ability-to-be*. I think that this picture of an affective state allowing a concrete circumstance to call for the actualization of a particular ability-to-be aptly captures the sense in which motivation, affectivity, and existence may be said to be tightly related to one another. Let me explain.

In saying that our affectivity always situates us in a particular world, we are asserting that at every point of our temporally extended existence we are affectively positioned in a more or less definite space of relations of import. As discussed above (in Sect. 5.2), these, in a way, *virtual* regions of import are co-constituted by *actual* emotions that compose patterns of evaluative attitudes tied together by rational connections. Our emotional responses bring us to, in a more or less consistent way, press ahead into the actualization of certain, and only certain, possibilities. The general terms in which the worldly occurrences one faces are likely to come to make a difference to one's existence are in some sense defined in advance by background affects that structure our experiences. So the sense in which affectivity can be said to be determinacy can be stated as follows. Our affective disclosure of the import things *already have* (as a consequence of our being beings to whom occurrences *can make a specific difference*) allows certain possibilities to, in the course of our emotionally motivated deeds, become actualities. In so doing, our affectivity brings us to exist in terms of those determinate possibilities that, in virtue of our projectively having understood ourselves in a particular way (and not in others), gain entrance into the realm of actuality.

But what is characteristic of Dasein's way of being, Heidegger is eager to observe, is not that, as long as it exists, Dasein is ineluctably confronted with its 'that-it-is', i.e. with the fact that it exists. Rather, what is characteristic of Dasein's existence is its being at every moment confronted with the concrete (and unique) 'there' 'that it is and has to be' (Heidegger [1927] 1962, p. 174). But what exactly does this mean, and why is this important here?

We can clarify the significance of this thought by elucidating the sense in which our affective attunement to the *specific* import things already have can be said to reveal to us our 'being delivered over' to *a particular* 'there'. That is, by elucidating the sense in which our attunement can be said to reveal (to us) our 'thrownness' [*Geworfenheit*], as Heidegger calls it.

We have characterized our human way of being in the following terms: Dasein exists in such a way that, in virtue of its having always already been thrown into certain projections, it is at all points understandingly situated in some specific realm of import. We can now elaborate on this idea in order to clarify the extent to which to exist (in the way Dasein does) means to be constantly confronted with the fact that one is and has to be a particular 'there'. Blattner begins to approach this issue by writing that 'Dasein has its being and must make something of it, must live it out *in a definite way*' (1999, p. 44; my emphasis). As he indicates, this idea of having to make something of one's own life is strongly related to Heidegger's characterization of Dasein as the entity for whom its own being is an issue. The crucial point is not immediately evident, but it can now be articulated as follows. The idea that Dasein *must* live out its existence in a definite way is related to the fact that everyday occurrences can make some more or less *specific* difference to us when we come to face them. The fact that occurrences can make some specific difference to us can, in turn, be understood as a function of a more fundamental fact. Moreover, it can be understood as a function of an ontological determinant of Dasein: it is normally our *qualified* being, i.e. our being *this or that way*, our being *a person of this or that kind*, and not our being *simpliciter* (i.e. not our mere persisting or continuing to occur), that is an issue for us.

Now, in order to be an issue for us in the manner just specified, our life has to already have been (at least non-thematically) understood by us as something that can 'be lived out' in a more or less adequate way. As Steven Galt Crowell puts it, we normally exist 'in light of what [in a certain respect] is best' (2008, p. 268). So Heidegger's proposal could be stated as follows: as long as we exist, what is an issue for us is our existing in terms of what seems to be best (in a certain respect), given not only the concrete situations we find ourselves in, but also the sort of person we are, at this moment, seeking to (continue to) be.[25] In what follows I shall specify the role our affectivity plays in this story in such a way as to, in the same move, finally explicate Heidegger's suggestion that, in coming to be affectively touched by something, we become confronted with the fact that we are and have to be a particular 'there'. That is, I shall explain the sense in which our affectivity may be said to disclose and constitute our 'thrownness' into the *particular* 'there' to which we have been delivered over in existing, and which we have to be (cf. Heidegger [1927] 1962, p. 173).

By motivating us to do certain things, our emotions make possible that we press forward into the actualization of certain possibilities (bringing other, less motivating, possibilities to remain unactualized). In so doing, however, they bring to light the following fact: it is only against the background of *certain already defined ways of valuing the worldly occurrences we face* that we can project ourselves into this or that ability-to-be and exist 'in light of what is best'. These ways of valuing that become manifest in one's affective responses, and which determine one's existence by offering a ground for one's projections, *only in certain cases* (and *only to a certain degree*) can be regarded as something one has actively determined. Hence, in coming to be affected by something, one comes to find oneself as a subject in the double sense of the term 'subject'. That is, one comes to find oneself as that which *serves as the ground for* a number of acts and experiences—acts and experiences one understands as one's own—and as that which *has always already been sub-*

---

[25] The respect in which a possibility can be taken to define the best terms in which one can exist at the relevant moment can, of course, be a moral one.

jected to certain ways of making sense; to certain ways of *bringing things to matter*. This, I think, is the picture of human affectivity Blattner is seeking to capture under the header of *The Affectivity Thesis*: '*Dasein's determinacy consists in the way things matter to it*' (1999, p. 52).

Following Crowell, we could restate this point by addressing the systematically ambiguous way in which, while addressing our human mode of determinacy in relation to what he calls *Gewissen*, Heidegger uses the term 'ground' [*Grund*] (cf. [1927] 1962, §58). As Crowell observes, this ambiguity is related to 'the age-old ambiguity between grounds-as-*causes* and grounds-as-(justifying)-*reasons*' (2008, p. 264). We can, I think, approach the issue as follows. As we have seen above (in Sect. 5.2), one's coming to be affected by something in a particular way can serve as a ground-as-a-(justifying)-reason for one's having acted the way one has. But at the same time our emotional responses may be said to reveal a particular way of *letting things matter*, which, in turn, can be seen as a ground-as-a-cause, i.e. as an inaccessible condition of our responding to certain occurrences the way we do.[26]

This fundamentally ambiguous character exhibited by our (affectively disclosed) evaluatively determinate existence is what allows Heidegger to propose that, in existing, Dasein is confronted, not merely with the fact that it exists in terms of a particular way of letting things matter, but with the intricate, though elementary, fact 'that it is and has to be' its concrete 'there'. This is the context in which we can take affectivity to amount to a very special kind of determinacy—to a form of determinacy that allows certain (and only certain) possibilities to begin to become actualities of (and in) our personal life.

We are now in a position to appreciate why Blattner deems it so important to emphasize that, for Heidegger, '[p]ossibility, as an *existentiale*, does not signify a free-floating potentiality-for-Being [or ability-to-be] in the sense of "liberty of indifference" [or "indifference of the will"] (*libertas indifferentiae*)' ([1927] 1962, p. 183; cf. Blattner 1999, p. 51). The crucial point is that, as Heidegger puts it, 'Dasein is, *as essentially affective*, in each case *already caught up in determinate possibilities*' ([1927] 2006, p. 144; as translated by Blattner 1999, p. 51; my emphasis).[27]

But if we are always caught up in determinate ways of letting things matter, which do not merely motivate, but, in a sense, determine our acts, to which extent can we speak of existential *possibilities*?

Crowell answers this question by writing that 'Dasein is not identical to its facticity; it is also existentiality or projection' (p. 267). The point can be restated by suggesting that a person is not *externally* determined by her specific evaluative pro-

---

[26] Moreover—and this, I think, is at the basis of a number of philosophical puzzlements that concern the relation between affectivity and rationality—, an emotion *in itself*, and particularly when considered atomistically, can be seen as a ground-as-a-cause for some of our responses; as something one just is in the grip of, or as something that is (almost) unresponsive to one's calm and allegedly more rational interpretation of the situation at issue.

[27] The reason for quoting the relevant passage from Blattner's translation here is that the affective character of the determinacy at issue here gets lost in Macquarrie and Robinson's translation of 'Befindlichkeit' as 'having a state-of-mind'.

file (by the specific way things already matter to her). For a person begins to understand herself *as the sort of person she is* in light of her capacity to, against (and only
against) this *determinate* evaluative background, *self-determinedly* exist as a subject
of a particular sort in terms of certain capabilities she is able to actualize.

Summing up, the reason why we can speak here of a *form of determinacy* is
because a person, as Blattner puts it, '[can never] get outside of [...] the way things
already matter to her' (1999, p. 52).[28] And the reason why we can speak here of a
peculiar form of determinacy is because this form of determinacy can be understood as that which makes possible our existing in terms of certain possibilities we
take ourselves to have. Trying to substantiate this suggestion, we could affirm that
the precise way in which the evaluative determinacy revealed by one's specific
affective responses makes possible the actualization of some of one's possibilities—
making out of them *existential* possibilities—is by allowing one to become the subject (or, if you prefer, the agent) of some of those ways of letting things matter one
is always already subjected to. Put another way, the peculiar character of the form
of determinacy that is at issue here is inextricably linked to a fundamental capacity
we human beings have—a capacity that is at the root of our self-understanding as
free beings: we *can* take over being this very ground that, in the way just specified,
determines us (cf. Heidegger [1927] 1962, p. 330).[29] This is the point Blattner is
seeking to make when he writes: '[a given person] can [...] live *as* this ground for
her projected abilities. To live as the ground is to live out the ground, to project on
the basis of the ground' (1999, p. 52).[30]

As I hope to have made clear, the idea that we can take over being the ground that
evaluatively determines us, thereby coming to actualize certain capabilities we possess, can be taken to spell out the suggestion that Dasein *is* its possibilities. At any
rate, in the course of our last reflection we have finally reached a position from
which we can offer a qualified answer to the question as to what Heidegger's notion
of care refers to.

To begin with, Heidegger's notion of care—and this is something we know from
the very beginning of our inquiry—is intended to capture the most basic unitary

---

[28] There are situations in which one can distance oneself from a given affective evaluation. But one
can do so only to the extent to which the relevant situation has *already* been evaluated in an affective way.

[29] 'To take over being a ground' is the phrase Crowell (2008) uses to translate Heidegger's 'das
Grundsein zu übernehmen' ([1927] 2006, p. 284). Macquarrie and Robinson use the expression
'take over Being-a-basis'.

[30] Drawing on Blattner, we could differentiate in this context between one's *factual* situation (what
I have often called the *circumstance* one faces) and what one could call one's *factive* situation. (I
have tried to reserve the expression 'the situation one finds oneself in' to refer to one's factive situation.) Indeed, the terms in which Blattner explains this difference allow us to further understand
the sense in which our affectivity can be said to *situate us*. Blattner writes: 'That [a given person]
is in a certain factual situation, say, having stolen something, does not itself have any motivational
import. She is motivated rather by shame, or pride or a fear in the face of this fact [i.e. by her factive
situation]. And shame pride and fear can have the motivational impacts only in virtue of the way
they reveal her possibilities to her' (p. 53). Blattner summarizes below: 'What situates her is *not*
the deed, but the affective interpretation of the deed' (ibid.).

structure of our human way of being; a way of being Heidegger calls existence. On the basis of the discussion developed so far in this chapter, we can now understand why Heidegger thinks that existing (in the way Dasein does) may be said to be a matter of Dasein's '[being]-ahead-of-itself-in-already-being-in-a-world' [*Sich-vorweg-schon-sein-in-(der-Welt-) als Sein-bei (innerweltlich begegnendem Seienden)*] ([1927] 1962, p. 236). To capture this idea, I have employed the expression 'grounded projective nature of our intelligible acts'.

But our discussion has brought us to furthermore appreciate the extent to which the idea of a care-defined mode of being may be taken to constitute the ultimate condition of intelligibility of the idea that our emotions disclose our evaluative perspective. The point is that the picture of our human way of being Heidegger's notion of care seeks to capture has to be seen as a picture that serves as a boundary condition of the very idea that things already matter to us in some specific ways when we come to be affected by certain occurrences. For worldly occurrences would have no import whatsoever, were our being 'in light of what is best' in some specific respect not always an issue for us. It is precisely to this extent—the extent to which it can be thought to be at the root of our being amidst things that matter to us in determinate ways—that care can be claimed to amount to the most fundamental ontological determinant of Dasein as the being that is always (and essentially) in-the-world.

7.4   Caring-with and Being Able to Exist as Our Group

Up to this point our efforts in this chapter have been directed to understanding the relation between the structure Heidegger calls care and the idea that, against the background of its fundamental affectivity, Dasein at every point exists in terms of some concrete possibility it takes itself to be able to actualize in the context of the situation at issue. Having understood this relation, in closing the present discussion, we can now turn our attention to those affective responses by means of which *on particular occasions* we emotionally express our joint concern about some object of import. We can begin to do so by elaborating on the general thought that caring about something on a particular occasion means being able to exist as such-and-such in the context of this situation. Let me begin to articulate the idea by reframing a claim that is central to my theory.

What characterizes those emotions by means of which we participate in an episode of collective affective intentionality, I have argued, is the '*our*self' that constitutes their oblique intentional reference.[31] To point to the tacit reference to a

---

[31] The grammatical inadequacy of combining the plural possessive adjective 'our' with the singular reflexive reference 'self' is intended to emphasize that the oblique intentional reference' of an emotion by means of which one participates in a moment of affective intentional community characteristically points back to us (the involved individuals), *as far as we (a definite plurality of people) as a (singular) group are concerned*. According to the *New Oxford American Dictionary*, '[the pronoun 'ourself' is] used instead of "ourselves," typically when "we" refers to people in general rather than a definite group of people'. The term 'ourself' as used here has, thus, a clearly technical character.

particular subject of concern emotions (qua intentional acts) always incorporate, Heidegger, as we have seen, employs the expression 'the for-the-sake-of-which of an emotion'. The emotional acts we are interested in can, hence, be said to characteristically have a for-the-sake-of-which that encompasses some plurality in some particular unity. It is in reference to this peculiar form of tacit self-awareness—which takes a plurality of people (one is a part of) to constitute a sort of unitary centre of concernful orientation towards something—that we can conceive of those emotions by means of which we participate in a moment of affective intentional community as affective acts that express the particular mode of caring-about I call caring-with.

Against the background of the discussion developed in this chapter, the proposal just summarized could now be reformulated as follows: our capacity to participate in concrete episodes of collective affective intentionality is grounded in our *ability to exist as our group* in the context of particular situations. In the course of an attempt to clarify this idea of a number of individuals actualizing their ability to exist (on a particular occasion) as some group they together constitute, we shall come to understand a fundamental issue: in order to jointly actualize on a particular occasion our ability to feel-towards together it is neither sufficient nor necessary that the group we (the participating individuals) jointly constitute be understandable as the common focus of our respective emotions.

The issue can begin to be tackled by noting that the participants in a collective affective intentional episode do not merely have to be able to understand themselves as individuals who care about the 'wellbeing' and 'flourishing' of *one and the very same group*—a group they together constitute. Furthermore—and fundamentally—, they have to be able to understand themselves as individuals who in the relevant situation are *jointly*, i.e. for the sake of the relevant group (or, if you prefer, *as* this group), caring about something. The point is that to care about the 'wellbeing' and 'flourishing' of one and the same group is definitely *not* sufficient for a number of individuals to come to understand their emotions as emotions that express a concern they share in a sufficiently demanding sense of 'sharing'; as emotions that bring them to participate in a moment of affective intentional community. Let me illustrate the point.

Imagine that Inna, the manager of the orchestra of our example, who understands herself as a person that cares about the 'wellbeing' and 'flourishing' of this group, on a particular occasion comes to worry about the fact that the theatre in which the orchestra is going to perform in a few minutes is almost empty. The target of her feeling of anxiety is this unexpected poor attendance at the concert. The background object of import that makes this emotional response intelligible is this group she cares about. Her worry is based, however, on her preoccupation concerning the possibility of being considered a bad logistic administrator. At this moment she is living in terms of 'what is best' with respect to her personal ability to, say, administer the public image of a group of musicians.

The fact that the theatre is so scantily visited this night is likely to also worry Cornelius, the conductor, who is deeply interested in promoting the 'wellbeing' and 'flourishing' of his orchestra. Cornelius' anxiety shares its target (the poor attendance at the concert) and its focus (the orchestra they both are a part of) with Inna's emotion. But his worry is based on his being afraid that the critics could interpret this emptiness of the theatre as a manifestation of the disagreement of the public with the way in which he has musically conducted the orchestra during the last months. It is his personal ability to conduct an orchestra that, in this context, is an issue to him.

Now, it is not the sheer fact that Inna and Cornelius have different reasons for being anxious in this situation that is relevant here. What is important is rather the fact that, having different reasons for doing so, we cannot assume that they *immediately* understand their emotions as emotions they share with one another in a demanding sense of 'sharing'; that they understand these feelings as *their* feeling-in-common. Although they both see themselves as members of one and the same group, although their emotions arise in the context of an attempt to promote the 'wellbeing' and 'flourishing' of this group, and although they both—let us assume—know that the pertinent other person also cares about the 'wellbeing' and 'flourishing' of this group, their emotions do not necessarily bring them to participate in some moment of affective intentional community.[32]

According to the view I have been defending, were Inna and Cornelius to not experience their respective emotions as contributions to some joint feeling of *theirs*, this would mean that, *as far as this concrete emotional response is concerned*, they would not be able to understand themselves as individuals who care with one another about something (but only alongside each other). This might sound strange, given that we are dealing with a situation in which, as just mentioned, first, the involved individuals both understand themselves as members of the group at issue, and second, these individuals are both emotionally responding to some occurrence in the context of an attempt to promote the 'wellbeing' and 'flourishing' of this group.

The key to understanding this apparently odd possibility is to understand the following thought. If, in the context of the situation just depicted, Inna and Cornelius do not come to jointly feel the relevance of a situation that is affecting them both, it is due to the fact that the group they together constitute *only* amounts to the shared focus of their emotions. That is to say, it is due to the fact that, in this situation, they are caring about one and the same background object of import (*their* group), in the case of Inna *ultimately* as the manager she takes herself to be, and in the case of Cornelius *ultimately* as the artist he takes himself to be.

Insofar as Inna and Cornelius are, in this situation, both 'carrying out their existence' in terms of some ability-to-be they *individually* have, we can affirm that each of them is caring about the 'wellbeing' and 'flourishing' of this group for her or his *purely individual* sake. So the fact that Inna and Cornelius have not come to jointly actualize their ability to feel-towards together in the situation of the example could be explained by invoking the following fact: in this context, it is not *ultimately* for

---

[32] As we have seen (cf. the example of Mrs. Harnett in Sect. 6.3), the sheer fact that two individuals have a different reason to emotionally respond to one and the same occurrence does not preclude them from understanding their respective feelings as contributions to some joint feeling of *theirs*.

the sake of the group they together constitute that Inna and Cornelius are doing a number of things aimed at promoting the 'wellbeing' and 'flourishing' of this very group. And the claim is that, in case they had been able to, in the relevant situation, exist as *their* group, i.e. in case they had been able to *ultimately* exist in this situation in terms of 'what is best' for the group they jointly are, the pertinent emotion would have been immediately experienced by them as an affective attitude had by *them together*.

In fact, the point in saying that the participants in a collective affective intentional episode have to care about something *ultimately* for the sake of some group they jointly constitute is to say that this group does not (necessarily) amount to the background object of import of the relevant emotion, but to the (phenomenal) subject—to the ultimate for-which—of this intentional act. In other words, strictly speaking, the participants in a collective affective intentional episode do not have to care *about this group*. Rather, they have to care *as this group* about some particular object that could, but definitively does not have to, be identical with the group they jointly constitute.

The issue can be clarified further in the course of an attempt to respond to the following objection. The theory articulated in this book is based on the idea that being able to care with one another about something is central to the possibility a number of individuals have to emotionally respond to certain occurrences in a genuinely joint manner. A good argument to this effect should show that being able to exist in the relevant situation as some particular group they together constitute is necessary for a number of people to experience the emotions they in this context have as contributions to a joint emotional response of *theirs*. On the basis of our last reflections, we could perhaps agree that, in order to come to understand their emotions as emotions that bring them to participate in a feeling-in-common, it would be *sufficient* that the participants took these emotions to be expressive of their caring about something for the sake of some group they jointly constitute. But it is not established yet that it is *necessary* for a number of individuals to participate in a moment of affective intentional community that they care about something for the sake of some group they jointly constitute.

Moreover, seeking to offer a counterexample to my claim to the effect that the participants in an episode of collective affective intentionality *have to* be able to understand their emotions as emotions that express their being ultimately concerned about the 'wellbeing' and 'flourishing' of a group they together constitute, someone could be inclined to point to the situation described by Scheler which was brought up at the very beginning of this debate. The point is that the emotions in virtue of which the parents of Scheler's example come to participate in a collective affective intentional episode are ultimately directed towards an object of import that does not amount to *their* group. The shared background object of import that warrants their (joint) emotional response is their dead child.

My imagined objector is definitively right. The problem is that he is confounding the for-the-sake-of-which of an emotion with its focus. Bennett Helm (cf. footnote 8 in Chap. 6) suggests that a particular sort of group—what he calls a 'community of respect'—has to be understood as the necessary common focus of certain sorts of shared emotional attitudes. But the focus of a joint emotional response is definitively not always the group the participating individuals take themselves to constitute. In other words, Helm's claim does not hold for every kind of shared emotion.

In general, the focus of an emotion and its for-the-sake-of-which do not have to coincide. On a given occasion, I can feel joy for my friend who has received an award that is important to him. In this case the focus of my joy is my friend, while the for-the-sake-of-which of my experiential act is myself. I do not experience my joy *for* my friend as the joy *of* my friend, but as a joy had by myself, given that this person (my friend) is important to me. What makes my joy intelligible is definitively the fact that this friend is a person who has import to me. But the particular existence that is an issue in this case—what Heidegger characterizes as the ultimate for-which of an emotion—is my personal existence, in this case, *as a friend of the awarded person*.

In this order of ideas, it can be claimed that what allows the parents of Scheler's example to experience their emotions as emotions in virtue of which they immediately come to participate in a moment of affective intentional community is definitively not the fact that the focus of their respective emotions amounts to one and the very same object of import, namely their child. Rather, the ultimate reason why they can participate in a feeling-in-common is because the for-the-sake-of-which of their respective emotions amounts to one and the very same '*our*self'. The existence that is an issue in this context is *their* common existence as this particular group.

To introduce a thought that will be central to the discussion I shall develop in the next chapter, I would like to suggest that the ultimate reason why the parents of Scheler's example can participate in a feeling-in-common is because their emotions self-referentially point back to a particular group which *as a group* has already begun to press ahead towards the actualization of some concrete possibility affected by the relevant occurrence (in this case, for instance, the truncated possibility of *jointly* raising a 'healthy and joyful' child). The point is that, in order to be able to experience their emotions as emotions in virtue of which they *immediately* come to participate in a moment of affective intentional community, the involved individuals *have to* be able to, *in their feeling*, understand themselves as constituting this group that has begun to press ahead towards the actualization of some particular possibility. This is what ultimately brings them to understand their feelings as feelings that contribute to a joint experiential act. To this extent to be able to exist as *their* group in the context of the relevant situation is necessary for a number of individuals to come to jointly actualize their ability to feel-towards together. In closing this chapter, let me indicate what has to be done in order to, on the basis of the discussion just developed, complete the present proposal.

In the course of an explication of Heidegger's notion of care, I have elucidated the sense in which Dasein can be said to essentially *be* its (existential) possibilities (i.e. to essentially be its *personal* abilities-to-be). In this context, I have discussed the relation between the way of being Heidegger calls existence and our capacity to become affected in particular ways by certain occurrences. This discussion ended up in the following thought: caring about something in a particular situation presupposes being able to exist as such-and-such in this situation. I elaborated on this thought by suggesting that jointly actualizing in a particular situation our ability to feel-towards together presupposes being able to, in this context, exist as *our* group. In the remainder of this study, I shall try to complete my account of collective affective intentionality by elucidating the sense in which it can be argued that we humans can, under certain circumstances, be *our* possibilities. Particularly, I shall clarify in how far, in asserting that we can be *our* possibilities, I am not denying that it is one's personal existence that ultimately (and as long as one exists as a Dasein) is an issue for one.

Chapter 8
Being Our Possibilities and Feeling Together

Abstract This chapter elaborates on the idea that, in order to jointly actualize our ability to feel-towards together, we have to be able to exist as our group. It articulates the following proposal: the faculty we human individuals have to emotionally respond to certain occurrences in a genuinely joint manner is grounded in the ability we have to exist in certain situations in terms of some possibilities we share with concrete others—the ability we humans have to jointly be our (shared) possibilities. The chapter begins with a clarification of what it means to have a justifiable sense to the effect that we (the involved individuals) constitute some particular social group. By means of a sort of case study I then explore some intuitions concerning the idea of a number of individuals caring with one another about something. I suggest that we can best cash out this idea in terms of the image of a number of persons existing in the relevant situation in light of some possibility they feel able to jointly actualize. I propose that in these situations the involved individuals are, in virtue of a non-purely instrumental actualization of their ability to be the relevant group, pursuing a joint actualization of some of their personal abilities—of some existential possibilities. To understand this idea is fundamental in order to make sense of the following suggestion: in those situations in which we are jointly actualizing our ability to feel-towards together we are caring about something ultimately for the sake of a group we take ourselves to co-constitute. This discussion allows me to further clarify the sense in which emotionally responding to some occurrence in a genuinely joint manner can be understood as a characteristically human ability.

Keywords Ability-to-be • Caring-with • Collective affective intentionality • Existential possibilities • Existing as a group • Feeling-towards together • Joint actualization • Shared possibilities • Social group

8.1 Introduction

The preceding chapter was organized around a discussion of Heidegger's notion of care, which aimed at explicating the idea that Dasein essentially *is* its (existential) possibilities (Sects. 7.2 and 7.3). It ended with the suggestion that jointly actualizing our ability to feel-towards together presupposes being able to exist as *our* group

H.A. Sánchez Guerrero, *Feeling Together and Caring with One Another*,
Studies in the Philosophy of Sociality 7, DOI 10.1007/978-3-319-33735-7_8

in the context of the relevant situation (Sect. 7.4). By means of this suggestion I began to spell out the main claim of the argument developed in Chap. 6. I am referring to the claim that, in order to be able to participate in an episode of collective affective intentionality, a number of individuals have to be able to, in the context of the relevant situation, care about something for the sake of some group they together constitute.

My main aim in this chapter is to elaborate on the idea that, in order to jointly actualize our ability to feel-towards together, we have to be able to exist as *our* group. I shall do so in such a way as to show that our ability to participate in moments of affective intentional community is grounded in a fundamental capacity we human beings have: we can be *our* (shared) possibilities. The discussion that follows, however, has a number of more wide-ranging goals. Up to this point I have taken for granted that we pre-theoretically understand not only what a social group is, but also what is implied by the idea of jointly being a group. In a first move I shall, therefore, try to clarify what it means to have a justifiable sense to the effect that we (the involved individuals) constitute some particular social group (Sect. 8.2). I shall do so by discussing Margaret Gilbert's influential account of what it is to go for a walk together. This discussion will make clear that my view of collective affective intentionality has no problem with smaller scale groups that are institutionally less clearly defined than those I have been appealing to in my previous examples. It will also allow me to dismantle a concrete worry that may have arisen in the course of our earlier discussion. This worry pertains to the suspicion that the account offered in this book might be circular in a vicious way. On this basis, in a second move I shall come back to my notion of caring-with. By means of a sort of case study I shall explore some intuitions concerning the idea of a number of individuals caring with one another about something—and not merely alongside each other. I shall suggest that we can best cash out this idea in terms of the image of a number of persons existing in the relevant situation in light of some possibility they feel able to jointly actualize (Sect. 8.3). In the last step, I shall propose that in the situations at issue the involved individuals may be taken to, in virtue of a non-purely instrumental actualization of their ability to be the relevant group, be pursuing a joint actualization of some of their personal abilities—of some existential possibilities. To understand this idea will be fundamental for us to come to appreciate why the following suggestion, which sharpens the main claim of my account of collective affective intentionality, should not be regarded as an implausibly exigent one: in those situations in which we are jointly actualizing our ability to feel-towards together we are caring about something *ultimately* for the sake of a group we take ourselves to co-constitute (Sect. 8.4).

I expect this discussion to clarify the sense in which it may be claimed that emotionally responding to some occurrence in a genuinely joint manner can be understood as a characteristically human ability.

8.2   The Minimal Feeling of Being (a Member of) a Particular Group

The notion of a social group has been employed in innumerably many ways in different sociological theories. In their attempts to spell out what a social group is (or what it is based upon), some sociologists have appealed to the image of a sort of *affective bond* holding a number of individuals together.[1] This link between the idea of constituting a group and the idea of having a feeling that ties one to the relevant others might seem to render my account problematic. The reason is as follows. In earlier chapters, I began to explicate the idea of a joint emotional response in terms of an affective motivation to pursue or avoid something for the sake of a group we (the participating individuals) take ourselves to jointly constitute. On pain of otherwise offering a viciously circular account, hence, in the context of my proposal, to understand oneself as a member of some particular group cannot mean to feel affectively tied to the relevant others in virtue of our emotional responses to some occurrence.

In view of this possible charge of vicious circularity, in what follows I shall make an effort to specify what we may call the minimal feeling of being (a member of) a group. My aim in this section and the next one is to tell this basic sense to the effect that one co-constitutes a particular group apart from the sense that one's emotional response is part of *our* emotional response—the sense that one is participating in an episode of collective affective intentionality. I shall do so by exploring some situations in which a number of individuals come to relate to certain worldly occurrences from 'within' the perspective of a member of a group they together constitute, without thereby coming to feel *emotionally* connected to one another in the manner that concerns us in this study. The point to be made in the course of this exploration is as follows: since a sufficiently demanding, though still intuitive, notion of a social group does not have to appeal to the image of a number of individuals feeling emotionally connected to one another, in order to explicate what it means to pre-thematically take oneself to be a member of a group, I do not have to (circularly) appeal to the idea of some affective bond tying together the individuals at issue in the context of the relevant situation.

---

[1] This image of an affective bond holding together a group of individuals has been particularly important for those sociologists and social psychologists who, elaborating on Charles Horton Cooley's ([1909] 1956) debated notion of a 'primary group', have sought to develop the idea of a *feeling of we-ness*. Max Weber's ([1921] 1972, pp. [220ff.] 238ff.) notion of *Gemeinsamkeitsgefühle* (usually translated as *'feelings of belonging to a community'*) also has to be mentioned here, despite of being a notion that is much more specific than the general idea of an affective bond—in that it refers to the peculiar bond that holds together individuals who share an *ethnic*, or at least a *political*, community. The reason why Weber's notion is worth mentioning here is because it aims at capturing the *genuinely affective* character of the tacit 'self-recognition of a people as a *demos* [that] has an empirical frame of reference, which encompasses a (usually undivided) territory settled together and a history understood as "concerning all of us"' (Offe 2000, p. 65). Weber is eager to differentiate these *Gemeinsamkeitsgefühle* from what he calls a *Gemeinsamkeitsglauben* (*a belief in community*).

Our leading question in this section will be the questions as to what it means—as to what it is like—to be (a member of) a particular group.[2] I shall try to answer this question by appealing to some of the insights gained in the course of a philosophical discussion aimed at solving an issue that is slightly different: what do we mean when we talk of a social group?

To try to spell out what we mean when we use the term 'group' in order to refer to a *social* group is important here for an additional reason. Most of the examples I have provided so far could be claimed to be too strongly marked by what we may call *institutional collectivity*. The problem is that, in focusing on these cases (the case of the orchestra or the case of the volleyball team), we might lose sight of expressions of collective affective intentionality that are likely to arise in contexts which involve groups of individuals that are less clearly defined by institutional formats—or so it could be objected.

Moreover, the examples offered may be considered problematic, not only because I have appealed to social groups that are clearly defined by institutional frameworks and regulations, but also because I have appealed to activities of a particular sort: activities in which one can *exclusively* engage in the context of a collaborative effort. In order to make a strong case for the claim that there is an essential difference between feeling towards something in a *merely parallel way (alongside other individuals)* and doing so *in a genuinely joint manner (with one another)*, it may be helpful to consider activities in which one could also engage *on one's own*, and try to spell out what is different about engaging in these activities solitarily and doing it together with someone else (or with certain other individuals).

In my attempt to tackle all the issues mentioned in a single discussion I will pay particular attention to Margaret Gilbert's notion of a social group. Most of the reasons for so doing are related to the considerations just presented. But let me make some of them more explicit.

First of all, Gilbert can be seen as one of the first philosophers who, in the context of the contemporary debate on collective intentionality, have devoted considerable and systematic efforts to spelling out the very notion of a social group, as opposed to just employing this notion, and taking for granted that we intuitively understand it.[3]

Moreover, Gilbert has developed a notion of a social group that is *just demanding enough*. That is, a notion to which I could appeal in order to block the objection concerning some vicious circularity present in my account, but which, compared

---

[2] I shall address the issue in terms of *what it is like for an individual* to be a member of a group. To offer an answer to this question, however, is to begin to offer an answer to the question as to what it is like *for a number of individuals* to jointly be a group. It is a mistake, I think, to believe that we have to be able to understand a group as a sort of supraindividual centre of conscious sentience in order to answer (or meaningfully pose) the question concerning whether there is something it is like to be a social group.

[3] Indeed, Gilbert presents herself as one of the first philosophers who have articulated an explicit notion of a social group. She writes: 'On the whole, those who have focused on the above questions have tended to work with a relatively inarticulate, intuitive understanding of the nature of social phenomena in general, and of social groups in particular' (1990, p. 1).

with other philosophical attempts to cash out the idea of a social group, could be seen as a relatively simple one.[4]

It is also important to note that, as she is eager to emphasize, the concept of a social group developed in the context of Gilbert's plural subject theory (cf. the discussion in Sects. 3.2 and 3.3) is the result of an attempt to analyze our *vernacular* notion of a social group, as opposed to being the result of an attempt to analyze one of the very special *terms of art* that are employed in the different sociological research programs.

A further point concerns the fact that Gilbert's notion of a social group can be applied to groups of different sizes and degrees of complexity, from dyads, i.e. groups that involve only two individuals, to large collectives. Moreover, Gilbert's concept of a social group can be applied in the analysis of activities carried out in the context of certain multipersonal settings that are *not* structured by explicit institutional frames and regulations. (Indeed, Gilbert's concept of a social group has to a great extent been developed by means of analyzing precisely such cases.)

Something from which I can especially profit in this context is the further fact that Gilbert develops her notion of a social group by discussing activities in which one can engage both solitarily or cooperatively.

The most important reason I have for drawing here on Gilbert's work, however, is the following: although there are a number of passages in her writings that strongly suggest that Gilbert is basically interested in making metaphysical claims— claims that concern the question as to *what kind of entity* a social group is—, Gilbert's account may be read in a 'phenomenological key'. For one thing, Gilbert's effort aimed at capturing in clear terms what it is to constitute a social group (a plural subject) basically amounts to an attempt to spell out how our engagement with the world (and with other human beings) *looks like from a personal perspective* in situations in which we adopt a particular point of view that we human individuals, as a matter of fact, are *able* to adopt. Here I mean, of course, the point of view of a member of a group. So, even if we take Gilbert's philosophical concerns to be fundamentally metaphysical in nature, we can read her work in such a way as to get some insights that pertain to *the particular way in which we make sense of worldly occurrences (and, as I shall argue, of our personal existence) in those situations in which we adopt the perspective of a member of a given group.* This is the reading of Gilbert's work which I shall try to exploit in this section—being aware that Gilbert is probably seeking to say much more than that which I am, in this context, taking her to be saying.

But there is at least one reason why one may be advised not to appeal to Gilbert's view when trying to dismantle the impression that one's own account is circular. As mentioned above (in Sect. 3.2), Gilbert's plural subject theory has itself been repeatedly charged with vicious circularity (cf. Sheehy 2002; Schmid 2014a; Tollefsen 2002; and Tuomela 1992).

---

[4] See, for instance, Seumas Miller's (1999, pp. 340ff.) and Raimo Tuomela's (2007, pp. 13ff.) attempts to spell out the notion of a social group.

For a particular reason that is related to my previous remark, however, in appealing to Gilbert's insights in the frame of this discussion I am not necessarily embracing those suggestions Gilbert's critics take to be profoundly problematic. The point is simply that, even if it turns out to be true that Gilbert's *metaphysical* account of social groups can be said to be viciously circular, her considerations concerning what it is for the participants to understand themselves as constituting a social group result illuminating in the context of a broadly *phenomenological* inquiry. Let me briefly explicate this point.

Gilbert is definitively committed—and perhaps, as her critics claim, by way of an assumption, and not by way of conclusion—to a particular view concerning the kind of entity a social group can be said to be. But her plural subject theory could be argued to be grounded in an unproblematic assumption along the following lines: we are beings that are capable of adopting a *collective standpoint*—and, in a number of situations, disposed to do so. At any rate, Gilbert sets out her account in such a way as to allow for a reading of her claims that is not motivated by the issue of what sort of entity a social group is, but by the question 'What it is *for us* (the participants) to have a justifiable sense that we constitute a group?'

In a characterization of her own work offered in the introductory chapter to the collection of essays entitled *Living Together*, Gilbert writes: 'The essays in this book [...] continue the defense and development of a particular interpretation of the collective' standpoint. This was introduced in my book *On Social Facts*' (1996, p. 1). It is, hence, a characterization of a particular *standpoint* or *perspective* what Gilbert has been after for years—or at least this is the way she wants us to conceive of her own philosophical efforts.

So it may be the case that Gilbert can be accused of having been playing a sort of philosophical double game.[5] But even if this were the case, one could certainly profit from many of her elucidating considerations in the context of an endeavor aimed at 'merely' spelling out the structural features of the sense of belongingness to a group that we are seeking to understand.[6] In determining these structural features, one would be answering the question concerning what it means for a number of persons to have a justifiable sense to the effect that they are (members of) the group at issue. This is the setting in which, ultimately seeking to argue for the idea that we can emotionally respond to certain occurrences in a genuinely joint manner only due to the fact that we can also be some of *our* (shared) possibilities, in what follows I shall discuss Gilbert's suggestions concerning what it is to constitute a

---

[5]Gilbert begins her influential paper 'Walking Together: A Paradigmatic Social Phenomenon' (1990) by pointing to what she characterizes as an *ontological* problem. But as Sheehy, who seems to be offering a criticism along the lines just mentioned, points out, Gilbert's basic goal is to specify the central features of a particular perspective. Sheehy writes: 'The *main aim* of plural subject theory is an interpretation and elucidation of the collective standpoint: the perspective from which we possess shared goals, beliefs, values, and so on' (2002, p. 378; my emphasis).

[6]By bracketing those claims of Gilbert's plural subject theory that clearly have a metaphysical intention, thereby focusing on her brilliant elucidation of what it is to adopt the perspective of a member of a group, I shall try to articulate an answer to the question concerning what it is like (for a number of individuals) to jointly be a social group.

social group. I shall begin to do so by discussing the central points of Gilbert's account of what it is to *jointly* engage in an activity one could, in principle, also *solitarily* engage in, namely going for a walk.

Gilbert's point of departure is an intuition she attributes to Georg Simmel: 'we can discover the nature of social groups in general by investigating such small-scale temporary phenomena as going for a walk together' (Gilbert 1990, p. 2). Note that, besides drawing our attention to 'small-scale temporary [social] phenomena', Gilbert is suggesting here that we can analyze our ordinary concept of a social group by trying to determine what is special about a particular sort of *acts* we are able to perform. The idea is that, as she writes, '[an] analysis of our concepts of "shared action" discovers a structure that is constitutive of social groups as such' (ibid.). In other words, the joint action of going for a walk together should be seen not only as a paradigm of a particular class of human acts, but also as an example of what we have in mind when we use the term 'group' in order to refer to a social group. But Gilbert's fundamental assumption is not easily recognizable in the passage just quoted. So let me try to make it explicit.

In suggesting that an analysis of what a shared action is amounts to an analysis of what a social group is, Gilbert is not merely seeking to point out that a group, in a way, only exists in and through the acts of its members. Rather, the point is that we cannot spell out the idea of a social group without referring to certain intentional attitudes of the individuals involved.[7] Put another way, the structure claimed by Gilbert to be constitutive of social groups *as such* is an *intentional structure*; a structure that configures the view of the world (and the view of themselves) the involved individuals have at the relevant moment.[8] But what is the peculiar feature of this intentional structure?

We have seen above (in Sects. 3.2 and 3.3) that Gilbert's plural subject account is to a great extent motivated by the following diagnostic impression: most of the circulating accounts of collective intentionality fail to make thematic the *normative nature* of genuinely collective acts. So we already have a rough idea of what the peculiar feature of this intentional structure is. But let us get a sight of the argumentative moves by means of which, by discussing what it means for two individuals to go for a walk together, Gilbert reveals this normativity that determines the intentional structure she takes to be constitutive of social groups as such.

In her often quoted paper 'Walking Together: A Paradigmatic Social Phenomenon' (1990), Gilbert takes advantage of the fact that going for a walk is an activity in

---

[7] Gilbert makes the following remark which suggests that she is concerned with elucidating a particular way of being-oriented-towards-worldly-occurrences; a form of intentionality that can be said to be at the heart of any social group: 'First, plural subject concepts apply only when certain individual people are in specific psychological states, that is only when they are jointly committed with certain others in some way. Second, one cannot employ a particular plural subject concept without employing the concept of the relevant psychological attribute [...] such as belief, having such-and-such goal, and endorsing such-and-such principle' (1996, p. 9). For a discussion on the position she calls 'Intentionalism', see Gilbert (1989, Chapter 3).

[8] This is an assumption many philosophers who understand themselves as 'realists about the social' find particularly problematic (cf. Sheehy 2002).

which one can engage solitarily or together with someone else (or with a number of other people). Her initial efforts are aimed at showing that, having determined as an analytic point of departure a *formally* individual intention (an intention expressed in this case in the form 'I intend to go for a walk'), we never reach the idea of a number of individuals going for a walk together. Put another way, we do not get a satisfactory picture of what is involved in such a joint act as going for a walk together by just rendering the idea of going for a walk alone gradually more demanding (by progressively introducing additional logical conditions). In what follows, I shall schematically reconstruct the four steps by means of which, in the mentioned paper, Gilbert discloses the normativity she takes to be central to any genuinely joint action.

In a first step, Gilbert addresses a very basic point: the mere physical proximity of two walking individuals is definitively not enough to make it the case that they are going for a walk together. As she observes, this proximity may in certain situations even disturb the involved individuals; the reason being 'precisely because they are *not* going for a walk together' (p. 2). It is important to understand that, in making this remark, Gilbert is not trying to make a suggestion along the following lines: were the two participants, on the contrary, glad of each other's presence, we would be allowed to assert that they are going for a walk together. The upsetting character of this co-presence is not an impediment to their doing something together, but a symptomatic expression of the fact that they do not take themselves to be doing so.

In a second move, Gilbert points out that doing something together is not merely a matter of having sufficiently similar, matching goals or intentions. Two individuals who, besides being physically close to one another, have the formally individual goal of going for a walk alongside each other are *not* walking together. They are precisely *just walking alongside each other*. Gilbert differentiates two sorts of cases; the point being that not even in the most demanding type of situations we should feel entitled to speak of two individuals going for a walk together.

In the first type of case, each individual's goal to walk in the company of the other person remains concealed to this other person. Gilbert writes that the problem here is that in such a situation 'giving both participants the personal goal that they walk alongside each other puts them no closer together *as far as they are concerned*' (p. 3). It is not easy to explicate the intuition captured by the emphasized phrase 'as far as they are concerned'. But the idea, as I understand it, might be clarified by appealing to the figure of a well-informed (non-participant) observer who knows the individual intentions of the persons involved; intentions that, as specified, are *not* common knowledge among the parties. Such an observer could, given the reciprocal nature of the participants' intentions, be inclined to conceive of these individuals as individuals who are going for a walk together. His assertion to the effect that they are doing so could, however, be questioned for the sole reason that the involved persons do not take themselves to be doing so.[9]

---

[9]A, to some extent, contrary intuition brings Sartre to suggest that a number of interacting individuals only come to constitute a group or community when an (external) observer—to whom Sartre refers using the term 'the Third'—brings them to see themselves as constituting a group by

As already hinted at, for Gilbert—who in this point, too, is following Simmel—, two or more persons can be said to constitute a group (a plural subject of a certain intentional act) just in case they can be claimed to understand themselves as constituting this group.[10] Put another way, the phrase 'as far as they are concerned', in this context, basically seeks to stress the following idea: togetherness is not primarily an observable feature of certain human constellations (of certain arrangements of entities of the human sort), but a character of the attitudes in virtue of which a number of persons participate in a joint intentional act.

Gilbert contrasts the situation just described with the case in which it is common knowledge between the participants that each one has the goal of going for a walk alongside the other participant. Gilbert spells out this Lewisian idea of a goal being common knowledge by exploiting the phrase 'as far as they are concerned'. She clarifies that what is special about this type of case is that 'each [participant's] goal is completely out in the open as far as the two of them are concerned' (p. 3). Appealing to our well-informed (non-participant) observer, one could be inclined to suggest something along the following lines: in the case in which the formally individual coincident goal of the participants is common knowledge between them, one could take these individuals to be at least as disposed as the observer to understand the situation at issue as a situation in which they are doing something together. What, then, prevents us from understanding such a situation as an exemplary characterization of what it is for two individuals to go for a walk together?

Seeking to bring to light the *essential* aspect of a shared action she is missing, Gilbert abandons the additive strategy—a strategy she has adopted mainly in order to show its inadequacy.[11] As her new point of departure she takes the situation an advocate of this additive strategy would, in her view erroneously, expect to be able to attain by progressively adding logical conditions to the idea of going for a walk on one's own.

In a third step, hence, Gilbert asks us to assume that at a given point the relevant logical conditions (whatever these conditions are) have come to be fulfilled, so that the involved individuals can be said to be going for a walk together. Gilbert's aim here is to show that an expectation we would have in this case—the case in which we take the parties to *really* be doing something together—would be absent in the most demanding scenario achieved by the procedure of gradually complicating the act of going for a walk alone. In order to specify what is missing, Gilbert explores a peculiar situation.

---

objectifying (or alienating) them (cf. [1943] [1956] 2001, pp. 389ff.). Arguing for the primacy of the experienced subject-we—of the pre-intentional sense of belonging together—, Schmid criticizes Sartre by writing: 'The experience of the third's view cannot *create* but only help to *reveal* or *discover* joint intentionality that was already there. A joint intention can be revealed in the third's view only if it was already *latent* in the original situation of action (i.e., before the third's appearance)' (2009, p. 176).

[10] This is the central tenet of the position to which I have referred above by the term 'Intentionalism'.

[11] By 'additive strategy' I mean the attempt to arrive at the idea of some individuals going for a walk together by complicating the idea of an individual solitarily going for a walk.

Gilbert asks us to imagine that one of the participants—to whom I shall refer by use of masculine pronouns—has begun to draw ahead, making no effort whatsoever to adjust his pace in order to allow the other party to come closer. She observes that in such a situation we would expect the other participant—to whom I shall refer by use of feminine pronouns—to make some remark (or to take some measure) aimed at rebuking the person who has begun to draw ahead. The expectation at issue here, she argues, would, however, not exhaust itself in the fact that we could easily imagine her to be inclined to reproach him. Rather, this expectation would be a matter of our taking her reproach '[to] be *in order*' (p. 3). This sense of appropriateness concerning this act of censure, Gilbert argues, shows that we expect both parties to be clear about the fact that, in such a circumstance, she would be *entitled* to rebuke him. The point is that the objective character of this entitlement could be taken to make clear that the persons involved in a joint act of going for a walk together have an *obligation* to, for instance, monitor and adjust their pace in reference to the other party.

According to Gilbert, we in general expect the individuals involved in a genuinely joint action to be aware of some obligations and corresponding rights they have in virtue of their taking part in this particular sort of activity. More concretely, we expect them to understand that, *in virtue of their having jointly accepted to take part in a shared activity*, they have acquired a number of rights and obligations. This is something, Gilbert thinks, we do not expect those individuals who merely are doing something alongside each other to take for granted; not even if they were aware of the reciprocal character of their intentions. The intuition is that in the latter case we would, given the situation just described, probably be able to *make sense* of her inclination to bring him to notice that he has begun to draw ahead, but it would be difficult to argue for the idea that she is *entitled* to rebuke him.

Having revealed by means of this example the normative structure that is proper to a joint action, in a last step, Gilbert makes an effort to show that this normativity is intrinsic to the very idea of doing something together. Gilbert's first point is that the obligations and rights at issue here cannot arise from a sort of *moral duty* each of the involved individuals has to promote both parties' individual goal to walk in the company of each other. For the entitlement to rebuke the other party, were she or he to fail to do certain things that pertain to *them* as individuals who are doing something together, would be valid even if none of them had a clue as to whether the other person also thinks that each of them has a moral duty to promote the individual goal of both parties.

But the normative character of genuinely joint actions, Gilbert claims, cannot be explained, either, in terms of a combination of prudence (or rational self-interest) and common knowledge between the parties concerning their respective intentions. Considerations based on sheer practical rationality may perhaps, under the assumption of common knowledge, require the involved individuals to monitor their situation and, if pertinent, to take action in order to keep close to each other. Correspondingly, if, as in the example we are considering, one of the participants were to fail to do so, the other party may deem him to be not only irrational, but also inconsiderate of her. Moreover, Gilbert observes, 'this could lead her to stop wanting to be with him' (p. 4). In other words, from a prudential point of view, given the fact that the participants' intentions to walk alongside each other are common knowledge among them, one certainly could take both of them to be *obliged* to do certain things. But this, Gilbert argues, would not explain the sort of normativity that is at issue here. What exactly is the problem now?

The point is definitely not an easy one. To explicate it, Gilbert appeals to Herbert Lionel Adolphus Hart's (1961) distinction between 'being obliged' and 'having an obligation'. In the case in which a person merely is obliged to do such-and-such in virtue of certain prudential considerations, it is instrumental rationality that obliges her or him to do so. Thus, in order to explicate the extent to which this person is obliged to do such-and-such, one simply has to specify what her or his goal is and explain, if not already evident, what she or he has to be disposed to do *in order to achieve this goal*. In the case in which someone has an obligation proper, Gilbert writes, 'such premises are insufficient' (p. 5). And what is, in my view, more telling, they are unnecessary. For, according to Gilbert, what brings us to recognize that in the case at issue here 'we are dealing with an obligation of the latter kind' (ibid.), and not with a mere being-obliged by certain prudential considerations to do something, is that the entitlement she has to rebuke him for having neglected the alleged obligation can be said to be *directly* related to this obligation. As Gilbert writes, '*the obligation is such that [his] failure to perform entitles [her] to rebuke him*' (ibid.; italics in the original). This points to the fact, Gilbert thinks, that the normativity at issue is constitutive of the joint action.

In closing her inquiry concerning the source of this normativity, Gilbert observes that the normative character exhibited by genuinely joint actions is not a function of both parties having *linguistically communicated* their respective intention to go for a walk in the company of each other. For if the relevant intentions were articulable as formally individual intentions (intentions expressed in the form 'I intend to go for a walk in your company') no normativity of the relevant sort (i.e. no obligation proper) would be generated by the verbalization of their 'matching' intentions. In cases in which the involved individuals share a formally individual goal (in a relatively weak sense of 'sharing'), Gilbert maintains, 'neither one seems to have to conclude that any one has any obligations to the other to perform satisfactorily, or that anyone is entitled to rebuke the other for not doing what they can to reach the goal' (p. 6).[12]

Gilbert summarizes this train of thought by writing:

---

[12] Gilbert continues this thought by writing: 'This is true even if each has averred: "I intend to do all I can to achieve my goal. For instance, if you draw ahead without noticing, I plan to call out to catch your attention. Given your own goal, this should help me attain mine." This does not seem crucially to change things. In the case now envisaged [he] will, if you like, be "entitled to expect" that [she] will call after him if he unknowingly draws ahead, and [she] will be "entitled to expect" that he will not be surprised at her doing so. This might make her less timid about doing these things. But here, saying that they are "entitled to expect" these things is just another way of saying that their evidence is such that they can infer that performance will take place, all else being equal. No one yet seems to have the right type of *obligation to perform* or the corresponding *entitlements to rebuke* and so on' (p. 6).

> As long as people are out on a walk together, they will understand that each has an *obligation* to do what he or she can to achieve the relevant goal. Moreover, each one is *entitled* to rebuke the other for failure to fulfill this obligation. [...] Importantly, [these obligations] seem to be a direct function of the fact of going for a walk together. Thus, though certain 'external' factors or considerations may lead to their being ignored, they are 'still there' (ibid.).

Both the expression 'as long as' and the expression 'to be a direct function of' stress the point of Gilbert's reflection: the normativity disclosed in the course of this analysis can be taken to be inherent to the very act of going for a walk together.

This normative character genuinely joint actions exhibit amounts, in Gilbert's view, to the characteristic feature of the intentional structure that is constitutive of a social group as such. At this point, we are, thus, already in a position to offer an answer to the question concerning what it means for a person to understand herself as a member of a given group. Against the background of Gilbert's analysis, it may be claimed that to understand oneself as a member of a particular group essentially means to *already have adopted* a perspective from which one sees oneself as having a number of obligations and rights (of a certain sort) that involve those other individuals one, at this moment, also understands as members of the group at issue.[13]

To the extent to which it can be claimed to 'be there', as Gilbert writes, as soon as one adopts this perspective (and as long as one maintains it), this sense of having certain sorts of obligations and rights that involve the pertinent others can be said to amount to a *structural feature of the very perspective of a member of a given group*. Correspondingly, those circumstances in which one understands oneself as doing something solitarily or alongside certain other individuals—and not with them together—can be understood as circumstances that, for whatever reason, do *not* bring us (the individuals involved) to, in the presence of each other, adopt the normatively structured perspective we have been discussing. But what is required for us to come to adopt the perspective of a member of a group (in this case of a group of individuals who intend to do something together)?

According to Gilbert, all that is required is that the involved individuals make explicit (by whatever means) that they are willing to *jointly commit themselves* to pursuing a given goal in a joint manner. Gilbert proposes considering an utterly quotidian communicative transaction. She writes:

> Suppose Jack Smith coughs to attract Sue's attention, and then asks if she is Sue Jones and would she mind if he joins her? 'No,' Sue says, 'that would be nice. I should like some company.' This is probably enough to produce a case of going for a walk together (pp. 6–7).

Gilbert takes such a conversation to be sufficient for both parties to feel entitled to assume that 'the attitudes and actions appropriate to their going for a walk together are in place' (p. 7). She considers crucial that in such an exchange 'each party has

---

[13] Gilbert observes that 'joint commitments are not necessarily brought into being with any clear conscious intent to do so' (2000, p. 6). That is to say, this already-having-adopted-the-perspective-of-a-member-of-*this*-group does not imply having at some point *decided* to do so. Very often it is, rather, a matter of, as we may say, 'having fallen into' or 'having been brought to adopt' this perspective.

made it clear to the other that he is willing to *join forces* with the other in accepting the goal that they walk in one another's company' (ibid.). Offering an alternative characterization of this very same point, Gilbert proposes that in the course of such an exchange 'each [party] has manifested his willingness to bring it about that the goal in question be accepted *by himself and the other, jointly*' (ibid.). The adverb 'jointly' is absolutely central here. For Gilbert's claim is that in the course of the exchange by means of which the plural subject of a goal comes to be constituted the participants express their respective will to join forces (in order to fulfill the goal at issue) in such a way as to tie these wills together in a very particular manner, namely in a *simultaneous and interdependent* manner. She explicates this point as follows:

> [W]e do not have, here, an 'exchange of promises' such that each person unilaterally binds himself to the goal in question, leaving himself beholden for release to someone else upon whom, through this particular transaction, he has no claim. Nor is it that one person in effect says: 'You may regard me as committed once *you* have made a commitment' leaving it up to the other person to make an initial unilateral commitment. Rather, each person expresses a special form of *conditional commitment* such that (as is understood) only when *everyone* has done similarly is *anyone* committed (p. 7).

It is particularly important to note that Gilbert's point here is completely independent from the idea that, in her view, warrants talk of a plural subject: the idea that 'each [of the individuals involved in a joint commitment to do something] must act as would the parts of a single person or subject of action in pursuit of the goal' (p. 8).[14] For Gilbert's remark does not concern the joint character of the *actions* the individuals involved, by means of the communicative exchange at issue, commit themselves to performing. Rather, this remark concerns the defining character of the *commitment* itself, which is not merely a commitment to do something together, but furthermore a *joint* commitment to do so.

At the latest at this point, Gilbert's account could be alleged to be circular. For the requirement Gilbert has in mind may be stated as follows: all that is required for a number of persons to *come to* constitute a group—in this case a group of individuals who aim at doing something together—is to express their willingness to, *as a group* (and not as distinct individuals), commit themselves to jointly pursuing the goal at issue. That is, before having come to constitute the relevant group, the participating individuals have to be able to see themselves as already constituting a group that is, at least, coextensive with the group they aim at constituting. They have to do so on pain of otherwise not being able to *jointly* commit themselves to pursuing together the goal at issue.

This arguably vicious circularity of Gilbert's account does, as already mentioned, not constitute a problem in the context of an inquiry concerning the minimal sense

---

[14] Gilbert completes this idea by writing: 'For now, let me sum up by conjecturing that in order to go for a walk together each of the parties must express willingness to constitute with the other *a plural subject of the goal* that they walk along in one another's company' (p. 7). Since this is not an exposition of Gilbert's plural subject theory, but an attempt to make fruitful some of her suggestions in order to spell out what it means to pre-thematically understand oneself as a member of a given group, I will not comment further on Gilbert's central—and controversial—notion of a plural subject.

of being a group. For, in order to begin to answer the question as to what it is like to be (a member of) a group, we only have to appeal to the following insight: a number of individuals who at least pre-thematically conceive of some intentional act they are performing as an act that would *immediately* entitle them to rebuke each other, were they to fail to perform the actions that are appropriate to *their* doing something together, *necessarily* understand themselves as individuals who jointly constitute a group. Put another way, the insight concerning what it is to be a group that from a phenomenological point of view is crucial integrates the very presupposition that from a metaphysical perspective can be argued to be problematic. In a phenomenological style, the point can be restated as follows: a number of individuals who in a given situation take themselves to be doing something together (in a broad sense of 'doing') have *always already* understood themselves as members of some particular group.[15] The mentioned sense to the effect that, in the relevant situation, one is entitled to assume that the attitudes and actions appropriate to *our* doing something together are in place can, thus, be taken to amount to what we may call the *minimal feeling of being (a member of) a particular group.*[16]

As already hinted at, this characterization of the *minimal* phenomenology of being (a member of) a group is intended to offer a basis for fleshing out the claim

---

[15] The phenomenological reading of Gilbert's account that I have been proposing averts one's eyes from the problem concerning how the normative expectations discussed above come to be a part of group membership. In claiming that this normativity can be understood as a structural feature of the very perspective of a member of a given group, i.e. as something that can be said to *always already be there* when a number of individuals come to constitute a social group, I do not mean to suggest that we do not need the idea of a joint commitment in order to account for the constitution of this experienced normativity. I am just pointing out that, as far as our purely phenomenological attempt to understand what it is like to be (a member of) a group is concerned, we can suspend this central ontological issue, thereby evading (and not solving) the problem of vicious circularity mentioned in the main text. Moreover, the discussion on the sense of togetherness that follows will be structured around an example that, in order to explain the participants' sense of togetherness, explicitly invokes a joint commitment. But the claim that this particular sort of normativity can be understood as a structural feature of the perspective of a member of a group could itself be objected to be controversial, as an anonymous reviewer of the manuscript of this book has made me aware of. For it may be argued that there are social groups without the kind of rights and obligations that Gilbert assigns to group membership. An example would be a cooperative endeavor that emerges in the frame of what Tuomela and Tuomela (2005) call I-mode cooperative action. I agree that we often use the expression 'group context' to refer to these sorts of situations. But to the extent to which the individuals involved in such a situation are cooperating with one another in order to achieve their *respective* (formally individual) intentions they can be said to be cooperating (with one another) alongside each other. Indeed, Tuomela and Tuomela observe that 'the assumption of a group context need not be made in the case of I-mode cooperation' (2005, p. 81). Moreover, they underscore that it is absolutely central to distinguish, in the first place, 'between acting fully as a group member and acting as a private person within a group context' (ibid.).

[16] Gilbert, as already mentioned, is interested in moving forward the discussion I have just reconstructed in such a way as to answer the question concerning what a social group *is*. She writes: 'I have argued that those out on a walk together form a plural subject, and that there is some reason to suppose that our concept of a social group—that concept by virtue of which we list families, guilds, tribes, "and so on" together—is the concept of a plural subject' (p. 12). As mentioned above (in Sect. 3.2), for Gilbert, a social group *is* a plural subject, and any plural subject *is* a social group.

that there is a basic sense of group belongingness that has to be differentiated from the feeling we are seeking to specify in this study: the feeling that we (the individuals involved) are participating in one and the same moment of affective intentional community. But the fact that we are still urged to offer some positive picture of the sense of togetherness that is at the heart of a joint affective intentional act can be made evident by way of the following objection: one could grant that the mentioned sense of having the sorts of obligations and corresponding rights Gilbert is pointing to amounts to *the* structural feature of the perspective of a member of a group and doubt that making an effort to relate to the world from such a perspective is sufficient for a number of individuals to immediately understand their convergent emotions as contributions to a joint emotional response.

By exploring the difference between *adopting* the perspective of a member of a particular group and *maintaining* this perspective, in what follows I shall try to distil the sense of togetherness that concerns us in this study. The difference I am really after is, however, the one between *merely 'taking up' the perspective of a member of some group* and *jointly existing (with the relevant others) as this group* in a particular situation. In the course of my attempt to draw this distinction, I shall bring back to the fore of the argument a number of issues I dealt with in previous chapters. My aim in doing so is to make plausible the claim that we can participate in moments of affective intentional community due to the ability we human individuals have to, in certain situations, exist in terms of some of *our* (shared) possibilities.

8.3   Jointly Existing as a Group and Being *Our* Possibilities

Let me begin the next series of considerations by emphasizing the following peculiarity of joint commitments: once established, joint commitments, in a sense, free themselves from the purely individual will of the parties. They do so to the extent to which they 'present themselves' to the involved individuals as something over which they can decide *only together (as a group)*.

As mentioned above (in Sect. 3.2), Gilbert makes the point by emphasizing that, once two (or more) individuals have jointly committed themselves to pursuing something together—having thereby come to constitute a plural subject of the goal at issue—, none of them can *unilaterally* rescind this commitment.[17] For, being a joint commitment, this commitment can only be rescinded *jointly*. The only way open to a member of the pertinent group who does no longer want to constitute this plural subject—provided the other member (or members) of the group is (or are) not prepared to terminate the joint commitment at issue—consists in violating or breaking it. This makes a big difference, since, in breaking a joint commitment, a person does not cancel all the obligations she has accepted by having come to constitute the

---

[17] Once a group has been constituted, Gilbert writes, '[none of the involved individuals] can release himself from the commitment; each is obligated to all the others for performance; each is (thus) entitled to performance from the rest' (1990, p. 8).

relevant plural subject. At any rate, she does not annul these obligations in the same way she would have done it, had they (the involved individuals) jointly decided to rescind their joint commitment.[18]

Now, Gilbert is certainly pointing to something fundamental here. But we should not overlook the fact that, in a number of situations, we are willing to incur the sorts of 'violations' just mentioned. In these situations we are willing to simply abandon the perspective of a member of *this* particular group and adopt either an individual perspective or the perspective of a member of another group.

Think about a person who, without having achieved an agreement with her husband concerning the convenience of separation, decides to leave home and break up the marriage. We can learn a lot, I think, by considering what the involved individuals may experience in such a situation.

To begin with, the mere separation could certainly be enough for both parties to feel annoyed (though probably to different extents and in different ways). However, one could plausibly take the experience of the person who has been 'left hanging'—to whom I shall refer by use of masculine pronouns—to be more upsetting. Moreover, we could plausibly take the experience of this person to be more annoying than the experience he would have had, had they (the two parties) jointly decided to dissolve the marriage. At least in part, this could be explained by the fact that, once the joint decision to dissolve the group has been taken, none of the parties would be inclined to continue to conceive of her- or himself as a member of this group. They might both be sad about this outcome, but, *as far as the joint commitment at issue is concerned*, none of them would feel that the other party *owes to her or him something*.

But having actually been 'left hanging', the individual whose experience we are considering may feel personally disrespected by the other party. What is more, this individual may feel that the other party—to whom I shall refer by use of feminine pronouns—has disrespected him by disrespecting *their* commitment to, say, spend the rest of their lives together. Although in such a dyadic case the act by means of which one of the parties has broken or violated the relevant commitment has, for practical purposes, also annihilated the group at issue, we could easily imagine him preserving in certain situations a sense to the effect that he has some rights that correspond to some obligations of the other party.[19]

Contrary to what one could be inclined to assume, as far as the existence of certain obligations and rights is concerned, the situation would not necessarily be much different for her—the person who has actively broken the commitment. Even if she were to take her decision to be definitively correct, this person may, for instance, feel that the other party has the right to reproach her and hold her accountable for

---

[18] At a minimum, this person could be made accountable for having broken the joint commitment at issue.

[19] Gilbert is aware that the situation is very special in the case of a dyad, since, in violating the relevant commitment, the party at issue is, in a sense, destroying the group (she or he is actually making it impossible that this concrete group persists). In this context, Gilbert refers again to Simmel (cf. Gilbert 1990, pp. 11–12).

having disrespected the joint commitment at issue. Correspondingly, she could be more than willing to offer the other party an explanation for why she has decided to 'violate' *their* joint commitment. And she could be more than willing to do so, even if she were absolutely clear about the fact that she does not feel any motivation to *maintain* the perspective of a member of this group.

So even in case she were to be convinced that she had good reasons for disrespecting the joint commitment at issue, no longer be motivated to care about the future of this marriage, and be aware that, at this point, it does not make much sense to talk of a 'we', this person may episodically 'fall again into' the normatively structured perspective of a member of the pertinent group—a group she used to be willing to co-constitute. Due to the fact that the actual dismantlement of the group has been the result of a violation of the joint commitment (or commitments) at issue, rather than being the result of a joint decision to rescind it (or them), at least episodically, this person could, in the presence of the other party, come to (passively) adopt a perspective that is marked by what certainly may be called a sense of togetherness.

What in this context warrants talk of a sense of togetherness is precisely the fact that, *as soon as* they 'fell again into' the perspective at issue, and *as long as* they related to the world 'from within' this perspective, both parties would feel (again) an obligation to do certain things which arise from *their* previous joint commitment. That is to say, at least during the periods we are considering, not only their relation to each other, but also their relation to a number of worldly occurrences would be organized around a sense that they owe something to (and are owed something by) each other in virtue of their having, at some point, come to agree to interrelatedly adopt the perspective of a member of a particular group.

Now, this finding concerning some remaining sense of togetherness might seem to be at odds with my account. I have been proposing that, in order to come to experience togetherness while responding emotionally to some occurrence, the involved individuals have to be able to understand themselves as individuals for whom the relevant group is an issue. Our last reflections suggest, however, that, even if they were to no longer 'give a damn' about the 'wellbeing' and 'flourishing' of the group that can be argued to be at issue, two individuals could have coincident experiences marked by some sense of togetherness—understood as a sense to the effect that one has some (non-derived) rights and corresponding obligations that pertain to the other members of this group. Does this not make evident that my account is much to demanding?

The key to understanding why my proposal is not implausibly exigent is the same key to understanding why it is not viciously circular. The key is to understand that the sense of togetherness invoked here is not identical with the *emotional feeling* in virtue of which the individuals of our example could have participated in a moment of affective intentional community, had, not only their relation to each other, but furthermore—and fundamentally—, their self-understanding been a different one at the relevant moment.

Indeed, the usefulness of the example just considered lies precisely in the fact that the *eminently affective* sense of togetherness we are seeking to understand can be expected to be elusive to the individuals in the example. Moreover, this elusiveness of the emotional experiences I call (joint) acts of feeling-towards together supports the claim that what is at issue is the for-the-sake-of-which of the participants' affective responses. For the problem, it may be argued, is precisely that at least the party who has violated the joint commitment at issue does no longer feel motivated to pursue certain things that seem to promote the 'wellbeing' and 'flourishing' of this group. She is no longer able to, together with her ex-partner, do (or avoid doing) certain things *for the sake of a particular group they take themselves to constitute.* Correspondingly, there is no framework in which she could emotionally respond to some occurrence as part of *their* (joint) affective assent to the import something has to *them* as a group.[20]

Seeking to connect this last insight to a number of reflections developed in the previous sections (particularly in Sect. 7.4), I would like to suggest that we can understand those situations in which a number of individuals are no longer able to emotionally respond in a genuinely joint manner as situations in which they are no longer able to *exist as some concrete group* they used to constitute. The point can be stated in such a way as to develop the main proposal of this chapter by arguing that these are situations in which the individuals involved are no longer able to exist in terms of certain possibilities they used to (at least pre-thematically) understand as *their* (shared) possibilities.

Now, I think that the polysemic character of the expression 'a sense of togetherness' can also be made visible by considering cases that do not involve an irregular orientation by the part of one or all of the parties towards a joint commitment they have agreed upon. Moreover, by appealing to a brief study case it is possible to, in one and the same move, elucidate a further and fundamental issue: it is not primarily the robustness of a collective that allows the members of this group to jointly actualize their capacity to feel-towards together.

For the sake of clarity, in what follows I shall differentiate between a social group and a collective*.[21] So let us say, following Gilbert, that we can speak of a social group in every conceivable situation in which two or more individuals (at least tacitly) agree on a joint commitment to do something together (in a broad sense of 'doing'), thereby simultaneously and interrelatedly coming to adopt a perspective from which they understand themselves as constituting a sort of supraindividual unity devoted to accomplishing this joint act 'as a body'. And let us reserve the word 'collective*' for social groups of a particular sort, namely for social groups that are not the result of a mere spontaneous impulse to, in a given occasion, undertake something with someone else. That is, let us reserve the technical term

---

[20] Note that he could not do so, either, even if he were willing to do or avoid certain things in order to promote the 'wellbeing' and 'flourishing' of the group they used to constitute.

[21] Most theorists involved in the debate on collective intentionality use the terms 'social group' and 'collective' interchangeably. I, too, take these two terms to be generally interchangeable. This is the reason for here introducing a technical notion. (The asterisk is intended to mark the technical character of this term.) This is a notion I will not really exploit after having made the point I am seeking to make here.

'collective*' for social groups that, due, among other things, to some constancy over time in the interrelated adoption of the perspective of a member of this group by the part of the involved individuals, have developed a higher degree of cohesiveness and cannot be easily broken down into pieces. So the difference between a social group that can be seen as a collective* and a social group that cannot may be expressed in terms of the robustness of the group at issue. As already mentioned, my goal in examining the case that follows is to support the claim that what ultimately matters is not this robustness, but the (in)capacity of the individuals involved to, at the relevant moment, exist in terms of some possibility or possibilities they can understand as *theirs*.

Suppose that you are attending a 1-week long conference in a town you have never been before. In the frame of the social events that accompany this conference you come to meet some colleagues you did not know before. During one of the informal and rather short communicative exchanges that take place in the first evening at a restaurant you tell your interlocutor that you are planning to go back to the hotel soon. You explain to her that the reason is because you normally begin your day by going for a walk early in the morning. With a bright smile on her face, the other person tells you that she also usually does so, and asks you whether you would mind if you were to go for a walk together the next morning. She adduces, ashamed by what she takes to be an act of excessive 'naturalness and spontaneity', that she cannot orient herself well geographically and does not know the town yet. You answer that you would be more than happy to do so, and seeking to cover her shame, avow that you would be glad if you managed to go for a walk together, not only because you, too, orient yourself rather badly. As we have seen, such an exchange may be sufficient for you and your conversational partner to make clear that you are willing to, in a simultaneous and interrelated manner, adopt the perspective of a member of a group you have jointly constituted this very moment.

The next day you meet, as agreed, early in the morning in front of the hotel and, for about an hour, go for a walk together. As we have seen, many of the experiences you and your walking partner have during such an episode may be taken to be structured by a sense of togetherness that involves both of you (and only you both). What in this context warrants talk of a sense of togetherness, we have also seen, is the fact that, in virtue of your having adopted in an interrelated manner the perspective of a member of this group, in the course of your conversation the evening before, you have come to see yourself (and the other person, too) as having certain obligations and some corresponding rights you did not have before.

Now, let us suppose that you both think of this episode as something circumstantial, and do simply not think about the possibility of making out of this incidental juncture something else. Although you do not care about the possibility of continuing this group beyond the temporal frame of this concrete episode, at least during the time span that begins with the conversation at the restaurant the evening before and ends with your shaking your hands in front of the hotel after having walked together for an hour, you understand some of your deeds in terms of the mentioned obligations and rights.

For example, both of you feel an obligation to show up at the agreed upon time and place. Moreover, once you have agreed on time and place, you would probably show up, even if you both were (independently) to prefer to begin the walk at a different moment. As Gilbert points out, during the walk you would probably not consider the possibility of simply drawing ahead, even if you were to think that your walking partner is walking much too slowly.

Of course, some of the attitudes I am pointing to here may be explained in terms of respect for the other person. But if we concede that some of the obligations and corresponding rights that have arisen in the course of the mentioned communicative exchange are best conceived of as the direct result of your having jointly agreed on a commitment to do something together, we could think of this joint commitment as something that has endowed you (both of you) with a motivation to do certain things you would probably not do, were you to engage in the activity at issue on your own.

Moreover, in order to explain to a good friend of yours why you have begun your routine this morning at 7:00 a.m., although you normally start your matinal walk at 6:00 a.m., you would probably not need to invoke some additional motives you and/ or your partner have *individually* had to do so. Particularly, you would probably not need to invoke motives that, so to say, go beyond your joint commitment to meet at 7:00 a.m. in order to go for a walk together. In other words, in appealing to the motivation that has arisen from this joint commitment, you would be able to satisfactorily explain many of the actions you have performed during this episode to someone that has *not* been involved in the episode at issue. This shows that not only you as involved individuals, but also a competent external observer could be immediately inclined to understand the perspective from which you both (jointly) relate to some worldly occurrences during the episode at issue as a perspective that is structured by a sense of togetherness to which a number of relevant motivations can be traced back.

But let us suppose that, understanding this joint activity as something incidental, neither you nor your walking partner feel an obligation to make it the case that you continue to go for a walk together every morning until the end of the week. Observe that this is something an external observer would also normally find understandable. We seem to understand without much explanation, first, that the sense of togetherness that is structural to the perspective from which a joint action is carried out can be more or less robust, and second, that, depending on the robustness of this sense of togetherness, in a given situation, some acts can be more or less warranted. Let me elaborate further on this point by modifying our example in a number of ways.

Our original scenario is as follows: although you have had an interesting conversation and have enjoyed the walk together, you both feel inclined to during the rest of the week just continue the routine you are accustomed to, and go for a walk on your own (you at 6:00 a.m. and your walking partner at 8:00 a.m.). The next day, without a new joint agreement you would probably not wait for her until 7:00 a.m. in front of the hotel. Nor would she wake up an hour earlier in order to meet you at this time and place. Moreover, neither you nor she would be justified in getting angry with the other party because she or he has not shown up at 7:00 a.m., and even if you had the vague impression that your partner could be inclined to be there at

7:00 a.m., you may feel comfortable with your decision to go for a walk alone an hour earlier.

But let us suppose that, in order to avoid possible misunderstandings, after your walk together you say: 'Well, as I told you, tomorrow I will go for a walk an hour earlier, since this is what I usually do. So it seems that I am condemned to repeat alone the beautiful route we have walked together today'. In answering that the next morning she was indeed planning to go for a walk at 8:00 a.m., your walking partner would be either making explicit that she agrees on jointly dissolving at this point the commitment you made the evening before or confirming that it was clear for both of you that the commitment was from the very beginning temporally limited, i.e. that, in a sense, at the very moment in which you made this joint commitment you jointly agreed on dissolving it once the goal at issue had been achieved.

Imagine now that before pronouncing these words you become unsure as to the adequacy of assuming that the temporally self-limiting character of your joint commitment is common knowledge between your walking partner and you. For a minute you hesitate to, in such a direct way, make explicit your *individual* intention to go for a walk the next morning an hour earlier. But you go on because you feel that, even if she had not understood the temporal limits of your joint commitment, your walking partner would understand your intention to proceed in such a way as to make it improbable that you jointly adopt again the perspective of a member of this group. But what exactly is it that you are expecting her to be able to understand?

You probably think that she would find it acceptable that you do not feel committed to making it the case that you both go again for a walk together the next morning. She would be able to understand that your joint commitment—provided there is, in virtue of a misunderstanding, some sense 'in the air' that you are still jointly committed to doing something—is not strong enough to prevent you from disregarding it. She would understand that the sense of togetherness that has structured many of the experiences you both have had during the last hour is, in a way, not robust enough.

In order to bring to the picture a more robust sense of togetherness—the sense of togetherness one could think of as grounding our being motivated to *maintain* the perspective of a member of a concrete group—, let us finally suppose that your intention to go for a walk the next morning at 6:00 a.m. is definitively not a matter of your preferring to go for a walk on your own. It is only that you are usually anxious about the possibility of not being able to, in the course of the day, complete all the tasks on your 'to-do list'. Having mentioned your intention to go for a walk the next day an hour earlier, with surprise, you hear the other party say: 'No, you're not condemned to a solitary walk. We can repeat our route together at 6:00 a.m.'. Realizing that she is also interested in extending the joint commitment beyond this episode—or confirming your suspicion that she has always understood this commitment as a commitment that goes beyond the activity of this morning—, and being aware that she is making an extraordinary effort to make it the case that you *continue* to jointly adopt the perspective of a member of this group, you say: 'Starting half an hour earlier should suffice. It would be great to repeat our matinal walk tomorrow at 6:30 a.m.'.

Victim of an abrupt attack of neurotic anxiety, for a moment you regret your 'excessive flexibility', and become inclined to let her know that you would definitively prefer to start at 6:00 a.m., and that you would understand if she were no longer feeling like waking up an hour earlier. But you have begun to feel not only motivated, but probably also obliged to make an effort to make it the case that you jointly maintain the perspectives of members of this group beyond the walk on this day. At any rate, at this point you feel uneasy with the idea of having to break your joint commitment. So you decide to rather try to bring your anxiety under control, and you manage to do it.

The third evening you do not feel that you need to double check that the joint commitment is not restricted to the two previous walking episodes. You only feel obliged to ask about the appointment's time. So, beating yourself, you just ask: '6:30 a.m. again or shall we begin at 7:00 a.m.?' Since 6:30 a.m. has become customary, the fifth evening you just cease to ask. The next morning you begin to get impatient because at 6:35 a.m. she is not in front of the hotel. But you feel that you have to wait for her. One minute later she arrives and apologizes for the delay—her apologies are very telling.

Now, one could think that, in elaborating in this way on Gilbert's example, I am only stretching the temporal limits of the relevant joint commitment. After all, both your walking partner and you are perfectly aware that after this week you will no longer constitute this concrete plural subject. To put it bluntly, there is no fundamental difference between being jointly committed to doing something for an hour and being jointly committed to doing it for a week.

I am not sure that this is true, but the difference is definitively not an obvious one. So let me complicate the situation in order to explore a thought that could bring us to see whether or not there is a fundamental difference between the situations we are comparing here; whether there is a fundamental difference between *circumstantially adopting* and *seeking to maintain* the perspective of a member of a given group.

The thought to be explored runs as follows. We can agree that, in the course of our repeated encounters with certain other individuals (or with a particular person), we may come to feel motivated to, as we may put it, *ideally perpetuate the possibility of jointly adopting the perspective of a member of a group we (the involved individuals) together constitute*. A typical example would be the motivation to start a family; a motivation that may gradually arise after having been together with another person for some time. We can answer the question as to whether there is a difference between circumstantially adopting and seeking to maintain the perspective of a member of a given group by trying to determine what changes when we come to feel motivated to perpetuate the possibility of interrelatedly adopting the perspective of a member of our group.

Let us imagine that in the course of the conversation you have during your first walk together your walking partner and you discover that you will, coincidentally, be moving to the same town soon. And let us suppose that some time after having (independently) established yourself in this town, you come to develop, on the basis of your earlier walks, the routine of going for a walk together every morning. In order to stress the motivational aspect, let us specify that you come to do so, despite the fact that you do not live in the immediate neighborhood of each other. So this, again, involves a number of personal efforts.

But we should be careful to construe our example in such a way as to avoid stipulating at the very beginning what we expect to find at the end of the analysis. So let us suppose that you are persuaded that the *ultimate* reason you have for maintaining this effortful routine is your *personal* health and wellbeing. Your reflection runs as follows: 'Thanks to this joint commitment, on those days on which I do not really feel like going for a walk, I manage to overcome my laziness, and feel better afterwards'.

Observe that, even if you were convinced, as just specified, that you care about the continuity of this group for purely instrumental and egoistic reasons, you would feel obliged to do certain things you would not do, had the (tacit) agreement to go for a walk together every morning not taken place. Moreover, you would be motivated (and perhaps even feel obliged) to do a number of things aimed precisely at making it the case that this possibility of jointly adopting the perspective of a member of this group *remains open in the future*. What is more, you could be interested in reaching the point at which the possibility of interrelatedly adopting the perspective of a member of this group becomes 'self-sustaining', as it were; the idea being that you could be interested in achieving the point at which this perspective, to put it metaphorically, would be able to 'possess you' in those moments in which you were inclined to skip your matinal routine.

But here we should ask: are the peculiarities of this situation grounded in a sort of conviction (or illusion) that the relevant group will never come to an end? I think they are not. In fact, the specification 'ideally' in the expression 'being motivated to ideally perpetuate the possibility of jointly adopting the perspective of a member of a given group' is intended to warrant talk of a motivation to perpetuate this possibility even in those situations in which it is foreseeable that the continuation of the plural subject at issue will *actually* become impossible at some point in the future.

Imagine that you are waiting for an answer concerning a position you have applied for. You are rather confident that you will get the position. Were the answer to indeed be positive, you would have to move again to another town. Being completely aware that this walking-collective*, as we may call it, may eventually (and probably) come to an end because of the sheer practical impossibility of maintaining it, you could still be motivated to make it the case that your partner and you interrelatedly maintain this shared perspective *as long as actually possible.*[22]

I think that we already are in a position to point to some differences between circumstantially adopting and seeking to maintain the perspective of a member of a given group. Particularly, I think that the joint commitment at issue in the case in which we are seeking to maintain the perspective of a member of a group may be taken to differ from the joint commitment that is at the heart of an agreement to go

---

[22] Observe that this would allow us to, given certain conditions, talk of a jogging-collective* even in the case that you and your partner were to jointly commit yourselves to going for a walk together every morning only until the end of the conference week.

for a walk together on a unique occasion. For, as I have tried to show, in the former case we could speak of additional non-individual motivations which may be thought to be constitutive of the joint commitment that has made out of this group of individuals a collective*. Here, I am alluding to the motivations associated with your feeling required to make it the case that both of you can continue to interrelatedly adopt the perspective of a member of this group you jointly constitute as long as actually possible.

Moreover, having for some time regularly met one another in order to share the matinal walk, your experience of the relevant encounters may have changed over time. Specifically, it would be plausible to assume significant differences between what we may call the sense of belongingness to this walking-collective* and the sense of togetherness that has structured your experiences during your very first walk together. Note that this is not merely a claim about a peculiar quality of the experiences your partner and you are now able to have when you go for a walk together. For the robustness of this felt togetherness is something that may become visible for a non-participating (though sufficiently well-informed) observer in those situations in which some conflict were to arise between the purely individual intentions or motives you and/or your partner have and *your* shared intentions.[23] The point is that during the initial phases of the process in virtue of which you have come to constitute this walking-collective* you could have been much more disposed to, in case of conflict, break your joint commitment than you are now.

Now, it might seem that I am trying to lead the discussion to the conclusion that the strength of the joint commitment in virtue of which a number of individuals constitute a collective* is a matter of their having come to develop some background structures of experience of the sort I call feelings of being-together. But I am not. I do not believe that we can decide on purely a priori grounds that our motivation to make it the case that we (the individuals involved) can continue to jointly adopt the perspective of a member of a group we constitute is *always* the result of our being affectively prepared to understand the situations in which we encounter certain other persons as situations in which we (the individuals involved) are pursuing something for the sake of our group.

Indeed, I think that we can agree, not only for the sake of argument, that there definitively are circumstances in which our motivation to make it the case that we can continue to jointly adopt the perspective of a member of our group is *not* a matter of our being affectively prepared to understand the situations in which we find ourselves as situations in which we (the individuals involved) can jointly care about something as members of a group we constitute. That is, I believe that we can take for granted that there are circumstances in which the experiential structures I call feelings of being-together are not a constitutive part (or a facilitating condition) of our being motivated to make it the case that we can continue to adopt the perspective of a member of our group.[24] Let us focus in what follows on those situations in

---

[23] This is something I have tried to show using the example of Dania (in Sect. 6.3).

[24] Note that, in making this suggestion, I am differentiating the sense of togetherness qua sense of being a member of a particular group (with certain kinds of rights and obligations) that we have

which we have to *make some effort* to understand our situation as a situation in which, in *individually* caring about something—e.g. in caring about waking up at time in order to carry out a matinal routine aimed at remaining 'fit'—, we are taking measures aimed at leaving open the possibility that we continue to jointly adopt the perspective of a member of our group.

To illustrate the point with a different example, let us imagine a number of individuals who are employed by a company that does not offer the conditions (whatever these conditions are) that bring them to develop a feeling that they belong together. Let us suppose that the involved individuals are all aware that the only reason each of them has for not being completely indifferent about the future of the company is because they are economically dependent on the persistence of this company (say, because this is the only source of money in this region). Put another way, let us suppose that it is common knowledge between the individuals involved that (ultimately seeking to survive) they all are constantly making an effort to see and present themselves as members of one and the same group.

Observe that, in such a case, the sustainability of the possibility of jointly adopting the perspective of a member of the company they work for may straightforwardly be said to be an issue for the individuals involved: the sustainability of this possibility could be seen as the most proximal telos of their efforts. So it can be argued that, in the course of their *selfishly motivated* deeds, these individuals often come to care about a number of things *for the sake of the company they all work for*. This is interesting, since I have sought to provide an example in which purely egoistic reasons and no affective structure of the sort I call feelings of being-together motivate the attempt to maintain the perspective of a member of a concrete group.

So it seems that we can affirm that *in any conceivable situation* in which a number of individuals are *interrelatedly seeking to maintain* the perspective of a member of a concrete group—in the sense of maintaining it *as long as actually possible*—, these individuals may be said to be doing something for the sake of *their* group. At

---

been discussing in this chapter from the structures of experience I call feelings of being-together discussed in Chap. 6. As specified above (in Sect. 6.4), the latter amount to a felt liability to experience certain emotions as feelings that are part of some joint feeling apt to manifest *our* joint caring. But the relationship between these two notions may be objected to remain obscure, since both the sense of togetherness discussed in this chapter and the feelings of being-together discussed in Chap. 6 may be understood as background structures of experience that allow the involved individuals to participate in what I call moments of affective intentional community. The key to understanding the extent to which these notions are not overlapping (but complementary) ones is to understand that the sense of togetherness discussed here, understood as a sense that experientially actualizes the participant's belief in the community they constitute, is experienced *as the discussed sense that there are some obligations and rights*—a sense that structures the relevant acts as a part of *their* doing something together (in a permissive sense of 'doing'). Put another way, the sense of togetherness discussed here does not consist of some *additional* feeling to the effect that we (the participants) are doing something together. On the contrary, the background structures of experience I call feelings of being-together are conceived as 'sedimented' *affects* that, so to say, experientially testify a common history of emotional meetings and dispose us (the participants) to have emotions that are experienced as *our* joint emotional responses to some occurrence: as we-emotions (or acts of feeling-towards together, as I call the emotions by virtue of which a number of individuals participate in a moment of affective intentional community).

least during these episodes, these individuals may be taken to be oriented towards a number of worldly occurrences in the mode of caring-about I have called caring-with—or so it seems. Let me exploit this insight concerning a close connection between the idea of being motivated to interrelatedly maintain the perspective of a member of a group and my notion of caring-with by considering a further objection.

It may be protested that the distinction between adopting the perspective of a member of a group and maintaining such a perspective, although probably intuitively sound, is tricky. For even in those cases in which a number of individuals come to adopt the perspective of a member of a given group *for an isolated occasion*, these individuals can be taken to jointly maintain this perspective *as long as the relevant episode perdures*. Being aware that your joint commitment to go for a walk together is restricted to the next sixty minutes, for instance, if something were to go wrong at the beginning of your walk, you would probably do something in order to enable *continuing* walking together. That is, even being clear about the fact that your group will not survive the next hour—and not being particularly interested in helping it survive—, your partner and you could be said to be doing a number of things for the sake of this group.

I think that there is an intuition behind this objection that is absolutely correct. Let me make the point as follows. As soon as two or more individuals came to understand some occurrence as an occurrence that affects some possibility they can jointly actualize, they would be able to experience their emotional responses to this occurrence as feelings that immediately connect them to one another. This possibility is *completely independent* of whether or not there are some prospects of continuing with this group beyond the actualization of the possibility at issue. In other words, such an occurrence would definitively be able to bring these individuals to emotionally respond in a joint manner, even in case they were not interested in maintaining the perspective of a member of this group beyond the temporal limits of this concrete episode. But it is crucial to note that not any occurrence that were to take place during the relevant episode would bring them to emotionally respond in a genuinely joint manner. In order to clarify this crucial point, let me elaborate further on the example of the walking group.

Suppose that both of you are perfectly aware that your joint commitment to go for a walk together is temporally limited: an hour later, you know, you will no longer constitute this plural subject. And let us assume that none of you has considered the possibility of making out of this concrete group another sort of group. The next morning each of you goes for a walk alone. Incidentally, you meet at a given place and greet each other. Precisely at this moment it begins to rain tempestuously. Both of you respond emotionally and in an extremely similar way to this unexpected event. More precisely, your reaction is such that any observer would assert that both of you are profoundly upset because of the rain. Now, suppose that both of you realize that you have responded in a very similar manner. The question is: could we assume that in the face of this occurrence your ex-partner and you have come to feel emotionally connected to one another in the immediate way that is at issue?

Assuming that both of you are aware that each of you is concerned about the possibility of having to cancel her or his *respective* walk, we may argue that, at any rate, you would *not* feel affectively connected to one another *in the very same way* you would have done it, had the rain bothered you the day before by interrupting *your* joint walk. Perhaps you have a feeling that your similar responses to one and the very same occurrence, in a way, bring you 'closer to one another'. This is not improbable at all. But in this case you would not feel emotionally connected to one another in the *immediate way* we are concerned with, but as a result of a second-order feeling. In other words, to the extent to which you were aware that your similar emotional responses exclusively concern your *individual* possibilities (or impossibilities) we would be urged to take this connectedness to be a matter of what Adam Smith calls fellow-feeling (cf. the discussion in Sect. 4.2).

Suppose, in order to consider the opposed scenario, that your first (and last) walk together is not over yet. That is, each of you is still regarding both of you as members of this walking group, although both of you are perfectly aware of the temporal limits of the joint commitment at issue, and are, indeed, not willing to extend these limits beyond this concrete walk. Imagine that you have been walking together for few minutes when it all of a sudden begins to rain. Your respective emotional responses to this unforeseen occurrence are very different in character. Being an explosive person, you respond with anger and have to control yourself to avoid giving a rather infantile impression. The response of your partner is less clear in character, but, if one had to characterize it, one could say that she looks rather sad about the possibility of having to terminate your walk. Given that we are dealing with affective responses of different emotional kinds the best, if not the sole, way of explaining any feeling of emotional connectedness that may arise in such a situation would be by arguing that you understand your *different* emotions as intelligible expressions of your interrelatedly being concerned about a possibility *you* have as a group. To support this claim, let me elaborate once more on this example.

Imagine that a minute later the rain has stopped and you can continue your walk together. Just to emphasize the crucial point, let me repeat that none of you is interested in making out of this incidental juncture something else. Few meters ahead you find a placard informing that during the next days this park—in which, as you think, you could in the future continue to go for a walk (though on your own)—will be closed for maintenance reasons. On this occasion, you both respond emotionally in a very similar way and become aware of this similarity. Here, we can (again) affirm something along the following lines: were you to, in this situation, come to feel 'close to each other' because of the similarity of your affective responses, you would probably not feel affectively connected to one another in the very same way you did a few minutes ago, when it began to rain. Understanding that each of you is concerned about a purely individual possibility (or impossibility), you would, for instance, not be inclined to out of this emotion—an emotion you, in a way, share—make an effort to reassure the 'wellbeing' and 'flourishing' of *your* group. This, I think, is an extremely interesting finding, given that we are not only considering emotions you in a certain sense share, but also emotions you experience while doing something together.

So we can agree that the distinction between adopting and maintaining the perspective of a member of a given group is indeed problematic. Since every temporal point has some duration, every adopting can be said to be a maintaining. But, as we have just seen, the distinction could be taken to be warranted on the following grounds: there is a fundamental difference between the shared emotional experiences we can have in those cases in which we maintain the perspective of a member of a group in the modus I have called a mere adopting and at least some of the shared emotional experiences we can have while understanding ourselves as individuals who are inclined to, as long as actually possible, continue to jointly adopt the perspective of members of a given group.

But in the course of our last reflection we have come to see something that is much more important: what is fundamental for us to come to emotionally respond in a genuinely joint manner is not the prospect of the possibility of continuing to jointly adopt the perspective of a member of the group at issue. Rather, in order to be able to jointly feel-towards together we (the participants) have to be able to understand the possibilities affected by the occurrence at issue as possibilities that can be *actualized by us as a group*. To this extent we can affirm that the robustness of a group does not play the decisive role. It is only because, in seeking to make it the case that the possibility of jointly adopting the perspective of a member of our group remains open, we bring a number of abilities-to-be to become possibilities we can actualize *together* that this possibility of continuing to jointly adopt the perspective of a member of our group has stricken us as central to our ability to emotionally respond to some occurrences in a genuinely joint manner. Hence, at the root of a collective affective intentional episode we find the ability of a number of human individuals to *interrelatedly* project themselves, in the frame of a given circumstance, into certain possibilities they share.[25] Put in a slightly different way, our capacity to emotionally respond in a genuinely joint manner is grounded in our human capacity to, in a circumstantially specific manner, exist—in the projected mode in which Dasein exists—in terms of some of *our* (shared) possibilities (i.e. in our capacity to exist in such a way as to see some of our possibilities as possibilities that can be jointly actualized by *us*). Let me try to further specify this idea of interrelatedly projecting ourselves into some of *our* possibilities.

As pointed out in the previous chapter (Sect. 7.3), to project oneself into certain possibilities means to, at this very point, be able to (at least pre-thematically) understand oneself in terms of—to conceive of oneself 'in light of'—these possibilities. In the concrete case we are considering right now, it means to understand oneself in terms of certain possibilities *we* have. But what is implied by this idea of existing in terms of some possibilities *we* have?

Coming back to the example of the walking-collective*, one may be inclined to assert that, thanks to your participation in the collective acts of the relevant group, both of you are able to 'live out' a particular understanding of yourselves. Both of you are able to, for instance, understand yourselves as persons for whom health is

---

[25] As we have seen above (in Sect. 7.3), in many cases this can be said to be a matter of our having come to be rather passively projected (by our situating affectivity) into these possibilities.

an issue precisely because you are capable of, in the context of *your* walks, actively and regularly doing something aimed at remaining fit. In a similar vein, it may be argued that Dania and her orchestra colleagues (cf. the discussion in Sect. 6.3) can understand themselves as good instrumentalists (each of them on her or his respective instrument) in the context of *their* being capable of jointly performing demanding symphonic works.

But this is not exactly the idea we are after. Projecting ourselves into some of *our* possibilities means understanding ourselves in terms of certain possibilities *we* have, and not merely understanding *oneself* in terms of certain possibilities *one* has in virtue of *one's* being a member of the group at issue. So what is actually implied by the idea that we can project ourselves into the actualization of some of *our* possibilities?

The crucial point can be articulated as follows: a number of individuals can, in a concrete situation, be said to jointly be on the pursuit of an actualization of a certain possibility they *together* have just in case they are, in the relevant situation, able to understand themselves as individuals who, by means of their acts, are jointly reassuring the 'wellbeing' and 'flourishing' of this concrete group they constitute. It is important to note that the claim is not that, in order to really exist in terms of *their* (shared) possibilities, the individuals at issue have to, in the relevant situation, suspend their personal possibilities. On the contrary, it is in jointly pressing ahead into the actualization of certain possibilities they *as a group* have (for instance, into the actualization of the possibility of making out of the orchestra they constitute an eminent orchestra) that the participants are living in terms of some personal abilities-to-be they have (for instance, in terms of the ability to be or become a prominent symphonic oboist).

In the last section of this chapter I shall address this complicated issue which pertains to what seems to be an incompatibility between my suggestion that the individuals involved in a case of collective affective intentionality are *ultimately* caring about something for the sake of a group they constitute and Heidegger's claim that, for Dasein, what is an issue is always *its own* being (i.e. an existence that essentially has an in-each-case-mine character). I shall tackle this issue by arguing for the idea that there are possibilities in terms of which we can exist and which are at the same time personal through and through as well as collective through and through.

8.4   Personally Caring About Something in a Genuinely Joint Manner

There are situations in which, by jointly pursuing a goal, a number of individuals come to express some central aspect of their psychological identity. Take, as an example, the case of a group of young men who, by trying to win a series of football games together, come to jointly express their self-understanding as professional sportsmen. Another example is the case of a pair of individuals who, in contributing to their shared aspiration to raise a healthy and joyful child, come in diverse situations to jointly exist in terms of their capability to be good co-heads of a family or of their capability to be sensitive parents.

In these situations, the participants, in the course of their joint acts, are co-actualizing some crucial ability-to-be and some possibility of a particular group they take themselves to jointly constitute. Put another way, the situations at issue are such that we can understand the deeds of the participants both as acts in virtue of which they are actualizing some capability that, as they take it, at least partially characterizes them as the sorts of persons they are and as acts they are performing as part of a genuinely collaborative effort.

In trying to better understand what is special about these sorts of situations we could come to characterize in more detail the essential feature of those moments in which a collective affective intentional episode can take place. The reason is not because a genuinely collective intentional episode requires of the participants that they pursue some goal that *centrally* defines their psychological identity. To suggest such a condition would be utterly implausible. Rather, the reason is as follows: what best explicates the *genuinely affective* nature of some of the collective responses that can originate in the situations just described is a peculiarity of the motivational force that guides the participant's acts. This peculiarity may be captured as follows: given that in the pertinent situation the participants are collaboratively pressing ahead towards the actualization of some existential possibility, being able to jointly co-actualize the relevant shared possibility—being able to, at this moment, jointly exist as this particular group—is an issue for them. In other words, the reason why the situations we are concerned with allow for moments of genuinely affective intentional community is because the acts of concernful-circumspection that frame them can be said to characteristically be *at the same time collective through and through as well as personal through and through.*

I believe that there is nothing mysterious in the claim that there are acts that can be argued to be at the same time genuinely collective and authentically personal, but the terms in which some of the discussions that constitute the debate on collective intentionality have been articulated make it difficult to be on familiar terms with a suggestion I take to be rather unproblematic: some of our goals can straightforwardly be said to be goals one *personally* pursues *in a properly joint manner.* This opens the door to a particular objection we shall consider below.

Margaret Gilbert, for instance, who, as we have seen (in Sects. 3.2, 3.3, and 8.2), defends an, in varied respects, demanding view of collective intentionality, evidently takes the adjective 'personal' to be serviceable for the purposes of contrasting the idea of something being collective or shared. In a paper, in which she seeks to challenge Michael Bratman's proposal that what a shared intention amounts to is 'a complex of [...] "interlocking" personal intentions' (Gilbert 2009, p. 171), Gilbert writes: 'One may believe [...] that singularist intentions are not always *personal intentions*, that is, intentions expressible by sentences of the form "I intend..."' (p. 169). Her point seems to be that 'singularist intentions'—and I take her to be referring here to the intentions particular human individuals are the ontic subjects of[26]—can also be collective *in form*, as opposed to being, in her terminology, personal.[27]

In addressing the pertinent distinction in these terms, Gilbert is not alone. At least Bratman, against whose account—not only in the context of the paper mentioned—Gilbert sets her arguments, seems to understand a shared intention as something that is *categorically* opposed to a personal intention (although, in his view, a shared intention is composed of what he calls personal intentions). Moreover, the contrast 'personal vs. collective' can certainly be taken to be part of our everyday discourse.

I believe, however, that the use of the adjective 'personal' in order to label that which stands out against what can be said to be collective can, at least in the context of our existentialistically framed discussion, be profoundly misleading. So, having used the *nouns* 'individual' and 'person' as synonyms, I would like to make a diagnostic claim. As just mentioned, there is a common assumption that obscures the general debate on collective intentionality, namely the assumption that an act can be *either* personal *or* collective, but not collective *and* personal. This, at least in certain contexts, definitively untenable assumption rests on the possibility we have to, in a number of situations, interchangeably employ the *adjectives* 'personal' and 'individual'.[28]

The key to understanding the relevance this general diagnostic claim has for our discussion is to understand that I am not merely trying to draw attention to the fact that there are situations in which, in endorsing some of the intentions of a group they constitute, a number of persons come to express what they are, at this moment, seeking to (continue to) be. The claim that there are situations in which a number of individuals can be said to be in personal pursuit of something in a genuinely joint manner involves a further idea. The point could be stated as follows: the situations we are interested in are such that the cooperative efforts of the participants cannot be said to be purely instrumental.

---

[26] Gilbert writes: 'I shall refer to the intention of a single human being as a *singularist intention*' (p. 169).

[27] Gilbert writes: 'a *personal intention* is understood here as an intention of a human being that is expressible by him in a sentence of the form "I intend..."' (p. 171). It is important to recall that Gilbert's account is not exhausted by the idea of some intentions being collective *in form*. In other words, and as we have seen (in Sects. 3.2, 3.3, and 8.2), Gilbert's approach is not a 'we-intentions approach', but a 'joint commitments approach'. (For a brief comparison of these two positions, see Gilbert 2010.) At the beginning of the paper I am quoting from, Gilbert characterizes the view she is seeking to oppose as follows: 'a popular option is what I shall call the *personal intentions perspective*, according to which the singularist-intentions in question are personal intentions' (2009, p. 171). The central assumption of this view, which Gilbert takes to 'probably [be] the most prevalent perspective among theorists' (ibid.), can be captured in a statement that does not employ the adjective 'personal': all the intentions of the ontic subjects involved in a case of collective intentionality are intentions that have a singular (or individual) phenomenal subject.

[28] I am not merely suggesting that, as many philosophers have observed (among them Gilbert and Bratman), some of our, in their terminology, 'personal' intentions could be thought to be embedded in (or derived from) a shared intention.

To address the issue in terms of the distinction between acts one instrumentally performs and acts one carries out for their own sake can be extremely elucidating here. For some of the worries I have not been able to calm as yet are presumably related to the following belief. An outlook on collective affective intentionality that takes seriously the idea that our emotional attitudes make visible what sort of projects we really care about, thereby indirectly making visible what sort of persons we are really seeking to (continue to) be, should, at a minimum, stick to the idea that we humans are *always* ultimately (or primarily) pressing ahead towards the actualization of some *individual* ability-to-be. This, it may be put forward, is precisely what Heidegger is anxious to emphasize when he, as we have seen, at the very beginning of his 'analytic of Dasein' makes thematic the in-each-case-mine character [*Jemeinigkeit*] of our personal existence (cf. the discussion in Sect. 7.2). Concretely, if we are to respect Heidegger's claim that it is our *own* existence that, in the end, is an issue for us, we have to conceive of any pressing ahead into the actualization of some possibility of a group we constitute as something that *necessarily* has a derivative nature. To formulate the problem in a slightly different way, it seems that if we are to stick to the suggestion that what ultimately grounds the import things have to us is our seeking to (continue to) personally exist in certain forms (and not in others), the only way open to us, while trying to make sense of the idea that an act can be at the same time personal and collective, consists in conceiving of our attempts to actualize some possibility we *as a group* have as acts that exhibit an instrumental character. It is *only* because we are—rather egoistically—seeking to (continue to) exist in this or that way that we are disposed to collaboratively actualize certain possibilities of the groups we constitute.

I would like to begin to rejoin to this objection by making the following suggestion: the situations we are interested in allow the participants to respond in an, at the same time, authentically affective and genuinely joint manner only because there is some possibility affected by the occurrence at issue that can be immediately understood by them as an existential possibility of *theirs*. The point is that, being an existential possibility—being an ability-to-be—, the possibility at issue is necessarily understood by the participants as a possibility that is primary, as opposed to being derived from some further possibility.[29] In other words, at the relevant moment the participants have a sense to the effect that they *are* this group; they have a sense to the effect that, in this situation, they *are* the shared possibility at issue. This is what ultimately permits them to emotionally respond to certain occurrences in a genuinely joint manner.

---

[29] The idea is that an occurrence that is apt to elicit a genuine emotion can be said to really be an issue for the person in question. If some worldly occurrence can be said to really be an issue for a given individual, it can be said to be so because her being a particular sort of person is an issue for her. Something can be said to *really* be an issue for someone in case it does not merely amount to a recognizable problem—to an unsettled or open question that is waiting for an answer, as it were—, but appears to the relevant person as something she *has to deal with*. That is to say, something that really is an issue for a given person cannot be easily ignored by her, for its 'being in her view' is accompanied by an imperative sense that she *has to do something with it*. This imperative sense that a certain sort of response is merited is what we call an emotion.

Now, this proposal basically aims at resisting the assumption that, being creatures for whom our personal existence is an issue, even in those situations in which we are collaboratively pursuing something, we are, in the end, necessarily caring about something that matters to us *individually*.[30] But this reflection should be seen, furthermore, as the key to understanding the suggestion that the individuals involved in a collective affective intentional episode are always caring about something *ultimately* on behalf of a particular group they jointly constitute. Indeed, in the context of the ideas we have been considering in this chapter, this suggestion can be reformulated along the following lines: a person for whom being the group at issue is not really a capability she at the relevant moment possesses can simply not come to understand her emotional feelings as feelings that connect her to the other participants *in the direct manner captured by Scheler's notion of an immediate feeling-together*. Taking her feelings to be, in some respect, similar to the feelings of these other individuals she may come to experience fellow-feelings. But she cannot come to jointly actualize with them her ability to feel-towards together. Let me illustrate the point.

Suppose that Gareth, a football player who is sufficiently indifferent to the 'wellbeing' and 'flourishing' of his team and who is basically seeking to, by way of his collaborative performances, increase the probability of becoming appointed by a better team, manages to score a goal that at the same time brings his team to advance to the next stage of the tournament and permits him to become the leading scorer of this tournament. He joyfully celebrates this goal, as the other members of the team also do. But being sufficiently indifferent to the 'wellbeing' and 'flourishing' of his team, Gareth is actually celebrating an event that, as he understands it, allows him to stand out from this group. Although his joy, in diverse respects, *coincides* with the joy of a number of other individuals involved in different ways in the relevant situation (not only with the joy of the other members of the team, but also with the one of the team's fans, for instance), there is a clear sense in which we could affirm that, in celebrating the scored goal, Gareth is not celebrating together with the relevant others. He is clearly doing so alongside these others.[31]

This finding is very interesting. For there seems to also be a clear sense in which it can be argued that, in scoring the goal at issue, Gareth has contributed to the 'wellbeing' and 'flourishing' of his team. In other words, it seems that we are confronted

---

[30] The intuition that is operative here concerns the idea that we—beings for whom our *own* being is an issue—seem to, in the end, always care about something that matters to us *personally*.

[31] For an observer who were not aware of the fact that Gareth is particularly interested in standing out from this team it would be difficult to recognize *in the face of this single episode* that Gareth is celebrating alongside those other individuals whose joyful response has been elicited by the event at issue. But by taking into account other episodes in which certain occurrences may be rationally expected to call for certain affective responses this observer could eventually come to recognize that, while celebrating his successful shot, Gareth was not celebrating *with* the relevant others. Were another player of his team, for instance, to score a goal just a few minutes after he has scored, Gareth could 'fail' to celebrate this joyful event. And were such a 'failure' to exhibit a repetitive character, the constancy of the 'failure' could come to undermine the initial impression that he was celebrating *with* the rest of the 'group of celebrants'.

with a result that is at odds with my theory: even if someone is, first, sharing *in* the relevant moment of multipersonal affectivity, and second, doing so by responding emotionally to an occurrence that affects the 'wellbeing' and 'flourishing' of the group that seems to be at stake, this person is not necessarily jointly actualizing with the pertinent others her or his capacity to feel-towards together. Does this finding not make evident that the requirements for what I call affective intentional community are much too high?

The key to understanding why my proposal is not an implausibly demanding one is to understand that Gareth could only functionally and only from an impersonal perspective be said to be contributing to the goal of the team to advance to the next stage of the tournament. The point is that to the extent to which *he is not able to understand himself* as someone who is contributing to the 'wellbeing' and 'flourishing' of the relevant group, we cannot really assert that, in this situation, Gareth is living out his capacity to (together with the relevant others) *be this group and exist in terms of their shared possibility to advance to the next stage*. Put another way, one could certainly affirm that Gareth's success while shooting to the opponent's goal has brought a group of individuals to which he could be taken to (at least formally) belong closer to an ambition they have as a collective (the ambition of winning this cup). Furthermore, one could assert that Gareth has achieved his individual purpose (the purpose of becoming the top goalscorer of this tournament) only thanks to the collaboration of other players of this team (and of the fans who at no point have ceased to cheer them). But being in the relevant situation exclusively concerned with his individual possibility to become the top goal-scorer of the tournament, so as to increase his chance to get hired by another team, Gareth is not really existing at the relevant moment in light of some possibility they (the members of the relevant community) jointly have.[32] And the point is that as soon as one becomes clear about this fact, one begins to feel disinclined to assert that Gareth is participating with the pertinent others in a moment of emotional community.

Note that our understanding of the situation would not change dramatically, were we to agree that we can take Gareth to, *at least instrumentally*, be in pursuit at the pertinent moment of the actualization of some possibility of the team at issue. Appealing to a distinction drawn by Raimo Tuomela, it is possible to restate part of the idea I am trying to articulate in completely different terms. I am referring to the distinction between I-mode and we-mode cooperation (cf. Tuomela 2003).

In I-mode cooperation, Tuomela writes, the participants are basically adjusting their *individual* goals in such a way as to benefit all participants, themselves included. In the I-mode case, hence, the central intention can be captured by means of a statement along the following lines: 'I will achieve my goal by cooperating with you' (Tuomela and Tuomela 2005, p. 82). In order to characterize this class of attitudes, Tuomela and Tuomela employ the expression '*I-mode pro-group* thinking and acting' (ibid.). This corresponds to the *instrumental* manner in which Gareth

---

[32] Indeed, despite the fact that he is in this context functionally contributing to a goal of a team to which he can be taken to belong, we could imagine Gareth to be inclined to, in a number of situations, refer to the group by using the pronoun 'them', rather than the pronoun 'us'.

could be argued to be involved in the cooperative endeavor of the example. On the contrary, the sort of cooperation Tuomela calls 'we-mode cooperation' requires of the participants that they really act as a group. But what does it mean to *really* act as a group?

In my view, we can spell out this requirement as follows: at least in the situation at issue, the involved individuals must have a justifiable sense that they are able to *jointly exist as the pertinent group*; a sense that, at this moment, they *basically are* the shared possibilities at issue. So the tacit claim that only in the context of some we-mode cooperation a number of individuals can come to jointly actualize their ability to feel-towards together could be rearticulated as follows: we simply cannot make sense of the idea that some individuals are emotionally responding to some occurrence in a properly joint manner, if we do not understand them as persons who at the relevant moment are able to interdependently *be* the shared possibilities at issue, i.e. the shared possibilities affected by the relevant occurrence. The point is that interdependently being the relevant group in the situations at issue is not something they can 'do' exclusively because this *promotes* a certain future condition; because this *brings them closer to some individual goal*. Rather, interdependently being their group is something they at least in part have to 'do' because this, in a way, is what being the kind of person they are at this moment seeking to (continue to) be *consists in*.

As already acknowledged, it would be utterly implausible to suggest that a collective affective intentional episode can only originate in situations in which each of the involved individuals is pressing ahead towards the actualization of an ability-to-be that is *absolutely central* to her or his psychological identity—whatever this turns out to mean. I do not, hence, mean to suggest that jointly actualizing our ability to feel-towards together is a matter of emotionally expressing that we (the participants) share a particularly 'deep' concern about something.[33] In sharing (in a strong sense of the verb 'to share') a relatively 'shallow' concern, a number of individuals can certainly come to jointly actualize their ability to feel-towards together. The reason is because every genuine act of caring-about—however 'shallow' the pertinent concern—makes the relevant subject prone to respond in a properly emotional way in the face of certain (and only certain) occurrences. Helm illustrates the point as follows: 'insofar as the local opera company has import to him, Albert devotes countless hours as a volunteer to ensure its success, and he does so in such a way as to "make himself vulnerable to losses and susceptible to benefits depending on whether [it] is diminished or enhanced" [Frankfurt 1988, p. 83]. [... T]his vulnerability or susceptibility is evident in the kinds of pleasures or pains— the kinds of felt evaluations—he feels in response to what happens to it. By making ourselves vulnerable to what happens to something in this way, Frankfurt says, we are in a sense identifying ourselves with it' (1988, p. 100).[34]

---

[33] For the distinction between relatively deep and relatively shallow forms of caring, see Helm (2001, pp. 100ff.).

[34] In the section from which I have taken this excerpt, Helm makes an effort to spell out the difference between mere caring and caring in the mode he calls 'valuing', i.e. the difference between

So the affected possibility has not necessarily to be such that, if it could not be actualized, the participants would lose some distinctive character of their personality, as it were. What is crucial, I have been suggesting in different ways, is that the self-referential aspect the participant's emotions *necessarily* exhibit—on pain of otherwise not being understandable as affective expressions of their concern about something—be plural in character. The point can now be made in such a way as to articulate the main claim of this chapter: the participants must be able to understand themselves as persons who, in the relevant situation, are *(jointly) existing as a particular group*, i.e. as individuals who, at the relevant moment, are *carrying out their (respective) care-defined existence in terms of some projection of a group they together constitute*.

We are now in a position to round out this discussion by claiming that there is a condition the possibilities affected by an occurrence apt to elicit a collective affective intentional episode characteristically fulfill: these possibilities can be understood not merely as abilities-to-be that can only in the course of genuinely collective acts become actualities, but furthermore—and essentially—, as possibilities in terms of which the participants are able to (at least in the relevant situation) jointly exist as a group. To the extent to which they are understandable as abilities-to-be proper, i.e. as possibilities in terms of which a number of individuals are able to, in the relevant situation, carry out their existence, these possibilities can be argued to be genuinely personal. At the same time, these possibilities are genuinely collective in the sense of being possibilities that are part of the collective self-understanding of the group these individuals jointly are, i.e. in the sense of being possibilities the participants (non-mistakenly) take themselves to be able to jointly actualize in virtue of their being able to, in the relevant situation, together exist as this group.

To sum up: if we are to make sense of the idea that we humans are able to respond to certain occurrences in a genuinely joint and, at the same time, authentically affective manner, we have to understand a human person as a being that, at least under certain conditions, can express her always being an issue for herself by caring in a non-instrumental way about something as some particular group she (together with certain others) constitutes. This, as we are now in a position to see, just is a way of saying that our capacity to feel affectively connected to certain others as an immediate result of the particular manner in which we are emotionally responding to the requirements of the world rests on the fact that some of our existential possibilities are at the same time personal and collective. That is, our capacity to emotionally respond to certain occurrences in a properly joint manner is grounded in the fact that we human individuals can (and are probably inclined to) in certain situations—and only together with certain others—be *our* (shared) possibilities. In closing this discussion, I would like to make explicit the extent to which the

---

'those things one [just] cares about and those things that have import to one at least in part because of an understanding of the kind of person one finds worth being' (p. 101). As he suggests, however, even if a person is merely caring about something, i.e. not taking the projection at issue to be 'fundamental to his sense of himself' (ibid.), this person is identifying himself with the pertinent pressing-ahead-towards.

proposal just summarized diverges from the main idea of Gilbert's account of what she calls shared guilt feelings.

As we have seen (in Sects. 3.2 and 3.3), Gilbert is not committed to the view that the individuals who constitute a social group necessarily have to share a *goal*. As she writes: 'the general, fundamental concept of a plural subject is not only embedded in our shared action concept, it can also be found, for instance, in our concept of a shared or collective belief and in the concept of a shared or collective principle' (1990, p. 9). This allows her to explore the idea of a collective affective intentional attitude by proposing an understanding of the attitude she calls a collective guilt feeling as an example of an emotional attitude that can be attributed to the relevant plural subject as such—as opposed to having to be attributed to the participating individuals. The idea is that in the same way in which a number of persons can come to constitute the plural subject of a goal, belief, or principle, a group of individuals can, in virtue of their having jointly committed themselves 'to feeling guilt as a body over [their] action A' (Gilbert 2002, p. 139), come to constitute the plural subject of a collective response of guilt.

As we have also seen (cf. the discussion in Sect. 3.3), the main problem of Gilbert's account as an account of a collective *affective* intentional response rests on her willingness to reduce our emotions to those judgments that cognitivists argue to be at the root of the relevant affective responses. In so doing, Gilbert has not merely rendered her account susceptible to a series of objections that are familiar from the debate on affective intentionality. Furthermore, she has become blind to a possibility suggested by her own theory. This is a possibility that would release her from having to invoke such a thing as a joint commitment to feel as a body an emotion of a particular sort.

Remaining faithful to Gilbert's terminology, on the basis of the discussion developed in this chapter, it can be suggested that the joint commitment that is at the heart of a collective affective intentional episode is rather a joint commitment to situatively maintain a particular shared evaluative perspective on something; a joint commitment to care as a body and maintain a joint orientedness towards the import of certain things. The point is that, on the basis of such a joint commitment, *genuine* emotions, i.e. proper acts of *felt* understanding, may come to arise in the face of certain occurrences.[35]

Appealing to a number of Heideggerian motives—of which I have made use in the course of the discussion developed in this book—, it is possible to elaborate on this last thought by articulating the idea of a joint commitment to care as a body in terms of joint actualizations of a capability we human individuals have: the capability to, in specific situations, jointly exist as some particular group, i.e. in terms of some shared possibility. The proposal I have tried to work out in this book is, hence, that the emotional feelings elicited by an occurrence able to affect an existential possibility a number of individuals are seeking to jointly actualize (as some

---

[35] In my view, exclusively in those situations in which (joint) acts of felt understanding can be argued to be involved we are allowed to talk of an episode of collective affective intentionality (or of a moment of genuinely affective intentional community).

particular group they together constitute) bring these individuals to *immediately feel* affectively connected to one another.

A central virtue of this proposal—and this remark should help me to dismantle any residual impression that there is some circularity in my account—is that it does not force us to conceive of the individuals who, at a given moment, come to jointly actualize their ability to feel-towards together as individuals who, *in advance*, understand themselves as members of some sort of *affective* community, as Gilbert's account requires us to do. Rather, the idea is that, on the basis of their (at least pre-thematically) understanding themselves as members of a particular group *for the sake of which they are able to jointly care about certain things*, the involved individuals can come to experience emotions that, in the context of certain occurrences, connect them in the instantaneous mode Scheler has pointed to in his 'anticipation' of the debate this book aims at contributing to.

Now, in this chapter I have basically sought to round out my account of collective affective intentionality by spelling out the main proposal articulated in the second part of this book: emotionally responding to some occurrence in a genuinely joint manner is a matter of emotionally expressing that we (the participants) care as a group about something. But my aim here has been a much more ambitious one. In the course of the argument developed in this chapter (and the previous one), I have elucidated the extent to which emotionally responding to something in a genuinely joint manner can be claimed to be a characteristically human ability, not only in the sense of being something we human beings are normally—under certain conditions—capable of doing, but also in the sense of being something that expresses our human nature. Moreover, I have brought the message home that, being an extremely rich and exigent expression of our care-defined nature, a collective affective intentional episode is something that, as mentioned in the remarks that opened this inquiry (in Sect. 1.1), can easily arise in the context of certain utterly quotidian situations.

References

Agamben, Giorgio. [1995] 1998. *Homo sacer: Sovereign power and bare life*. Stanford: Stanford University Press.

Anderson, Ben. 2009. Affective atmospheres. *Emotion, Space and Society* 2: 77–81.

Aristotle. 1984. Rhetoric. Trans. W. Rhys Roberts. In *The complete works of Aristotle: The revised Oxford translation*, vol. 2, ed. Jonathan Barnes. Princeton: Princeton University Press.

Baber, Chris, Paul Smith, James Cross, John Hunter, and Richard McMaster. 2006. Crime scene investigation as distributed cognition. *Pragmatics and Cognition* 14(2): 357–385.

Baier, Annette. 1997. Doing things with others: The mental commons. In *Commonality and particularity in ethics*, ed. Lilli Alanen, Sara Heinämaa, and Thomas Wallgren, 15–44. New York: St. Martin's Press.

Baird, Bryan. 2006. The transcendental nature of mind and world. *Southern Journal of Philosophy* 44(3): 381–398.

Bedford, Errol. 1956–1957. Emotions. *Proceedings of the Aristotelian Society* 57: 281–304.

Ben-Ze'ev, Aaron. 2000. *The subtlety of emotions*. Cambridge, MA: MIT Press.

Blattner, William. 1996. Existence and self-understanding in being and time. *Philosophy and Phenomenological Research* 56(1): 97–110.

Blattner, William. 1999. *Heidegger's temporal idealism*. Cambridge: Cambridge University Press.

Blattner, William. 2006. *Heidegger's being and time: A reader's guide*. London: Continuum.

Bourgois, Patrick, and Ursula Hess. 2008. The impact of social context on mimicry. *Biological Psychology* 77: 343–352.

Brandom, Robert. 1997. Dasein, the being that thematizes. *Epoché* 5(1/2): 1–38.

Bratman, Michael. 1993. Shared intention. *Ethics* 104(1): 97–113.

Bratman, Michael. 1999. I intend that we J. In *Faces of intention: Selected essays on intention and agency*, 142–162. Cambridge, MA: Cambridge University Press.

Brentano, Franz. [1874] 1995. *Psychology from an empirical standpoint*. London: Routledge.

Brooks, David. 1986. Group minds. *Australasian Journal of Philosophy* 64: 456–470.

Calcagno, Antonio. 2012. Gerda Walther: On the possibility of a passive sense of community and the inner time consciousness of community. *Symposium* 16(2): 89–105.

Caminada, Emanuele. 2014. Joining the background: Habitual sentiments behind we-intentionality. In *Institutions, emotions, and group agents: Contributions to social ontology*, ed. Anita Konzelmann Ziv and Hans Bernhard Schmid, 195–212. Dordrecht: Springer.

Caputo, John. 1986. Husserl, Heidegger, and the question of a 'hermeneutic' phenomenology. In *A companion to Martin Heidegger's 'being and time'*, ed. Joseph Kockelmans, 104–126. Washington, D.C.: University Press of America.

Carman, Taylor. 2003. *Heidegger's analytic: Interpretation, discourse and authenticity in being and time*. Cambridge: Cambridge University Press.

© Springer International Publishing Switzerland 2016
H.A. Sánchez Guerrero, *Feeling Together and Caring with One Another*,
Studies in the Philosophy of Sociality 7, DOI 10.1007/978-3-319-33735-7

Carr, David. 1973. The 'fifth meditation' and Husserl's cartesianism. *Philosophy and Phenomenological Research* 34(1): 14–35.

Cerbone, David. 2000. Heidegger and Dasein's 'bodily nature': What is the hidden problematic? *International Journal of Philosophical Studies* 8(2): 209–230.

Chartrand, Tanya, and John Bargh. 1999. The chameleon effect: The perception-behavior link and social interaction. *Journal of Personality and Social Psychology* 76(6): 893–910.

Chelstrom, Eric. 2011. Pluralities without reified wholes: A phenomenological response to Hans Bernhard Schmid's collectivism. *Investigaciones fenomenológicas* 3: 87–106.

Collingwood, Robin George. [1942] 1947. *The new leviathan*. Oxford: Clarendon Press.

Cooley, Charles Horton. [1909] 1956. *Social organization: Human nature and the social order*. Glencoe: Free Press.

Crane, Tim. 1998. Intentionality as the mark of the mental. In *Current issues in the philosophy of mind*, ed. Anthony O'Hear, 229–251. Cambridge: Cambridge University Press.

Crane, Tim. 2001. *Elements of mind*. Oxford: Oxford University Press.

Crowell, Steven. 2008. Measure-taking: Meaning and normativity in Heidegger's philosophy. *Continental Philosophy Review* 41(3): 261–276.

Damasio, Antonio. 1994. *Descartes' error: Emotion, reason, and the human brain*. New York: G.P. Putnam's Sons.

Damasio, Antonio. 1999. *The feeling of what happens: Body and emotion in the making of consciousness*. New York: Harcourt Brace and Company.

Damasio, Antonio. 2001. Fundamental feelings. *Nature* 413: 781.

Damasio, Antonio. 2003. *Looking for Spinoza: Joy, sorrow, and the feeling brain*. Orlando: Harcourt, Inc.

de Gelder, Beatrice, John Morris, and Ray Dolan. 2005. Unconscious fear influences emotional awareness of faces and voices. *PNAS* 102: 18682–18687.

Dennett, Daniel. 1978. *Brainstorms*. Montgomery: Bradford Books.

Dennett, Daniel. 1991. *Consciousness explained*. New York: Penguin Press.

Deonna, Julien, and Fabrice Teroni. 2009. Taking affective explanations to heart. *Social Science Information* 48(3): 359–377.

de Sousa, Ronald. 1987. *The rationality of emotion*. Cambridge, MA: MIT Press.

de Sousa, Ronald. 2010. Emotion. *Stanford encyclopedia of philosophy*. URL = http://plato.stanford.edu/archives/spr2010/entries/emotion/. PDF of the spring edition 2010 downloaded on 25 February 2011.

Donagan, Alan. 1987. *Choice: The essential element in human action*. London: Routledge and Kegan Paul.

Dreyfus, Hubert. 1991. *Being-in-the-world*. Cambridge, MA: MIT Press.

Ekstrom, Laura. 2010. Ambivalence and authentic agency. *Ratio* 23(4): 374–392.

Fontaine, Philippe. 1997. Identification and economic behavior: Sympathy and empathy in historical perspective. *Economics and Philosophy* 13: 261–280.

Frankfurt, Harry. 1988. *The importance of what we care about: Philosophical essays*. Cambridge: Cambridge University Press.

Friedman, Bruce. 2010. Feelings and the body: The Jamesian perspective on autonomic specificity of emotion. *Biological Psychology* 84: 383–393.

Gallagher, Shaun. 1995. Body schema and intentionality. In *The body and the self*, ed. José Luis Bermúdez, Anthony Marcel, and Naomi Eilan, 225–244. Cambridge, MA: MIT Press.

Gallagher, Shaun. 2008. Direct perception in the intersubjective context. *Consciousness and Cognition* 17: 535–543.

Giere, Ronald. 2002. Scientific cognition as distributed cognition. In *The cognitive basis of science*, ed. Peter Caruthers, Stephen Stich, and Michael Siegal, 285–299. Cambridge: Cambridge University Press.

Gilbert, Margaret. 1987. Modeling collective belief. *Synthese* 73(1): 185–204.

Gilbert, Margaret. 1989. *On social facts*. New York: Routledge.

Gilbert, Margaret. 1990. Walking together: A paradigmatic social phenomenon. In *The philosophy of the human sciences*, Midwest studies in philosophy, vol. XV, ed. Peter French, Theodore Uehling Jr., and Howard Wettstein, 1–14. Notre Dame: University of Notre Dame Press.

Gilbert, Margaret. 1996. *Living together: Rationality, sociality, and obligation*. Lanham: Rowman and Littlefield.

Gilbert, Margaret. 1997. Group wrongs and guilt feelings. *The Journal of Ethics* 1: 65–84.

Gilbert, Margaret. 2000. *Sociality and responsibility: New essays in plural subject theory*. Lanham: Rowman and Littlefield.

Gilbert, Margaret. 2002. Collective guilt and collective guilt feelings. *The Journal of Ethics* 6: 115–143.

Gilbert, Margaret. 2004. Collective epistemology. *Episteme* 1(2): 95–107.

Gilbert, Margaret. 2007. Searle and collective intentions. In *Intentional acts and institutional facts*, ed. Savas Tsohatzidis, 31–48. Dordrecht: Springer.

Gilbert, Margaret. 2009. Shared intention and personal intentions. *Philosophical Studies* 144: 167–187.

Gilbert, Margaret. 2010. Collective action. In *A companion to the philosophy of action*, ed. Timothy O'Connor and Constantine Sandis, 67–73. Malden: Wiley-Blackwell.

Gilbert, Margaret. 2014. How we feel: understanding everyday collective emotion ascription. In *Collective emotions: Perspectives from psychology, philosophy, and sociology*, ed. Christian von Scheve and Mikko Salmela, 17–31. Oxford: Oxford University Press.

Glendinning, Simon. 1998. *On being with others: Heidegger, Wittgenstein, Derrida*. London/New York: Routledge.

Goldie, Peter. 2000. *The emotions: A philosophical exploration*. Oxford: Clarendon Press.

Goldie, Peter. 2002. Emotions, feelings and intentionality. *Phenomenology and the Cognitive Sciences* 1: 235–254.

Goldie, Peter. 2012. *The mess inside: Narrative, emotion, and the mind*. Oxford: Oxford University Press.

Gordon, Robert. 1987. *The structure of emotions: Investigations in cognitive philosophy*. Cambridge: Cambridge University Press.

Greenspan, Patricia. 1988. *Emotions and reasons: An inquiry into emotional justification*. New York: Routledge, Chapman and Hall.

Greenspan, Patricia. 2004. Emotions, rationality, and mind/body. In *Thinking about feeling: Contemporary philosophers on emotions*, ed. Robert Solomon, 125–134. Oxford: Oxford University Press.

Griffiths, Paul. 1997. *What emotions really are: The problem of psychological categories*. Chicago: University of Chicago Press.

Guignon, Charles. 1983. *Heidegger and the problem of knowledge*. Indianapolis: Hackett.

Gurwitsch, Aron. 1979. *Human encounters in the social world*. Pittsburgh: Duquesne University Press.

Gutiérrez Alemán, Carlos. 2002. *Temas de filosofía hermenéutica: Conferencias y ensayos*. Bogotá: Ediciones Uniandes.

Hardin, Russell. 1988. *Morality within the limits of reason*. Chicago: University of Chicago Press.

Hart, Herbert Lionel Adolphus. 1961. *The concept of law*. Oxford: Oxford University Press.

Heidegger, Martin. [1921/22] 1985. *Phänomenologische Interpretation zu Aristoteles: Einführung in die phänomenologische Forschung. Gesamtausgabe*, vol. 61. Frankfurt a.M.: Klostermann.

Heidegger, Martin. [1921/22] [1985] 2001. *Phenomenological interpretations of Aristotle: Introduction to phenomenological research*. Trans. R. Rojcewicz. Bloomington: Indiana University Press.

Heidegger, Martin. [1925/26] 1976. *Logik, die Frage nach der Wahrheit. Gesamtausgabe*, vol. 21. Frankfurt a.M.: Klostermann.

Heidegger, Martin. [1927] 1962. *Being and time*. Trans. J. Macquarrie and E. Robinson. New York: Harper and Row.

Heidegger, Martin. [1927] 1996. *Being and time*. Trans. J. Stambaugh. New York: State University of New York Press.

Heidegger, Martin. [1927] 2006. *Sein und Zeit*. Tübingen: Max Niemeyer.

Heidegger, Martin. [1928/29] 1996. *Einleitung in die Philosophie. Gesamtausgabe*, vol. 27. Frankfurt a.M.: Klostermann.

Heidegger, Martin. [1929/30] 1983. *Die Grundbegriffe der Metaphysik. Welt – Endlichkeit – Einsamkeit. Gesamtausgabe*, vol. 29/30. Frankfurt a.M.: Klostermann.

Heidegger, Martin. [1934] 1998. *Logik als die Frage nach dem Wesen der Sprache. Gesamtausgabe*, vol. 38. Frankfurt a.M.: Klostermann.

Heinnonen, Matti. 2016. Minimalism and maximalism in the study of shared intentional action. *Philosophy of the Social Sciences* 46(2): 168–188.

Helm, Bennett. 2001. *Emotional reason: Deliberation, motivation, and the nature of value*. Cambridge: Cambridge University Press.

Helm, Bennett. 2002. Felt evaluations. A theory of pleasures and pains. *American Philosophical Quarterly* 39: 13–30.

Helm, Bennett. 2008. Plural agents. *Noûs* 42: 17–49.

Helm, Bennett. 2009. Emotions and motivation: Reconsidering neo-Jamesian accounts. In *The Oxford handbook of philosophy of emotion*, ed. Peter Goldie, 303–323. Oxford: Oxford University Press.

Helm, Bennett. 2010. *Love, friendship, and the self: Intimacy, identification, and the social nature of persons*. Oxford: Oxford University Press.

Helm, Bennett. 2011. Affektive Intentionalität: Holistisch und vielschichtig. In *Affektive Intentionalität: Beiträge zur welterschließenden Funktion der menschlichen Gefühle*, ed. Jan Slaby, Achim Stephan, Henrik Walter, and Sven Walter, 72–99. Paderborn: Mentis.

Helm, Bennett. 2012. Accountability and some social dimensions of human agency. *Philosophical Issues* 22(1): 217–232.

Helm, Bennett. Forthcoming. Truth, objectivity, and emotional caring: Filling in the gaps of Haugeland's existentialist ontology. In *Mind, meaning, and understanding: The philosophy of John Haugeland*, ed. Zed Adams. Cambridge: MIT Press.

Hess, Ursula, Stephanie Houde, and Agneta Fischer. 2014. Do we mimic what we see or what we know? In *Collective emotions: Perspectives from psychology, philosophy, and sociology*, ed. Christian von Scheve and Mikko Salmela, 94–107. Oxford: Oxford University Press.

Hochschild, Arlie Russell. 1983. *The managed heart: Commercialization of human feeling*. Los Angeles: University of California Press.

Huebner, Bryce. 2011. Genuinely collective emotions. *European Journal for the Philosophy of Science* 1(1): 89–118.

Hursthouse, Rosalinda. 2002. Review: Emotional reason. Deliberation, motivation and the nature of value. *Mind* 111(442): 418–422.

Husserl, Edmund. [1929] 1999. *Cartesian meditations: An introduction to phenomenology*. Dordrecht: Kluwer Academic Publishers.

Hutchins, Edwin. 1995a. *Cognition in the wild*. Cambridge, MA: MIT Press.

Hutchins, Edwin. 1995b. How a cockpit remembers its speeds. *Cognitive Science* 19: 265–288.

Hutto, Daniel. 2002. The world is not enough: Shared emotions and other minds. In *Understanding emotions: Mind and morals*, ed. Peter Goldie, 37–53. Aldershot: Ashgate Publishing.

Inwood, Michael. 1999. *A Heidegger dictionary*. Oxford: Blackwell.

James, William. 1884. What is an emotion? *Mind* 9: 188–205.

Jaspers, Karl. [1947] 2001. *The question of German guilt*. Trans. E. Ashton. New York: Capricorn Books.

Kenny, Anthony. [1963] 2003. *Action, emotion, and will*. London: Routledge.

Kisiel, Theodore. 1993. *The genesis of Heidegger's being and time*. Berkeley: University of California Press.

Knobe, Joshua, and Jesse Prinz. 2008. Intuitions about consciousness: Experimental studies. *Phenomenology and the Cognitive Sciences* 7: 67–83.

Knorr Cetina, Karin. 1999. *Epistemic cultures: How the sciences make knowledge*. Cambridge, MA: Harvard University Press.

Konzelmann Ziv, Anita. 2007. Collective guilt feeling revisited. *Dialectica* 61: 467–493.

Konzelmann Ziv, Anita. 2009. The semantics of shared emotion. *Universitas philosophica* 52: 81–106.

Krebs, Angelika. 2010. Vater und Mutter stehen an der Leiche eines geliebten Kindes. Max Scheler über das Miteinanderfühlen. *Allgemeine Zeitschrift für Philosophie* 35(1): 9–43.

Kutz, Christopher. 2000a. Acting together. *Philosophy and Phenomenological Research* 61(1): 1–31.

Kutz, Christopher. 2000b. *Complicity*. Cambridge: Cambridge University Press.

Lange, Carl. [1885] 1922. The emotions: A psychophysiological study. Trans. I. Haupt. In *The emotions*, ed. Knight Dunlap, 33–90. Baltimore: Williams and Wilkins.

Lazarus, Richard. 1991. Cognition and motivation in emotion. *American Psychologist* 46: 362–367.

LeDoux, Joseph. 1996. *The emotional brain*. New York: Simon and Schuster.

Lehrer, Keith. 1990. *Theory of knowledge*. Boulder: Westview Press.

Leighton, Stephen. 1986. Unfelt feelings in pain and emotion. *The Southern Journal of Philosophy* 24(1): 69–79.

Lévinas, Emmanuel. [1935] 2003. *On escape: De l'évasion*. Trans. J. Rolland and B. Bergo. Stanford: Stanford University Press.

Lipps, Theodor. 1905. Das Wissen von fremden Ichen. In *Psychologische Untersuchungen* Bd. I, Heft 4, 694–722. Leipzig: Verlag von Wilhelm Engelmann.

Luckner, Andreas. 2007. Wie es ist, selbst zu sein. Zum Begriff der Eigentlichkeit (§§54–60). In *Martin Heidegger: Sein und Zeit*, Klassiker Auslegen Bd. 25, ed. Thomas Rentsch, 149–168. Berlin: Akademie-Verlag.

Lycan, William. 1987. *Consciousness*. Cambridge: Bradford Books/MIT Press.

Lyons, William. 1980. *Emotion*. Cambridge: Cambridge University Press.

Marks, Joel. 1982. A theory of emotion. *Philosophical Studies* 42: 227–242.

McDowell, John. 1979. Virtue and reason. *The Monist* 62: 331–350.

McDowell, John. 1985. Values and secondary qualities. In *Morality and objectivity: A tribute to J. L. Mackie*, ed. Ted Honderich, 110–129. London: Routledge.

McDowell, John. [1994] 1996. *Mind and world*. Cambridge, MA: Harvard University Press.

Meijers, Anthonie. 1999. Believing and accepting as a group. In *Belief, cognition and the will*, ed. Anthonie Meijers, 59–71. Tilburg: Tilburg University Press.

Meijers, Anthonie. 2002. Collective agents and cognitive attitudes. *Protosociology* 16: 70–86.

Meijers, Anthonie. 2003. Can collective intentionality be individualized? *American Journal of Economics and Sociology* 62: 167–193.

Merker, Barbara. 2007. Die Sorge als Sein des Daseins (§§39–44). In *Martin Heidegger: Sein und Zeit*, Klassiker Auslegen Bd. 25, ed. Thomas Rentsch, 117–132. Berlin: Akademie-Verlag.

Merleau-Ponty, Maurice. 1964. In *The primacy of perception*, ed. James Edie. Evanston: Northwestern University Press.

Michael, John. 2011. Shared emotions and joint action. *Review of Philosophy and Psychology* 2(2): 355–373.

Miller, Seumas. 1992. Joint action. *Philosophical Papers* 21(3): 275–297.

Miller, Seumas. 1999. Collective rights. *Public Affairs Quarterly* 13(4): 331–346.

Montague, Michelle. 2009. The logic, intentionality, and phenomenology of emotion. *Philosophical Studies* 145(2): 171–192.

Neu, Jerome. 2000. *A tear is an intellectual thing: The meaning of emotions*. Oxford/New York: Oxford University Press.

Nisbett, Richard, and Timothy Wilson. 1977. Telling more than we can know: Verbal reports on mental processes. *Psychological Review* 8: 231–259.

Nussbaum, Martha. 1990. *Love's knowledge*. Oxford: Oxford University Press.

Nussbaum, Martha. 1994. *The therapy of desire: Theory and practice in Hellenistic ethics.* Princeton: Princeton University Press.

Nussbaum, Martha. 2001. *Upheavals of thought: The intelligence of emotions.* Cambridge: Cambridge University Press.

Obhi, Sukhvinder, and Preston Hall. 2011. Sense of agency and intentional binding in joint action. *Experimental Brain Research* 211(3–4): 655–662.

Offe, Claus. 2000. The democratic welfare state in an integrating Europe. In *Democracy beyond the state? The European dilemma and the emerging global order*, ed. Michael Greven and Louis Pauly, 63–90. Lanham: Rowman and Littlefield.

Pacherie, Elisabeth. 2011. Framing joint action. *Review of Philosophy and Psychology* 2(2): 173–192.

Pacherie, Elisabeth. 2012. The phenomenology of joint action: self-agency vs. joint-agency. In *Joint attention: New developments in psychology, philosophy of mind, and social neuroscience*, ed. Axel Seemann, 343–389. Cambridge, MA: MIT Press.

Pacherie, Elisabeth. 2014. How does it feel to act together? *Phenomenology and the Cognitive Sciences* 13(1): 25–46.

Panksepp, Jaak. 1998. *Affective neuroscience: The foundations of human and animal emotions.* Oxford/New York: Oxford University Press.

Pettit, Philip. 2002. Collective persons and powers. *Legal Theory* 8: 443–470.

Pocai, Romano. 2007. Die Weltlichkeit der Welt und ihre abgedrängte Faktizität. In *Martin Heidegger: Sein und Zeit*, Klassiker Auslegen Bd. 25, ed. Thomas Rentsch, 51–67. Berlin: Akademie-Verlag.

Prinz, Jesse. 2004a. Embodied emotions. In *Thinking about feeling: Contemporary philosophers on emotions*, ed. Robert Solomon, 44–58. Oxford: Oxford University Press.

Prinz, Jesse. 2004b. *Gut reactions: A perceptual theory of emotion.* Oxford: Oxford University Press.

Quinton, Anthony. 1975–1976. Social objects. *Proceedings of the Aristotelian Society* 75: 67–87.

Ratcliffe, Matthew. 2005. The feeling of being. *Journal of Consciousness Studies* 12: 43–60.

Ratcliffe, Matthew. 2008. *Feelings of being: Phenomenology, psychiatry and the sense of reality.* Oxford: Oxford University Press.

Ratcliffe, Matthew. 2010. Depression, guilt and emotional depth. *Inquiry* 53(6): 602–626.

Ratcliffe, Matthew. 2012. The phenomenology of existential feeling. In *Feelings of being alive*, ed. Joerg Fingerhut and Sabine Marienberg, 23–53. Berlin: De Gruyter.

Reinach, Adolf. 1922. Die apriorischen Grundlagen des bürgerlichen Rechts. In *Jahrbuch für Philosophie und phänomenologische Forschung*, vol. I, ed. Edmund Husserl, 685–847. Halle: Niemeyer.

Rizzolatti, Giacomo, and Laila Craighero. 2004. The mirror-neuron system. *Annual Review of Neuroscience* 27: 169–192.

Roberts, Robert. 1988. What an emotion is: A sketch. *Philosophical Review* 97: 183–209.

Rorty, Amélie. 1980. Explaining emotions. In *Explaining emotions*, ed. Amélie Rorty, 103–126. Berkeley: University of California Press.

Ryle, Gilbert. 1971. Feelings. In *Collected papers*, vol. II, 272–286. London: Hutchinson.

Salmela, Mikko. 2012. Shared emotions. *Philosophical Explorations* 15(1): 33–46.

Sánchez Guerrero, H. Andrés. 2011. Gemeinsamkeitsgefühle und Mitsorge: Anregungen zu einer alternativen Auffassung kollektiver affektiver Intentionalität. In *Affektive Intentionalität: Beiträge zur welterschließenden Funktion der menschlichen Gefühle*, ed. Jan Slaby, Achim Stephan, Henrik Walter, and Sven Walter, 252–282. Paderborn: Mentis.

Sánchez Guerrero, H. Andrés. 2012. Affektive Intentionalität, die fundamentale Begründbarkeit unserer Emotionen und die Unbeschreibbarkeit des depressiven Erlebens. In *Psychoanalyse: Texte zur Sozialforschung*, vol. 30, ed. Brigitte Boothe, Lina Arboleda, Nicole Kapfhamer, and Vera Luif, 369–380. Lengerich: Pabst Science Publisher.

Sánchez Guerrero, H. Andrés. 2014. Feelings of being-together and caring-with. In *Institutions, emotions, and group agents*, ed. Anita Konzelmann Ziv and Hans Bernhard Schmid, 177–193. Dordrecht: Springer.

Sartre, Jean-Paul. [1939] 2002. *Sketch for a theory of the emotions*. Trans. P. Mairet. New York: Routledge.

Sartre, Jean-Paul. [1943] [1956] 2001. *Being and nothingness: An essay in phenomenological ontology*. Trans. H. Barnes. New York: Citadel Press, Kensington Publishing Corp.

Schachter, Stanley, and Jerome Singer. 1962. Cognitive, social and physiological determinants of emotional states. *Psychological Review* 69: 379–399.

Scheler, Max. [1913] 2008. *The nature of sympathy*. Trans. P. Heath. New Brunswick: Transaction Publishers.

Scheler, Max. [1913–1916] 1973. *Formalism in ethics and non-formal ethics of values*. Evanston: Northwestern University Press.

Schmid, Hans Bernhard. 2001. Gemeinsames Dasein und die Uneigentlichkeit von Individualität: Elemente einer nicht-individualistischen Konzeption des Daseins. *Deutsche Zeitschrift für Philosophie* 49: 665–684.

Schmid, Hans Bernhard. 2003. Can brains in vats think as a team? *Philosophical Explorations* 6(3): 201–218.

Schmid, Hans Bernhard. 2005. *Wir-Intentionalität: Kritik des ontologischen Individualismus und Rekonstruktion der Gemeinschaft*. Freiburg: Alber.

Schmid, Hans Bernhard. 2008. Shared feelings: Towards a phenomenology of collective affective intentionality. In *Concepts of sharedness: Essays on collective intentionality*, ed. Hans Bernhard Schmid, Katinka Schulte-Ostermann, and Nikos Psarros, 59–86. Frankfurt a.M: Ontos.

Schmid, Hans Bernhard. 2009. *Plural action: Essays in philosophy and social science*. Dordrecht: Springer.

Schmid, Hans Bernhard. 2014a. Plural self-awareness. *Phenomenology and the Cognitive Sciences* 13(1): 7–24.

Schmid, Hans Bernhard. 2014b. The feeling of being a group: Corporate emotions and collective consciousness. In *Collective emotions: Perspectives from psychology, philosophy, and sociology*, ed. Christian von Scheve and Mikko Salmela, 3–16. Oxford: Oxford University Press.

Schmid, Hans Bernhard, and David Schweikard (eds.). 2009. *Kollektive Intentionalität: Eine Debatte über die Grundlagen des Sozialen*. Suhrkamp: Frankfurt a.M.

Schmitt, Richard. 1969. *Martin Heidegger on being human*. New York: Random House.

Schmitz, Hermann, Rudolf Müllan, and Jan Slaby. 2011. Emotions outside the box—the new phenomenology of feeling and corporeality. *Phenomenology and the Cognitive Sciences* 10(2): 241–259.

Schweikard, David, and Hans Bernhard Schmid. 2013. Collective intentionality. *Stanford encyclopedia of philosophy* (summer 2013 edition). URL = http://plato.stanford.edu/archives/sum2013/entries/collective-intentionality/.

Searle, John. 1980. Minds, brains and programs. *Behavioural and Brain Sciences* 3: 417–424.

Searle, John. 1983. *Intentionality: An essay in the philosophy of mind*. Cambridge: Cambridge University Press.

Searle, John. [1990] 2002. Collective intentions and actions. In *Consciousness and language*. Cambridge: Cambridge University Press.

Sebanz, Natalie, Harold Bekkering, and Günther Knoblich. 2006. Joint action: Bodies and minds moving together. *Trends in Cognitive Sciences* 10(2): 70–76.

Sellars, Wilfrid. 1956. Empiricism and the philosophy of mind. In *Minnesota studies in the philosophy of science*, vol. 1, ed. Herbert Feigl and Michael Scriven, 253–329. Minneapolis: University of Minnesota Press.

Sellars, Wilfrid. 1963. Imperatives, intentions, and the logic of 'ought'. In *Morality and the language of conduct*, ed. Héctor-Neri Castañeda and George Nakhnikian, 159–218. Detroit: Wayne State University Press.

Sellars, Wilfrid. 1968. *Science and metaphysics*. London: Routledge and Kegan Paul.

Sellars, Wilfrid. 1980. On reasoning about values. *American Philosophical Quarterly* 17: 81–101.

Shaffer, Jerome. 1983. An assessment of emotion. *American Philosophical Quarterly* 20: 161–172.

Sheehy, Paul. 2002. On plural subject theory. *Journal of Social Philosophy* 33(3): 377–394.

Shockley, Kevin, Daniel Richardson, and Rick Dale. 2009. Conversation and coordinative structures. *Topics in Cognitive Science* 1: 305–319.

Sizer, Laura. 2006. What feelings can't do. *Mind and Language* 20(1): 108–135.

Slaby, Jan. 2007. Emotionaler Weltbezug: Ein Strukturschema im Anschluss an Heidegger. In *Gefühle – Struktur und Funktion*, ed. Hilge Landweer, 93–112. Berlin: Akademie Verlag.

Slaby, Jan. 2012. Emotional rationality and feelings of being. In *Feelings of being alive*, ed. Joerg Fingerhut and Sabine Marienberg, 55–78. Berlin: De Gruyter.

Slaby, Jan, and Achim Stephan. 2008. Affective intentionality and self-consciousness. *Consciousness and Cognition* 17: 506–513.

Smith, Adam. [1759] 2000. *The theory of moral sentiments*. Amherst: Prometheus Books.

Smith, David. 2003. *Routledge philosophy guidebook to Husserl and the Cartesian meditations*. London: Routledge.

Solomon, Robert. 1976. *The passions: The myth and nature of human emotions*. New York: Doubleday.

Solomon, Robert. 1993. *The passions: Emotions and the meaning of life*. Indianapolis: Hackett.

Solomon, Robert. 2004. Emotions, thoughts, and feelings: Emotions as engagements with the world. In *Thinking about feeling: Contemporary philosophers on emotions*, ed. Robert Solomon, 76–88. Oxford: Oxford University Press.

Stack, George. 1972. Basis of Kierkegaard's concept of existential possibility. *The New Scholasticism* 46(2): 139–172.

Stein, Edith. [1922] 1970. Beiträge zur philosophischen Begründung der Psychologie und der Geisteswissenschaften. Zweite Abhandlung: Individuum und Gemeinschaft. In *Jahrbuch für Philosophie und phänomenologische Forschung*, vol. V, ed. Edmund Husserl, 116–283. Halle: Niemeyer.

Steinbock, Anthony. 1995. Generativity and generative phenomenology. *Husserl Studies* 12(1): 55–79.

Stocker, Michael. 1983. Psychic feelings: Their importance and irreducibility. *Australian Journal of Philosophy* 61: 5–26.

Stoutland, Frederick. 1997. Why are philosophers of action so anti-social? In *Commonality and particularity in ethics*, ed. Lilli Alanen, Sara Heinämaa, and Thomas Wallgren, 45–74. New York: St. Martin's Press.

Strasser, Stephan. 1977. *Phenomenology of feeling: An essay on the phenomena of the heart*. Pittsburgh: Duquesne University Press.

Sugden, Robert. 2002. Beyond sympathy and empathy: Adam Smith's concept of fellow-feeling. *Economics and Philosophy* 18: 63–87.

Sutton, John. 2006. Distributed cognition: Domains and dimensions. *Pragmatics and Cognition* 14: 235–247.

Taylor, Charles. 1978–1979. The validity of transcendental arguments. *Proceedings of the Aristotelian Society* 79: 151–165.

Taylor, Charles. 1985. Self-interpreting animals. In *Human agency and language: Philosophical papers I*, 45–76. Cambridge: Cambridge University Press.

Theiner, Georg, and Timothy O'Connor. 2010. The emergence of group cognition. In *Emergence in science and philosophy*, ed. Antonella Corradini and Timothy O'Connor, 78–117. New York: Routledge.

Thompson, Evan. 2007. *Mind in life: Biology, phenomenology, and the sciences of mind*. Cambridge, MA: The Belknap Press of Harvard University Press.

Tollefsen, Deborah. 2002. Collective intentionality and the social sciences. *Philosophy of the Social Sciences* 32(1): 25–50.

Tollefsen, Deborah. 2004. Collective intentionality. *The internet encyclopedia of philosophy*. http://www.iep.utm.edu/coll-int/. Retrieved on 22 December 2010.

Tollefsen, Deborah. 2005. Let's pretend! Children and joint action. *Philosophy of the Social Sciences* 35: 75–97.

Tomasello, Michael. 2008. *Origins of human communication*. Cambridge, MA: MIT Press.

Traue, Harald, and Henrik Kessler. 2003. Psychologische Emotionskonzepte. In *Natur und Theorie der Emotion*, ed. Achim Stephan and Henrik Walter, 20–33. Paderborn: Mentis.

Tsuchiya, Naotsugu, and Ralph Adolphs. 2007. Emotion and consciousness. *Trends in Cognitive Science* 11(4): 158–167.

Tuomela, Raimo. 1984. *A theory of social action*. Dordrecht: D. Reidel Publishing Company.

Tuomela, Raimo. 1992. Group beliefs. *Synthese* 91: 285–318.

Tuomela, Raimo. 1995. *The importance of us*. Standford: Standford University Press.

Tuomela, Raimo. 2003. The we-mode and the I-mode. In *Socializing metaphysics: The nature of social reality*, ed. Frederick Schmitt, 93–128. Lanham: Rowman and Littlefield.

Tuomela, Raimo. 2005. We-intentions revisited. *Philosophical Studies* 125(3): 327–369.

Tuomela, Raimo. 2007. *The philosophy of sociality: The shared point of view*. New York: Oxford University Press.

Tuomela, Raimo, and Kaarlo Miller. 1988. We-intentions. *Philosophical Studies* 53(3): 367–389.

Tuomela, Raimo, and Maj Tuomela. 2005. Cooperation and trust in group context. *Mind and Society* 4: 49–84.

van Hooft, Stan. 1994. Scheler on sharing emotions. *Philosophy Today* 38(1): 18–28.

Velleman, David. 1997. How to share an intention. *Philosophy and Phenomenological Research* 57: 29–51.

Vendrell Ferran, Íngrid. 2008. *Die Emotionen: Gefühle in der realistischen Phänomenologie*. Berlin: Akademie Verlag.

Vesper, Cordula, Stephen Butterfill, Günther Knoblich, and Natalie Sebanz. 2010. A minimal architecture for joint action. *Neural Networks* 23: 998–1003.

Vikhoff, Björn, Helge Malmgren, Rickard Åström, Gunnar Nyberg, Seth-Reino Ekström, Mathias Engwall, Johan Snygg, Michael Nilsson, and Rebecka Jörnsten. 2013. Music structure determines heart rate variability of singers. *Frontiers in Psychology* 4(334): 1–16.

von Hildebrand, Dietrich. [1930] 1955. *Metaphysik der Gemeinschaft: Untersuchungen über Wesen und Wert der Gemeinschaft*. Regensburg: Habbel.

von Scheve, Christian, and Mikko Salmela. 2014. Collective emotions: An introduction. In *Collective emotions: Perspectives from psychology, philosophy, and sociology*, ed. Christian von Scheve and Mikko Salmela, xiii–xxiv. Oxford: Oxford University Press.

Walther, Gerda. 1923. Ein Beitrag zur Ontologie der sozialen Gemeinschaften. In *Jahrbuch für Philosophie und phänomenologische Forschung*, vol. VI, ed. Edmund Husserl, 1–158. Halle: Niemeyer.

Weber, Max. [1921] 1972. *Wirtschaft und Gesellschaft: Grundriß der verstehenden Soziologie*. Tübingen: J. C. B. Mohr (Paul Siebeck).

Wegner, Daniel, Toni Giuliano, and Paula Hertel. 1985. Cognitive interdependence in close relationships. In *Compatible and incompatible relationships*, ed. William Ickes, 253–276. New York: Springer.

Wilkins, Burleigh. 2002. Joint commitments. *The Journal of Ethics* 6: 145–155.

Wilson, Robert. 2001. Group-level cognition. *Philosophy of science* 68 (suppl.): S262–S273.

Wittgenstein, Ludwig. [1953] 2001. *Philosophical investigations*. Oxford: Basil Blackwell.

Wollheim, Richard. 1999. *On the emotions*. New Haven: Yale University Press.

Wray, Brad. 2001. Collective belief and acceptance. *Synthese* 129: 319–333.

Zahavi, Dan. 2005. *Subjectivity and selfhood: Investigating the first-person perspective*. Cambridge, MA: MIT Press.

Index

Note: References to footnotes are indicated by the suffix 'fn' followed by the footnote number

© Springer International Publishing Switzerland 2016
H.A. Sánchez Guerrero, *Feeling Together and Caring with One Another*,
Studies in the Philosophy of Sociality 7, DOI 10.1007/978-3-319-33735-7

Printed in Great Britain
by Amazon